IMAGES OF MAN

IMAGES
OF MAN

A History of Anthropological Thought

ANNEMARIE

DE WAAL MALEFIJT

Alfred A. Knopf New York 1974

This is a Borzoi Book published by Alfred A. Knopf, Inc.
Copyright © 1974 by A. de Waal Malefijt
All rights reserved under International
and Pan-American Copyright Conventions.
Published in the United States
by Alfred A. Knopf, Inc., New York,
and simultaneously in Canada
by Random House of Canada Limited, Toronto.
Distributed by Random House, Inc., New York.

Grateful acknowledgment is made to
Harcourt Brace Jovanovich, Inc.,
for permission to reprint an excerpt from
A Diary in the Strict Sense of the Term,
by Bronislaw Malinowski (1967).

Library of Congress Cataloging in Publication Data
De Waal Malefijt, Annemarie (Date)
Images of man; a history of anthropological thought.
Bibliography: p.
1. Ethnology—History.   2. Anthropology—History.
I.   Title.
GN17.D44   301.2'09   74-7182
ISBN 0-394-48330-8
0-394-31903-6 (text)

Manufactured in the United States of America
First Edition

CONTENTS

INTRODUCTION

One of the recent discoveries in anthropology is that of its own historical perspective. For a while, anthropologists held a narrow view of the history of their science, fixing its birth date somewhere in the nineteenth century. This presumed youthfulness was often invoked as an excuse for paucity of data and inconclusive findings. It is now generally recognized that anthropology did not begin with Tylor, Frazer, or Morgan, but that it has its roots in the ancient past. Anthropological questions are timeless because they center around the universal concern to understand human existence and human behavior. Writing in 1904, Boas said, "Up to ten years ago we had no trained anthropologists." Yet, two millennia earlier, scholars were already speculating on the origin of man and his culture, analyzing and comparing social institutions, writing grammatical analyses of old languages, and reporting on foreign peoples and their customs. The study of man—anthropology writ large—is one of the oldest subjects of serious thought. Nevertheless, the development of anthropology has not been arrested in time, but has brought about refinement of methods and increased insights into the nature of man and his culture. This evolution has taken place not by repudiating older questions, but by raising problems that were inherent in earlier formulations and by seeking alternative solutions. If a true understanding of the foundations of our discipline is to be reached, it is necessary to consider its whole history rather than that of the last hundred years.

This book is an attempt to expose some of the historical sources of anthropology as a Western cultural phenomenon. I do not presume that it represents a conclusive history of anthropology, but only offer a somewhat sketchy map of that history. Every map leaves out many aspects of the real environment, and different map makers emphasize different features. Critics will have an easy task in pointing out the many deserts and empty quarters, and undoubtedly will also find errors of commission. Nevertheless, I hope that the descriptions in this book will not only enrich our knowledge of the past, but will also enable readers to discover the patterns of past concerns and thus provide further insight into the present status of anthropology. One important fact emerging from a historical perspective is that the conditions that gave rise to anthropology as it is now were marked by an intrinsic sharing of concerns. Philosophers, historians, theologians, statesmen, economists, medical doctors, and many others were often enough in sharp disagreement with one another, but they generally recognized the intellectual relevance of the other points of view. Early-twentieth-century anthropologists, carried away perhaps by their own exciting discoveries, developed a strong degree of professional ethnocentrism. They tended to acknowledge the existence of other disciplines only insofar as their findings stood in the service of anthropological explanations. This self-imposed isolation is now breaking down, and communication between anthropologists and other scientists is once again taking place. A deeper understanding of the past may help to accelerate that process.

Not all older theories and data are acceptable in the light of our present knowledge. For that matter, modern anthropologists are certainly not of one mind about current theoretical approaches and interpretations. Although the shortcomings of earlier writers are sometimes pointed out, I have stressed the positive over the negative, in the conviction that the history of anthropology is not a history of errors, but a reflection of the growth of our understanding of man and his culture. To my mind, anthropology is "an astonishing achievement," not merely of the last hundred years, but of mankind.

I have aimed at giving a broad view, hoping that others will become inspired to make analyses in depth. The emphasis is on cultural anthropology, and the other subdisciplines receive short shrift. Furthermore, although fully aware of the many important outside influences, I have limited my descriptions to Western developments only.

In writing this book I have drawn on the knowledge of many scholars, and the length of the bibliography indicates the scope of my indebtedness. I wish to thank my friends and colleagues for their advice and suggestions, and am grateful to Ray Dunstan for his work on the bibliography.

IMAGES OF MAN

CHAPTER I

IN THE

BEGINNING

The earliest Greek myths known to us display a lively interest in the origin of man. One myth relates that Athena advised Cadmus to sow the teeth of a serpent into the earth, from which a crop of armed men arose. Another one tells that Zeus ordered Deucalion and Pyrrha to throw stones behind their backs and these stones became men and women. In a third well-known myth the hero Prometheus fashioned men out of earth and water. In fact, not only the origin of man but the existence of the whole universe was explained by mythology: it was said to have been created by the gods, either by fiat or by causing heaven and earth to mate and thus to bring forth the rest of nature.

Thales of Miletus in Ionia (c. 636–c. 546 b.c.) is generally credited with being the first to break away from mythological explanations. His reputation rests on his statement that everything in the world arose from one single substance, namely water. The importance of this claim does not rest in its contents, but rather in its being an explanation of ultimate origins in other than mythological terms. Thales was the first materialist philosopher: he presented a thesis that could be verified or rejected by science (unlike posited divine origins, which cannot be subjected to such verification).

Mythical thinking certainly did not suddenly disappear, and in fact it is still present in our own midst. Nevertheless, nonmythological theories about the origin and evolution of man and nature followed on the heels of Thales' insight. Anaximander (c. 611–c. 547 B.C.), a younger friend and pupil of Thales, agreed with his master that the universe must have been derived from a single basic matter, but he held that this was neither water nor any of the other known elements. He theorized that everything arose from some indefinite and boundless stuff, for which he could find no better term than "the infinite." This undifferentiated matter was in constant motion, eventually sifting out of itself hot and cold, moist and dry, earth and sky, sun, moon, and stars. Life on earth originated in water, and man originally resembled a fish, or perhaps he was born inside a fish, emerging on dry land when he became capable of feeding himself there.

Hints about a theory of evolution by natural selection are present also in the writings of Empedocles (c. 495–c. 435 B.C.). In his view, various parts of bodies existed first in separation and were scattered about in space. In his own words:

> *many heads sprang up without necks,*
> *arms wandered bare for lack of shoulders,*
> *and eyes strayed alone in want of foreheads . . .*

These parts combined at random, often producing monstrosities:

> *many creatures came into being with double*
> *faces and double breasts,*
> *ox-kinds with the foreparts of men,*
> *and men with the heads of oxen . . .*

The minotaurs, sphinxes, centaurs, and sirens of Greek mythology thus received a status in zoology. But these arbitrary combinations were doomed to extinction since they were unable to assimilate food and could not reproduce their kind. Only appropriate and functional combinations survived and became the adapted species of animals and of man as we now know them. However imaginary the depicted process of evolution was, it took place without divine intervention. More than two millennia later, Darwin's theory had to overcome mythical preconceptions before it could find general acceptance.

It is anthropologically significant that the first formulations of social rather than physical evolution came from scholars who had made extensive travels and thus had been confronted with different modes of life. Xenophanes of Colophon (c. 570–c. 475 B.C.) was such a traveler, and after visiting many places he settled in Elea, in what is now southern Italy. Explicitly rejecting the mythological ideas of Homer and Hesiod that the gods had made all important cultural inventions and had bestowed them on men, he wrote: "The gods did not reveal to men all things in the beginning, but in course of time, by searching, they find out better."

This is the earliest known statement presenting society as man-made, and the idea of progress is implicit in these lines. Xenophanes even considered religion as a social creation. Ridiculing Homer and Hesiod for their anthropomorphic representations of the Greek gods, he wrote:

Yea, and if oxen and horses and lions had hands, and could paint with their hands, and provide works of art, as men do, horses would paint the forms of gods like horses, and oxen like oxen, and make their bodies in the image of their several kinds.

The Ethiopians make their gods black and mule-nosed; the Thracians say theirs have blue eyes and red hair.

Another early traveler, much better known than Xenophanes, is Herodotus (c. 484–c. 425 B.C.). Often called the father of history, he could with equal justice be called the father of ethnography. It has been calculated that his travels covered some seventeen hundred miles east to west and sixteen hundred miles north to south—no small accomplishment in his day and age. In his various writings he described more than fifty different peoples, some in greater detail than others. Unlike many of his contemporaries, he did not speculate about origins, but, similar to modern functionalists, he dealt with societies as efficient wholes. The list of cultural items to which he paid attention would not be out of place in a modern ethnography. Usually beginning with descriptions of environment and physical types, he made observations about the spoken languages, material culture, marriage and divorce rules, laws, government, war patterns, and religion. He was the first to report couvade (the custom in which the father goes to bed as if for childbearing when his wife is having a baby), and his descriptions of marriage patterns cover the whole Tylorian range from promiscuity to patrilineal monogamy.

A proud Greek, Herodotus felt that his own culture was in many ways superior to the surrounding barbarian ones, but he wrote, nevertheless: "All men, if asked to choose the best way of ordering life, would choose their own." His tolerance for other customs becomes nowhere more clear than in his treatment of the sensitive topic of religion. Employing what now would be called the comparative method, Herodotus showed how gods in various religions, while having different names and attributes, possessed basic functional similarities. He boldly concluded that these gods were the same, and of the same origin: the Egyptian Amon is Zeus, Isis is Demeter, Horus is Apollo, Osiris is Dionysus. This canon of the equivalence of the gods was later on widely accepted in Rome, and became known as the *interpretatio romana*. Herodotus explained the similarities by the principle of diffusion. He wrote: "I will never admit that the similar ceremonies performed in Greece and Egypt are the result of mere coincidence," and Babylonian funeral songs so strongly resembled those of Egyptians that "imitation must have played a role." He paid lip service to evolution by mentioning three successive historical eras—the ages of gods, of heroes, and of men; but he left it to later scholars to elaborate on this theme.

Herodotus thus used many principles that are still central in modern anthropology: he was not ethnocentric, he aimed at universality, he did not reject any human habits as unimportant, he made use of comparison, and he gathered many of his data by asking questions of the natives in the countries he visited. When he received different answers, he recorded them all. He described the great changes that took place in history as caused by human will or whim, but he acknowledged that Destiny stood behind all human acts.

From Herodotus' time onward, Greek scholars turned their attention increasingly toward society, and they often attempted to explain both physical and social evolution by the same basic principles. Democritus (c. 460–c. 370 B.C.), for one, theorized that all reality consisted of atoms, describing them as indivisible bodies of similar substance, but differing in shape, size, and velocity. The cosmos and all it contained had come into being by the impact of free-moving atoms, and the various combinations produced an endless variety of forms. Man himself, and even his mind, had such a material basis. His atoms were similar to those that constituted fire: they were smooth, fine, and lively. Plants and animals also possessed some of these smooth and lively atoms, but in lesser numbers; the difference was one of degree, not of kind. In fact, animals had been our masters for many important cultural practices: man had learned weaving from spiders, housebuilding from swallows, music from nightingales, and singing from swans. In Democritus' view, society itself had risen through necessity. Alone, man was helpless to defend himself against the much stronger wild beasts, and he sought strength in numbers. Such social cooperation could not be effective without communication, and so language came into being, followed by many technical inventions. Society thus advanced slowly but steadily from a primitive level of existence to civilization. Democritus thus accounted for the development of society itself in terms of survival. But he felt that man's moral faculties needed to be accounted for too. In his view, the atoms that constitute the mind were capable of different degrees of motion, and unethical or antisocial acts produced violent motions, while correct social behavior resulted in gentle and delicate movements of the atoms, setting the mind at rest. The peaceful state of mind being much more pleasurable, it stands to reason that man will seek the right kind of social behavior. In this remarkable theory, Democritus thus accounted for ethics on purely physical-materialistic grounds.

Because of his strong convictions about progressive evolution, Democritus departed from earlier held concepts of a past Golden Age. Social life began in a state of brutishness, and successive technological innovations led to civilization. Man was endowed with reason and inclined to seek what was good and pleasurable. These ideas were very congenial to the Greeks, and found wide acceptance. The chorus in Sophocles' *Antigone* celebrated technological progress, mentioning speech, hunting, housebuilding, agriculture, seafaring, cattle breeding, and medicine, and stressed that these were human inventions rather than divine gifts:

> *Language, and thought like the wind*
> *and feelings that make the town,*
> *he [man] has taught himself . . .*

Until the fifth century B.C.—the time of Herodotus and Democritus—most Greek speculations about the origin and development of nature, man, and society had been intellectual exercises launched in a spirit of scientific curiosity, but not generally applicable to practical life. This situation changed drastically when the Greek lineages, and their larger kinship organizations, the tribes, lost their political power, and democracy became established in Athens. This new form of government instituted universal suffrage without property restriction and universal eligibility for office. Thus the need for education arose: public speaking, legal ability, and knowledge about social affairs became important prerequisites for political and social success. This demand was answered by a group of professional itinerant teachers known as Sophists. Although their individual views and methods were quite diverse, they all taught social effectiveness and practical skills. To them and their pupils the search for knowledge was not an end in itself, but it was valuable only because it formed a means to master the arts of life and the control thereof. The teaching of social proficiency demanded that society itself should be understood, and social studies, together with rhetoric ("the art of persuasion"), were prominent in the Sophists' curricula.

These practical concerns caused Sophists and their followers to become skeptical and even scornful about all older speculations, which appeared to them rather useless. Searching for objective knowledge rather than for ultimate truth, their philosophies of social conduct were marked by an absence of religious scruple and of any universal moral principles.

Both sentiments are clearly recognizable in the teachings of Protagoras of Abdera (c. 480–c. 410 B.C.), who is famous for two pronouncements in particular: "Man is the measure of all things" and "I have no means of knowing whether gods exist or not." The former statement appeared as the opening sentence in his work *Truth or the Rejection*, and what needed rejection were all useless speculations. If man is central, and gods have no influence upon human affairs, social behavior becomes relative only to the specific circumstances under which man lived. In terms of society itself, this implied that its laws, morals, and values are cultural conventions, pertinent to the existing situation, but not representing universal truth or validity. Many modern anthropologists share this view, and call it cultural relativism, by which they mean that every society has its own worth and its own cultural rules.

To justify his relativism, Protagoras presented an evolutionary scheme that explained how different social norms came into existence. Early society was homogeneous, unified and undifferentiated, and the basic cultural inventions such as language, the family, justice, and morality were made in this early stage. Increase in population caused fission, and new societies were established elsewhere, each developing its own elaborations of the basic institutions, and adopting its own fitting modifications of law, government, family life, religion, and ethics. Absolute standards could thus not be found: they simply did not exist. People must accommodate themselves to the rules and patterns of the society in which they lived, and such adaptation Protagoras called "social virtue," meaning efficiency in the conduct of life. Even religion was a useful social institution, and the gods should be worshiped, no matter if one believed in them or not.

Protagoras and most other Sophists were outspoken evolutionists, mainly because this served as a convenient theory for the explanation of the diversity of customs, and it implied progress as well. Their secular worldviews were justified by euhemeristic theories about the origin of religion. Prodicus of Ilius, a younger contemporary of Protagoras, wrote that religion had its origin in object worship, or what de Brosses and his followers much later on called "fetishism." Man first worshiped those objects that were useful to him, but in a later stage of development the discoverers of the useful arts became deified. Demeter, having invented agriculture, became the goddess of grain; Dionysus, the discoverer of wine agriculture, was similarly deified after his death. In Prodicus' view, religion was a useless error, and it would be much better for people to study language, because it was the most important tool of law, government, and education. Prodicus himself was a linguist: he classified the parts of speech into nouns, verbs, articles, particles, and participles, and he is credited with founding the science of etymology.

The "enlightened" relativistic views of the Sophists eventually led to social nihilism. Callicles maintained that there were no norms of morality and thus social virtues could not exist. The laws of society had been invented by the poor and the weak in an attempt to break the power of the rich and the strong. Another Sophist, Thrasymachus, said that justice was nothing but a name given to whatever action furthered the advantage of the elite and the rulers. The ultimate expression of nihilism came from Gorgias, who wrote that nothing exists, if anything did exist it could not be known, and if anything were known it could not be communicated. Such a view is clearly not conducive to education, and cannot further knowledge about the nature of society. In the long run, Sophists raised more questions than they could solve. Nevertheless, their contributions were important in several ways. They fully understood that the study of sociocultural phenomena bears on the understanding of human existence, and that it is a necessary prerequisite for the solution of social problems. They argued convincingly that social practices possessed a large element of convention, so that it became impossible to assume that cultural behavior was due to human nature. Moreover, they stressed the importance of language as a precondition of cultural development and as an instrument of progress, and of course they were fully convinced that education in general was advantageous. Their concepts of evolution also strike us as modern, and their explanation of the diversity of cultures as a function of fission and adaptive specialization is also widely accepted today. Sophists' teachings served as a progressive force, but their skepticism about the validity of all social life was soon challenged. The clearest and strongest opposition to their views came from Socrates and Plato.

Socrates (470–399 B.C.) was appalled by the attempts to teach social success and the disregard for social morals. Faced with the variance of social practices in various cultures, he held that every society was nevertheless guided by certain universal values that transcended the different social customs. Universal ethics stood behind social morals, universal justice guided social laws, and universal principles were present in every other form of social life. These absolutes could not be perceived by the senses, and it was even difficult to express them in words. Every individual must discover these principles for himself, by training his mind to do so. Education was thus important, not for the sake of social climbing, but in order to achieve understanding about the principles of life that transcended local varieties of social behavior. Man's fundamental error was to live in ignorance, as a slave of unanalyzed and ununderstood social rules. The study of social phenomena was of particular importance because it would stir people into consciousness about their own social norms, which was the necessary first step toward the discovery of absolute values.

Socrates' most gifted pupil, Plato (427–347 B.C.), agreed with his master that social behavior was linked to universal values. He went further, however, by attempting to answer Socrates' unsolved question as to how man can acquire knowledge about these values. He first demonstrated that universal values must indeed exist. In everyday life people are confronted with variable particulars—many different kinds and types of dogs, for instance. Nevertheless, dogs are always recognized as such, no matter how different they may be in size, color, or breed. It followed, to Plato, that the human mind possesses an image of an "ideal" dog, one that has never been encountered in reality, but which combines all doglike qualities in itself so that all existing varieties become immediately recognizable. This was true also for cultural rules and social institutions. The ideals of law, forms of government, rules of conduct, goodness, beauty, and truth were equally present in the human mind, and the various institutions found in real life were imperfect reflections of the absolutes. Man could thus discover universal values because they were already present in his mind. This implied that man was not born with an empty mind, but possessed certain innate ideas at birth. Not eschewing the question of where these ideas themselves may come from, Plato said that they were given to man by a divine creator, a transcendental First Cause that had created man, nature, and the universe. Man was part of nature, which was a living whole, and there were no sharp contrasts between men and animals, or between the natural and the social world.

Man's innate knowledge about absolute ideals made him also aware of the faults of his own society. In the *Republic* Plato attempted to visualize a more ideal society, one in which all ultimate values would be implemented as best as humanly possible. He realized that all societies must have practical functions if man is to survive, and in order to discover the basic functional prerequisites of social life Plato dealt with the origin and evolution of society. In his view, food, shelter, and clothing served man's most fundamental survival needs, but since not everyone was equally skilled in producing those commodities, the first social institution to arise was occupational specialization, or a division of labor. Growing needs made other specializations necessary, and in the end there were three classes: producers, protectors, and political leaders.

Plato was definitely not interested in the origin and the evolution of society for its own sake, and he does not present it as a scientific theory. Rather, it was an intellectual construct that he used to illustrate and support his ideas about an ideal society. Where the Sophists stressed cultural diversity, Plato depicted the developments as unilineal changes in complexity. He reconstructed the past in order to discover which elements had remained constant through time, in the conviction that these universals were the necessary components of any form of society, and should thus not be neglected in the ideal republic. Plato stressed innate individual differences, and one of the first requirements of a good society was a just division of labor, everyone carrying out those tasks to which he was most suited by nature, taste, and temperament. This not only would contribute to personal satisfactions, but was of great value to the well-being of the whole society because the goods produced by specialists would be superior. Slaves were also needed to make for a perfect state, and since some people were slaves by nature, they too would be satisfied by doing what they could do best. His picture of an ideal society also reflects the Greek concepts of demography: the city-state could not be too populous. Plato thus recommended controlled and limited selective breeding, presenting the first comprehensive scheme of eugenics in the history of the Western world.

Plato's speculations on the origin and development of society are not in agreement with the findings of modern anthropology; they more resemble nineteenth-century evolutionism, except that the latter was more interested in evolution per se. Like Maine, Plato posited a patriarchal origin of the family, and his account of the developments from pastoralism to agriculture to industrial society returns in the writings of Morgan, Tylor, and V. Gordon Childe. Most important was his insight that a great amount of time is needed for the course of evolution. Later Christian scholars labored for a long while under the conviction that the world had been created around 4000 B.C., and the lack of proper time perspective was a great barrier to the understanding of the processes of evolution.

Like Plato, Aristotle (384–322 B.C.) intertwined his views of man and society with his whole philosophy of life. Acknowledging that society had obvious survival values, he stressed that its true function went far beyond man's material needs: "a city comes into being for the sake of mere life, but it *exists* for the sake of the good life." Man shared the need for nutrition with plants and sensation with animals, but man alone possessed wisdom, reason, and virtue. "Man is by nature a social being," by which Aristotle meant that man was born with social potential that would develop as surely as the acorn grows into an oak tree. Man's social potential was rooted in language and rational thinking.

Society then evolved naturally to realize its higher goals. The necessity for perpetuation of the human race accounts for the early appearance of the family, "an institution established by nature for the supply of man's everyday wants." Next, families united to form villages, but the third and highest development was the full-fledged state organization, and only here could man's nature find its fullest development. Society was thus not an artificial construct as the Sophists would have it, but a natural entity, created through and by man's inherent sociability. Neither could society be explained by reference to a transcendent realm as Plato had tried to do, because such a realm, even if it did exist, would be external to man and society and thus could not be a key to social behavior. Society was not merely a state of mind, but a substantial reality to be observed and analyzed.

Aristotle's approach to the study of society was more in line with modern thinking on the matter than with that of Plato. Plato was more speculative, and his concept of innate knowledge is at variance with the anthropological insight that culture is acquired by learning. Aristotle stressed the empirical method in his studies, stressed the social nature of man, and pointed out that society can best be studied by observing and analyzing social relationships.

Brief mention should be made of Aristotle's contributions to biology. His several essays in this field include "On the descent of animals," "History of animals," "On the movement of animals," and so on. Even the essay with the not so modern sounding title "On the soul" was based upon empirical data, because "soul" meant to Aristotle the principle of life, or the natural force moving all organisms. But most remarkable is the fact that he used his biological findings to attain insights into social life, thus aiming at what we now call anthropology's "holistic" approach, namely the attempt to understand the relationship between man's physical and cultural properties.

Aristotle died one year after Alexander the Great, who had been his pupil. From this time onward, Athenian political life and power rapidly declined. The resulting disintegration and uncertainties of life caused a radical shift in outlook and attitudes toward scholarship. A great many different schools of thought arose, some stressing resignation, others depicting society as subordinate to the individual.

The Epicurean school was named after its leader, Epicurus (341–270 B.C.). He was strongly influenced by the mechanistic materialism of Democritus, and emphasized that society is strictly a human phenomenon. Any attempt to explain it by reference to the gods or to abstract powers such as fate or destiny is both erroneous and dangerous: man himself created his social existence, and he alone can alter it, and strive to happiness. Man exists only in the here and now. His body as well as his soul dissolve after death and are reabsorbed by nature. Life should thus be pleasurable, and pain should be avoided. Yet, Epicurus was not an "epicure" in the sense of how we now understand the word. He did not seek after short-lived sensual pleasures—among them, good food—because they are only of the moment and often have painful aftereffects. To the contrary: in order to live a happy life man should renounce his passions, eat only simple and natural foods, and seek satisfaction in the pursuit of knowledge and in friendship.

Society should not impose any unnecessary restraints upon human existence. Man should not have to adapt himself to society; society exists for the sake of man, and must thus be adapted to his needs. Why then do social laws and rules exist at all? Epicurus felt that if everyone possessed wisdom, rules would indeed be superfluous. Unfortunately this was not the case, and laws were made to lead and to protect the unenlightened masses. This elitist view of society recurs in the Enlightenment, for instance in the writings of Voltaire.

Epicurus' mechanistic and utilitarian worldview led him to the formulation of one of the earliest social contract theories. To support his arguments, he followed the now customary practice of reconstructing the evolution of society. Man began his career as a wild animal-like creature and engaged in frequent fighting. Eventually, men entered into mutual contracts of protection in order to avoid frequent injuries. Government was needed to enforce these laws, and society and the state thus arose as necessary survival mechanisms.

The best-known representative of the Epicurean school is the Roman poet Lucretius (c. 99–55 B.C.), who fully accepted and endorsed the radical materialism of Democritus and Epicurus. In his famous poem *On the Nature of Things*, he drew upon several earlier notions, arriving at a system of biological and cultural evolution of all-encompassing scope. The universe was created "by no tool of gods," but by a confluence of atoms, "the primal germs of things." The first plants and animals arose by spontaneous generation from the moist and warm soil; man and his soul both had material substance and material origins. At first, men lived like beasts, without clothing or tools, gathering berries and acorns as food. Later, arming themselves with clubs, the first tools, they hunted animals, eating the flesh, and using the hides to cover themselves. They lived in sexual promiscuity, but the invention of hut building made men and women cohabit, marking the beginnings of family life. Eventually, groups of families agreed to cooperate, forming village organizations that in due time developed into cities and kingdoms. The early kings and their lineages were wealthy, and the fierce jealousies of the underprivileged groups led to war, and subsequently to anarchy and chaos. It was then that social contracts were deemed necessary and made binding:

> Some wiser heads instructed men to found
> The magisterial office, and did frame
> Codes that they might consent to follow laws.
>   (Lucretius 1957:231)

From this time onward, civilization took its course. Lucretius also dealt with the origin of language, believing that it began with gestures, and that speech developed naturally from animal communication. Throughout he stressed that all developments had demanded long periods of time and could not be considered as sudden changes or one-time inventions.

His long and beautiful poem foreshadowed many later theories and concepts, among them Hobbes' origin of society as the war of all against all; the social contract theories of Hobbes, Spinoza, and Locke; Darwin's struggle for existence and survival of the fittest; Marx's class struggles; the stage theory of evolution of Tylor and Morgan; as well as later oft-repeated concepts about the origins of tools, agriculture, family life and language. Although progress was somehow implicit in this scheme of evolution, Lucretius was no optimist, and was skeptical about the enduring value of civilization.

On the whole, Epicureans were unconcerned with science. It is true that Epicurus wrote on physics, but his system was largely taken over from Democritus, and displayed little original thought. Most of his followers were indifferent to mathematics, logic, astronomy, linguistics, and biology. In this they differed from the Stoics, a school of thought founded by Zeno (c. 340–c. 265 B.C.). Born on Cyprus, Zeno came to Athens as a young man, attracted by the teachings of Socrates. But Socrates' followers, the Cynics, had become rather extreme in the interpretation of the teachings of their master. Emphasizing Socrates' independence of character, they were anarchistic and indifferent to any values. Disappointed, Zeno established his own school, and found many followers.

Like the Epicureans, the central concern of the Stoics was the discovery of the correct and happy way of life. They eagerly sought to advance all knowledge in the conviction that every branch of science would give insights leading to increased social understanding and thus also to increased social well-being. Basic to their theories was the conviction that social behavior is not random, but patterned and orderly. Without this premise it was useless to study society. On this point they thus opposed the Epicureans, who, following Democritus and the atomists, denied the existence of order, seeing only blind random forces at work. The Stoics observed that nature was subject to laws, as evidenced by the regular change of the seasons, the phases of the moon, and the predictability of sunrise and sunset. This order was not man-made, and the power that regulated nature must also be the one that ordered society, since man was also part of nature. They thus developed the theory that "natural law" was the dominant force in the universe and also controlled social relationships. They variously called this ordering principle Zeus, Reason, Providence, Nature, or Logos.

In early Stoicism these explanations were not necessarily of a theological nature. They did not intend to prove the existence of a higher power, but merely wanted to explain the rational order of the world and society. The transcendental was not supernatural, but an explanatory principle, which also explained why man should lead a moral life. It was not that the transcendental demanded morality, as was the case in later Christian doctrine. Instead, the Stoics felt that man would attain happiness if he acted in accordance with the laws of nature and of society. These laws were not necessarily those that governed human relations as set forth by human rulers

CHAPTER 2

MEDIEVAL VIEWS

OF MAN

The late Roman period witnessed the beginning of a fundamental change in the conceptualization of man and society. This change is often explained in terms of a shift from philosophy to religion, culminating in the establishment of Christianity. The fundamental difference between a philosophical and a religious worldview does not rest in the recognition of transcendental powers. The Greeks had recognized these also, but their explanations of society were not predicated on such beliefs. The transcendental formed part of their speculative cosmogony, but man determined his own life and destiny by his social interactions and his search for knowledge. The emerging religious ethos taught that the relationships between man and the gods determined human and social destiny, and that the gods must be obeyed and worshiped. Man could obtain salvation not by knowledge but by piety.

Such a transformation in worldview did not take place overnight, although it went hand in hand with the worsening conditions of life. This brought about a feeling that the world was an imperfect place that could not bring true happiness, and that man was powerless to change his own destiny. The Stoicism of Seneca or of Marcus Aurelius reflected the begin-

nings of the disenchantment and the concomitant turning for
help to higher powers. When Marcus Aurelius died in A.D. 180,
the Roman Empire was beset by civil strife, its government
was weakened, and there were invasions, wars, and plagues.
Many foreign cults formerly outlawed in Rome now were
tolerated, and some became very popular. The general loss of
self-reliance caused many people to seek solace in the promise
of a better life, and this hope was held out in the various cults,
even if they were otherwise very different. Orphism proclaimed man's innate depravity and offered an eschatology in
which he could escape from the evils of his carnal nature. The
Great Mother cult, centered around the worship of Cybele,
included a baptism that purged man from his sins so that he
could be reborn in eternity; the cult of Isis and Osiris promised redemption and resurrection after death; while Mithraism
saw its god Mithra as a savior whose worship would lead to
eternal life in a region of light and beauty. Hundreds of other
cults invaded Rome, among them Christianity. It too emphasized the wretched conditions of man and offered hope for
a new and better life.

This is not the place to discuss why Christianity survived
and other cults gradually disappeared, but it is certain that
it filled an important social need. Not only did it promise a
better life in the hereafter, but in its earliest beginnings it
also attempted to improve the conditions of the deprived lower
classes here on earth.

Although Christianity was first considered an outcast sect
in Rome, and its adherents were persecuted by hostile emperors, it rose from its humble beginnings to a state religion
under Constantine the Great (280?–337). The general lines
of Christian orthodoxy were not firmly established until the
fourth century. Early Church Fathers disagreed not only on
matters of doctrine, but also about the nature of man and of
society. Some of the more urbane Fathers did not escape from
the influences of Greek and Roman humanism. The social
theories of Ambrose (339?–397) and of Origen (185?–254?)
were close to those of the pagan Stoics, and Lactantius (c.260–

340) even thought Stoic ethics much too strict, arguing that passions should not be suppressed but channeled into the right direction.

The much more severe views of Augustine (354–430), however, were the ones that became the most influential, and they dominated the West for centuries to come. In broad terms, Augustine's views of the universe, society, and man were constructed on the assumptions of the perfection of God and the inherent sinfulness of human nature. To the Greeks, the universe possessed a basic unity whose various parts were in essential harmony with one another. In Augustine's view, the cosmos was not at one with man. The universe was made by an omnipotent and perfect Creator, who was also inscrutable, and His work and purposes could never be fully understood by man. It was thus useless to study the universe and nature, and it was similarly superfluous to study society. After an initial period of happiness in the Garden of Eden, Adam and Eve had disobeyed God's commands and brought damnation to all posterity. Coercive social institutions such as the monogamic family, laws, government, and slavery were divinely instituted after sin had entered the world, both as punishments and as remedial measures to counteract man's evil will. The study of man's social life was thus useless, because the only thing that mattered was God, His commands to man, and man's relationship to the Divine. Greek ethics had been man-centered, aimed at happiness through correct social behavior. In the Christian view social behavior was to be judged not by men but by God.

Man himself was, in Augustine's famous words, "crooked, sordid, besotted, and ulcerous," essentially evil, and devoid of reason. Augustine thus closed the door to almost any form of independent scientific inquiry. Whatever God had wanted man to know about nature and society was revealed in the Scriptures, and whatever was not so revealed was intended to remain hidden. Clearly, a true science of man cannot be reared upon Augustinian views. They contradict the premise upon which all modern sociology and anthropology is based, namely that sociocultural phenomena are governed by *discoverable* lawful principles. His views of man and society were, in fact, antianthropological. One of the intentions of his *The City of God* was to destroy any respect for culture: there was no place there for scientists, statesmen, poets, artists, and certainly not for anthropologists. On the whole, Augustine was fairly indifferent to man's social and physical surroundings. In his scheme, faith replaced comprehension, and God's revelations were the only pathways to knowledge. These revelations were mainly contained in the Scriptures, but they could also be found in history, because God's dealings with the world could be observed from the past. The study of history thus became the only intellectual exercise suitable to Christians, and Augustine made significant contributions here. Greeks and Romans had tended to a cyclical view of history, holding that all events recur in endless identical cycles, an outlook that makes study of the past rather useless. Augustine explained that history was linear and goal-directed, and that the nature and actions of historical persons should be observed and analyzed, because they were important as vehicles for God's purposes with the world. Augustine also radically changed the particularistic outlook of earlier historians. History was to him the drama of mankind, not of individual nations, and it should thus be universally conceived. It should begin with the origin of man, and describe all inventions, developments, and the rise and fall of civilizations and powers. It was moreover the task of historians to discover the intelligent pattern in the general course of these events: history is not mere description, but it has meaning and direction. This direction can best be delineated by dividing history into epochs, each one unique, nonrepetitive, and with its own characteristics. The logical succession was from Creation to the end of time, i.e., the Last Judgment, but Augustine also compared the course of history with the life of man, from infancy to childhood, youth, early manhood, late manhood, and old age.

All modern studies of history and of evolution are predicated on Augustine's conceptions. The division of history into unique periods is now commonplace, as is the idea of universal history. Modern historians and evolutionists fully agree that the importance of their research rests not in description, but in the interpretation of the meanings of events, whose occurrences cannot be considered as random.

Augustine's own historical writings dealt mainly with biblical peoples, but he asked Orosius (c. 385–420), one of his disciples, to write a more complete history. The resulting *Seven Books of History against the Pagans* dealt with many different peoples, including barbarians, and contained ethnographic descriptions. The work was officially approved by the pope in 494, and remained a major source of information throughout the Middle Ages.

The period following Augustine's death was one in which the Empire was invaded and eventually conquered by peoples who were still called barbarians and pagans. Although they were feared, they were also a major source of interest and curiosity. The lineal view of history led to the inevitable question about the role of other peoples in the historical process, and the Christian doctrine of the universal brotherhood of men and their common descent from Adam posed questions that were difficult to answer. Some were led to deny this common descent and espoused theories of polygenesis. They speculated that the pagans might be the offspring of the Antipodes, who were supposed to live on the other side of the (flat) earth, and perhaps some had managed to climb over the edge. A more orthodox explanation was that the devil had corrupted the pagans as he had indeed corrupted mankind from the fall of Adam onward, but he had been more successful with some than with others. The various descriptions of barbarians also served to point up moral lessons and as warnings of what horrors would befall those who strayed from the Church. But no matter for which purposes the descriptions of barbarian cultures were used, and no matter how slanted they may have been, they kept alive the ethnographic interest that had begun with Herodotus. Even those authors whose main purpose it was to denounce the pagans served posterity by liberally quoting from older "pagan" documents, thus preserving many descriptions that would otherwise have been lost.

Early Christian historians tended to be more hostile toward the pagans than later ones. The still young Church needed to defend its position and to prove the falsehood of other religions. Euhemerism was a favorite weapon. This was in fact an old Greek theory of mythology holding that gods were deified heroes. Christian writers declared again and again that all pagan gods were thus mere human beings, and diligently collected examples to prove their point. But around the seventh century, when the Church was firmly established, euhemerism took a different turn and became used as an important instrument of reconstruction. If the pagan gods were once historical persons, important kings, or early inventors, much could be learned about the past by reconstructing their lives.

This was one of the methods used by Isidore of Seville (c. 560–636), who attempted to write a complete and universal history. Perhaps following the suggestion of Augustine, who had said that it would be good if someone would compile a description of unknown places, animals, plants, minerals, and other things mentioned in the Scriptures, Isidore intended to summarize all human knowledge and thus help to preserve all learning of the past. He cast his monumental work, the *Etymologies*, in the form of an encyclopedia, and brought together a large collection of excerpts from existing documents under headings such as agriculture, anatomy, architecture, arithmetic, astronomy, cosmology, geology, law, and so on. Although there were no separate entries on customs and manners of people, ethnographic data were scattered about in these volumes. He brought in a wealth of detail concerning ancient Egypt, Assyria, Greece, Rome, the Germans, Franks, Saxons, Africans, and many others. He dealt with their languages, food habits, arts, warfare, worship, laws, trade patterns, and similar items still expected to be included in present-day monographs. While the material thus collected was not always reliable, the effort is interesting, and gives much information about the extent of knowledge in the early Middle Ages. It also marks the beginning of an interest in a universal body of knowledge, or what Isidore called a *scientia universalis*.

The *Etymologies* achieved great popularity, and was still one of the standard authorities in Shakespeare's youth. It was but the first in a long line of medieval histories and encyclopedias, such as Ado of Vienne's (799–874) *Chronicle of the Six Ages of the World,* the works of Peter Comester (fl. 1148–78), the *Speculum naturale* and *Speculum historiale* of Vincent of Beauvais (1190–1264), and the works of Albert of Bollstadt (1193?–1280). The efforts culminated in Bartholomaeus Angelicus' (fl. 1230–50) *On the Properties of Things*. In it, he dealt with 170 nations, including modern ones such as the English, Irish, Scots, Norwegians, Swedes, and Frisians. He was careful to give the references for all his statements, so that it was also a good bibliographical source. The work was translated into six European languages, and reached forty-six editions, thus testifying to the widespread interest in such matters. Bartholomaeus' work contains a quantity of information that had not been brought together before.

Of course, it is easy to find fault with these various compilations. Margaret Hodgen (1964:chapter 2) points out that the authors often relied upon out-of-date sources such as Herodotus, Pliny, or Solinus; that misinformation was thus compiled, and culture change not taken into account. Once Herodotus had typified Egyptians as "very religious," they remained so stereotyped. But the compilers also attempted to bring in new materials, and diligently read accounts by travelers, traders, and missionaries who had resided in other lands. Unfortunately, these eyewitnesses were also often far from reliable. Tending toward sensationalism, they included stories not only about natural races, but also of monstrous ones, with dogs' heads, or with ears so large that they could be used as coverlets during the night (Malefijt 1968). Nevertheless, the information about existing peoples was partially correct. Merchant traders had to know the customs of the people with whom they traded, missionaries realized that they would be more successful if they knew the cultures and religions of the peoples they set out to christianize. But even so, medieval ethnographic descriptions would not pass the test of modern anthropological scrutiny. Not only were they anecdotal, but they were also fraught with preconceived notions of value. Although many showed an increasing degree of tolerance toward exotic customs, the writers were always ethnocentric. The importance of the medieval compendia is that they preserved knowledge about peoples who have now disappeared, and that they kept ethnographic interests alive. They stressed cultural diversity and stirred many later scholars to seek answers to the hidden problems. Before being all too critical of the medieval branch of "ethnology," it would be well to remind ourselves that modern anthropology also began with unverified and unsifted data—witness Frazer's *Golden Bough*.

Although the early Middle Ages are sometimes called "dark," this value judgment overlooks many important developments that took place. There were many technological inventions; Charlemagne (c. 742–814) founded a number of monastic schools in which higher learning was pursued; and the study of nature was made respectable by John Scotus Erigena (c. 810–c. 877), who wrote that God revealed himself not only in history, but in the whole universe. Optics, magnetism, metallurgy, medicine, anatomy, the planets, the rainbow, all were subjects of investigation and lively debates. Many revolted against Augustine's view that man was deprived of reason and evil by nature, and there was a general desire to preserve past knowledge and to learn from it.

When Aristotle's and other Greek writings were rediscovered during the twelfth century, they were enthusiastically studied. It became clear that the Greeks had made many important discoveries in physics, ethics, logic, and politics, and that they possessed splendid art and architecture. The Greeks also depicted man as a rational being, capable of improving his own lot as well as his social conditions. This was radically different from the Augustinian views.

Thomas Aquinas (1225–74), who admired Aristotle so much that he always referred to him as "The Philosopher" (as if others did not exist), was worried and struck by this entirely different view of human existence. Through very complex arguments he concluded that man was intelligent, endowed with reason, and capable of selecting higher or lower life goals. Since man's innate reason was bestowed upon him by God, it was man's duty to exercise his divine gift and to apply it not only to theological questions, but also to the study of nature, society, politics, ethics, and all other realms of science.

In Thomas' universal scheme of things, man occupied a position just below the angels. With them he shared the potential for universal knowledge, but he shared his sensuous appetites with animals. Much of Thomas' thinking was centered around the interrelationships and interactions within man's dual nature, a problem we still study in terms of relating man's biology to his cultural faculties. Thomas Aquinas also noted man's helplessness and lack of instincts at birth, argued for the psychic unity of man since "by nature all men are equal," believed in the social contract theory, used the organic analogy, made a distinction between the law of nations and civil law, and discussed man's upright posture, his senses, his brain, and his extremities, in terms of comparative anatomy. Although theology remained central in all his writings, we find in them many views about man's social and physical nature that are original and thought provoking. Aristotelianism was officially condemned by Bishop Tempier three years after Thomas' death, but his influence was nonetheless enduring, and his views of man's rational nature, without which social sciences could not exist, prevailed in the long run.

The comparative studies of man and his cultures slowly moved in the direction of greater objectivity and empiricism. Roger Bacon (c. 1214?–94), who taught at Oxford, wrote that experience and observation were the *only* ways to arrive at reliable truths. Boasting that he had spent two thousand pounds on books and various instruments for experiments, he clearly was not a man relying on tradition alone. He wrote essays on mathematics, optics, anatomy, astronomy, and comparative linguistics, and advocated the study of manners and customs of peoples in the whole habitable world. From his hands came the first comparative universal history of religion, and his objectivity in dealing with this still very sensitive topic is truly remarkable. Among other things, he constructed a typology that was meant to include all known forms of religion: nature worship, idol worship, fire worship, Islam, Judaism, and Christianity. He calculated that monotheism was more common than polytheism, and monotheism thus must be the basic principle of true religion. As a Christian, he held that Christianity was superior to Judaism and Islam, but he was willing to accept that these other monotheistic religions were valid in their own rights.

As the Middle Ages came to an end, religion was still a central power, but a trend toward secularization was quite noticeable. Other cultures and religions were generally recognized as significant, and the Augustinian idea that history should be universal was interpreted to mean that there was a basic unity of mankind. By extension there was also a basic unity of the pagan gods.

Giovanni Boccaccio's (1313–75) *Genealogy of the Gods* represented this view. In this book, written at the request of Hugues IV, king of Cyprus, Boccaccio attempted to reduce all classical mythology to one coherent system. He was fully aware of the necessity to consult original sources, and claimed that all his data were so gathered. Later commentators on his work said that in fact he knew only very little Greek, and that he had made extensive use of secondary sources (Seznec 1961: 220–21). He presented Demogorgon as the progenitor of all gods, but this "mighty father of the race," to whom every god, demigod, and hero was related, was wholly unknown in classical times. Nevertheless, Boccaccio showed that a myth can be interpreted in more than one way: its meanings may be literal, moral, or symbolic. The myth of Perseus decapitating the Gorgon and rising into the air by the aid of his winged sandals could be read as an account of actual events, it could be an allegory of a wise man's virtue after the conquest of evil, or it could be seen as a symbol of Christ's ascension into heaven after overcoming the evils of a sinful world.

The *Genealogies* was not dissimilar to Frazer's *Golden Bough*, either in scope or in method. Like Frazer, Boccaccio tried to make sense out of a general mass of varied but related data for which so far no systematic relationship had been put forward. Like Frazer also, Boccaccio was uncritical of his sources, using all the writings of the past with equal confidence. Frazer correctly noted that ceremonies, taboos, and magical practices had meanings beyond the literal ones, as Boccaccio saw that myths possessed several possible meanings. His great insight was that myths are not merely irrational stories, and the later organized study of mythology was rooted in this premise.

CONCLUSIONS

Most writers dealing with developments in the history of anthropology have neglected the Middle Ages in the conviction that nothing in that period contributed to the understanding of man and society. While the intellectual climate in Europe was not favorable to scholarship of any kind, it was certainly not a period of utter stagnation. During the Middle Ages excellent heroic poetry was written, Gothic art and architecture developed, logic and mathematics were elaborated, the first universities were established, many technological inventions were made, and knowledge was preserved in encyclopedic works. Moreover, many ideas basic for later development of the social sciences were formulated or strengthened.

Stripped of its religious implications, medieval thought expressed the conviction that man and society did not exist for their own sake alone, but had meanings beyond their existence. Modern social studies would be barren without this conviction, no matter what these meanings might be. For medieval thinkers the meaning was the attainment of salvation; anthropologists study men and cultures to acquire a sense of social responsibility, to provide guidance in circumstances of inevitable change, to discover universal values, or to mitigate human suffering.

The Christian ideal of the brotherhood of man was not always put into practice, but its principle proclaimed the basic unity of mankind and the conviction that other peoples were not mere brutes, so that their customs were worthy of study and scrutiny. The interest in foreign peoples remained lively throughout the period, although for a variety of reasons. Augustine and Orosius wrote about the pagans in order to refute them, the encyclopedists were often moved by a curiosity about the diversity of habits, missionaries wrote their reports to counteract culture shock of their successors, others wrote in a spirit of adventure or sensationalism.

Compared to earlier periods, the spatial horizons were widened, since more geographical areas had become known. The temporal views, however, became much narrower, because Christian doctrine dictated that Creation had not taken place so very long ago.

The study of history took important new turns from cyclical to lineal and from particular to universal. The seeds of unilineal evolutionism were contained in many historical accounts since they implied a degree of progress and refuted the idea of a past Golden Age. The periods the accounts depicted were unique and followed each other in logical succession.

While the dogmatic and pessimistic worldview of Augustine is not very congenial to anthropology, or for that matter to all modern science, his extreme views were challenged and almost completely reversed by the end of the Middle Ages. One of the major points of social dispute during the period was the question of the supremacy of church or state in political matters. In the course of these debates it became necessary to consider the origin and nature of political organization, and the first systematic theory concerning this was that of social contract. Scattered statements of interest to social scientists can be found in many medieval writings, i.e., on population growth, on the nature of laws, on the divinity of kings, on racial differences, on etymology and linguistic change, and many others.

Although most anthropologists will be inclined to feel that their own views are more closely related to Greek thought than to medieval ideas, the latter should be neither despised nor overlooked, but studied in much greater detail.

CHAPTER 3

WIDENING

HORIZONS

Anthropology as it exists now was forged out of the encounter with exotic peoples. It is obvious that the science of man cannot achieve competence without knowledge about the existing varieties of peoples and cultures. The travels and discoveries of the fifteenth and sixteenth centuries, culminating in the discovery of the New World, are thus very germane to the development of anthropology.

It is fortunate that so many travelers wrote detailed accounts of their experiences and the peoples they encountered. Even in their own time, the astonishing array of peoples and cultures that no one knew existed caused great excitement. Europe was shaken out of its provincialism, the outlook was widened, and the creative imagination of scholars was stimulated.

Of course, there had also been travelers in medieval times. Some merchants traveled as far as China, missionaries settled in Asia and Africa, pilgrims journeyed to the Holy Land, often on foot. The Crusades, beginning in 1097, brought about large-scale contacts with the East and North Africa, and the participants brought back a great deal of information about different religions, customs, and life styles of the peoples they encountered. The best known of these accounts came from the crusaders William of Tyre (c. 1130–c. 1190), Robert de Clari (d. 1240), Jean Joinville (c. 1224–c. 1317), and Jacobus Vitriarco (d. 1240). The latter even discussed problems of acculturation.

A good deal of information about Asia came from missionary-diplomats. After the Mongolian conquests, the politically powerful Church realized that the new Mongolian Empire could not be ignored. Innocent IV, the ruling pope, sent Giovanni de Plano Carpini (c. 1182–1252) to Mongol courts to establish diplomatic relations. Upon his return he wrote *History of the Mongols,* in which he described people's physical appearance, manners of living, "good and bad habits," laws, customs, superstitions, and taboos. The exotic was emphasized: people were forbidden to thrust a knife into the fire, to touch arrows with a whip, to kill young birds, and to spill milk on the ground. William Rubruquis (c. 1215–70; the spelling of his name varies, and he is also known as Friar William) traveled in Asia for similar purposes, and in his later *Journals* he wrote about items of material culture, food habits, the duties of women, manners of burial, and he mentioned that "certain people are wont to eat their own parents." The journal of Friar Odoric (d. 1331) is particularly strong in its emphasis upon "great and miraculous things" that he encountered in the East. Chapter titles include "Of a strange and uncouth idol," "Of a monastery where many strange beasts live upon a hill," but also, more practically, "Of certain inns appointed for travelers." The reports of the friars include some comparisons with their own culture. Rubruquis notes with some amazement that pagan idol worshipers used strings of shells to count their prayers, not unlike his own rosary; and the chests upon which candles and oblations were placed reminded him of the altars in Catholic churches.

A great deal of factual information came from the *Book of Diversities,* dictated by Marco Polo (c. 1254–1323) at the end of his life. His seventeen years of service at the court of Kublai Khan had given him broad knowledge about Asian conditions, and he wrote about trade relationships, market systems, money values, types of houses, division of labor, marriage practices, religion, burial rites, and so on. He also yielded to sensationalism and included many fabulous stories about monsters and freaks. The title of his book reflects its purpose as well as the status of ethnography in his age: customs were collected for entertainment rather than for analysis.

Another famous book was *The Travels of Sir John Mandeville*. No birth or death records have been found of this mysterious figure. He began his "travels" in 1322, but it appears that Mandeville, whoever he may have been, was a clever and artistic compilator who probably never saw the marvels he so vividly described. Richly illustrated with woodcuts, the book achieved great popularity, went through many editions (the last one in 1964), and was translated into ten different languages.

Such accounts, however fanciful some of their information, served to make people aware of human diversity. But it was not for this reason that travels increased. Important improvements were made in shipbuilding and the art of sailing, and there were economic reasons to find a sea route to India, and to explore Africa further. The Portuguese ruler Henry the Navigator (1394–1460) ordered his fleet to explore the west coast of Africa, and the mouths of the Gambia and Senegal rivers were discovered. Accounts by these maritime explorers, such as the *Chronicle of the Discovery and Conquest of Guinea* (1453) by Gomez Eannes de Azurara, provided the world with new data.

It became established custom that at least one literate person should accompany such expeditions, and the author of the *Journal of the First Voyage of Vasco da Gama, 1497–1499* described not only the perils of the journey, but also the appearance, dress, language, ornaments, food habits, and trade items of the peoples encountered. The explorers were also anxious to discover the fabled kingdom of Prester John, the legendary devout Christian ruler of a land that contained all treasures of the world, harboring not only the richest mineral and natural resources, but also the fountain of eternal youth. The Prester John legend had come into being in the twelfth century when a letter was received by the Byzantine emperor Manuel Comnenus, purportedly written by this wise and wealthy monarch, who invited all Christians to visit him, but did not include his address. It is quite sure that European leaders asked the members of their expeditions to be on the lookout for the location of this friendly realm. The author of the Vasco da Gama journal relates that on the island of Monocobique (Mozambique) they received the information that "Prester John resided not far from this place," that he held many cities along the coast, and that the inhabitants of these cities were merchants who owned great ships. He added: "This news rendered us so happy that we cried with joy, and prayed to God to grant us health so that we might behold what we so much desired."

Even before da Gama set sail on his epoch-making journey, Christopher Columbus (1451–1506) was diligently studying available maps and travel literature. A museum in Seville still proudly displays a copy of Marco Polo's *Diversities* with notes in the margins in Columbus' handwriting. Columbus knew that the world was round, and since the southern limits of Africa had not yet been reached it seemed more plausible to sail westward. Marco Polo had described Cipangu (Japan) as fabulously rich, but had placed it much too far east of Cathay (China). The exaggeration of the eastward projection of Asia and the underestimation of the circumference of the earth made Columbus believe that a relatively short trip would bring him to Asia.

Unable to convince Portuguese rulers, he persuaded Ferdinand and Isabella of Spain to finance the undertaking. In August 1492 Columbus sailed out with his now famous ships *Niña, Pinta* and *Santa Maria,* and in October of that same year San Salvador in the Bahamas was sighted. Sailing southward, Columbus reached Cuba, which he assumed to be part of China, and then, turning east, he found Hispaniola, which he believed to be India.

Upon his return to Europe, Columbus wrote a letter to his royal patrons that contained the first information about the "Indians." He remarked that they walked around naked, although some women used coverings of leaves or small cotton aprons. They had no iron and no weapons, were well formed, timid, simple, and extremely liberal with their possessions. Columbus kidnapped seven Taino Indians and brought them to the Spanish court. It is certain that the monarchs were more intrigued by Columbus' promise to procure them "as much gold as you need," than by ethnographic details. But attached to their court was an Italian scholar, Pietro Martire d' Anghiera (1457–1526), who immediately grasped the importance of the discoveries for ethnography and linguistics, and he became the first systematic reporter on the Indians. Collecting a vocabulary from the Taino Indians whom Columbus had brought back, he produced the earliest European record of any New World language. He interviewed many explorers, examined their captives and the objects they brought with them. His reports were objective, and he condemned only the practices of cannibalism and human sacrifice. Although he never visited the New World himself, he entreated all explorers to make extensive notes on their observations of native life. His writings were largely descriptive, but he hinted at the possibility that Indians might be descendants of the Jews, and he suggested a "noble savage" image when he wrote that Indians "seem to live in that golden world of which the old writers speak so much, where men lived simply and innocently, without enforcement of laws, without quarreling, judges and libels . . . without toil, living in open gardens, not entrenched by dikes, divided with hedges, or defended with walls." Like so many before him, he also took delight in reporting gruesome tales: "Such children as they take they fatten like we do chickens and young hogs, and eat them when they are well-fed . . . they first eat the intestines and extremities as hands, feet, arms, neck, and heads. The fleshier parts they dry and store as we do with pork or bacon . . ."

Columbus himself remained fairly restrained in his descriptions. He was not amazed by the presence of people in the New World, simply because he did not know that it was a new world. Amerigo Vespucci (1451–1512), after whom the new continent was eventually named, was much less sympathetic in his descriptions of the native inhabitants. The Indians were cruel, warlike, and cannibalistic, and he described their cultures in negative terms: they were ignorant of law, government, private property, religion, and the immortality of the soul. This evaluation implied that the Indians lived much like early men, and gave rise to the idea that early cultures can be reconstructed from the study of contemporary savage ones. Louis Le Roy (c. 1510–77) gave early expression to this concept when he wrote that the Indians of the New World lived "as the first men, without letters, without laws, without kings, without government, without arts . . ." But even the more favorable reports were written in the conviction that Indian cultures were far inferior to European civilization, no matter if the natives were friendly or cruel. This ethnocentric confidence was not shaken when the higher civilizations of Mexico and Peru were discovered. Diego Velásquez (c. 1460–1524) reached Yucatán in 1517, Hernando Cortés (1485–1547) seized what is now Mexico City in 1521, and Francisco Pizarro (c. 1476–1541) conquered Peru in 1527. Although these lands were certainly not without government, laws, or art, the cruel conquistadors rationalized their acts by saying that the people were not Christians, and thus to be despised.

When Vasco Núñez de Balboa (c. 1475–1517) reached the Pacific shore in 1513, it became relatively certain that America was a separate continent, and not an extension of Asia. Ferdinand Magellan's (1480–1521) voyage around the world settled this without a doubt. Now the question of the origin of the Indians became more acute than it had been before. Almost inevitably, the debates were first carried on in theological terms. On the one hand, Christian doctrine dictated that Creation had been a single event, and that all men descended from Adam. But it seemed difficult to accept that these cruel cannibals were related to civilized Europeans. Discussions centered around the question of monogenesis versus polygenesis, and were devoid of interest in the origin of Indians for their own sake.

Polygenists, aware that they were stepping on dangerous grounds, attempted to reconcile their views with the Scriptures. Paracelsus (1493–1541)—whose real name was Theophrastus Bombastus von Hohenheim—observed that the book of Genesis stated that all people were created by one God, but argued that this did not necessarily mean that all are born from Adam. He postulated that the New World was populated through another ancestor outside Adam's creation, arguing that "it is impossible to conceive that the newly found people are of Adam's blood." One of his disciples, who wisely remained anonymous, stated blandly that Moses "understood no physics," and had thus described creation in a wholly unscientific manner. A century later, Isaac de La Peyrère (1594–1676) espoused the much better known "pre-Adamite" theory, attempting to prove that only the Jews descended from Adam while the gentiles came from a different and earlier ancestor.

Monogenists accepted the single origin of all mankind, but were now faced with the question of how the Indians had reached America. A popular early answer was that they had come from Atlantis, a mythical continent that had stretched from Spain to Africa, but had sunk beneath the sea around 1320 B.C. Pedro Sarmiento de Gamboa's *Historia de los Incas* (completed in 1572 but first published in 1906) may serve as one example out of many possible ones championing the Lost Continent theory. The author explained that Atlantis was first settled by descendants of Noah who had reached it via Spain and North Africa. It became a very rich and wealthy empire, with a well-developed civilization. When it disappeared beneath the ocean in a flood, only the westernmost inhabitants survived, who became thus the forebears of the present American Indians. The Incas had preserved some of the civilized traits of Europe, and the fact that they had myths about a flood was sufficient proof to Gamboa that the drowning of Atlantis was a historical fact.

Another very popular monogenist theory was that the Indians were descendants of the lost tribes of Israel. In 1511 Pietro Martire had hinted at a possible Jewish origin of Indians, and the missionary Bartolomé de las Casas had also discussed this as a possibility. The many later advocates of the idea (which survives in some circles even today) were convinced that similar practices, however superficial, were conclusive proof of close relationships. They pointed out that both ancient Jews and Indians carried out animal sacrifices and purification rites, both held fasts, had food taboos, bride-service, endogamy, and, most startling of all, both practiced circumcision. Linguists bolstered the convictions by showing that some words in Indian languages resembled Hebrew.

Of course, some similarities exist between all peoples, and the comparative method survives until the present day. Archaeologists and ethnologists still attempt to establish historical connections between peoples with like artifacts or customs. But they do not base their conclusions on superficial similarities, because they may be accidental, or due to diffusion, historical circumstance, or adaptation to similar environments. Moreover, before culture traits can be compared they must have similarity in function. Direct descent is often very difficult to establish. In fact, the presence of Indians in the Americas antedates the desert wanderings of the Jews by many millennia. Nevertheless, a host of rival theories sprang up, relating Indians to most any known ancient or modern nation, including China, India, Egypt, Africa, Ireland, Wales, Scotland, Scandinavia, France, Italy, Troy, and so forth (Wauchope 1962). The positive result of these attempts was that they did much to improve ethnographic data gathering since detailed descriptions were needed to prove the supposed relationships.

Present-day anthropologists generally accept the theory that the peopling of America took place via the Bering Strait, with possible minor contacts with Southeast Asia across the Pacific. Without the supporting evidence of archaeology and oceanography that we now possess, the Bering Strait theory was proposed as early as the sixteenth century, when Edward Brerewood (c. 1565–1613) argued that the Indians had probably crossed from Siberia to Alaska. Thomas Jefferson (1743–1826) wrote in his *Notes on the State of Virginia* that the peopling of America had taken place in that manner.

It became generally realized that whatever the theory, accurate data collecting was crucial. As early as 1575, Jerome Turler admonished those who make journeys to "mark down such things in strange countries as they shall have need to use in the common trade of life." A few years later (1578), William Bourne gave directions still valid for modern field workers: "They should be steady men, not attracted by banquetting and play and gain and dancing and dallying with women." Soon afterward a number of full-fledged manuals appeared, forerunners as it were of the *Notes and Queries* handbook for anthropologists (first published in 1874, now in its sixth edition). Albert Meier wrote such an early guidebook in German in 1587, and it was almost immediately translated into English under the title of *Certain brief and special instructions for gentlemen, merchants, students, soldiers, mariners, etc.* (1589). Its goals were somewhat pompously stated: "... it purports to enroll every traveler abroad in the Catalogue of Homer as seers of many regions and of the manners of many nations." The twenty-one-page syllabus contained twelve sections, each with some twenty to thirty subheadings. In addition to marriage customs, burial practices, and food habits, many other important items were pointed out as worthy of attention, including systems of weights and measures, coinage, taxes, market days, crimes, punishments, recreation, political relationships to neighboring countries, and "all other capabilities and habits of man." Anticipating the much later interest in personalities, Meier also demanded studies of "the disposition and spirit of the people" to note whether they were valiant or faint-hearted and effeminate, and to observe their honesty, humanity, hospitality, love, and all other moral virtues. A full year of intensive field work would hardly suffice for the recording of everything mentioned in these "brief instructions." About a century later, Bernard Varen (1622–50) wrote *Geographica generalis* (1650), which became the standard handbook for all travelers. His categories are still adhered to by modern ethnographers, namely:

1 Stature, shape, skin color, food habits
2 Occupation and arts
3 Virtues, vices, learning, wit
4 Marriage, birth, burial, name giving
5 Speech and language
6 State and government
7 Religion
8 Cities and renowned places
9 History
10 Famous men, inventions and innovations
(1682:3)

The great geographer left environment out, but perhaps he took that for granted.

As the number of travel accounts increased, they began to be published in collections. The most famous series in English is that begun by Richard Hakluyt (1552–1616). Others attempted to deal with the mass of materials through compendia, among which Sebastian Münster's (1489–1552) *Cosmographia universalis* (1544) is perhaps best known. Some compilations became specialized and dealt with one topic only. Samuel Purchas (1575–1626), a country clergyman who never traveled outside his native England, dauntlessly proposed to compile a complete work on religion, namely the "religious rites of all religions before the Flood, any form of worship, any fetishism, any idolatry anywhere and at any time." In *Purchas, his Pilgrimage* (1613), he wrote that the diversity of cultures and religions could be explained easily, because nations had become divided after the confusion of languages at the Tower of Babel. Like many other writers of his times he translated all pagan customs into European terms. Among the pagans of Mexico there were "virgins" serving in temples, rising for "Matins," doing "penance"; there were "monasteries" for men and "convents" for women, and the religious hierarchy included priests, bishops, and even a pope.

Hundreds of other descriptions and compilations appeared on the scene preserving a great deal of information about peoples and conditions that no longer exist. They differed widely in scope and emphasis, and while some displayed greater sympathy and understanding of native peoples than others, most took the superiority of Western civilization over all others wholly for granted. Some early writers had been inclined to believe that "wild savages" were more closely related to animals than to man, but the pope quickly ended those speculations by declaring that Indians were fully human. But this official pronouncement did nothing to shake the prevailing ethnocentrism. If Indians were no beasts, they were in any case inferior human beings, and it rarely occurred to anyone that they were worthwhile studying for their own sake or for the intrinsic interests of their own cultures.

One exception to this general rule can be found in the writings of the French essayist Michel de Montaigne (1533–92). In his essay "Of Cannibals," he criticized this cruel practice of South American Indians, but quickly added that if we want to call them barbarians for that reason we must include ourselves as well, because we surpass them in every kind of cruelty and barbarity. A great many anthropological insights can be found throughout Montaigne's essays. He came close to a modern concept of culture because he held that "the force of custom" determines behavior to a very large degree. He also said that the customs of his own culture were neither more nor less rational than those of others. Skeptical of supernatural causation of social phenomena, he sought instead for naturalistic explanations. It was man's nature to be social, but since his mind was plastic at birth, different cultural habits were learned, and personalities were formed by these learning patterns. Geography and climate also influenced human habits, with the result that some nations are more warlike and others more peaceful, some are inclined to freedom, others to slavery. While modern anthropologists disagree with such geographical determinism, it should be noted that racial determinism was unknown to Montaigne; he stressed that the different behavior patterns were not dependent upon complexion, stature, or countenance, but that people assumed new dispositions if they moved into different environments. While seeking naturalistic explanations, Montaigne was skeptical about the existence of invariable natural laws. The diversity of human customs and habits spoke against such laws, but Montaigne was at a loss to explain similarities and correspondences between peoples. Montaigne also warned against premature theorizing, and scorned those writers who built vast edifices of systems, explaining all of mankind on the basis of a few scraps of evidence.

Montaigne's thoughts were strongly influenced by the contemporary discoveries, and the whole Renaissance period received much of its impetus from the expansion of travel and exploration, particularly from the discovery of the New World. Many other authors concentrated their efforts on describing and explaining the amazing variety of plants, animals, peoples, and customs. Horizons became widened in another way, too, namely through the rediscovery of the writings of ancient Greeks and Romans. Many scholars began studying those pagan documents rather than steeping themselves in the teachings of the Church Fathers, and to them the revelation of the wisdom of the Greeks was a far greater event than the discoveries of new places and peoples.

The new intellectuals soon were called "humanists," but their secularism did not signify an open rebellion against religion, as was the case in the later Enlightenment. The diligent reading of non-Christian writings brought about the awareness that social problems had a secular as well as a religious side. Like Thomas before them, early humanists tried to reconcile current religious doctrines with the world-views of the Greeks. This in turn necessitated a revaluation of contemporary social conditions. Side by side with ethnographic writings, others appeared that were more society oriented, often critical of their own social conditions, and, like the Greeks, proposing ways and means to alter unwarranted or unacceptable social conditions.

One effect of the rediscovery of the ancient writings was an almost boundless admiration for the Greeks and Romans. They were viewed as the source and fountainhead of all learning. It seemed that many humanists, while rejecting medieval religious authority, willingly exchanged this for submission to the supremacy of the ancients. Thus they looked backward rather than forward in their quest for knowledge. Galen (c. 130–c. 200) was called "the Prince of physicians" and his teachings remained unassailed and unaltered for a long period of time. Aristotle himself was so exalted that one of the statutes of Oxford University decreed that bachelors and masters who did not follow Aristotle faithfully were liable to a fine of five shillings for every point of divergence (quoted by R. Jones 1965:4).

The admiration of the past was in keeping with the prevalent Renaissance view that the world was old and decaying. Human accomplishments paralleled that downward movement. Looking for evidence, people found it almost everywhere. John Donne (1572–1631) noted that the life span of people had shortened considerably as compared to that of early man: Adam lived 930 years, while Methuselah reached the age of 969 years. Edward Brerewood (1565–1613), examining the Greek language, noticed its increasing "corruption" in style, purity, and elegance. It did not particularly astonish him, because language, too, followed the "law of nature." Even Sir Walter Raleigh (1552?–1618), after his famous expedition up the Orinoco River, concluded that the world was senile, run down like a clock, and men, fallen away from undoubted truth, "descend lower and lower, and shrink and slide downwards . . ." (1614).

Social criticism was not incompatible with this pessimistic outlook, nor with the admiration of the Greeks and Romans. They too had often enough focused their attention upon man's adjustment to society and had offered plans for betterment.

It was much more difficult to reconcile Christian doctrine with the new outlook, and religious persuasions were by no means lost. How could the worship of God be brought in line with the worship of the ancient philosophers and the basic principles of Christianity with the secular worldviews of Greeks and Romans?

Perhaps no humanist suffered more from these contradictions than Desiderius Erasmus (1469?–1536). A devout Christian, his admiration of the ancients verged on veneration. He considered the appellations "Saint Socrates" and "Saint Cicero" highly appropriate and found their writings so "chaste, holy and divine" that he convinced himself that they must have been inspired by the same Spirit that inspired later Christian writers. What impressed him so much about the saintly ancients was their concept of original human goodness, which was so far removed from the Augustinian concept of original sin. Erasmus tried to show that Greek virtue and Christian virtue are one, and that the knowledge of the Greeks could thus be used in the service of Christian piety. He felt that early Christians had been much closer to the Greek ideal than his contemporaries, and in his *The Praise of Folly* (1511) he fiercely criticized the Church, the formalism of priests, the stupidity and greed of monks, as well as all misdirected social efforts such as people marrying dowries instead of women, and old flabby-breasted females chasing their own lost youth.

The book was dedicated to his friend Thomas More (1478–1535) because the surname More was so near to *moriae* (folly). More himself was very critical of his own society, but rather than expressing his discontent with the ironic humor of Erasmus, he took the course of presenting an imaginary ideal society in *Utopia* (1516). Influenced by accounts of travelers about the newly discovered Indians, More became convinced that these primitive savages were happier than his so-called civilized contemporaries.

In his book he pretends to have heard about Utopia from a scholarly man, the Portuguese adventurer Raphael Hythlo-

day, and through the mouth of this imaginary spokesman
More contrasts the goodness of Utopia with the evils of his
own society. Utopia is an agricultural city-state. Its streets
are commodious and handsome, the houses very beautiful
and their doors never locked because private property does
not exist. Money has been abolished, precious stones are mere
playthings for children, meals are communal, but the family
is the central unit of social organization. Residence rules are
patrilocal, resulting in extended families of which the oldest
male is the household head, unless he has reached his dotage.
Working hours are only six a day, eight hours are appointed
for supervised and institutionalized education and entertainment; the remainder of the day is free, although idleness is
not permitted. The society is ruled by a democratic monarch,
elected for life unless he becomes old and useless.

More's Utopia is not very attractive to modern man: as in
most utopias, there is little personal freedom. Not only are
taverns and alehouses banned from the country, but travel is
severely restricted, possible only by special permission.
Strangers are not welcome, and allowed to come only if
they bring in something useful. Even then they have no
freedom of movement for fear that they will infect the
Utopians with a desire for change. There is no place for
science, for creative activity, or for new discoveries. Change is
frowned upon, and those who disobey the rules are sentenced
to a condition of slavery.

More cannot be called a modernist. His ideal society was
more static than that of the Middle Ages, and its social order
was a straitjacket, closed to outside influence. Nevertheless,
More believed that his Utopia was "immediately practicable."
While this seems very doubtful, he may yet be counted as a
representative of the new spirit of his age, which developed a
greater concern for social life here on earth than for life after
death.

Another contemporary writer concerned about social evils
was Niccolò Machiavelli (1496–1527). Like Thomas More, he
accepted classical authors as his models, simultaneously de-

veloping a rigorously secular attitude toward social and political life. But Machiavelli was not interested in utopias. In his most famous book, *The Prince* (1513), he made it clear that he dealt with reality. To him, it was useless to fancy utopias or imagine republics that never existed. Any possible improvement of societies could be effective only if their present conditions were faced squarely and without sentimentality. Social institutions existed to fulfill the needs of society, and political power could be effective only if it concentrated on its own goals, i.e., to be a power for the good of the people.

Machiavelli is thus not the advocate of immoral political unscrupulousness, but he separates political action from ethical and religious considerations. Political leadership cannot be based upon lofty but unrealistic ideals, and if the state requires a strong and powerful prince, this leader should know how to remain strong and powerful. Rather than an exercise in deception, *The Prince* was an effort to improve the social and political conditions of contemporary peoples. Many consider Machiavelli the first truly scientific thinker on politics and thus also the first modern social scientist (Bronowski and Mazlish 1962:30).

Perhaps the most basic aspect of his advice to a prince is that—if he wants to retain his power—he should know how to employ the nature of man. Machiavelli felt that human nature is very much the same everywhere. It has both its good and its bad sides, but has grown worse through the corruption of civilization. This corruption came about through the insatiability of human desires, which are the major moving powers of social activities. Nature created men so that they desire everything, but since they are unable to attain this goal, desire will be always greater than the faculty of acquiring, and discontent will be the inevitable result. This will always incline men to fighting and war, and hence they need a strong political power to keep them in check. Machiavelli also believed that people are easily deceived. Proceeding from these two conclusions about human nature—ambition and gullibility—he laid down the rules of conduct for a prince who should avail himself of the knowledge of human nature and human motivations. His advice included:

A prince ought to be a fox in recognizing snares and a lion in driving out wolves.

A wise prince should not and cannot keep his pledge when it is against his interest to do so and when his reasons for making the pledge are no longer operative.

He must stick to the good as long as he can, but, being compelled by necessity, he must be ready to take the way of evil . . .

It will be well for him to seem, and actually to be merciful, faithful, humane, frank, religious. But he should preserve a disposition which will make a reversal of conduct possible in case the need arises.

(Machiavelli 1971:62–63)

These are the kinds of statements we now equate with Machiavellianism; but they should be understood in the light of Machiavelli's conviction that the safety and liberty of a country depends upon strong government. He wrote in one of his *Discourses*:

Where the well-being of one's country is at all in question, no consideration of justice or injustice, of mercy or cruelty, of honor or shame must be allowed to enter in at all. Indeed, every other consideration having been put aside, that course of action alone which will save the life and liberty of the country ought to be wholeheartedly pursued.

(*Ibid.*:121)

All his advice about statecraft was thus ultimately for the benefit of the whole nation, and not merely to show a prince how to obtain power.

An objective approach to social and political phenomena is Machiavelli's great contribution to the development of social science. He pronounced no judgment on the moral value of individual deeds, but merely judged their practical results. He anticipated many later theories, including those on the evolution of political organization, on population growth and class struggles. But most important of all was Machiavelli's discovery of the individual not as a creature one step removed from the angels, but as a human being out for his own advantages. Mario Praz, in a lecture to the British Academy (1928:9) put it this way: Machiavelli's hero is the counterpart of the nudes by Signorelli or sketched by Leonardo. The artists revealed man's physical nudity; Machiavelli bared his social nature.

Less known but not less remarkable than Machiavelli was the Spanish reformer Juan Luis Vives (1492–1540). Vives made it very clear from the outset that he had constructed his theories from the observation of nature and the study of history, and would not invoke divine oracles or other unobservable entities to account for development and change.

He presented one of the earliest post-Lucretian secular schemes of evolution, and similarities between his scheme and that of nineteenth-century evolutionists are clearly recognizable. He made many common-sense observations, reasoning, for instance, that language could not have its origin in gestures or mute nods. Since communication is the building block upon which all social life rests, gestures could never have produced the cooperation and interaction necessary for a functioning society. According to Vives, language began by the use of single words and the combination of these soon gave rise to sentences and grammar. But if speech was the necessary condition for the emergence of social life, society itself rose from the need of subsistence. Once this was successfully accomplished, other physical needs were attended to. Early men soon found means to fortify themselves against disease, learned to protect their bodies by clothing and coverings and build barricades of some sort to protect themselves from wild animals. But people started to realize that their greatest strength came from social cooperation, and began to live together in caves. This daily contact with their fellow men brought greater mutual understanding, and fostered closer ties also between a man and his wives and children. Coming out of the communal caves, they began to build huts in which they lived with their own families. The need for mutual assistance urged them to construct their huts close together in a kind of village settlement. Disagreements were brought before the oldest male, and political leadership was thus first established on the criterion of age. But it happened that not all old men were equally wise and benevolent. It was then that people began to seek out their headmen on the basis of individual qualities of leadership. While this was an advance in political organization, it also gave rise to a great deal of conflict, because people were not of one mind as to what the best qualities of leadership should be. Some held that eloquence was most important, others considered birth order, physical strength, wealth, or a reputation for justice as the best qualifications. This difference of opinion unleashed violent emotions and excited passions that often overshadowed all reason. The disputes were settled by elections of some kind, but the seeds of social and political discord had been planted in the hearts and minds of men.

When men had duly provided for the necessities of life through inventing speech, the family, community and political organization, they turned to the contemplation of the world. Curiosity led to study of the constellations, plants, animals, metals, and of the human mind itself. Some people were so anxious to unlock the secrets of nature that they sought the help of evil spirits and resorted to magic. More capable minds asked questions about the final goal of knowledge; from inability to find answers arose a need of God, and thus religion developed.

Vives' scheme is remarkable for its objectivity. He had no preconceived ideas about progress or degeneration. Later evolutionary theories were often biased by such views. Those who championed progress were forced to place early men in a most unfavorable position, while degenerationists were obliged to place them in a more favorable light. Vives realized that human nature at all times had contained elements of good and evil, and in his view society evolved as a tension between the two. Primitive man, to Vives, was neither a nasty brute nor a happy and innocent child of nature living on the lands without a thought for the future.

Vives used his evolutionary scheme as a kind of platform from which to denounce the social evils of his time, which arose in his view from the passions unleashed by politics. Moving from criticism to constructive proposals, he held up the ideal of a kind and just ruler and endorsed state organization. All land and immovable property should be placed under its immediate jurisdiction so that the discrepancies between the wealth of monasteries and feudal lords and the dire poverty of the masses would be diminished. In the interim period the poor should receive welfare assistance and in his book *On the Relief of the Poor* (1526) he outlined a modern-sounding system of such welfare organization, emphasizing that dependency upon such aid should be avoided.

Most writers placed their social theories within the framework of their own society. In France the issue of sovereignty was crucial, and Jean Bodin (1530–96) addressed his theories to this problem. Like Machiavelli, he felt that the primary task of political theorists was the analysis of the nature of power; Bodin considered it their duty to make their insights available to rulers. Such understanding was not for the benefit of political leaders, but for the good of the whole nation.

Bodin supported sovereignty and reconstructed evolutionary history in order to show that the power of kings is a natural development. In his scheme family organization started from one original family which grew in size and formed larger groups. At that time, every man was master in his own house, having complete power over his wives and children, unrestrained by any law. Sovereignty was thus an early and necessary component of social life. The several extended families first dispersed, but later reunited through the recognition of strength in numbers. But the first results were violence, ambition, and desire for revenge, and it became clear that power should be legalized and invested in the hands of one capable leader. Early state organization thus became modeled upon family organization. While family heads possessed no recognized legal power, a sovereign ruled by generally accepted legal power.

More clearly even than his predecessors, Bodin was aware of cultural diversity, not only stressing the differences between Greeks, Romans, and his contemporary France, but also between them and nonliterate peoples. He sought to explain these differences not in theological theories of original sin, but in a number of empirical factors. Notable among those was the influence of environment. Earlier writers had often stated that direct one-to-one correlations existed between climate and mentality, but Bodin's environmentalism was much more sophisticated. He denied that temperature or any other climatic factors directly influenced the human mind, but said rather that barrenness of soil in some environments had made people flock to cities. City dwellers in poor natural environments were forced to work hard and to carry out trade, so that they became strong and alert. Peoples living in fertile valleys where nature is bountiful became soft and lazy. Related to these views were his attempts to analyze the processes of change itself. In relatively peaceful times change was slow and adaptive, but under conditions of war, conquest, or other upheavals change was drastic and upsetting. In the latter instances, personalities might change also.

Bodin also saw progress in evolution, which meant that he rejected the notion of degeneration as well as that of the infallibility of the ancient Greeks. He divided human history into three great periods: Mesopotamian-Egyptian, Greco-Roman, and Northern. He characterized each period by a dominant worldview rather than by material criteria; the first one was ruled by religion, the second by warfare, the third by inventive skill. It was the latter that had been most important. The Northern invention of the compass had made circumnavigation of the world possible, and the invention of printing alone was more important than anything achieved by the ancients.

CONCLUSIONS

In the centuries after the Middle Ages two kinds of writings came to the foreground, both of interest to later developments in the social sciences. The first were ethnographies, accounts by travelers and explorers of places and peoples. They are of interest to us not only because they represent a storehouse of information about cultures that became drastically altered or passed out of existence, but also because they focused the attention of scholars on cultural diversity. A number of theories were advanced to explain the puzzling differences in customs and social institutions; others attempted to account for the origin of American Indians and their presence in the New World. Although most of these theories are untenable, they generated further research and more accurate data collecting. The issue of monogenesis versus polygenesis was sometimes brought up, but there were not many dissenters from the orthodox belief in the single origin of man. The debates on this question were much less violent than those that followed in later centuries when the question became wedded to theories of race. Racism itself was not yet a serious issue. Although very few doubted the superiority of their own Western civilization—Montaigne being a notable exception—this supposed superiority was not generally considered to be innate and thus was not correlated with physical characteristics.

The other group of writers were somewhat influenced by the new discoveries, but they were more troubled by the social conditions of their own societies than by questions of Indian origins. Like ancient Greeks they used their ideas about evolution to extract lessons for contemporary situations, to illustrate concepts about human nature, or to predict future events.

The whole period was marked by an increase in secular explanations of society: it was seen as a product of history and environment, rather than divinely guided. Although early humanists relied strongly upon the authority of the ancients, later scholars were more progressive and repudiated ideas of degeneration.

The main ingredients for an objective approach to the study of society and culture were present by the end of the sixteenth century: a separation from theology, a waning reliance upon older authorities, and a consideration of literate as well as nonliterate cultures for comparative purposes. Still lacking were systematic, objective observations, and a conscious application of scientific principles. These principles were discovered in the next century.

CHAPTER 4

THE RISE
OF SCIENCE

Seventeenth-century scholarship was marked by a general spirit of optimism and self-reliance and by conceit. Optimism led away from earlier convictions that the world was old, decrepit, and decaying; self-reliance came to imply that something could be done to help the forward movement of events; while conceit repudiated every form of knowledge and scholarship that had gone before. In other words, the age was modern and attempted to make a complete break with the past.

The earlier adoration of the classics eventually gave way to contempt. George Hakewill (1578–1649) wrote that admiration of the past had persuaded man to feel hopeless and inferior, and had smothered all impulses and motivations to become creative in thought and action. He even considered degeneration theories to be basically irreligious, since they not only debilitated man's creativity, but also indicated a lack of trust in divine providence. He was not the first to contest the superiority of the ancients, but he emphasized that comparative judgments of competence should not be colored by emotions, but should be rooted in hard facts of unbiased observation. His conceit was that he claimed to be the first to have such insights:

I have walked, (I confess), in an untrodden path, neither can I trace the prints of any footsteps that have gone before me . . .
(Quoted by R. Jones 1965:29)

Yet it is very unlikely that he was unacquainted with the writings of his great contemporary, Francis Bacon (1561–1626), who broke with the past in a much more radical way. Hakewill merely compared the past with the present, demonstrating the superiority of moderns over ancients. Bacon, however, wanted to make a new start altogether. He not only assailed the ancients, but was highly dissatisfied with the state of knowledge in his own days. His conceit rested in the conviction that *everything* that had so far passed for knowledge was erroneous, that a total reconstruction of the sciences, arts, and all human knowledge was necessary, and that he himself was the only person who could achieve this revolution.

During his life, Bacon kept working at a grandiose scheme which he called a Great Instauration, or Total Renovation of the Sciences. It would constitute "the true end and termination of infinite error" (Bacon 1939:13). In 1605 he published *The Advancement of Learning,* in which he classified all existing sciences and revealed their deficiencies. His famous *Novum organum* ("A new tool for science," 1620) contained the fullest exposition of his new experimental methods. Basic to his theories was the recognition of the human mind as rational and thus capable of passing beyond old errors. First he sought an answer to the question why earlier rational minds had fallen into error. In his view, the mind was originally like a fair sheet of paper with no writing on it, or "like a mirror with a true and even surface, fit to reflect the genuine ways of things." This was not, however, the ancient *tabula rasa* theory. Bacon's "fair sheet of paper" did not refer to the state of mind of an individual at birth, but it was a phylogenetic idea, symbolic of the original condition of mankind in the beginning of time. Created perfect, the mind soon became corrupted by wrong cultural training and learning, but it was possible to restore it to its original state by ridding it of prejudices. The false notions that had spoiled the mind Bacon called "idols," and he recognized four different kinds. The "idols of the Tribe" falsely assert that man is the measure of all things, the "idols of the Cave" are those of individual idiosyncrasies, the "idols of the Theatre" are the result of reliance upon authority, while the "idols of the Marketplace" obstruct understanding through linguistic ambiguity. The last ones are the most troublesome of all. Once all idols are recognized and overthrown, scientific observation becomes possible. Observations cannot be random, but must be systematic and experimental, and conclusions should be made by inductive logic, leading from the particular to the general. Bacon's passion for experimentation is made dramatic by the fact that he died of pneumonia brought on by an experiment with the antiseptic properties of snow.

Bacon's examples of experiment and induction were all in the realm of the natural sciences, but he was guided by a social concern, for he believed that the progress of science would have a salubrious effect upon social conditions. Where the Greeks had studied nature in order for men to learn to act in harmonious conformity to its laws, Bacon asserted man's dominance over nature, since "knowledge is power." The understanding of the true laws of nature would give rise to many scientific inventions that would overcome the miseries of humanity to a significant degree. In his unfinished utopian book *New Atlantis* (1622), he described an imaginary island, Bensalem, where a wise lawgiver had organized a happy kingdom on the basis of applied science. The busy scientists had artificially constructed metals; built a weather observation tower half a mile in height, desalinization plants ("pools of which some strain fresh water out of salt"), and experimental agricultural stations; developed techniques to make fruits and plants larger and yielding better crops, wonderful drugs and medicines, sound houses to reproduce all natural and musical sounds, and so forth. Although most scientific prophecies have been fulfilled in our own age, they have not brought us the promised happiness. Bacon apparently did not realize that man must learn to live in harmony with his neighbors, an art that science cannot teach. Bacon's contributions to social science are thus indirect. Only much later did people realize that the Baconian "idols" are as detrimental to the development of anthropology as to the natural sciences.

Like Bacon, René Descartes (1596–1650) also envisaged a reformation of knowledge. In his early years he studied classics, philosophy, mathematics, and physics, but when he was twenty-three years of age he went through a mystical experience that revealed to him that the structure of the universe is mathematical and logical. This event shaped his own life and exercised a strong influence upon the further development of science, which hinges on the view that the world is orderly and thus also understandable.

Descartes' theory was mechanistic insofar as everything in the universe was to him explainable by cause and effect. He broke with anthropomorphic concepts of nature as an entity endowed with emotions of love, anger, or abhorrence. Instead, Descartes saw nature as a machine in perpetual motion, and these motions were regular and predictable. Animals were machines also, and their activities could be explained as necessary reactions to external stimuli. Man differed from animals only in that he possessed a soul, an entity that cannot be perceived by the senses. But except for this soul (or mind— Descartes did not always differentiate between the two), man was also a machine, and cause and effect were thus operative in his physical behavior. Physically, man was part of nature, ruled by natural laws, but with a soul or mind that stood outside it.

Although Descartes himself did not apply his insights to the study of society, his mathematical-materialistic views of nature exercised a very strong influence upon social theories. Thomas Hobbes (1588–1679), who in his younger years had been in the service of Francis Bacon, resembled Vives and Bodin in placing his social theories in the framework and service of contemporary political polemics. But Hobbes rose far above such practical concerns. Incorporating the methods of the new science, he was the first seventeenth-century scholar to present a consistent materialistic and scientific explanation of man and society.

He disagreed with the Cartesian dualism of body and mind, and rather extended the materialistic outlook by treating the soul simply as another body in motion. It was not the mind or the soul that distinguished man from other animals, it was man's ability to speak that marked the basic difference. In Hobbes's view, neither animals nor men were social creatures by nature. In fact, it was in their nature to fight rather than to cooperate. Hobbes described the early brutish natural conditions of mankind in the *Leviathan* (1651) in this famous passage:

During the time men live without a common power to keep them all in awe, they are in that condition which is called war; and such a war as is of every man, against every man. . . . In such condition there is not place for industry; because the fruit thereof is uncertain: and consequently no culture of the earth; no navigation, nor use of the commodities that may be imported by sea; no commodious building; no instruments of moving, and removing, such things as require much force; no knowledge of the face of the earth; no account of time; no arts; no letters; no society; and which is worst of all, continual fear, and danger of violent death; and the life of man, solitary, poor, nasty, brutish, and short.

(1967:100)

Social life, which did not exist from the beginning, came into being for purely selfish reasons, namely to alleviate man's continual fear, and to secure life and liberty. Society was formed by social contract. Hobbes did not further speculate on the evolution of society, because he felt that nature had made men equal in body and mind. All were moved by two basic natural emotions: the desire for power and the fear of death. Fear led to the construction of the commonwealth, Leviathan, which resembles a large organism created for the enforcement of social rules and for the provision of security against violent death. In this social body the sovereign is the soul, judges are the limbs, reward and punishment are the nerves; it is fed by economic pursuits and its children are the colonies. Leviathan becomes diseased when the system is upset by false doctrines, unnatural laws, and by wars. All social institutions are thus governed by natural laws, including war, justice, civil laws, human rights, religion, and the power of the sovereign.

This purely naturalistic and mechanical description of human action and social institutions is difficult to defend. Even in his own time, Hobbes was severely attacked, and even the most materialist-minded modern anthropologist cannot accept the idea that man and his society are nothing but engines moved by only two basic human emotions. *Leviathan* is, nevertheless, a very important book which influenced many generations of scholars of all different persuasions. Hobbes's great contribution to social studies is that he saw society as a dynamic changing force whose movements and changes could be examined and understood. Many scholars after him continued the search for explanations of the natural laws that seemingly ruled both society and the human mind itself.

One of the generally accepted scientific principles was that the understanding of complex phenomena can be accomplished only if they are first reduced to their simplest and most basic elements. General conclusions were thus to be drawn from the particular and not from unanalyzed complex situations. This principle, although often modified, became applied also to the analysis of social institutions, giving rise to an early form of comparative method.

Herbert of Cherbury (1583–1648) analyzed religion in this new and objective way, searching for the "natural laws" underlying this social institution. He was among the first of his age to recognize "paganism" as a legitimate form of religion, so that it could be examined on a par with Christian and other so-called great religions. Viewing religion thus as a cultural universal, Herbert felt that it must constitute an inherent aspect of human nature. Yet religious systems and forms of worship differed greatly. In order, then, to find the true nature of religion, its different manifestations must be compared, and whatever they had in common must be the invariable principles of religion as a whole. Herbert found five such common elements: all believed in a supreme power, worshiped it, demanded virtue and piety, punished sins, and meted out punishments in life as well as after death. Not all pagan religions were in full conformity with these principles, but Herbert explained this as due to venal priests who, sometimes purposely, sometimes unwittingly, had perverted the true nature of religion. Herbert did not write in order to defend his own religion as so many had done before him; he made *all* forms of religion worthy objects of study, analysis, and comparison (Herbert 1705).

Hugo Grotius (1583–1645) applied the same method to the study of international law. He was convinced that natural law is the basis of all social life. In order to discover its basic natural principles all existing laws should again be compared in order to find what they had in common. His book *Of the Rights of War and Peace* (1625) is based upon this method, and it is generally considered the first definite text on international law. In a similar manner, Thomas Mun (1571–1641) tried to discover the universal natural principles of economy and trade.

From these and many other comparative studies with universal orientations, the concept of culture as learned behavior began to emerge. Samuel Pufendorf (1632–94), a follower of Grotius, turned the theory of natural law completely around. Where Grotius had felt that natural law is the basis of all social life, Pufendorf wrote that, to the contrary, social life is the basis of natural law. This position was also at variance with Hobbes's theory that man was by nature *not* social. Pufendorf explained that it was precisely man's nature to lead a social life, and society and man were coterminous: "The race of man never did live at one and the same simple state of nature, and never could have" (quoted by Slotkin

1965:152). Again opposing Hobbes, Pufendorf argued that early (or natural) man did not live in a state of constant war, but early society was one of cooperation and friendship, because without this the human race could not have perpetuated itself. Political organization evolved because natural peace is weak. But state organization is not a necessary development. It occurred in some societies, but certainly not in all. Many known smaller societies managed very well to get along without the state. Societies were thus not ruled by invariable natural laws which in themselves were as inscrutable as divine laws. While it was man's nature to *be* social, social life itself could take different forms, as was amply demonstrated by the many existing cultural varieties. Pufendorf's awareness of cultural differences and his realization that different forms of society each had their own intrinsic functions and survival values made him appreciative of the powerful force of what we now call cultural learning. He put it this way:

. . . to have been brought up from infancy on some idea is so powerful an influence that, even though the idea be fallacious, the thought of questioning it scarcely ever occurs to man . . .

(Quoted by Slotkin 1965:152f)

The year in which Pufendorf was born (1632) produced three other important scholars: Locke, Spinoza, and van Leeuwenhoek. The contributions of the last were important for the later development of physical anthropology. Of the others, John Locke (1632–1704) exercised the greatest influence upon later thought. According to one historian of anthropology, Marvin Harris (1968:10), it was Locke who provided the metaphysical foundation upon which anthropologists later reared their formal definitions of culture. Although Harris' position underestimates all earlier contributions and overlooks the importance of Pufendorf, it is true enough that Locke is much better known. He was explicit in rendering the study of man and society as an undertaking based upon empirical observation. Like Hobbes, he looked upon man as an object of nature to be explained by principles of natural science; like Bacon, he stressed empiricism and the reliance upon sense observations; and like Descartes he applied the principle of reducing complex phenomena to their basic elements.

Locke felt that the most basic element of all social phenomena was the human mind itself, and thus he turned first to the examination of its properties, convinced that the natural condition of the mind was the key for understanding all social institutions. His *Essay concerning Human Understanding* (1690) was basically epistemological, asking the question from where human knowledge arises. His basic premises were that the human mind is by nature rational, and that at birth it resembles a "fair sheet of paper," or "an empty closet." Knowledge comes about by experience: sense perceptions impress themselves upon the blank paper and fill the empty closet. Locke argued that this must be so, because if men were born with innate ideas human behavior and human cultures would be identical everywhere. Instead, there is a bewildering variety of customs, determined by different experiences, and in turn experience depends much upon local circumstances and situations. This insight brought Locke very close to an anthropological understanding of culture. He wrote:

Had you or I been born at the Bay of Soldania, possibly our thoughts and notions had not exceeded those brutish ones of the Hottentots that inhabit there. And had the Virginia king Apochancana been educated in England, he had been perhaps as knowing a divine, and as good a mathematician as any in it; the difference between him and a more improved Englishman lying barely in this, that the exercise of his faculties was bounded within the ways, modes, and notions of his own country, and never directed to any other or further inquiries.

(Locke 1849 I:3, 12)

In this manner Locke attempted to free social thought from extraneous conditions, so that it might become scientific. The human mind itself was not innately equipped with any preconceived notions, did not contain any rules of natural laws, but was formed exclusively by external experiences and observations, or what we now would call cultural learning.

Locke's contemporaries Benedict Spinoza (1632–77) and Blaise Pascal (1623–62) both held much more pessimistic views about the innate rationality of the human mind. Spinoza observed that human passions generally act much more powerfully than human reason, and Pascal similarly observed that although man was naturally endowed with reason, he rarely acted by its guidance.

Although the materialistic worldview and the theories that posited the existence of natural laws were secular in orientation, they did not clash with beliefs in a divine creator who had set the world in motion and ordained the natural laws. Even Locke, generally known as a skeptic, admitted that the rationality of the universe and the order of nature were of divine origin.

But the study of religion itself by scientific methods—the comparative approach initiated by Herbert—eventually led to relativism. If many different forms of religion were valid in their own right, the ultimate truth of any religion could be doubted. This problem received particular attention from mythologists, who had retained an interest in the myths of the classical past. Bacon had condemned the reliance on the past and had downgraded the learning of the Greeks, but even he felt that ancient myths should not be forgotten and might reveal some deep wisdom.

Mythological compilations remained immensely popular. Following Boccaccio, myths were, most often, interpreted allegorically and moral lessons drawn from them. When the myths of newly discovered peoples were added to the already existing repertoire, it seemed to many collectors that they were often strikingly similar to those of the ancients.

The new scientific method, however, initiated quite a different approach to myth interpretation. Pierre Bayle (1647–1706), for one, agreed with Hobbes that religion was born of fear. If this was the case, all allegorical interpretations of myth were beside the point. Bayle proposed that myths were neither allegorical, nor symbolic of some hidden wisdom, but depicted the beliefs of people in a direct and matter-of-fact manner. Mythical accounts of divine deceptions, robberies, adultery, and rape were not symbolic of a struggle between good and evil, did not depict moral conflicts of a higher order, but reflected the literal beliefs of the peoples in whose midst those myths arose about how their gods behaved. Bayle took great delight in seeking out the most perverse activities of gods and goddesses, retelling tales of divine incest, castration, homosexuality, lust, and debauchery. After dealing in this manner with the well-known Greek and Roman myths, he examined those coming from Africa, Oceania, and the Americas, and found them to be equally perverse. In other words, Bayle attempted to prove the absurdity of every pagan religion. He was much less outspoken about Christianity. Nevertheless, he made some daring comparisons between paganism and Catholic beliefs and practices. (It should be added here that Bayle was a Protestant.) Calmly, he wrote that savages believed in the miracles of their gods as literally as Catholics believed in the liquefaction of the blood of Saint Januarius. He also pointed out that there were great similarities between pagan trances and the reported ecstasies of Christian saints and mystics.

Bayle tended to the belief that many religious phenomena were psychopathological, thus foreshadowing Freud, who, much later, called religion "an infantile neurosis." The frenzied fury of the bacchants, the convulsive trance of shamans, the mass tortures of Indians during initiation, and the hysterics of some nuns were not explainable otherwise, he thought.

Bayle thus considered all religions to be irrational, a trend that culminated in the Enlightenment. While hostility is as poor a guide to an objective study of religion as dogmatic commitment to specific religious truths, the implication of Bayle's work was that all religions and myths should be analyzed by the same methods, and that myths were social phenomena, "charters of reality" as Malinowski said later on.

Different conclusions were reached by Bernard Fontenelle

(1657–1757). He also examined Greek and pagan mythology, and concluded that all were patently false. Myth making was thus an irrational trait, common to all early peoples throughout the world. The primitive inventors could, however, hardly be blamed, because they had no scientific experience: myths were the result not of a diseased mind, but of an inexperienced one. They were simply erroneous understandings of causality, because primitives were like children that had not yet had the experience of adult life, and were thus unable to think in abstract terms. For that reason they also anthropomorphized their gods: gods were conceived as superhuman creatures that caused natural cataclysms. Only later, when the human mind progressed, were people capable of thinking about their gods in more abstract terms.

Fontenelle's ideas reappear in nineteenth-century anthropology. Myth was a kind of mistaken science also to Frazer, Durkheim, and Lang; and the concept of primitives possessing a "prelogical mind" was vigorously taken up by Lévy-Bruhl. These erroneous concepts were seriously challenged by Malinowski in the twentieth century.

CONCLUSIONS

In this chapter we have attempted to show how much the development of the social sciences depended upon the rise of scientific method, and how they were modeled on the example of the physical sciences. The latter strove consciously to discover laws of nature and of the universe, and the emerging social sciences equally attempted to find laws of human nature and of social life. Both took it for granted that regularities did in fact exist, and that the human mind was rational and thus capable of discovering these laws. Hobbes was perhaps the first to write about society in this new scientific spirit, and attempted to show how social theories could be brought in line with the nature of physical reality. This view of necessity demanded that man and society be viewed as natural phenomena, and this is indeed how Hobbes and many after him considered them. But Hobbes also felt that the nature of man and that of society were not in harmony with one another; human nature, in his view, was ill-adapted to social living. Hobbes's social theories concentrated on showing how human nature could be reconciled to the demands of social living. This reconciliation was far from voluntary: the social was a constraint on human nature. Yet it followed the laws of nature: laws which were eternal and immutable, resulting from the nature of fundamental human drives. Hobbes's view of human nature excluded the possibility of a concept of culture in the modern anthropological sense of the word. Society was to him a mere conglomerate of people who allowed the drive for security to take the upper hand over their more warlike instincts.

The concept that human nature is the same everywhere led to the search for universals in social behavior. Those culture items or behavior patterns that were most common were also believed to be closest to original human nature. It was in this spirit that Herbert looked for universals in religious beliefs, that Grotius searched for universal truths in laws, and that Mun tried to find universal principles of trade and economy.

Such typical universal orientations brought about an identification of the social domain as a distinct area of scientific investigations. These were not carried out in a spirit of idle curiosity; the study of society was considered to have many practical consequences. Bacon had stressed the utility of natural science in the conviction that it would give rise to a better society. Hobbes, writing in the midst of rebellion and political upheavals, showed how the first and absolute need of society was order, and order was to be enforced by a ruler with absolute authority. Grotius saw the utility of just international laws, and mercantilists such as Mun of course had practical interests in mind when they tried to establish universal rules for international trading.

Pufendorf reversed the Hobbesian concept that man and

society were at heart inimical, and wrote that it was left to the
choice of men to establish different types of society. Although
the idea that the form of society depends on free choice sounds
overly rationalistic, Pufendorf's approach had the advantage
of seeing human society not as incontrovertibly determined by
natural laws, but changing as man's "choices" were changing.
Locke also stressed that the human mind was not innately
equipped with natural laws, but rather formed by experience,
and Spinoza similarly analyzed society as a human invention.

All these and other attempts to understand man's social
life took their impetus from the Baconian and Cartesian
emphasis on a new departure in the quest for knowledge. The
reliance upon former authorities was eschewed, Greeks and
Romans were derogated, but Greek myths were still studied
with great diligence and allegorized to show how noble—
albeit unscientific—was the Greek mind. But even this was
placed in doubt by the writings of Bayle and Fontenelle, who,
each in his own way, scorned allegorical interpretations. Bayle
set the stage for a science of religion, Fontenelle developed
a concept of primitive mentality not unlike that of Lévy-Bruhl.

All in all, the study of nonliterate peoples became increasingly important. Still, they were not observed for their own
intrinsic interest, but were considered as the best example of
original human nature. This was, nevertheless, an advantage
over previous considerations, which had looked at primitive
men only as exotic specimens.

The increasing secularism of social interpretations did not
yet lead to attacks on religion, except perhaps in the case of
Bayle. Although some scholars were more devout than others,
none made overt breaks with religious tradition. Instead,
causality became a step further removed. In medieval times
it was believed that God ruled every step of social life, while
in the seventeenth century the Divine was the creator of the
laws of nature, but left it more or less up to man to develop
his own social institutions. These trends continued in the following century, eventually leading to a complete separation
between theology and the study of society.

CHAPTER 5

THE PROPER STUDY
OF MANKIND IS MAN

The great advances in mathematics, medicine, astronomy, and technology from the time of Bacon and Descartes onward inspired a good deal of confidence in the Cartesian mathematical worldview. The theories and discoveries of Isaac Newton (1642–1727) completed this image. If the gravitation of the earth kept the moon in orbit and that of the sun regulated the course of the planets, the whole universe must be ruled by mathematically calculable laws.

It was generally accepted that man and society were equally subject to natural laws, and the emerging science of statistics lent further support to this belief. John Graunt (1620–74) was an early exponent of statistical regularities in society. Soon afterward, Veit Ludwig von Seckendorf (1626–92) in Germany and William Petty (1623–87) in England developed full-scale systems of social statistics. The predictability of birth and death rates and of life expectancies seemed a clear proof of the existence of social laws, and it appeared to some that all concerns of human life could be understood in terms of numbers.

Although Hobbes had already written that human reason was nothing but "reckoning" (Hobbes 1967:41), the idea that men were machines found its ultimate expression in the writings of a French doctor, Julien O. de La Mettrie (1709–51). During his medical practice he became struck by the idea that high fever caused an intensification of thinking, evidenced by the continuous "ravings" of fevered patients. He concluded that the mind (or the soul) was as physical as the rest of the body. The brain produced thoughts in the same manner as the liver excreted bile. His first book, with the startling title *Natural History of the Soul,* caused a scandal. It was publicly banned, and La Mettrie fled to Leiden in the Netherlands. Here he wrote his famous book *Man a Machine,* published toward the end of 1748. Excluding any spiritual principles from the universe, he sought to reconfirm his materialistic views by describing experiments with decapitated frogs whose muscles remained irritable, and by giving case histories of patients whose thought processes were altered by physical causes.

More important for further developments was his insistence that men and animals were composed of the same elements, so that they not only were subject to the same natural laws, but they were also biologically related. He wrote that all organisms contained within themselves the power that produced their activity, and also the power to transform into some other organism. Mankind thus belonged to nature and to the animal kingdom, and the transition from animal to man had not been violent. In his last book, *L'homme-plante* (1748; the book was not translated into English but its title would read *Man a Plant*), La Mettrie took one more step toward building the eighteenth-century theory of transformism. Nature was dynamic and self-determining; it consisted of an unbroken gradation of beings from the simple to the complex, and transformational evolution was the necessary conclusion. He felt that polyps formed the link between plants and animals, and apes between animals and man. He proposed that attempts should be made to teach apes to speak in order to prove that link, a suggestion followed up only in the twentieth century.

The prevalent idea that nature, man, and society were ruled by uniform laws made it difficult to explain change. Newton had accepted the traditional 4000 B.C. creation date, and the limited time depth allowed little opportunity for change. Moreover, it was believed that the wise Creator who had set all laws in motion would not change what He had once so perfectly established.

While the physical laws of the universe appeared stable enough, it was obvious even to the most casual observer that societies were in a state of constant flux. The Italian scholar Giambattista Vico (1668–1744) proposed a most ingenious solution to this dilemma, namely that change itself was regular and thus subject to laws. Vico set out to discover these laws, engaging himself in the gigantic task of reconstructing all human history, in the conviction that only this vast panorama could reveal the regularities of change. What is more, he also felt it necessary to start from the point where society first took shape, which meant that he began to search for historical origins.

The title of his magnum opus was *The New Science* (first published in 1725, with two subsequent revised editions). He believed not only that his theory was new, but also that it constituted a true science, more scientific than physics or mathematics. This was in opposition to Descartes, who had rather despised history, philology, and social studies, holding that these undertakings could never lead to absolute truth. Vico countered that physics and mathematics could not lead to absolute truths precisely because, as Descartes himself avowed, the laws of the universe were created by God, and how could mortal men ever understand the principles of creation? At best, physics could perceive and describe, but man can truly *understand* only what is of his own making, namely history and society. The fact that society was man-made was Vico's triumphant discovery, and no one before him had made it so explicit:

But in the night of darkness . . . there shines the eternal and never failing light of a truth beyond all question: *that the world of civil society has certainly been made by men,* and that its principles are therefore to be found within the modifications of our own human mind.

Whoever reflects on this cannot but marvel that the philosophers should have bent all their energies to the study of the world of nature, which, since God made it, He alone knows; and that they should have neglected the study of the world of nations, or civil world, which, since men had made it, men could come to know.

(Vico 1961:52–53)

In order, then, to discover the "perennial springs of change," Vico started with a study of "remote and obscure" periods of history. Turning to ethnographic literature, he was among the first to take nonliterate peoples into account as full members of the social tradition.

His Christian scruples demanded that the creation story of Genesis be taken into account, but he soon departed from orthodoxy. Some of Noah's sons, dispersed after the flood, wandered in the vast forests of the earth. They forgot all cultural learning, even language, and descended to the level of wild beasts. From this zero point, Vico developed his history of cultural evolution. Startled by thunderclaps, the savage creatures took shelter in caves, and here family life began. In Vico's own words:

. . . they forcibly seized their women, who were naturally shy and unruly, dragged them into their caves, and, in order to have intercourse with them, keeping them there as perpetual lifelong companions. Thus . . . they gave a beginning to matrimony.

(*Ibid.*:376)

With the settling of habitation came language, agriculture, ownership, property, morality, and burial of the dead. Fathers were the rulers of extended families, and all important undertakings were accompanied by rituals in order to appease the fearful thundergods. Vico called this early stage "the age of the gods." It was followed by "the age of heroes," in which social inequalities caused quarreling, raiding, and wars. The war captives became slaves, thus enlarging the family units, and forcing them to add the distinctions of consanguinity and class to those of sex and generation. Families united to form "heroic states," in which only fathers and their families were citizens, and not the slaves. This in turn gave rise to feudalism, and even greater inequalities. The lower classes began to press for land tenure, legal marriage, citizenship, and eligibility for office. Eventually they won their points, and the heroic states became democracies, which, together with the invention of writing, ushered in the third stage of evolution, "the age of men." At first it was characterized by respect for law, discipline, and social solidarity. Equality first led to tolerance, then to license, and the softening of laws eventually resulted in disintegration and a reversal to early savagery. A new cycle of the three ages then began: in Europe, Christianity replaced the pagan age of the gods, feudalism recurred in the Middle Ages, and the seventeenth century was the second "age of men." Although Vico held that there was a succession of these stages, he also posited multiple origins, and thus multiple parallel developments.

No matter what the flaws of his scheme may have been— and they are obvious enough—it possessed great internal coherence, and at every point of transition Vico produced logical explanations for the change from stage to stage, and from substage to substage. The primary importance of Vico's work rests not so much in his evolutionary views, but in his strong opposition to rationalism. Many evolutionists before him had depicted evolutionary changes as made by men who consciously fashioned new institutions or social contracts, as if motivated by the same intellectualistic rationality as that of modern Western men. Vico moved the explanation of social change from an individual psychological level to a truly social level, accounting for the past not in terms of modern thought, but in terms of social circumstances as they had existed in the past.

It is true that Vico's ultimate law somewhat resembled natural law after all. His overall principle of change was what he called the law of *corsi e ricorsi*, "course and recourse," or "flux and reflux," better called "the law of historical recurrence." He meant that social change was regular, resembling the flow and ebb of tides. This law itself was not man-made, but guided by providence, one of God's attributes. Left wholly to himself, man would destroy his social existence. Providence supervised the law of change, but did not interfere with social affairs as such. It did not act by force of external laws, but was always "making use of the customs of men, which are as free of all force as the spontaneous expressions of their own nature."

All in all, Vico is a very important figure, with specific significance for anthropology. This discipline could not exist without the insights that society is man-made, that its changes are best explained within their own social context, that a historical perspective is necessary if culture is to be understood, and that nonliterate peoples are full members of the sociocultural tradition. His three-stage theory anticipates many later ones, the concept of parallel developments recurs in many modern writings, and Vico also contributed to the later sciences of linguistics and mythology. Any attempt to write a complete social history must have its flaws, and these are certainly not wanting in *The New Science*. His theories of origins are by necessity conjectural, he often contradicts himself, and the number three was in his writings endowed with almost magical powers: there were three types of languages, of myths, of customs, of laws, of governments, of religion, of reason, and so forth. But he rescued social history and cultural evolution from the Cartesian disparagement, returning them to their proper places among the sciences.

Soon after Vico's death, his writings fell into obscurity. Although several of his ideas can be found in those of other writers, it is a strange fact that almost no one acknowledged his influence. He was rediscovered in the early 19th century, but is still relatively unknown in anthropological circles, although the recent *Vico Symposium* (Tagliacozzo 1969) contains two anthropological articles, one by Leach and one by Bidney. In our discipline, Vico's French contemporary Baron de Montesquieu (1689–1755) is much better known. Evans-Pritchard (1964:21) named him the founder of the lineage of social anthropology, and sociologists also recognize him as one of the founding fathers of their discipline (Aron 1968:13). Although it is likely that Montesquieu knew of Vico's work, he never mentioned him. Yet, there are certain striking resemblances between the two thinkers, because both attempted to discover the intelligible order of history, and both treated social phenomena within their own settings. Montesquieu, however, did not attempt to reconstruct all human history, but concentrated on the examination of laws. He used this term with various meanings, and discussed not only written laws of government, but all other forms of social control, be they sanctions, customs, or morals.

In his well-known book *The Spirit of the Laws* (1748), Montesquieu, like Grotius before him, set out to discover the universal properties—the "spirit"—of all laws, but rather than searching for correspondences and similarities, Montesquieu attempted to grasp the underlying causes that could account for their existence and their specific forms. He stated his thesis in the very first sentence of his book: "Laws, in their most general signification, are the necessary relations arising from the nature of things" (Montesquieu 1966 I:1). These "things" included forms of government, religion, occupation, commerce, manners, customs, morals, and environment. In other words, the nature of laws was determined by their own sociocultural frameworks, and they interacted with all internal and external elements that form a culture. In a sense, the rest of the book is a demonstration of this thesis. Since laws took their specific forms from the social reality in which they appeared, Montesquieu tried to explain why societies themselves differ from one another. He mentioned such factors as population density, geographical barriers, degree of isolation from other societies, stage of technological development, religion, subsistence patterns, state of commerce, climate and soil.

The introduction of factors of climate and soil into discussions about the nature of laws and of society has been branded by some as gross environmental determinism. Many of his statements on the subject are indeed untenable, particularly when read out of context. But it is untrue that Montesquieu's

approach was essentially an attempt to explain to legislators
how they should adjust their laws to climate and soil, as
Harris (1968:42) maintains. Montesquieu understood that
environment was one factor among many others, and wrote:

Mankind are influenced by various causes: by the climate, by the
religion, by the laws, by the maxims of government, by precedents,
morals, and customs; whence is formed a general spirit of nations.

(Montesquieu 1966 I:293)

He noted that nature and climate ruled much more strongly
in savage societies than in technologically developed nations
such as China, Japan, and ancient Rome. In the final analysis,
Montesquieu felt that forms of government were chiefly
responsible for the spirit of the laws of a nation. Although he
advocated equal tolerance of all forms of government, he also
made it clear that he himself preferred certain forms of government over others, and argued in favor of a limited, balanced constitutional government based on the English model.
One of the effects of *The Spirit of the Laws* in France was that
it increased the general dissatisfaction with the old regime,
which eventually led to the Revolution.

Montesquieu may be considered as an early modern
functionalist, because he stressed the functional interrelationships between social institutions. Of course he was not the first
to notice such relationships, but he was not satisfied with mere
observation. He analyzed the nature of the connections, and
saw them as orderly processes, subject to laws, and thus having
explainable regularities. These regularities existed in every
form of society, and not merely in Western cultures:

All countries have a law of nations, not excepting the Iroquois
themselves, though they devour their prisoners: for they send
and receive ambassadors, and understand the rights of war and
peace.

(*Ibid.*:5)

Consequently, he also realized that all sorts of exotic
customs had a legitimate basis of existence within their own

society. Even polygamy, cannibalism, idol worship, and slavery (customs Montesquieu abhorred) had their functions within the cultural framework in which they appeared.

While many of Montesquieu's methodological principles were sound, the promise of his theories was not fulfilled in the actual working out of his ideas. His logic is often false, his facts wrong, he regularly contradicts himself, and the presentation of his data is so unsystematic and confused that it does not seem to follow any logical order. He admitted, almost proudly, that he had followed his objectives "without any fixed plan" (*ibid.*:lxix), and indeed *The Spirit of the Laws* is a most difficult book to read. But he stressed again and again his major thesis, namely that social institutions do not derive from divine laws, nor from human nature, but from the nature of societies themselves. His "laws" are thus no abstractions, but are derived from the comparison of actual societies. All laws are functional social elements, and all societies, primitive and modern, are thus comparable to one another.

The period from Hobbes to Montesquieu witnessed an increasing secularization of social explanations. Most scholars, however, brought their theories into alignment with current religious beliefs. In a way, this was not so difficult, because although the natural order of the universe and of society could be analyzed, the fact that there was any order at all remained unexplained and could thus be relegated to a divine creator. Even Vico assigned the ultimate laws of change to a non-human power. The most consistent secular theory came from Montesquieu. Admitting that God had created the laws of nature, he felt that man, as soon as he entered into a state of society, had broken the divine order, establishing laws of his own making. In the study of society it was thus unnecessary to take God into account.

Voltaire (François Marie Arouet, 1694–1778), however, was more impatient than his predecessors with theological interference in any scientific explanations. Yet, he too professed a belief in a personal God who had created natural laws such as those discovered by Newton. But it was utterly useless to study

such divine laws, because the riddle of God's purpose was un-
answerable, and no scientific undertaking should be predicated on the presumption of scanning God's thoughts. In fact,
Voltaire felt very strongly that all previous scientific theories
had been confounded by such efforts. It was thus necessary to
begin anew, under the slogan *Écrasez l'infâme,* i.e., do away
with all theological interpretations. *L'infâme* was not so much
natural religion itself, but rather the "superstitions" of the
Church which had caused countless scientific errors.

A new social science should thus be initiated, and it was to
be the "philosophy of history," a phrase Voltaire coined and
introduced in his *Essay on the Customs and Spirit of Nations*
(1756). What he meant by "philosophy" was an employment
of critical, empirical, and objective methods, thus to be distinguished from "theology," which was always biased and
conjectural. All sociohistorical events were to be explained in
terms of men, not in terms of providence. Moreover, a true
philosophy of history should be explanatory of social facts
and events rather than a mere listing of the successions of
kings or wars.

In his *Essay,* Voltaire struggled with a number of questions
that remained very important in later years—questions about
progress, evolution, human reason, and social reform. He was
very uncertain about the status of the first three of those. Although he felt that his own age was certainly advanced as
compared to early barbarism, there had not been any steady
progress. Religious prejudices, superstitions, wars, crimes, and
human folly had often obstructed advance, and human reason
was thus also in doubt. Progress in history had been more
often the result of lucky accidents than of rational action.

Voltaire was inclined to believe that reason was a scarce
commodity even in his own age, and that it was to be found
only in the minds of enlightened individuals such as he considered himself to be. "Cobblers and kitchenmaids" certainly
did not apply their reason in any constructive manner, and
one could not expect that social reforms would be initiated by
them. Neither would it be very useful to educate the masses.

Only kings and emperors possessed the power to introduce better laws. In Voltaire's view it was thus the task of cultivated and enlightened philosophers to educate rulers, and indeed several rulers began to pose as enlightened monarchs. They practiced toleration and religious freedom in their respective lands, and often patronized artists and scholars.

In his historical works Voltaire paid particular attention to social phenomena. He was more interested in forms of family life or in the technology and arts and crafts of a period than in its battles and politics, and he used etymology to trace the wanderings of peoples. He increased understanding about the new empiricism by his critical treatment of historical data, and by concentrating on cultural rather than on political traits. In his philosophy he linked Descartes' method with the theories of Newton and Locke, achieving a branch of science usually labeled as the French Enlightenment.

Later historians have often characterized the Enlightenment as a period in which the belief in reason and progress reigned supreme. This assessment is only partially true. Enlightenment philosophers certainly did not believe that human beings had been reasonable at all times. Their rationalism was of a specific type because they generally believed that they themselves had discovered reason, and that their methods were thus rational, while older ones could not be so considered. In fact, the concept of progress was somewhat in conflict with a belief in universal human reason. Progress posits by definition an increasing improvement of social life, and early man was thus often depicted as crude and not very reasonable. This position, in turn, is at odds with a conviction that human nature is basically similar.

Anne Robert Jacques Turgot (1727–81) presented a theory in which these seemingly irreconcilable premises were brought together. In his view, progress always moved toward a higher degree of perfection, human nature was fixed, and man was and had always been a rational creature. But human reason itself operated within the framework of its social setting. Differences between human behavior patterns were not due to greater or lesser amounts of reason, but resulted from the interaction beween biological and social forces. Of these, biological ones were the least important. Some individuals were more talented than others, perhaps because of "a lucky combination of the fibers of the brain," or "a greater or lesser quickness of the blood." Social conditions, however, caused some people to develop their talents while leaving others buried in obscurity. Small and isolated societies could not advance at a great rate because they had to depend upon their own inventions alone, and in these relatively simple and homogeneous societies talent was neither encouraged nor easily expressed. It was quite different in societies that were in contact with others. The larger numbers, the wider context, and the exchange of ideas made such societies progress at a much quicker pace. Trade and commerce brought about social connections, but more often than not social interactions were accompanied by war and conquest. The occurrence of war had been a great stumbling block for earlier evolutionists who believed in progress, but Turgot saw that even deplorable social institutions may possess positive functions. He felt that the human race would have remained in mediocrity if conquests and revolutions had not commingled peoples, tongues, and manners in a thousand ways.

So far, Turgot had explained why societies differed in their respective degrees of progress, but not why they were different in customs and habits. Talent could not account for it, and the reasons why some individuals were more capable than others could not be known. But apart from this:

All the rest is the effect of education, and that education is the result of all our sense experiences, of all the ideas we have been able to acquire from the cradle onward. All the objects which surround us contribute to that education; the instructions of our parents and teachers are only a small part of it.

(Turgot 1844:645)

In other words, Turgot clearly recognized culture as socially learned behavior, and further statements reveal that his other insights into the nature of culture are also close to modern ones:

> The succession of men . . . offers from century to century, an ever varied spectacle. Reason, passions, liberty, give rise unceasingly to new events: All the ages of mankind are enchained, one with another, by a sequence of causes and effects that binds the present to the whole preceding past. The arbitrary signs of speech and writing, by giving men the means wherewith to make sure of the possession of their ideas and to communicate them to others, have formed from individual stores of knowledge a common treasure, that one generation transmits to another, like unto a heritage continually augmented by the discoveries of each century; and the human race, considered from its origin, appears to the eyes of a philosopher to be an immense whole, having like every individual its own childhood and its own stages of growth.
>
> (Quoted by Slotkin 1965:358)

Turgot thus formulated a number of principles that constitute the building blocks of modern anthropology. Although his terminology was different, he said in fact that culture is learned, that it constitutes a whole, that it is transmitted from generation to generation by means of symbolic language, and that it is cumulative in as far as past achievements are added to the common store of knowledge. Turgot also saw that each cultural advance accelerates the rate of change, that diffusion plays a larger role than independent invention; he gave cogent explanations for the existence of cultural and personal differences, and he stressed the relationships between cultures instead of considering them as separate entities.

Turgot planned to demonstrate his theories in a universal history, but the project was never completed. In 1750 he published the outline as *Plan for Two Discourses on Universal History*, and the scope resembled that of later anthropology:

> Universal history embraces the conditions of the successive progress of humanity, and the detailed causes which have contributed to it: the earliest beginnings of mankind, the formation and mixture of the nations; the origins and revolutions of government; the development of language; of morality, custom, arts and

sciences; the revolutions which have brought about the succession of empires, nations and religions.

(Turgot 1844:627)

He dealt in some detail with the evolution of sciences and art, government, and religion, and he wrote a separate book on the evolution of economy (1769–70). His ideas on the evolution of the mind clearly anticipate Comte's famous "law of the three stages" (cf. Bury 1955:157). In his description of cultural rather than mental development, Turgot saw leisure time as an important factor in evolution and progress. The natural resources were scarce for early nomadic hunters. They lived in small and widely dispersed bands, and their constant wanderings in search of food left them little time for creativity. When animal domestication and agriculture were invented, sedentary living became possible, food supplies increased, and larger populations could be supported. Not everyone was kept busy with tilling the soil, and the extra time was used first to build houses, later temples and cities as well. Civilization was ushered in, writing was invented, more and more people were brought together, and progress accelerated.

Turgot's belief in progress was surpassed by that of his friend and biographer Marie Jean de Condorcet (1743–94), who wrote his *Outline of the Intellectual Progress of Mankind* (first published in 1795) under the menace of the guillotine. Caught in 1794, he died in jail in that same year; yet, the French Revolution ushered in the last of his ten stages of historical progress.

His design was as ambitious as that of Turgot. He wrote that he wanted to show

the successive changes in human society, the influence which each instant exerts on the succeeding instant, and thus, in its successive modifications, the advance of the human species towards truth or happiness.

(Quoted by Bury 1955:208)

He described history as progress through ten epochs: (1) hunting and fishing, (2) pastoralism, (3) agriculture, (4) commerce and science in Greece, (5) the Roman Empire, (6) from the fall of the Roman Empire to the Crusades, (7) from the Crusades to the invention of printing, (8) from the invention of printing to the time when philosophy and the sciences shook off the yoke of authority, (9) from Descartes to the foundation of the French Republic, and (10) the future stage of progress from the Revolution onward.

The last seven stages represent European rather than universal history, but Condorcet was convinced that the development of the mind had culminated in Europe. He agreed with Turgot that culture contact was the mainspring of progress, and Europe was the place where more different nations had come together than anywhere else in the world. Condorcet was more dogmatic about progress than his friend Turgot. He held that the perfectibility of man is absolutely indefinite, and can never be retrogressive. If the earth were to retain its position and the laws of nature remain unaltered, the future would bring a prolongation of the human life span and the abolition of slavery, freedom would be restored to Africa and Asia, the inequalities between nations would be destroyed, and, "since nature has fixed no limits to our hopes," progress would even bring about the liberation of women.

To Condorcet, progress moved ahead by its own power. Where Turgot had stressed such important factors of change as diffusion, migration, population density, environmental changes, increase in productivity and economic surplus, Condorcet saw progress as an independent power, marching on despite human reason or unreason, leading man inevitably in the right direction. Condorcet's "progress" thus was the secular counterpart of Vico's "providence."

British scholars of the age were strongly influenced by Locke, and tended to feel that the question of how the mind acquires knowledge was the most basic of all. They were less inclined than the French *philosophes* to take human nature for granted. To them, the human mind was a subject not of speculation but of empirical analysis. The title of David Hume's (1711–76) *An Enquiry Concerning Human Understanding* (1748) expresses such a concern. His aim was to "discover, at least in some degree, the secret springs and principles, by which the human mind is actuated in its operations." Hume dismissed the concept of innate ideas with observations such as "a blind man can form no notion of colors; a deaf man no notion of sounds," and "a Laplander or Negro has no notion of the relish of wine . . ." This had been also Locke's position, and apart from the fact that Hume was more systematic and attempted to classify types of experiences and their mental results, there was no great difference between the two scholars. But Hume was bothered by a problem that had not occurred to Locke. Hume became painfully aware of the fact that not all forms of behavior and thought can be explained in terms of previous experience. It was true that man learned by experience that a specific loaf of bread was edible and nourishing. But later on man acquired the faculty to recognize any bread as such, no matter if it was different in shape, size, and color from the bread of his experience. This involved a process of mind about which Hume said that he "would willingly know the foundation," but he had to admit that it passed his comprehension. Of course, one could say that the recognition of the general comes about by inference from the particular, but this was a mere observation. Hume wanted to know *how* the mind made such inferences.

In recent years, Noam Chomsky has addressed himself to the same question. He too acknowledges that part of man's ability to use language is learned by experience. A child will learn the word "doll" through association with particular dolls. But eventually the child will recognize all dolls, no matter if they are entirely different from the ones previously encountered. This linguistic "creativity," as Chomsky calls it, is further extended in as far as people learn to use and interpret strings of words never heard before in that combination, and Chomsky concludes that this creative faculty of man cannot be explained by simple stimulus-and-response mechanisms. But Chomsky also has not yet discovered the "secret springs" of this human capability.

Hume also applied his principles of the mind to the analysis of religion. He turned to this social institution because religious thought seemed to be one of the strangest mental phenomena, appearing to be devoid of any rational order. Moreover, although it was a universal institution, present in all known cultures, it did not seem to have the obvious utility of technology or of family life. In *The Natural History of Religion* (1757), Hume examined religion not in order to attack its doctrines, but merely to understand the human thought processes that gave rise to this social phenomenon. Hume found it difficult to perceive any order and rationality in religious behavior, and concluded that religion is not born of reason. Even if early men were capable of rational thought, they possessed neither the knowledge nor the leisure time to develop it:

But a barbarous, necessitous animal (such as a man is on the first origin of society), pressed by such numerous wants and passions, has no leisure to admire the regular face of nature, or make inquiries concerning the cause of those objects, to which from his infancy he has been gradually accustomed.

(Hume 1964:35)

Earlier, Hume had reached the conclusion that man was born with a blank mind, so that neither could religion be explained by referring to innate knowledge about God or the divine. Tracing religions back to their origins, Hume concluded that early men were not brooding over the world order, were not contemplating the infinite goodness or supreme wisdom of a creator, and were also not moved by ethical considerations. Instead, early men were subject to emotions, passions, and appetites. The strongest emotion was fear—fear of demons, or of powers that would destroy them—and hence they attempted to propitiate these powers. These sentiments were present not only in early religions, but fear was a universal property of the mind. The fear of demons and the hope to overcome them rested at the roots of all religions. The difference between primitive and modern religions rested in their external forms only. Religion had begun as polytheism, because primitive man assigned a separate cause to each problem that confronted him, and therefore he conceived of many deities. Some of those appeared more powerful than others, and they were addressed more frequently in times of stress. Eventually, the minor spirits were forgotten, and a single deity emerged who combined in his person the powers and qualities of all others.

Hume's explanations about the origin and evolution of religion are not so important in themselves. The theory that religion originates in fear is one of the oldest explanations in existence, and remains unproven and unprovable. His description of the evolution from polytheism to monotheism was equally conjectural. But he examined religion as a social phenomenon on a par with all other social institutions, and was a detached observer. More important was his insight into the fallacy of using the preconceived and unproven similarity of human nature as a tool for the explanation of social phenomena. To Hume, human nature itself was to be examined, and its understanding would come from the observation of human behavior rather than from speculating about ideas. His approach revealed that the human mind was not an orderly storehouse of religious truths and social wisdom. Instead, human natures were products of an interplay between appetites and emotions on the one hand, and physical and social experiences on the other.

The Natural History of Religion offended many people who misread Hume's intentions and accused him of atheism and impiety, branding his work as that of an Antichrist. For the same reasons the book was acclaimed by the French Enlightenment philosophers, who also read it as a deliberate assault on revealed religion. Charles de Brosses (1709–77) decided to use Hume's method to further unmask the errors of ancient and modern religions. In his book *Du Culte des dieux fétiches, ou, parallèle de l'ancienne religion de l'Egypte avec la religion actuelle de Nigritie* (1760) he began with attacking all previous interpretations of myth and worship.

Scholars dealing with Egyptian religion had interpreted their pictorial imagery as symbolic of secret wisdom. Athanasius Kircher, for one, had written *Oedipus Aegyptiacus* in four volumes, attempting to show that every hieroglyph and picture signified Egyptian knowledge about medicine, architecture, music, theology, and geometry. Animals were seen as symbols of Christian virtues and vices, and everything else also assumed concrete scientific or moral significance (Manuel 1959:190–91). De Brosses dismissed these and all other allegorical interpretations as well as those that had explained paganism in terms of a degeneration of original monotheism. Objective study of Egyptian art showed clearly that Egyptians were animal worshipers, said de Brosses. Animals were not symbolic of anything; they were literally the gods of the Egyptians, who literally worshiped them. De Brosses found animal worship so repulsive and irrational that he could find no better explanation than to assign it to fantasies of rather debilitated minds.

Comparing Egyptian animal worship with other pagan religions, he discovered that all adored natural objects of some kind: mountains, rivers, trees, stars, stones, snakes, birds, and beasts. From this observation de Brosses concluded that religion had begun as object worship, for which he coined the term "fetishism." His definition of a fetish was so all-embracing that it covered nearly every material object, and soon he saw fetishes everywhere: the Islamic black stone of the Kaaba, Greek and Roman statues, the fire of Zoroastrianism all were instances of fetishism. Many fetishes also appeared in the Scriptures: the Urim and Thummim, the sacred grove of Abraham, the stone anointed by Jacob; de Brosses even dared to conjecture that the Holy Cross itself might be of fetishist origin. Reconstructing the evolution of religious worship, de Brosses held that astrolatry was earliest, followed by pure fetishism, anthropomorphic polytheism, and monotheism. The third section of *Du Culte des dieux fétiches* was a literal translation of Hume's *Natural History of Religion*, except that the term "polytheism" was replaced by "fetishism." But de Brosses's purposes differed from those of Hume. De Brosses wanted to attack religion while Hume wanted to understand human nature. De Brosses emphasized the irrationality of early man, who was in his eyes not just "barbarous and necessitous," but "in a state of ferocious stupidity," debilitated, mad, sick, and terror-struck. At best, early men were like children who, devoid of reason, imagined their dolls to be alive. Children, however, mature, while savages passed their lives in eternal infancy: their mental development did not go beyond that of a four-year-old civilized child.

In a sense, de Brosses adumbrated all negative aspects of nineteenth-century evolutionists. The theory of primitive stupidity returned in the writings of Lévy-Bruhl, Freud, Frazer, Tylor and Radin; and his views about the unilineal direction of progress were more dogmatic than those of later "unilineal" evolutionists. His conviction that the evolution of the mind had culminated in his own enlightened society was a sentiment not wholly unknown to nineteenth-century anthropologists either.

De Brosses also anticipated Tylor's famous survival theory. Perhaps because he did not want to break openly with the Church, he wrote that many contemporary religious practices were probably fetishist in origin, but could no longer be so considered because they had survived only by tradition or force of habit and had lost their earlier meanings. He achieved a good insight into the nature of religious syncretism in seeing that most religions retain older elements even if their interpretations change radically. Finally it should be said that de Brosses must have felt that contemporary primitives were in any case *capable* of improvement. He called upon the French government to conduct new expeditions to the South Sea islands, not for the greater glory of France, but to deliver savages from their fetishism and to raise them to rationality.

In de Brosses's writings the distinguishing features of Enlightenment appear in exaggerated form. He hailed the triumph of reason, stressed empirical scientific methods, held a very dismal view of primitive life and mentality, attempted to be objective, and believed that progress could be accelerated by enlightened education. Although he fell short of the ideals of scientific objectivity, there is no doubt that he possessed the quality that Kant felt to be the epitome of the Enlightenment spirit, namely "daring to know." Alexander Pope expressed the mood of the age in his famous lines:

> *Know then thyself, presume not God to scan,*
> *The proper study of mankind is man.*

CHAPTER 6

THE FATE
OF REASON

Although the eighteenth century is often called "the age of reason," scholars of that period were by no means certain about the universal rationality of the human mind. Those who believed in progress were inclined to think that reason itself had evolved, and often posited an early stage of human irrationality verging on brutishness. But the evolution of reason posed problems. When social scientists began to search for the emergence of reason they could certainly point to the many advances in technology, but not to an ever increasing improvement of social conditions. The conclusion was either that man was not endowed with much reason at all, or else that he had not used it properly, which in itself was not very reasonable. Several Enlightenment scholars indeed tended to the conviction that reason had been recognized and put to good use in their own era only, and that they themselves were the discoverers and carriers of that human quality.

While they were not always certain about social progress in the past, they were generally more optimistic about the future. Many enlightened rulers had introduced more humane laws, and even de Brosses had held out hope of raising the fetishist primitives whom he so despised to rationalism.

Progress could certainly be sped up by enlightened education —or so it was thought until the outbreak of the French Revolution. The horrors that attended it and the failure to fulfill its promises seemed to deny both the social reason of man and the constancy of future progress. Post-Revolution discussions centered around these problems, and eventually reason became denounced or denied. Also progress was not an obvious factor of everyday life. These considerations tended toward the idea that the past may have been a better time than the present. This notion took different forms, turning some into romanticists, others into reactionaries.

Of course, doubts about universal reason also existed before the Revolution, and the arguments of Immanuel Kant (1724–1804) about the limited scope of reason had been hard to refute. Kant agreed with Locke and Hume that human knowledge comes from experience. But early empiricists had been at a loss to explain how these experiences became organized in the human mind. Locke had made it appear as if every individual learned in isolation from others, filling the blank pages of his mind only by personal sense perceptions. But if this were the case, human communication and social behavior in general could not exist. In his *Critique of Pure Reason* (1781) Kant proposed that the human mind not only possessed the capability of registering experiences, but also had the innate ability to organize them. There were then both universal and innate principles of the human mind: all human beings organized their experiences by the same principles and in the same manner, no matter what the experiences themselves might be.

These universal ordering principles were, according to Kant, of two basic kinds, namely "the forms of intuition" and "the forms of understanding." The former had to do with man's ability to conceive of time and space. Since these entities could not be experienced directly, their forms must be present in the mind at birth, and they caused man to place every sense impression within a framework of time and space.

While Kant knew that different peoples conceptualized time in different ways, all expressed awareness of its existence and passing, and this was also true for space. The second set of ordering principles, the "forms of understanding," comprised what Kant called the "categories," namely the relationships between experiences. These included concepts of unity, comparison, reality, cause-and-effect, and so forth.

With this universal equipment—Kant called it the "transcendental consciousness"—man perceived his world and organized his experiences. Since the categories were universal and pregiven, people could understand each other's behavior and thoughts, and social life thus was possible. Man had no certainty, however, that his observations were true, because he could not know the things in their own rights, but only in terms of the a priori transcendental consciousness. It followed then, that human reason, although not absent, was conditioned and thus also limited by the preexisting nature of the mind itself. If human thought processes were so conditioned, human actions also could not be entirely under man's control. Social statistics helped to bolster Kant's argument that societies possessed laws not of man's own making: births and marriages occurred as regularly as the changes of seasons, and what appeared to be of human volition was in fact outside it.

Kant's theories exercised a strong influence upon early sociologists such as Comte and Durkheim, who also stressed the social over the individual. But in the early nineteenth century Kant's arguments were often used to bolster attacks on human reason.

There was another well-known pre-Revolution writer who was skeptical about human reason and its progress. Less analytic than Kant, Jean-Jacques Rousseau (1712–78) felt that the unsatisfactory conditions of his own time were proof enough that reason had not been the prime mover of history. Consequently he expressed the idea—for his time still uncommon—that the past may have been more pleasant than the present. In his *Discourse on the Origin and Foundation of Inequality among Mankind* (1755) he sketched the early conditions of mankind as a state in which people had dwelled harmoniously with one another, living in small groups, unencumbered by laws or other social constraints, not knowing the value of gold and silver, living by their emotions, and thus achieving a simple and happy life that civilization had since destroyed. The social life of "natural man," however, had little survival value, because man was physically inferior to ferocious animals. He differed from them in that he possessed the faculty of improvement, so that he did not have to abide by the laws of nature. Eventually concepts of family life, property, government, law, and mutual cooperation were developed. While these institutions made his existence more viable, they also destroyed freedom and happiness:

. . . but from the moment one man began to stand in need of another's assistance; from the moment it appeared an advantage for one man to possess enough provisions for two, equality vanished; property was introduced; labor became necessary; and boundless forests became smiling fields, which had to be watered with human sweat, and in which slavery and misery were soon seen to sprout out and grow with the harvests.

(Rousseau 1967:220)

It is untrue, however, that Rousseau advocated a "return to nature," to earlier and happier conditions, as is often believed. He felt that man was basically good, and he sometimes said that people ought to live naturally, responding to their own emotions and following their own conscience; but this does not mean a return to primitive social conditions. Rousseau realized all too well that the clock could not be set back, and of course he also admitted that the inventions of agriculture, art, and family life were desirable ones. Instead he suggested possibilities to improve present social conditions, and in *The Social Contract* (1762) he described an ideal state society, namely one ruled by mutual agreement and legal equality. If this were accomplished, society would be in a condition vastly superior to the earlier state of nature, because man would enjoy the fruits of technological progress while living in peace and harmony.

A description of Rousseau as a romantic primitivist is inaccurate. He never even used the term "noble savage"* and he was realistic enough to admit that his "natural man" was a hypothetical construct for which no empirical evidence was in existence. Rousseau appealed to the later romanticists because of his positive evaluation of the past, and because his views about reason put its power into serious doubt. Although Rousseau did not deny that man was endowed with reason, and that the proper use of it could perhaps have worked toward social improvements, something had gone wrong, and technical inventions had contributed to social discontent and human unhappiness.

Romanticism itself was a movement that arose as a reaction against Enlightenment. It developed into a widespread and complex school of thought that became strongly associated with art and literature. Many of its spokesmen were poets: Herder, Matthew Arnold, Lessing, Goethe. But it was also a social philosophy, a worldview that exercised great influence upon nineteenth-century thought in every field of the humanities. More strongly than Rousseau, romantic writers denied reason and qualified progress. This led to a glorification of the past. Progress was not denied, but it was not depicted as accelerating in time and cumulative in its effects. At best it was seen as a slow and gradual process, sometimes at a standstill, sometimes retreating to earlier levels. But since its movements were not guided by human reason, other explanations of social change were in order. Romanticists did not return to theological explanations, but tended to depict cultural evolution as an unconscious process whose movements were sometimes held to be inscrutable, sometimes explained as adaptation to environment. But the most outstanding feature of romanticism was nostalgia for the past. Unhappy about the results of the Revolution and questioning the values of their own times,

---

* The poet John Dryden (1631–1700) first used this phrase when he wrote:
> I am as free as nature first made man,
> Ere the base laws of servitude began,
> When wild in woods the noble savage ran.

(*The Conquest of Granada*, Act i, sc. 1)

many felt that former social conditions had been better, more harmonious, less encumbered, less threatening. This nostalgia became even more poignant through the awareness that the past is irrevocably gone and cannot be brought back. But the past could be recollected and vicariously relived through studies and reconstructions of earlier conditions. These sentiments led to a strong upsurge in the study of nonliterate cultures, which were considered to be the best relics of the past. Primitive peoples were no longer depicted as superstitious fanatics, poverty-stricken in material skills and resources, half-crazed by fear, and continuously at war. They were now described as naturally good, living from the fruits of nature, well adapted to their environments, and above all poetic and creative. As such they stood in stark contrast to modern city dwellers, who were slaves of their own institutions and laws, corrupted by their own technology and science, and decadent in their morals. Folk poetry and folk art were admired and imitated; folklore and mythology became separate branches of study.

Many of these ideas converged in the voluminous writings of Johann Gottfried Herder (1744–1803). Like so many before him, Herder was convinced that a reconstruction of a universal history of culture was the best empirical demonstration of theory, and in his four-volume *Ideas about the Philosophy of the History of Mankind* (1784–91) he set out to write such a history. While most earlier scholars had envisaged the evolution of culture in terms of stereotyped stages or periods (as Morgan and Tylor would do again later on), Herder was convinced that history was an uninterrupted process of natural development. This process was, however, neither mechanical nor automatic. Where Locke's or Hume's primitives were almost undifferentiated, Herder stressed the diversity of cultures, in the conviction that each group of people had enacted a separate and different version of cultural development.

The beginning of society was not a divine act, not an unexplainable sudden awakening of reason, but a natural development. Man's upright posture was a necessary first step for the existence of culture, and early man, a single species with but a few closely related members, lived in a homogeneous society. At that time the similarities of human nature were the most pronounced. In this early stage the basic social institutions without which human life could not be perpetuated were established, but the romantic Herder added the making of poetry to the traditional list of language, religion, technology, and family life. Inventions of clothing, fire, and shelter made it possible for men to live in the most diverse types of climate, and when population increase made it necessary for people to move apart, small groups of people settled in various physical environments. Each of these small communities adapted to new surroundings in a durable and harmonious manner and reached a near-perfect equilibrium. In Herder's terms, each of these *Volk* cultures established its own "genius," or what we now would call its "ethos" or "national character."

All *Volk* cultures were different because they were formed through an interaction between environment and the creative capabilities of man. Climate and environment did not operate in a vacuum, but acted upon the already existing genius and creativity of a people. Creativity was a universal property of man, but it found different expressions under the influence of different physical conditions. These processes were unconscious in the *Volk* cultures, and only in the Western world had historical self-consciousness been achieved.

In Herder's views, *Volk* cultures encompassed the greatest amount of time and space in history. The early homogeneous pre-*Volk* condition had been of relatively short duration, and the historical self-awareness of the Western world was of rather recent date. The *Volk* also captured Herder's own strongest sympathies. Convinced that even the most exotic forms of human behavior had value, meaning, and often even beauty, he was far removed from the often blatant ethnocentricism of Enlightenment scholars. Although the historical consciousness achieved by Western civilization was a progressive step, Herder did not extol the superiority of his own culture. He lamented Europe's missed opportunities to achieve excellence, and at times even predicted that Western civilization would decline and disappear. Herder pleaded for sympathetic and unprejudiced evaluations of all cultures:

Is there any species of barbarity, to which some man, some nation, nay frequently a number of nations, have not accustomed themselves; so that many, perhaps most, have even fed on the flesh of their fellow-creatures? Is there a wild conception the mind can frame, which has not been actually rendered sacred by hereditary tradition, in one place or another? . . . I am persuaded, no form of human manners is possible, which some nation, or some individual, has not adopted . . . . If, then, we would philosophise on the history of our species, let us reject, as far as possible, all narrow modes of thinking, taken from the constitution of one region of the Earth . . .

(Quoted by Slotkin 1965:287)

Herder was full of admiration for the poetic manifestations of *Volk* societies, and translated many poems, myths, and tales into German so that everyone could come to know and admire them.

In spite of this humanistic outlook, Herder is sometimes accused of incipient racism (Stocking 1968:36, 65, 214; Collingwood 1956:91–92). Collingwood found Herder's conception of human nature too static, so that it appeared to him as if the psychological peculiarities of *Volk* societies were inherited together with physical ones. For this reason, Collingwood even considered Herder "the father of anthropology," and compounded his errors by defining anthropology as a science that "distinguishes various physical types of human beings, and studies the manners and customs of these various types as expressions of psychological peculiarities going with physical ones" (Collingwood 1956:91). To the contrary, Herder anticipates the modern anthropological concept of cultural learning as a major determinant of human behavior, a view that strongly contradicts racistic ideas about biologically inherited behavior. Herder wrote:

. . . our specific character lies in this, that, born almost without instinct, we are formed to manhood only by the practice of a whole life.

. . . living beings like ourselves contribute to instruct us, fashion us, and form our habits.

. . . everyone becomes a man only by means of education.

. . . throughout his whole life, he is not only a child in reason, but a pupil of the reason of others. Into whatever hands he falls, by them he is formed.

(Quoted by Slotkin 1965:289)

These statements belie the idea that Herder believed human nature to be fixed and unalterable. He stressed that *Volk* was a historical development, not a biological one. All societies were to him equally legitimate, and if he is to be accused of bias at all, it could be said that he seemed to love *Volk* cultures more than all others. He treated them as beautiful and exotic flowers, worthy of study in their own right, a sentiment not wholly unknown among modern anthropologists either.

Herder was not the only writer of his time to view history as the unfolding of cultural developments. A number of universal histories appeared whose writers were generally more intrigued by cultural variations than by progress. Like Herder, they tended to give natural explanations for cultural differences, sometimes using the biological analogy and comparing cultural growth with the ages of mankind, sometimes attempting to establish stages of development by comparing cultural institutions such as technology, subsistence, arts, beliefs, myths, laws, forms of government, and grading them on a scale of increasing complexity.

Johann Christoph Adelung's (1732–1806) *History of the Culture of the Human Species* (1782) is an example of the first approach. He compared stages of culture with stages of individual development as follows:

1 From origin to the flood. Mankind an embryo.
2 From the flood to Moses. The human race a child in its culture.
3 From Moses to 683 B.C. The human race a boy.

4 683 B.C. to A.D. 1. Rapid blooming of youth of the human race.
5 A.D. 1 to 400 (Migrations). Mankind an enlightened man.
6 400–1096 (Crusades). A man's heavy bodily labors.
7 1096–1520 (full enlightenment reached). A man occupied in installation and improvement of his economy.
8 1520–present. A man in enlightened enjoyment.

> (Quoted by Kroeber and Kluckhohn 1963:36)

Christoph Meiners (1747–1810), however, stressed the study of cultural institutions, customs, and habits "at all times and in all places" (1785), and the importance of studying cultures empirically was made even more explicit in the writings of D. Jenisch (1762–1804), who wrote that there was a world of difference between the examination of actually existing primitive cultures and conjectures about ideal developments. Reconstruction of cultural evolution should thus not begin with positing stages and fitting all customs of mankind within this preconceived framework, but all developments should be traced as they actually occurred in history.

The emphasis on the study of primitive customs and habits became increasingly pronounced, so that several scholars began to feel that this field of investigation constituted a separate branch of learning. Meiners called it "the history of humanity," which, as he himself admitted, was close to being a *Völkerkunde* or ethnography (Kroeber and Kluckhohn 1963:41). Lowie began his *History of Ethnological Theory* (1937) with Meiners. Although admitting that a point of departure is always arbitrary, Lowie felt that the recognition of anthropology as a separate discipline should stand at the beginning of its history. It is at this time also that attempts to define culture began to emerge, and although culture was often equated with improvement, there was also a general recognition that culture was something learned or to be learned.

Admiration of the past took quite a different form in France. This country had suffered most from the Revolution, and it appeared to many that the old regime had been much better than postrevolutionary chaos. These sentiments were strongest among intelligentsia and nobility, and it is thus not surprising that two noblemen, Count Joseph de Maistre (1754–1821) and Viscomte V. G. A. de Bonald (1753–1841), became the best-known spokesmen for the return of the monarchy. De Maistre, a Savoyard of French origin, fled to Switzerland when Savoy was invaded, and later went to Russia, waiting for the defeat of Napoleon and hoping for the restoration of the French monarchy. During that time he wrote voluminously, never tiring of attacking the "satanic" Revolution and its creators, among whom he counted not so much the political rebels as Rousseau, Voltaire, and the whole Enlightenment philosophy. Their claim that society was a human creation and that man thus could play a decisive role in the course of history was, according to de Maistre, not only false, but pernicious. "Man is but an instrument of God" (1959:15), but had fallen into the trap of Enlightenment arrogance, believing that he could change the natural order of society. All he had done, however, was to upset that order, and the aftermath of the Revolution clearly showed that such attempts inevitably led to chaos and misery. Society and the course of history were ruled by natural laws, wisely ordained by God, and thus should not be tampered with. Constitutional monarchy was part of the divinely in-stituted social order, and hence it should be not only restored but safeguarded forever afterward. If necessary, even freedom of speech and of press should be curtailed.

While de Maistre's reactionary views were neither scientific nor very appealing, his writings contained ideas that were taken up by later French sociologists and filtered through to twentieth-century British functionalism. Since de Maistre was convinced that man was not very reasonable, not important in history, and had not created the laws of society, it followed that social laws could be studied without taking people into account. Comte inherited his thoroughgoing anti-individualism to a large extent from de Maistre. Moreover, since people should obey the laws of society, the implication was that society possessed a moral force of its own, constraining man in his actions. These ideas were also fundamental for Durkheim, who stressed that social science dealt with social phenomena and not with the minds of individuals (Durkheim 1960:17); that social conduct was external to the individual, and society was endowed with coercive powers, which themselves were moral (Durkheim 1958:2). Although Durkheim named Montesquieu as his master and did not mention de Maistre, the theories of the latter are closely related to Durkheim's views. To Montesquieu, laws did not exist outside the individual. He wrote: "Law in general is human reason" (1966 I:6), and he related social laws to such other psychological factors as "inclinations" and "dispositions" of people and the "intent" of legislators. De Maistre was much more dogmatic: for man to believe that he is the author of society is "as if the trowel thought itself an architect" (de Maistre 1959:15).

The writings of de Maistre also indicated another growing trend, namely that the study of social phenomena could be placed in the service of social reform, an ideal pursued also by Marx, Saint-Simon, and Comte. Before discussing their theories and programs, some brief mention must be made of George Wilhelm Friedrich Hegel (1770–1831).

Like many Enlightenment scholars, Hegel conceived of world history in terms of progressive evolution. But the former had encountered difficulties in upholding progress when they examined the human record for affirmation. Hegel obviated such doubts by starting at the opposite end, making social history itself part and parcel of reason, thus setting it apart from everyday human reason. To explain his system, Hegel began by stating that the moving power of history was its own spirit, its *Weltgeist,* by which he meant that history possessed an inherent predisposition to move and develop in a certain given direction. This predisposition was "reason" and the direction it took was toward the increase of human freedom. This freedom was not, however, the ability to do what one likes. In fact, it was almost the opposite: freedom was the free obedience to social laws. "Only that will which obeys laws is free, for it obeys itself" (Hegel 1956:39). These laws need not concur with the desires of the individual; but while some people obey laws without understanding—as children obey their parents—the realization that obedience is freedom is the fullest manifestation of reason.

Hegel's evolutionary scheme is but a variation on a theme. He used biological analogy, saw progress as an increase of consciousness, felt that his own German civilization had gone farthest in this development, and sought the cause for social change in history itself. But his specific explanation of the regularities of change—his famous dialectic—was new. Social change followed a patterned course: when an entity or event —the thesis—appeared, it was countered by the emergence of its opposite, the antithesis. The conflict between the two resolved itself in a synthesis which, taking some elements of both thesis and antithesis, "elevates" both, bringing about a new and higher event. In turn, synthesis becomes thesis, is negated again by its antithesis, resolving again in a new synthesis. The direction of history was determined by these movements, and progress spiraled upward. In Hegel's view, this process was guided by reason and thus worked toward the development of human reasoning and toward human freedom.

Hegel insisted on concrete demonstration of his dialectics, and in *The Philosophy of History* (1956) he placed all his most basic notions within the framework of actual historical events, showing that cultures are in conflict, and that the resolution of these conflicts brings about a higher order. He stated unequivocally that theory must be subordinate to the realities of fact, so that the laws of change can be demonstrated only in the realities of history.

Hegel's philosophy is still widely debated, but the complexities of his theories need not to concern us here. His importance for the further development of nineteenth-century social science rests mainly in his influence upon Karl Marx (1818–83) and Friedrich Engels (1820–95). Marx accepted the dialectical process as the moving power of history, and believed, with Hegel, that this process was marked by conflict. But where Hegel had identified reason as the ultimate power behind the dialectical process, Marx strongly denied this.

Looking around him, he saw many social conditions that contradicted the idea that reason had led men everywhere to greater freedom. The lower classes—the proletarians—were oppressed, and their lot was anything but a fulfillment of human potentialities: they lacked freedom and even the awareness of it. The causes of change must be sought in society itself, in concrete social and economic institutions. Marx boasted that he had taken Hegel's dialectic and "stood it on its head." Hegel had started from above, from reason and philosophy; Marx began with "real active men" and wanted to show how their real life processes displayed the developments of the social. On this basis Marx called his system "historical materialism," namely the idea that the meaning of social and historical developments was to be found *nowhere else* but in social facts. In his view, social change cannot be understood by speculative philosophy, nor by intuition, but only by materialistic social science.

Marx's own speculation was that all social activities were ultimately reducible to economic motivations and processes. Since economics can be studied concretely and empirically, Marx considered his materialism a victory over philosophical speculation. Although it is certainly true that economy is a category that lends itself better to empirical research than reason or world spirit, Marx proceeded to prove his thesis in a manner similar to that of Hegel. Hegel demonstrated his dialectic of reason in history; Marx similarly demonstrated his dialectic of economy in social history, and saw it as an independent power that continually negated earlier conditions.

Both Marx and Hegel neglected early and nonliterate societies, Hegel because he felt that the world spirit had not yet manifested itself on that level, Marx because he thought that tribal societies were classless, and thus not very interesting. Upon reading Morgan's *Ancient Society* (1877), Marx and Engels became convinced that economic forces had also been at work in primitive times. Moreover, Morgan had shown that private property and the state appeared late in history, which seemed to prove that these institutions were not *necessary* components of society and might be abolished again in a future more ideal state. In his book *On the Origin of the Family, Private Property, and the State, in the Light of the Researches of Lewis H. Morgan* (1884), Engels hailed Morgan as the American discoverer of the material conception of history.

The importance of Marx and Engels does not rest in their version of dialectics, nor in their evolutionary schemes, but in the fact that they elevated social studies to the rank of science. Although it is true that ideology crept into their system, that they did not always abide by their own scientific canons, and that their principles were not entirely removed from metaphysics, they objectified the world of man and ushered in a new era of interpretation. It cannot be said that they forever banned metaphysical explanations from social studies, but the distinction between social philosophy and social science could no longer be neglected by any serious scholar. Modern anthropology and sociology are materialistic insofar as they seek the causes of social and cultural change in concrete phenomena, although the question of what constitutes concreteness has not been solved.

One answer was provided by a school of thought that developed during Marx's own lifetime and announced itself as "positive philosophy." It considered itself "positive" on several counts. First, it was a reaction against Hegel's (and later Marx's) concepts that history moves in terms of negations. Early positivists called Hegel's theory "negative philosophy," and charged that it denied the real factors of society and history, seeing it only as a chain of negations. Instead, positivists wanted to create a study of reality, of what actually existed and was directly observable. "Essences" or other abstract ideas could never give true knowledge, but led only to useless speculation. Examination of patterns of society and its changes would lead toward the understanding of laws that had caused prevailing conditions, and such understanding would make it possible to improve society according to its own laws.

In France, Claude-Henri de Saint-Simon (1760–1825) was

the most vocal spokesman of this social philosophy. Durkheim acknowledged him, rather than Comte, as the true founder of positivism. In his early writings, Saint-Simon attempted to formulate a unified theory of science and thus to align the study of society with the natural sciences. Astronomy, physics, chemistry, and biology had long been working on the basis of positivism and had made rapid strides. Their method should become the guideline for all intellectual undertakings, and particularly for social science:

In all portions of my work, I shall be occupied with establishing series of facts, for I am convinced that this is the only solid part of our knowledge.

(Quoted by Marcuse 1960:331)

This statement became as it were the positivist's manifesto: science was the study of observable sense data only. It followed that a close relationship between natural and social sciences was perceived and that both were subject to the same kind of natural laws. Both should thus employ the same methods of observation and deduction, and relate themselves to all other branches of physics. Saint-Simon felt that his new science deserved a special name, and he called it "social physiology."

Like Marx, Saint-Simon felt that economy was the major determinant of society. But where Marx had seen the industrial system as one of exploitation, Saint-Simon looked upon it in a "positive" sense, claiming that it was the foundation of social existence and the source of all wealth. Eventually, Saint-Simon developed the idea that science should rule supreme over all human affairs. He called upon scientists, artists, and industrialists to form a society for the promotion of this ideal, and constructed a plan for the total reorganization of Europe on this basis. The present forms of government would be replaced by one consisting of three "Houses," manned by "captains of industry," to examine, promote, and utilize inventions (Saint-Simon 1814). Still later, he proposed that science should replace religion, so that all scientific undertakings would attain an aura of sacredness. This *New Christianity* (1825) would do much to put science into action, mainly through the promotion of industry. He found a number of followers, mostly wealthy industrialists, who also became convinced that industry was the major pathway to progress. After Saint-Simon's death, they formed an organization working toward this end. They financed the building of railroads, aided in the construction of the Suez Canal, and developed many international commercial banks.

In more than one way, Saint-Simon set the tone for the development of sociology. His interest was in contemporary Western society and in contemporary social problems, he studied society in abstraction from its human members, was interested in observable facts, and stressed that social physiology was a strictly scientific undertaking.

Most sociologists, however, look upon Auguste Comte (1798–1857) as the founder of their discipline. No discipline can claim to be fathered by any one person, and Comte was in any case strongly influenced by Saint-Simon, with whom he collaborated for a period of six years. Comte was equally convinced that the scientific study of society was a new departure, but after quarreling with Saint-Simon, and from there on writing independently, he did not want to call this science "social physiology," and in fact tried to suppress all evidence of his connections with his former friend. First he used the term "social physics," but when another writer, Adolphe Quételet, began to use this same phrase, Comte coined the term "sociology."

His most important work appeared between 1830 and 1842, namely his famous *Positive Philosophy*. Although it is certain that he took many of his ideas from Saint-Simon, these volumes contain many new and creative insights.

Comte took the positivist method already more or less for granted, and did not spend much time on the justification of its principles. Instead, he worked out the relationships between the sciences in great detail, thus firmly integrating sociology with natural sciences. Sciences, in his view, were of two basic types: some were static, others dynamic. Sociology was unique in that it participated in both types, and formed a bridge between the two. Static sociology studied the given social order, dynamic sociology examined the causes of change and progress. Comte's own major interest was in the latter, and he began to search for the laws of social change.

These laws were "natural," but yet not identical to the physical laws of nature. Rather, they were to be found in the development of the human mind, as it was reflected in the evolution from theology to positivism. In the first stage, the theological one, everything was explained by referring to supernatural causes, or to the activities of personified deities. This stage had its own subdivisions. Fetishism, treating physical objects as if they were alive, gave way to polytheism, while the third substage of monotheism unified all deities and spirits into one godhead. In the second major stage, the metaphysical one, the gods became replaced by abstract and impersonal principles such as "essence" or "reason." The positive stage was reached when explanations became scientific and were made in terms of laws that describe the relationships between observable phenomena. Since Comte was not interested in developments outside Western history, he could assign absolute dates to his stages. The theological stage ended around 1400, the Renaissance ushered in the metaphysical stage, the positive stage was only just beginning.

Comte looked upon his "law of the three stages" as one that reflected the natural order of society as well as social reality. Processes of change were both orderly and progressive, and every stage possessed a harmonious internal organization. Positivism was to Comte definitely the most efficient type of understanding, and closest to the truth. He was convinced that all forms of society should be studied objectively, because value judgments had no place in science. Positivism "neither admires nor condemns political facts, but looks upon them as simple objects of observation." All one could say about societies in earlier stages was that they were less evolved and less perfected, but balanced and adjusted to the intellectual capabilities of their members.

Since evolution was guided by naturally developing and invariant social laws, it was best to let nature take its course. Comte did not advocate social or political actions, and the "positive politics" he recommended would tend to consolidate the existing social order by "wise resignation." Genuine science had no other aim than "constantly to establish and fortify the intellectual order which . . . is the indispensable basis of all true order," or, again, positivism was "the real and only means of raising the social organization, without disruption, into the realm of daylight." Comte was certain that his theories could and eventually would influence the world, but he understood that sociology itself had to be systematized before it could be put into action. This attitude marked the greatest difference between himself and Saint-Simon. The latter was much more impatient, and wanted to start his reforms right away, before his theories had been properly examined.

Comte's faith in the orderly process of both natural and social evolution led him to compare society to a biological organism. Both possessed inner structures of balanced harmony. Society was a kind of collective organism, where families formed the cells, social forces the tissues, while the state comprised various organs. The important difference between the two was, however, that biological organisms were static in their existence, while social ones were dynamic, capable of and indeed destined to progress.

Comte's positivism was an expression of the Kantian insight that absolute notions cannot be grasped by the mind. He renounced the vain search for origins: since they cannot be witnessed they are not amenable to scientific analysis. Scientific research should combine empirical observation with logical reasoning, and from the relationships between social phenomena thus observed their natural laws could be deduced.

Comte felt that religion had played an important role in the march of progress. The early theological stage was a necessary beginning for the evolution toward positivism. Man could not have begun as a scientist, and religion had provided the stimulus for the human mind to correct earlier ideas. Religion itself had thus also progressed and nudged general progress. In his later years, Comte came to regard positivism itself as a kind of religion, one acceptable to scientific men. Traditional religion required the acceptance of unscientific beliefs in supernatural powers, but "the new religion of humanity" was to be based upon altruism and dedicated to the principles of service and love. Unfortunately, Comte was not satisfied merely to advocate his new religion; he began to outline its rituals and overall organization in detail. Eventually he regarded himself as the Supreme Pontiff of his world religion, and sought ten thousand priests to be posted all over Europe, who should both guard the morals of their charges and supervise their scientific education. While these matters became objects of ridicule to his critics, they have not diminished Comte's reputation as a profound thinker who consolidated sociology as an independent science and launched it on its future career.

CONCLUSIONS

This chapter has given some indications about the separation between anthropology and sociology that began to emerge in the beginning of the nineteenth century. Before that time sociological and anthropological interests were not strongly differentiated, but after the French Revolution the divergent trends became more clearly recognizable. These may be considered as alternate reactions to Enlightenment philosophy.

Both movements distrusted reason. During his short reign of terror, Robespierre had proclaimed Reason as a supreme deity in whose honor masses were held in the cathedrals of Paris. But since his reign ended in less than two years by his own execution, it appeared that his goddess was rather powerless. Moreover, the Revolution not only cost many lives, but its *liberté* was in many respects a poor substitute for the liberties enjoyed under the monarchy. Trade became restricted, prices rose sharply, black markets flourished, and the distance between rich and poor remained unaltered. When Napoleon involved almost all European nations in war, the Continent fell into a state of confusion and chaos. After his defeat at Waterloo, the nations formed alliances to prevent resurgence of the masses, and the restored monarchs tended to conservatism, curtailed social reforms, and looked to principles of pre-revolutionary days as their guidelines.

In the face of these innumerable odds, Hegel still proclaimed reason to be the moving power of history. Critical of the terrors the Revolution had engendered, he remained convinced that it was a manifestation of the activity of reason—the historical force working toward the realization of human freedoms. Even if it had not reached its overt goals, it had brought about a much greater awareness of freedom.

Intellectually, one reaction against Enlightenment, reason, and revolution manifested itself as romanticism. Enlightenment philosophers had hoped to discover universal laws of human development in the conviction that what was uniform and natural was also the most rational. Romantics rejected that notion: man was not uniform, but diverse. Peoples and their cultures were very different, and rather than minimizing this, uniqueness should be cherished. In some instances this viewpoint resulted in rather blatant nationalism, but it also led to an appreciation of the kaleidoscopic variety of cultures, including exotic and early ones. Not only were reconstructions of the history of mankind to be universal, but they began to stress the importance of nonliterate cultures in the realization that these occupied the largest time span in history and the biggest geographical area, even at present. These cultures and peoples should thus be studied intensively if present situations and history as a whole were to be fully comprehended. This task was so large and the undertaking so new that it seemed to warrant the creation of a separate discipline, which was first named "history of mankind" (*Völkerkunde*) or "ethnology."

Romanticism was not merely a nostalgia of dreamers. Its adherents insisted upon the dignity of cultures and of individuals, and acknowledged their rights to achieve self-realization. Although with detours and modifications, these principles remained preserved in the discipline that soon would become known as anthropology.

In contrast, scholars who were the direct forerunners of Comte were interested in the Western world only. They were generally assured that the study of society was useful and practical, and could lead to social improvements of the civilized nations. In this frame of mind, non-Western peoples appeared to be totally unimportant, because they seemed to have had little influence upon present European conditions. If they were taken into account at all, it was not because they were important in their own right, but because the laws of nature could possibly be deduced from studying the degrees of their social development. Individual people were equally unimportant for the understanding of the social. To de Maistre, man was but an instrument of God; to positivists, man was but an instrument of the laws of nature, which were also the laws of progress.

Comte's successors remained more concerned with problems of modern complex societies, and although less optimistic about their powers to cure social ills, sociologists still tend to be problem-oriented, analyzing divorce patterns, labor relations, class struggles, race relationships, crime, delinquency, and suicide. Sociology also tends to derive structure from social phenomena, without taking individuals into account, and the search for laws of change continues.

In recent years sociology and anthropology have strongly influenced one another, so that earlier differences have become somewhat blurred. Nevertheless, the different ideologies and methods of the separately emerging disciplines gave each its own distinctive coloring, which has not faded in the intervening years.

CHAPTER 7

EVOLUTION
BEFORE TYLOR

The perspectives of the history of anthropology are complex. In the previous chapter the influence of romanticism was emphasized, but although appreciation of all cultures as important in their own rights was a basic prerequisite, other insights were necessary before anthropology could become, in the words of Tylor, "the general science of man."

Throughout the century, interests in history and evolution prevailed. Where some scholars concentrated their attention primarily on Western developments, others endeavored to understand the entire range of humanity. A more realistic estimate of the amount of time it had taken for man and his culture to evolve was essential for such understanding. Earlier explanations had suffered from the assumption that the creation of the world had taken place in six days, that plant and animal species had been created separately from each other and from man, and that these events had taken place about six thousand years ago. James Ussher (1581–1656), archbishop of Armagh, placed the beginning of the world at 4004 B.C., but similar figures had been popular long before his time. Ussher's chronology attained particular acceptance because it was printed in the margins of some editions of the King James Version of the Bible.

This Christian view of history was first challenged by evidence of a geological nature. Although several other scholars had begun to suspect that the earth was quite a bit older than some six millennia, this fact became firmly established when James Hutton's (1726–97) *Theory of the Earth* appeared in 1788. In it, he explained how natural processes of erosion, deposition, and consolidation of sediments had formed the various strata of the earth, and that these processes had taken hundreds of thousands of years, so that the earth must be at least several million years old. Most scientists who followed Hutton's arguments accepted this expanded chronology. But the idea that organic life would be equally ancient met with greater resistance. Xenophanes' recognition of fossils as indicators of ancient life had long been forgotten, and many different theories had since been advanced to account for these troublesome leftovers. Most common among those was that they were animals drowned during the Noachian deluge. A popular alternative was that they were "sports of nature," created, perhaps, by the "plastic virtue" of the earth, or else by "astral forces" that had attempted to imitate nature or its Creator. Other possible explanations were that God Himself had planted the fossils in the earth to furnish the regions below the surface with plants and animals corresponding to life on the exterior; or that they were remnants of an earlier experiment of God before He began creating in earnest. It was of course also deemed possible that the devil had placed the fossils in the soil with the express purpose to confound man and to make him doubt the truth of the Holy Scriptures. Even in those instances where fossils were recognized for what they were, their age was not surmised. Fossil mammoth bones found in England were considered to be proof that Julius Caesar's army under Claudius had entered England on giant elephants.

It was an engineer by the name of William Smith (1769–1839) who discovered the age of fossils. In order to trace coal measures or to ascertain the direction of earth layers for draining purposes, he found it useful to identify strata by the types of fossil organisms that were found in them. In Germany, von

Schlotheim independently discovered the importance of fossils for dating techniques, while in France Georges Cuvier (1769–1832) and Jean Baptiste de Lamarck (1744–1829) employed fossils as a means of reconstructing the history of organic life. Unlike Lamarck, Cuvier was a catastrophist, believing that a series of worldwide cataclysms in the past had destroyed some species, and postulating that new creations had occurred after these events. Although he is generally considered to be the founder of vertebrate paleontology, Cuvier never accepted the antiquity of the human race.

The first recognition of the age of man did not come from his human remains, but from his handiwork. Ancient Greeks had been aware that some peoples in the past had made and used stone tools, but this knowledge had been lost. When tools were found they were not recognized as such. It was generally believed that they were "thunderstones" hurled from the sky by lightning bolts, or else that lightning had transformed some rock material on earth. Although Michel Mercatus (1541–93) was among the first to recognize that flint arrowheads were man-made, he did not think that they were very old. William Conyers, who found a handax in association with the already mentioned mammoth bones, explained in 1690 that it was a spear point used by the British to attack the giant elephants of Claudius' army. John Frere (1740–1807), who discovered many flint artifacts in Suffolk, wrote that he was "tempted" to refer them to a very remote period, even beyond that of the present world, but he resisted this temptation. Benjamin Smith Barton (1766–1815), who wrote the first book on North American archaeology, found so many stone tools that he became convinced that various parts of the New World "must have formerly been inhabited by a people who had made considerable advances towards those arts which are almost inseparable from the dawn of Civil society." But the ultimate conclusions were not drawn.

Significantly, the acceptance of the antiquity of stone tools (and thus also of human culture) came in 1858, the year when Darwin first announced his theory of evolution, Marx wrote his preliminary statement of historical materialism, and when both Boas and Durkheim were born. Jacques Boucher de Perthes (1783–1868), a French customs officer and amateur archaeologist, had been digging in tertiary strata near Abbeville. Finding many stone hand axes imbedded in that layer, he became convinced that they must belong to that ancient period. A prolific writer, he published his findings in many books, but encountered scorn and ridicule until he met an English geologist, H. Falconer, who inspected the evidence and accepted the conclusions. In the next year several of Falconer's British colleagues, among them the influential Charles Lyell (1797–1875), visited the sites. All confirmed de Perthes's findings, and presented them to the Royal Society and the British Academy. French and English newspapers now hailed the great discovery.

Lamarck, however, published his theories of organic development even before the expanded chronologies were generally accepted. In his *Philosophie Zoologique* (1809), he departed from the older ideas about fixity of species and special creation which he himself had held until 1800. In his new view, he presented the theory that all organic nature was an indivisible whole. Species had evolved by transformation, i.e., by successive change. The mechanisms of this change were summed up in his two most famous laws, namely the development or decay of organs through use and disuse, and the inheritance of characteristics acquired by organisms during their lifetime. The law of use and disuse meant that those parts of the body that were intensively exercised during the life of an individual would increase in size and complexity, while those organs that were useless in a specific situation diminished in function. The giraffe, needing to reach its food high up in trees, thus developed a very long neck, while the mole, living underground and not exercising its eyesight, was nearly blind. The law of inheritance simply meant that those changed physical conditions were passed on to the offspring of those individuals.

While these Lamarckian laws are well-known, it is im-

portant to point out how his system was in full agreement
with current beliefs in the order and lawfulness of nature. In
his views, nature always developed in the direction of an
increase in the complexity of the organization of organisms.
On the one hand, the growing complexity was triggered by
the increased "needs" of organisms in relationship to their
environments, but over and above that stood the master plan
of nature itself. Lamarck did not refer to a deity as the in-
itiator of those laws, but instead posited the equally metaphysical concept of a "plastic force" inherent in nature. It
was this force that both enabled and directed species in their
transformations. Nature was thus fulfilling its own purposes,
enacting the evolutionary sequence, changing existing forms,
and creating new organisms and species on its way. Animals
were thus mere tools in the hands of nature, which worked
its wonders through them. In Lamarck's own words:

> They [i.e., organisms] feel certain needs, and each felt need,
> stirring their inner consciousness, immediately causes fluids and
> forces to be directed toward the point of the body where an action
> capable of satisfying the need can take place. But, if there exists
> at this point an organ appropriate to such an action, it is stimulated
> to act; and if no organ exists and the felt need is pressing and
> sustained, little by little the organ is provided and develops by
> reason of its constant, vigorous use.
>
> (Lamarck 1809:185)

The stimulus of change was not the environment itself,
but an internal dynamism reacting to the environment. Evolution was thus not abrupt, did not represent a struggle, but
was a development of a potential that had been there from
the beginning, requiring only the right physical conditions
for its unfolding. The life principle thus expanded along lines
of infinite progression.

Lamarck's theory plainly implied that man was the latest
product of the process of evolution. He described how a race
of apes, "moved by the need to dominate and to see far and
wide," might slowly become adapted to an upright posture,
while the further need for communication would lead to the

development of speech organs and thus to language. But he quickly added:

Such would be the reflections which one might indulge if man, considered here as the preeminent race, were distinguished from animals only by organizational characteristics and if his origin were not different from theirs.

(Lamarck 1809:357)

The panorama that Lamarck put before us is a history of life forms, a presentation of the whole tableau of the organic series. He felt that his classification of species represented a natural taxonomy that accurately reflected the plan and laws of nature. It thus reflected reality, since it showed how developments had actually taken place. Evolution was also progressive: "apathetic" invertebrates had developed into "sensitive" invertebrates, who in turn became vertebrates, "the intelligent animals."

Although a number of Lamarck's contemporaries had begun to realize that biological evolution was possible and indeed probable, the concept of cultural evolution was already old and well established long before then. Biologists usually do not mention this fact, and anthropologists themselves believed for some time that their discipline had received its major impetus from biological theories of evolution. It might be the other way round: Lamarck and other naturalists of his time were strongly influenced by the notion of cultural evolution, and fitted their theories into the prevalent concepts of process and progress, perfectibility, stages, unfolding, and natural laws. Lamarck also assigned the cause of natural laws to an external power. His "plastic force" was axiomatic, and resembled Vico's "Providence," Condorcet's "progress," Hegel's "world spirit," and so forth.

The parallels between Lamarck on the one hand and Saint-Simon and Comte on the other are not less striking. Lamarck's concept of the inward urge of the organism to develop to its capacities is fully compatible with Saint-Simon's and Comte's ideas about the development of the human mind which increasingly more reaches its capacity toward better understanding of causal factors.

Charles Darwin (1809–82) announced his theory of evolution a year after the death of Comte, but during the lifetimes of Marx, Engels, Spencer, Tylor, and Morgan. It has often been said that Darwin did not invent evolution but proved it. Scientific discoveries are usually built upon foundations laid down by predecessors, but no one before Darwin amassed so much factual material bearing on the question, and no one had thought about such a logical conclusion as natural selection. With his insight, the historical perspective of the age of the earth, life, and man, reached its fullest potential, even if the antiquity of man was much greater than Darwin suspected. His theory may simply be summed up as the idea that living organisms become differentiated through a universal process of change that favors the perpetuation of those organisms that are better adapted to survival than others.

When the *Origin of Species* appeared in print in 1859, Marx, Maine, McLennan, Spencer, and Morgan had already published, and Tylor was probably writing his first book, which appeared in 1861. Those who reacted to Darwin's work did not seem to feel that it altered their own theories, but found in it a confirmation of their own already established ideas. Marx wrote to Engels: "Darwin's book is very important, and serves me as a basis in natural selection for the class struggle in history." Engels too was more impressed by the struggle for existence than by natural selection. Spencer warmly welcomed the book and found that it supplied massive support for his own theories, while the famous linguist Max Müller said: "In language I was a Darwinian before Darwin."

It cannot be said, therefore, that Darwin's theory represented a turning point for cultural evolution. Neither Tylor, Morgan, nor Frazer made use of the concept of natural selection, which was the core of Darwin's explanations. Of course, the later "Social Darwinists" did derive their theories from natural selection, but theirs was an intellectual movement standing somewhat outside the mainstream of anthropological developments. It almost constituted for a while a separate branch of social science, and is now discredited by anthropologists and sociologists alike. Apart from this, Darwin's influence on anthropological theory is diffuse rather than direct. His proof that man was related to the animals, and thus not separately created and not standing outside of nature, is of course relevant to all social sciences. The greatly enlarged time scale of man's existence could find acceptance through his proven relationship with the rest of nature, and the concept of continuity in culture history was considerably strengthened by Darwinian theories. It may also be noted that Darwin's scientific method was exemplary. Without attacking ideas of creation or divine purpose, Darwin simply accepted natural phenomena as given, and examined them as they presented themselves. Unable to explain his observations on the basis of prevailing ideologies, he started afresh, placing his arguments entirely outside the framework of speculative philosophy. He thus demonstrated that the methods of science were of a different order than those of theology or philosophy. *The Origin of Species* was the product of more than twenty years of scientific observation and experimentation. His scientific canons were recognized by most scholars after him, and the ideal of scientific method for the study of social life was strengthened by Darwin's example, because of his clear-cut distinction between assertion and proof.

Apart from these important implications, Darwin was less important to the development of evolutionary cultural anthropology than Maine, McLennan, and Bachofen, all lawyers who dealt with the evolution of specific social institutions.

Sir Henry James Sumner Maine (1822–88) declared in the preface of his *Ancient Law* (1861) that he wanted to examine "some of the earliest ideas of mankind as they are reflected in ancient law, and to point out the relationship of those ideas to modern thought" (Maine 1888:v). In other words, Maine wanted to explain the evolution of law in the Western world, but the difficulty involved was that not much could be known about the laws of people before the invention of writing. Maine attempted to solve this problem by devising a method of reconstruction. He was a specialist in Roman law, and discovered that these laws had developed gradually, so that changes in law were not immediately made manifest in codification. Older forms continued to exist as "legal fictions," and these thus pointed back to earlier times when they were real functioning laws. Legal fictions could thus serve as tools for reconstruction.

Primarily by this method, Maine found a number of sequences of development: from kinship organization to territorial organization, from status to contract, from civil law to criminal law, and from decree to case law to true legislation. Of those, the first is most often discussed by anthropologists, because it related to early forms of family organization.

Maine reasoned as follows: In Roman law, the legal fiction existed that a father was *patria potestas*, which meant that he had absolute power—even of life and death—over his wife, children, and servants. In the period for which documentation existed, fathers no longer possessed such powers, but they must have existed at earlier times. It followed that patriarchy was the earliest form of family organization, and in the absence of true government and legislation, this must also have been the form of political organization in those early societies. When groups began to unite around common land holdings, the territorial notion developed by necessity. But patrilineal kinship reckoning remained the organizing principle, and societies thus remained kinship-based until the time when nations developed, which were by definition determined by territoriality exclusively.

Maine was not very well acquainted with ethnographic literature, and believed that the book of Genesis gave a good and reliable picture of early life. He was reasonably assured that he had covered the whole range of Western history, because in his view early societies were largely stationary, and only later ones changed faster and became progressive. Although he wrote later on that he had not intended to determine the absolute origin of human society, this was only in reaction to criticisms.

These criticisms had been launched most strongly by another lawyer, John Ferguson McLennan (1827–81), whose most famous book was *Primitive Marriage* (1865). He, too, was interested in the early history of society, and charged that no one before him had attempted to reconstruct the social conditions of primitive peoples. All we know about them, he said, were their food habits, their ornaments, and their weapons. He was much better acquainted with ethnographic literature than Maine, and was convinced that "rude" contemporary peoples were good examples of early social conditions.

His major item of reconstruction was bride capture, which was still carried out in mock battles in some contemporary societies. Thus, among the Kalmucks, a prospective groom would go to the village of his bride, pay the bride price, and then carry the girl away on his horse, while the people of her village pursued them or made mock resistance. Or again, among the Welsh, the groom and his friends engaged in a mock battle with the friends of the bride, until the latter inevitably lost. Postulating that these customs were survivals from former actual situations of bride capture, McLennan set out to explain why women should have been taken in this manner. He arrived at the logical conclusion that there must have been a shortage of women. This was so, he argued, because primitive peoples practiced female infanticide, neglecting or sometimes outright killing their newborn daughters. This was not mere cruelty, but rather a functional necessity. The groups were small, men were the hunters and food providers, and immature women were a burden upon the meager subsistence economy. Female infanticide necessarily resulted in an unfavorable male-female ratio, and therefore bride capture became the common rule. Moreover, the shortage of women led to polyandry: a number of men took one woman as their common wife.

This was, however, not the earliest stage of society. In the beginning, marriage and kinship did not exist at all, and mating was fairly random. Such promiscuity made it impossible to recognize paternity, and kinship was thus reckoned through females only, or what we now would call a system of matrilineality. The next step was the development of a more regulated (and thus less "rude") form of promiscuity, namely polyandry, where several men had a wife in common. This existed in two forms: Nair polyandry, where the various husbands were unrelated, and Tibetan (or fraternal) polyandry, where the husbands were brothers. The latter form implied patrilocality: the woman went to live in the camp of the brothers. This situation then also marked the beginning of patrilineal descent. Although fraternal polyandry was no longer actually practiced, its former existence was attested by the occurrence of the institution of levirate, the custom that a younger brother is obliged to marry the wife or wives of his deceased older brother.

Early groups were also homogeneous, so that captured wives were at first regarded as strangers. But when kinship through females became strengthened, the women, no matter what their origin, were recognized as full members of the group into which they had married. McLennan coined the terms "endogamy" and "exogamy" to indicate rules of marriage with women from inside the group or without; but his arguments about the evolution of these institutions were not always clear. Marriage by capture of course indicated exogamy, but when these foreign women became recognized as members of the group, their offspring could be considered as marriage partners, and exogamy was thus practiced "under the guise of endogamy."

Eventually kinship became reckoned through males. In the instance of Tibetan (fraternal) polyandry, this development was most clear: the oldest brother assumed responsibility for all children, and thus became the legal father. Children inherited from him rather than from the mother.

When agriculture came to replace hunting and gathering, subsistence became less precarious and female infanticide could be abandoned, so that the sex ratio evened out. At that time property became more important, and inheritance was thus a focus of concern. The best solution was monogamy, because it clearly solved the relationship of children to their parents.

In the nineteenth century, a period in which the dominance of men over women was unquestioned, McLennan's theory that at one time in history women had the upper hand was quite startling. McLennan was not the only one to maintain that matrilineality had preceded patrilineality. Johann Jacob Bachofen (1815–77), a Swiss lawyer, presented the same point of view in his book *Das Mutterrecht* (1861). His arguments were more mystical and certainly more speculative than those of Maine and McLennan. Taking his cues from Greek classical writings, he noted that ancient scholars testified to the fact that in early societies children were named after their mothers. Ethnographic literature confirmed that this is still the case in some nonliterate societies, and Bachofen became convinced that "matriarchy" must have preceded patriarchy. It was, however, the second stage of development. Before that he postulated a period of "hetarism," or sexual promiscuity. This he deduced from evidence of formerly existing temple prostitution, where priestesses gave themselves freely to male worshipers. This practice must have been a survival of earlier promiscuous conditions.

From this base line, Bachofen developed the following scheme: in the earliest period of hetarism, women were mere sex objects. Kinship lines were of necessity "gynaecocratic," reckoned through females, because in random mating it was impossible to know the real father of the child. But the ancient women's liberation movement revolted against such submissiveness, and managed to get the upper hand in social affairs, ushering in the period of "Amazonian assertiveness," where mother rights prevailed. For a while, women ruled the world, female deities were worshiped, the female left was exalted over the male right side, the moon (female because it regulated menstruation) was more important than the sun, earth ruled over ocean, sorrow over joy, death over life, darkness over light, and the youngest born was preferred over the oldest, expressed in ultimogeniture.

Eventually, however (women's liberationists take note!), women tired of the whole business, and wanted husbands to care for them. Simultaneously, men strove to overthrow the female reign. First, men pretended that they, too, could give birth and invented the couvade, a custom where the father goes to bed as if for childbearing when his wife is giving birth, so as to make believe that he has delivered a child and is thus equal to women. But even without such conceits men succeeded in their dominance, and the assertion of patriarchy and patrilineality reversed all former symbolism: the sun ruled the moon, and the heavenly light prevailed over the darkness of the earth.

Considering Maine, McLennan, and Bachofen together, they have in common, first and foremost, an interest in the history of social institutions and in the dynamic dimensions of time. Although their evolutionary schemes were to a great extent deductive and speculative, they were aware of the necessity of proof and explanation of the processes of change. They seriously aimed at showing that mankind was a unity, and that lower stages of development were directly related to later ones. When written documentation was lacking, they devised means to fill the gap by their concepts of "survivals," which also came to play an important role in Tylor's reconstructions. It simply meant that items of culture that were no longer active or functional must have had meanings before, and were thus indicators of conditions in earlier periods.

On the whole, they focused attention on the importance of the development of social institutions. Not only did they thus contribute to the analysis of culture history, but they clearly understood that law, marriage, kinship, and so on, were to be understood in relationship to each other and to social conditions in general.

In their views as well as those of most other nineteenth-century evolutionists historical explanations were sufficient to the understanding of the varieties of culture. Their method became known as "the historical method," which meant, in the nineteenth century, the attempt to show that human culture had undergone progressive and cumulative growth. It was thus necessary to reconstruct the total panorama of human history. They relied also on the "comparative method," which postulated that contemporary primitive peoples reflect early conditions of mankind. Evolutionary sequences could thus be established by comparing and analyzing certain aspects or institutions of primitive cultures, and ordering them in a sequence from the simple to the complex. The equation of primitive with early was justified by the idea that primitive populations were conservative to an extreme degree. Maine wrote:

Vast populations, some of them with a civilization considerable but peculiar, detest that which in the language of the west would be called reform. . . . The multitudes of colored men who swarm in the great Continent of Africa detest it, and it is detested by that large part of mankind which we are accustomed to leave on one side as barbarous or savage. . . . To the fact that the enthusiasm for change is comparatively rare must be added the fact that it is extremely modern. It is known but to a small part of mankind, and to that part but for a short period during a history of incalculable length.

(Maine 1890:132–34)

Although Maine, McLennan, and Bachofen intended to give an overall picture of the evolution of specific social institutions, and were rather convinced that progress had taken place in an orderly way so that higher forms of organization followed lower ones almost by necessity, they were not strict unilineal evolutionists. They recognized that environmental or social conditions sometimes impeded change, sometimes accelerated it. McLennan outlined at least two lines of development from Tibetan and Nair polyandry, while Maine wrote on this matter that societies did not advance concurrently, but at different rates of progress.

In general then, the aim of these evolutionists was to

present an overall view of culture history, but they did not attempt to reconstruct unequivocal stages of total cultural development. Instead, they focused attention upon the separate but related phenomena of law, family organization, marriage, and kinship.

No such restrictions were made by Herbert Spencer (1820–1903). To him, evolution was a cosmic process, operating in the sociocultural sphere as well as in organic and inorganic realms. In his early essay "The Development Hypothesis" (1852), he firmly rejected creationism and expressed agreement with Lamarck's theory of transformation. In the same year, after reading Thomas Malthus' *Essay on Population* (1798), Spencer wrote another article called "A Theory of Population Deduced from the General Law of Animal Fertility," in which he came very close to formulating natural selection. Malthus had warned that the "natural power of mankind to increase" would lead to disaster if it remained unchecked, because food production would soon fall behind. Darwin and Wallace also were prompted to conceive of the idea of natural selection after reading Malthus' essay, but where they applied it to the evolution of the species, Spencer became convinced that "struggle for existence" and "survival of the fittest" were the efficient causes of all progress. Population pressure made progress inevitable, because, in the words of Spencer:

those prematurely carried off must, in the average of cases, be those in whom the power of self-preservation is the least. It unavoidably follows, that those left behind to continue the race are those in whom the power of self-preservation is the greatest—the select of their generation.

(Quoted by Carneiro 1967:xx)

Armed with this insight, Spencer developed his "law of evolution," namely that it represents "a change from a state of relatively indefinite, incoherent homogeneity to a state of relatively definite, coherent heterogeneity" (quoted *ibid.*: xvii). In other words, evolution was progressive because in any circumstance the fittest would survive, and their adaptation was in the direction of greater complexity.

The idea of the essential unity of this process dawned upon Spencer in 1857, when his assistant read several of Spencer's older essays to him. He found development from simple to complex implicit in all his writings, and became convinced that it was the key to the understanding of all phenomena in the entire cosmos:

> The advance from the simple to the complex through a process of successive differentiations, is seen alike in the earliest changes of the Universe . . . it is seen in the geologic and climatic evolution of the Earth, and of every single organism on its surface; it is seen in the evolution of Humanity, whether implemented in the civilized individual, or in the aggregation of races; it is seen in this evolution of Society in respect alike of its political, its religious, and its economic organization; and it is seen in the evolution of all . . . products of human activity.
>
> (Spencer 1857:465)

After this discovery, Spencer set himself the enormous task of demonstrating the truth of his thesis in all fields in a series of volumes under the general title of *Synthetic Philosophy*. The first of those, *First Principles* (1862), contained the plan and explained the system. It was followed by *The Principles of Biology* (1864–67), *The Principles of Psychology* (1870–72), *The Principles of Sociology* (3 volumes, 1876, 1882, 1896) and *The Principles of Ethics* (1892–93). At the time of his death only two volumes were missing, namely on astronomy and geology.

When Darwin's *Origin of Species* appeared, Spencer was "overwhelmed in the gratification . . . at seeing the theory of organic evolution justified," and he considered it as firm support for his own theories. Yet, he remained an avowed believer in the Lamarckian inheritance of acquired characteristics, because he found it easier to explain the evolution of the mind, and thus also of culture, by transformation than by selection. Nevertheless, both biological and cultural evolution displayed a struggle for survival, and both evolved through the same process of growth, differentiation, integration, and transformation. While he often compared society to an organism, he did not go to extremes, because he was well aware of the differences also. In a biological organism, the seat of consciousness is only in a small part of the whole (the brain), while in a social organism all members possess consciousness. Moreover, a society does not form a concrete whole, but its living units are free, not necessarily in physical contact, and more or less dispersed. Cooperation between members of a society comes about by language, and as such the parts of a social organism remain mutually dependent, but in a discrete rather than a concrete manner.

In early societies, cooperation was geared primarily toward survival, and in this "militant phase" people were trained for warfare, the individual was submerged in the group, status was the basis of social relationships, and cooperation was compulsory. Those who were best adapted to this kind of life became dominant, and those societies that were strongest conquered the weaker ones. Larger and larger social units were thus created, until a kind of equilibrium of powerful nations was achieved. At that point, the industrial society emerged. It was more peaceful, individual differences became respected, contract regulated social relationships, and economic cooperation between nations and between individuals became favored. This cooperation was no longer compulsory, but voluntary. Struggle for survival no longer selected the physically strong, but rather the personality that sought security for life and property, and was altruistically inclined.

The organic analogy of Spencer was thus more pertinent to an explanation of the mechanisms of change than to social analysis per se. As a matter of fact, he considered social phenomena to be of a different order than those of the organic and inorganic realms: he called them "superorganic." Although the superorganic had arisen from the organic, once so established it had evolved in a different manner, namely through an increase of interaction between many individuals, so that social phenomena became ever more complex and heterogeneous. While the social behavior of bees and ants was also superorganic, in man these developments had taken such strides that social behavior superseded biological requirements and processes in many ways.

Evolution is thus clearly the hallmark of Spencer's writings. Organic evolution arose from the inorganic, and the superorganic from the organic. Within each of these realms separate processes of development took place, but always working into the direction of greater complexity. Spencer demonstrated that this had been the case in separate societies and dealt with the "evolution" of Mexicans, Peruvians, African and Asiatic races, Hebrews, Chinese, Phœnicians, French, Chinese, Egyptians, Greeks, and many others. He also treated the evolution of specific institutions in the same manner, including marriage, the family, religion, language, political organization, fashions, customs, morals, as well as the origin and development of handshakes, tattooing, and wearing black as a sign of mourning.

Functional explanations were not absent either. Evolution was to him not a mere sequence, but a *system* of change. He branded as erroneous the idea that organisms and societies should have an intrinsic tendency to become something higher. Instead, evolution was determined by the mutual dependence of parts, or by "the cooperation of inner and outer factors." Evolution established both in organisms and in societies "such differences that each makes the other possible. The changes in the parts are mutually determined, and the changed actions of the parts are mutually dependent." Part 2 of *The Principles of Sociology* was almost entirely devoted to a discussion of these principles. What is more, Spencer felt that without an understanding of such functional interrelationships a true science of sociology would not be possible. But he treated these interactions on an abstract level, because in his view human individuals had not played a great role in evolution. Since evolution was a natural process, even "great men"—inventors, leaders, conquerors—had had no perceptible influence upon the course of history. The human mind itself was a product of evolution and had evolved through stages of increasing complexity. In early or contemporary simple societies, people themselves were simpler, and men were thus not equal in physical or mental endowments.

There were, however, other nineteenth-century evolutionists who, although believing in progress, did not draw the conclusion of unequal mental endowment. To them, progress was not the moving power of evolution, but its result. Theodor Waitz (1821–64), who wrote a six-volume work called *Anthropologie der Naturvölker* (1851–71, the last volumes published posthumously), championed this position. In Volume 1, significantly titled *On the Unity of the Human Race and the Natural Condition of Mankind* (1858), he wrote: "We are irresistibly drawn to the conclusion that there are no specific differences among mankind with regard to their psychical life."

This position became known as the doctrine of the "psychic unity of mankind" and it was a subject of heated discussion among later anthropologists. Waitz explained that there were a number of interacting factors contributing to progress, including environment, diffusion, migration, and inventions. The latter are of course made by individual people, and the question whether or not "great men" had aided in the course of progress became another topic of anthropological debate in later years. Waitz took the reasonable position that there were individual differences between members of a group, but renounced the idea that uncivilized groups as a whole should be mentally inferior to civilized ones. This clashed, of course, with the concept of natural laws of progress, which saw the advance of history as inevitable and moved forward by powers external to human beings. To Waitz, however, progress was caused by specific historical, social, and human factors, and societies that were isolated, situated in poor physical environments, and had not produced "great men" remained backward for those reasons rather than through overall mental inferiority.

Another German ethnographer who strongly championed the psychic unity principle was Adolf Bastian (1826–1905). Rejecting both Lamarck's and Darwin's theories of evolution on the ground that no one had ever seen a species change into another, he was an empiricist and a field worker, or if not that, in any case an ardent traveler. He was much more impressed by similarities between peoples than by their differences, and explained these similarities by man's psychic unity. In his view there was a restricted number of basic ideas common to all mankind—a theory presently examined by Lévi-Strauss and Chomsky. Bastian called these basic ideas *Elementargedanken* (elementary thought patterns), but since these ideas develop in different environments, they always find their specific expression as *Völkergedanken* (folk ideas). Those areas with similar folk ideas constituted "geographical provinces," a concept foreshadowing the later American culture area concept. Bastian admitted that these provinces had not remained pure, because migration and diffusion had introduced different culture traits.

Bastian's writings are virtually unknown to present-day anthropologists, and perhaps with good reason, because his style was confused, obscure, ornate, bombastic, and untranslatable. Yet it must be admitted that he was better aware of the complexity of cultural evolution than many other nineteenth-century evolutionists. He clearly realized that simple "stages" of development could not exist, because too many different factors had intervened. On his many travels he also collected various objects of material culture which eventually found their way into the *Museum für Völkerkunde* in Berlin, which he helped to establish. Together with Rudolf Virchow he founded the German Society for Anthropology. Bastian also founded the German African Society, and began publication of the *Zeitschrift für Ethnologie*.

An American advocate of the psychic unity principle was Daniel G. Brinton (1837–99), who wrote of the "nigh absolute uniformity of man's thoughts and actions, his aims and methods, when in the same degree of development, no matter where he is or in what epoch" (Brinton 1896:12). The question of psychic unity became very important in discussions about racial inferiority, as will be shown later.

CONCLUSIONS

The major purpose of this chapter has been to indicate the interaction between concepts of biological and social evolution in the nineteenth century, and to explode the myth that cultural evolution took its major cues from biology. Since the beginning of the Christian era it had been generally accepted that man and society had a single origin, and that all existing forms and variations were derived from it, so that discussions of cultural evolution were orthodox and not in conflict with Genesis.

In biology the situation was entirely different. The Scriptures depicted creation of animals as separate divine acts, and for a long time biologists simply could not accept the idea that species had evolved from one another. Similarities between organic structures were often recognized, but were explained by parallelism rather than by evolution. Ray and Linnaeus, the great classifiers of nature, arranged all life forms in a hierarchical order that fitted well with a concept of evolution, but the conclusion was not made. They searched for the master plan of nature, and although nature might be a unity, it was not a connected whole. Only toward the end of the eighteenth century did some biologists begin to realize that biological evolution was possible and indeed probable. Lamarck himself accepted creationism and the separate origin of species until 1800, when he was fifty-six years old. Neither his transformation hypothesis nor Darwin's evolution by natural selection conflicted with the already existing theories of cultural evolution, and the outcry against Darwin's theory did not come from cultural evolutionists but from theology.

Even the biological analogy was rarely used by cultural

evolutionists after Darwin. In fact, ahistorical-minded functionalists such as Durkheim, Radcliffe-Brown, and Malinowski
were much more inclined to compare societies to organisms
than were Tylor, Morgan, and Frazer, who had no need to
support their theories in this manner. These developments will
be dealt with in the next chapters.

CHAPTER 8

TYLOR, MORGAN
AND FRAZER

It should now be abundantly clear that anthropology did not begin with the writings of Edward Burnett Tylor (1832–1917). Yet the mere fact that he has so often been called the "father" of this discipline indicates that his contributions were quite important. Among those, his clarification and definition of the notion of culture is most outstanding.

The word "culture" itself was not new. Originally it was a biological term, related to breeding and improvement of animals and plants, surviving in words like "agriculture" and "horticulture." Its application to human societies occurred first in Germany in the eighteenth century (Kroeber and Kluckhohn 1963:13) and at that time it still carried the connotation of improvement. Long before that, the idea of culture had been recognized, albeit under different terms such as "customs," "traditions," or "social habits" of peoples. Certainly from Herodotus onward it was known that human behavior patterns were different from place to place, and many attempts were made to account for these variations. Some proposed explanations in terms of climate or environment, others believed that there were differences in mental endowment, or else it was thought that natural laws had caused some people to progress more than others. In the eighteenth century, if not earlier, the idea that diversities of conduct were correlated with racial differences entered the picture, implying that culture was part of man's physical equipment. In this view, culture traits, like physical ones, were passed on from generation to generation by some biological mechanism of inheritance, so that the hierarchy of races and of cultures was depicted as constant and unalterable. Finally, there was the degeneration theory, which posited that peoples were different because they deviated, in different degrees, from original perfect conditions.

Tylor took particular issue with the latter view, which during his lifetime was championed strongly by Archbishop Whately of Dublin. He pronounced that civilization was the original condition of mankind, bestowed by divine intervention. Savages and barbarians had degenerated from this original state, while civilized nations had retained and perfected the higher culture. Tylor did not argue against this position for reasons of his belief in progress alone; he also stated firmly that science could not be based upon religious convictions (Tylor 1958 I:ii).

Tylor's definition of culture obviated all erroneous explanations. The very first sentence of his *Primitive Culture* (1871) reads:

Culture or civilization, taken in its wide ethnographic sense, is that complex whole which includes knowledge, belief, art, morals, law, custom, and any other capabilities and habits acquired by man as a member of society.

(Tylor 1958 I:1)

"Acquired" is the key word of this definition, because it meant that culture was the product of social learning rather than of biological heredity, and that the differences in cultural development were not the result of degeneration, but of progress in cultural knowledge. Moreover, Tylor's insistence that culture was a "complex whole" implied that it included *all* socially learned behavior, no matter if it seemed trivial or not.

Every facet of social life was thus worthy of study, because it contributed to the understanding of mankind.

Although Locke and others had been conscious of the fact that culture was learned and not inborn, they had not sufficiently seen that such learning was social, but attributed it instead to individual sense perceptions and experiences. Tylor realized that man learns in social context, and his definition is thus not merely a recognition of the existence of culture, but contains theories about it. Later anthropologists constructed hundreds of additional definitions, but few would disagree with Tylor's assessment of culture as a socially learned entity.

While Tylor was convinced that progress had taken place, he did not conceive it to be the moving power of history, but rather used it as a tool for reconstruction of past conditions. Monogamy, for instance, was the marriage rule of his own highly evolved civilization, and the earliest human condition must thus have been one at the farthest possible remove from it, namely primitive promiscuity.

Yet Tylor was careful to note that not all cultural inventions had of necessity been good:

> To have learnt to give poison secretly and effectually, to have raised corrupt literature to pestilent perfection, to have organized a successful scheme to arrest free enquiry and proscribe free expression, are works of knowledge and skill whose progress toward their goal has hardly conduced to the general good.
>
> *(Ibid.*:28)

Nevertheless, on an overall scale progress had occurred and worked toward betterment:

> . . . on the whole the civilized man is not only wiser and more capable than the savage, but also better and happier, and the barbarian stands in between.
>
> *(Ibid.*:31)

The difference was not due, however, to unequal mental equipment. Tylor's belief in psychic unity assured him that all peoples were equally *capable* of progress. The differences between cultures were "those of development rather than of origin, rather of degree than of kind" (Tylor 1865:232). Various groups of people would eventually progress along similar lines, because their minds were uniform.

Since Tylor envisaged various lines of development in which groups of people would each progress in similar sequences, it followed that he was happier with independent invention than with diffusion, although certainly not denying the latter. He gave many examples of similar culture traits between peoples without known historical connections:

[Australian aborigines] raise scars on their bodies like African tribes; they circumcize like the Jews and Arabs; they bar marriage in the female line like the Iroquois; they drop out of their language the names of plants and animals which have been used as the personal names of dead men, and make new words to serve instead, like the Abipones of South America . . .

(Tylor 1964:233–34)

Shortly, whatever was found in the world could be matched more or less closely elsewhere, particularly among lower cultures.

His evolutionary scheme of progress consisted of the by now well-known stages of savagery, barbarism, and civilization, but his was not a dogmatic system. Whenever Tylor mentioned these developments he was careful to note that it was an *ideal* scheme, presenting a *possible* order of evolution, that there was a *tendency* in this direction, that the course of progress was not always uniform, and that evolution could take place along many different lines (Tylor 1958 I:6, 27). He did not attempt to force specific cultures into savagery or barbarism, although he harbored no doubts that his own Victorian England had reached the stage of civilization. But by and large he was more inclined to reconstruct the evolution of particular culture traits or institutions than to establish overall stages.

He used a number of different techniques for such reconstructions. One of those was the assignment of conditions opposite to the present ones to early stages of development, another was his concept of survivals, which he used in a manner similar to Maine's and McLennan's. Survivals were processes, customs, and opinions that persisted by force of habit even when they had lost their utility, and they thus remained proofs of earlier conditions. He found such survivals in superstitions, children's games, proverbs, riddles, and nursery rhymes. The custom of saying "God bless you" to someone who sneezed, for instance, indicated an earlier belief that sneezing was an attempt of the soul to leave the body, and this danger was counteracted by a spell.

In his 1889 essay "On a Method of Investigating the Development of Institutions, applied to the Laws of Marriage and Descent" (note that it is the development of *institutions,* not of cultures), Tylor used statistics. Taking data from 282 societies, and correlating postmarital residence patterns with the custom of in-law avoidance, he concluded that matrilineality and matrilocality had preceded patrilineality and patrilocality. Also the custom of couvade pointed in this direction. Matrilineal societies did not practice it at all, because the woman's position was dominant. Most societies in the intermediate patri-matrilineality stage adopted this custom, because men needed to establish their authority over women, and thus imitated their habits. Going into childbed like women, they symbolically stated their paternity. In pure patrilineal societies, some still practiced couvade as a survival, others had already dropped the custom because it had lost its function. Matrilineality must thus have been the earlier form.

Although Tylor reconstructed possible sequences of many cultural institutions, his most comprehensive treatment was in the field of religion. We may follow his reconstructions because they constitute the clearest example of his overall methods. He began with defining religion in such a way that all forms of it could be included, namely as "the belief in Spiritual Beings." He firmly stated that religion was a cultural universal, because no known cultures were without such beliefs. Next, he sought for an explanation of how the belief in spirits could have arisen.

Picturing early men as rationalists who did not possess the necessary knowledge to reason scientifically (he called them "savage philosophers"), they must have noted the difference between a living body and a dead one. They pondered about this as well as about phenomena of sleep, trance, and visions, and concluded that every man possessed not only a material body but also a life and a phantom. Life enabled the body to think and act, the phantom was its image or second self. Both were separable from the body: life went away after death, the phantom could appear to people at a distance, as in dreams. Soon enough, savages began to consider the two identical, and conceived of the idea of soul. After death the soul left the body permanently, but it sometimes appeared in dreams, acting as if it were alive. Thus the belief grew up that souls continued to exist after the death of the body. This belief was easily extended to include all other living beings and even nonliving objects, because plants and animals, as well as weapons, boats, and clothes, sometimes appeared in dreams. Early man thus began to believe that everything possessed life and a soul, and this early stage of religion Tylor called "animism." He went on to explain that early man soon recognized that the soul was superior to the body, because of its greater mobility and durability of existence. First merely admiring the souls of the dead, early man later on ascribed additional powers to them. It was believed that they protected their own families and tribes, and watched over their moral behavior. Attempts to communicate with these souls led to prayer and active worship. The idea that souls and spirits must reside somewhere gave rise to belief in an afterlife, while their freedom to move about and to appear everywhere led to the idea that they could enter into the bodies of the living, and thus also to the notion of "possession" and the practice of exorcism. Since spirits could also take up residence in material objects, these would acquire special powers and become fetishes. Eventually, fetishes were given the shape of images, and idolatry was born, elevating spirits to the rank of gods. Each god controlled a specific aspect of nature or of life: this was the stage of polytheism. But not all gods were of the same importance, and a hierarchy emerged, with one god as supreme deity. Later on, all minor gods receded into the background, and when they disappeared altogether, the final stage of monotheism was reached.

Tylor's treatment of religion shows both the strengths and the weaknesses of his methods. On the positive side stands his abundant use of ethnographic material, illustrating each point he wanted to make in rich detail. In the preface to *Primitive Culture* he stressed the importance of presenting "wide and minute evidence" (1958 I:xvi), which served both as proof of his theories and accounted for formerly meaningless ethnographic data. His useful "minimum definition" of religion is still generally accepted, as are his views on religion as a cultural universal and on the relationships between Western and earlier religions. His scheme of development was not rigid, and he did not attempt to place any particular religious system in the straitjacket of barbarism or savagery. As a matter of fact, he did not deal with religious systems as wholes, but rather reconstructed the origin and development of beliefs in supernatural powers, souls, afterlife, and of religious practices such as prayer, offering, sacrifice, and various other selected aspects. This practice was perhaps his greatest weakness. All religious phenomena were taken out of their cultural settings and used as isolated items of proof for his contentions. Moreover, Tylor's treatment of religion focused only on its cognitive aspects. Religion was to him mainly an attempt to understand the events of human experience, and the "primitive philosopher" was also a kind of primitive logician, rationally analyzing the world in the same manner as Western scientists, hampered only by a lack of experience and knowledge. In this rational exercise, Tylor sought the difference between earlier and later forms of religion in content and degree of knowledge, and the essentially social character of religion remained untreated and unexplained.

On the whole, Tylor's evolutionary reconstructions were more closely related to Lamarckian transformationism than to Darwinian natural selection. In the preface to the second edition of *Primitive Culture* (1958 I:xvi), Tylor acknowledged the importance of Darwin and Spencer, but added that his work was arranged on its own lines and not directly influenced by their writings. In fact, Tylor rarely recognized any of his predecessors, although many nineteenth-century trends converge in his theories. His treatment of anthropology as history, his interest in exotic phenomena, his belief in progress, his stages, his concept of survival, his emphasis on empirical data and on the scientific nature of anthropology all had been adumbrated. But the synthesis of all these trends into one coherent whole was Tylor's great achievement, and he thus established anthropology as an independent and scientific field of study in Europe. He championed it so strongly that many of his contemporaries half-jokingly referred to it as "Mr. Tylor's science." But his science did not remain without academic recognition. Tylor occupied Britain's first recognized university post, first as the Keeper of the university museum of Oxford, and a year later, in 1884, as Reader in anthropology at Oxford.

In the final analysis, Tylor is then not unjustly named the founder of modern anthropology. Not only did he establish its existence in Europe as an academically recognized science, but he also stressed the importance of firsthand data-collecting which has since become the hallmark of anthropology. Although Tylor spent a year in the United States, six months in Mexico, and a shorter period in Cuba, he himself was not basically a field worker, and he relied strongly on secondary sources for his own reconstructions. But he was not uncritical of these data and often attempted to test their accuracy by the comparative method. Precisely because he often found them wanting he sensed the need for scientifically oriented field work and he was instrumental in the founding of organizations fostering this practice.

Furthermore, the holistic four-field approach that is particularly strong in American anthropology was present also in Tylor's work. His book *Anthropology* (1881) included chapters on the antiquity of man, his relationship to other animals, on the races of mankind, and on language, and he often referred to archaeology. His examination of communication among deaf-mutes provides a model for the study of exotic systems of communication, and his insights into the nature of symbolization and its importance to human life are crucial for an understanding of the nature of culture and of man.

His student R. R. Marett (1866–1943) wrote Tylor's biography (1936), and summed up his theoretical contributions: his concept of animism, his inclusive definitions of culture and of religion, his use of comparative method, his attempts at statistical correlations, his stress on material culture, his historical reconstructions, and so forth. Perhaps none of these was entirely original with Tylor, but he brought them together in a coherent whole. In his hands, anthropology became "the science of culture."

Lewis Henry Morgan (1818–81) and Tylor are often mentioned in one breath as "nineteenth-century cultural evolutionists." Yet there are many differences between these two scholars. Although Morgan never gave a formal definition of evolution, he became much more dogmatic about it than Tylor. But before discussing that, it will be useful to describe Morgan's own evolution.

Born in Aurora, New York, he studied law in Albany, and settled as a lawyer in Rochester. All his life he was in close proximity to Iroquois Indians. Like many Americans of his time, he was attracted by clubs, lodges, and similar fraternal societies. While he was a student he formed the Order of the Gordian Knot, the purpose of which was to study ancient Greek myths and to imitate Greek customs. But when he became interested in the Iroquois, the lodge was remodeled, and now named the Grand Order of the Iroquois. Morgan himself was elected as its chief under the lodge name of Skenandoah. The members called themselves "warriors," they wore Iroquois costumes at their meetings and carried little tomahawks. Several of them, including Morgan himself, soon began to study Indian customs in earnest. Luck would have it that Morgan met a young Seneca Indian, Hä-sa-no-án-da, in a bookstore. Ely Parker (his non-Indian name) was a law student, spoke fluent English, and brought Morgan in contact with Indian chiefs, later also introducing him in several Indian communities. When Parker was invited to lecture at a meeting of the Grand Order, he did not describe the songs and myths and ancient lore of his tribe, as had been expected, but told instead how his people were being driven from their land and farms, were poor, unhappy, and desperate. Impressed, Morgan took their side and assisted the Senecas in their legal struggles with the government over land rights. But Morgan also became aware that Indian cultures were rapidly changing, and that their customs should be recorded before it was too late. Visiting and interviewing many Indians, notebook in hand, Morgan collected a great many data, and published them in his first book *League of the Ho-dé-no-sau-nee, or Iroquois* (1851). Major J. Wesley Powell (1834–1902) said of this book that it was "the first scientific account of an Indian tribe ever given to the world" (Fenton 1962:xviii), and Fenton, the foremost living scholar on the Iroquois, called it "the best general book on this classic people" (*ibid.*:v). In it, Morgan carefully described not only the dances, games, religion, language, and material culture of the Iroquois, but also their form of government and family organization. It was the latter topic that interested him most keenly. He probed deeply into Indian marriage rules and systems of matrilineal descent, but was particularly struck by their system of naming relatives. An Iroquois child called all his mother's sisters "mother," all his father's brothers "father," all his grandmother's sisters "grandmother," and so on. Children of two or more sisters called each other "brother" and "sister," and the same was true for children of two or more brothers. Morgan called this a "classificatory" kinship system, contrasting it with the "descriptive" system of his own culture. First believing that it was a system of their own making, he soon discovered that Ojibwa Indians possessed a very similar system. Both must be derived from a common source, because it seemed unlikely to Morgan that such a "strange" system could have been invented twice. It followed that if this system was prevalent or universal among all American Indians the unity of their origin would be proved. Furthermore, if the same system could also be found to exist in Asia, it would prove that the Indians were of Asiatic origin, a question that was by no means firmly settled in Morgan's time.

In order to establish the data Morgan constructed a seven-page questionnaire with more than two hundred questions, and with financial aid from the Smithsonian Institution those were mailed to foreign missions and diplomatic representatives in the United States and all over the world. The answers that trickled in—not everyone had time and energy to complete the complex form—tended to confirm that other American groups used a similar kinship terminology. When he also received information that the Tamil in India used a classificatory system, Morgan was happily convinced that his hypothesis had obtained its definite proof.

These findings became the topic of his *Systems of Consanguinity and Affinity of the Human Family* (1870). In the words of Meyer Fortes, this book "broke open for the first time in the history of the human sciences the golden vein of kinship and social organization for scientific mining" (Fortes 1969:19). Yet serious criticisms came almost at once. Maine (whose own theory was that patrilineality came first, while Morgan felt that matrilineality did) politely demurred that he was not convinced. McLennan more rancorously argued that Morgan misunderstood kinship terms altogether and had overestimated their importance. They were mere forms of address and had no other significance, and hence Morgan's scheme was totally without foundation. John Lubbock (later Lord Avebury, 1834–1913) more pertinently observed that, even according to Morgan's own data, classificatory kinship systems were present in Australia and Polynesia. Why then did American Indians originate in Asia, rather than in other parts of the world?

Morgan did not immediately grasp the significance of

Lubbock's remarks. It was a minister and Sanskrit scholar by the name of Joshua McIlvaine who pointed out to Morgan that a widespread occurrence of the classificatory system did not merely indicate American Indian relationship to Asia, but would prove that all primitive groups who used it were related, and thus it might well signify an earlier stage of human development.

Although Morgan now began to understand the wider implications of his discovery, he waited three years before publishing in a true evolutionary vein. Since it is known that Morgan bought a copy of Darwin's *Origin of Species* immediately after receiving McIlvaine's letter, it is possible that he had not read Darwin before that time. He wrote later on that he first "resisted" Darwin's theory, because he accepted the views of the permanence of species and the divine creation of man. It is not known at what precise moment Morgan felt "compelled" to change his mind and to "adopt the conclusion that man commenced at the bottom of the scale from which he worked himself up to his present status" (quoted by Resek 1960:99). Even this statement does not indicate a wholehearted acceptance of natural selection, although later on Morgan explained the evolution from endogamy to exogamy in terms of deleterious biological consequences of inbreeding.

In any case, Morgan emerged as a full-fledged evolutionist with a paper published by the American Academy of Arts and Sciences in 1868 under the title "A Conjectural Solution to the Origin of the Classificatory System of Relationships." Here he traced the history of the human family from primitive sexual promiscuity through fifteen stages of evolution to modern monogamy. In his reconstruction he used a vast array of different types of kinship nomenclature. From this time onward he began to work on the reconstruction of world history rather than that of American Indians alone. The result was his famous *Ancient Society,* subtitled *Researches in the Lines of Human Progress from Savagery through Barbarism to Civilization* (1877). The first of his two stages were subdivided, so that seven periods were distinguished, each with its own diagnostic characteristics, as follows:

Lower Savagery: Invention of speech, subsistence on fruits and nuts

Middle Savagery: Fishing and the use of fire

Upper Savagery: Bow and arrow

Lower Barbarism: Pottery

Middle Barbarism: Domestication of animals in the Old World; cultivation of maize by irrigation, adobe and stone brick buildings in the New World

Upper Barbarism: Iron smelting, use of iron tools

Civilization: Phonetic alphabet and writing

                                        (Morgan 1963:12)

He wrote further that

Each of these periods has a distinct culture and exhibits a mode of life more or less special and peculiar to itself. This specialization of ethnical periods renders it possible to treat a particular society according to its condition of relative advancement, and to make it a subject of independent study and discussion. It does not affect the main result that different tribes and nations on the same continent, and even of the same linguistic family, are in different conditions at the same time, since for our purpose the *condition* of each is the material fact, the *time* being immaterial.

                                        (Morgan 1963:12-13)

Unlike Tylor, Morgan at once assigned specific known cultures to his various stages. Lower Savagery had passed out of existence, Australians and most Polynesians were in Middle Savagery, Indian tribes east of the Missouri river were generally in the stage of Lower Barbarism, village Indians in Mexico,

Central America, and Peru were in Middle Barbarism, while Homeric Greeks, Germanic tribes of Caesar's time, and ancient Italians were Upper Barbarians.

Except for Civilization, Morgan used criteria of subsistence and material culture for the recognition of his periods. Next he established sequences of family organization, kinship terminology, descent patterns, sociopolitical organization, and rules of inheritance of property. Although not all of those exhibited all seven stages, he fitted their reconstructed sequences into his original scheme so that a fairly complete picture of human progress emerged.

His correlations and sequences were by no means faultless, and later research has pointed up his many errors. But although many of his conclusions were wrong, they were carefully thought out. At every point he asked himself how far and why institutions changed from one form to the next, and his answers were of a functionalist nature, namely that aspects of sociopolitical organization were interrelated with one another and were tied to technological developments and economic pursuits. The overall scheme was thus internally quite coherent. Present-day anthropologists have dropped the offensive words "savagery" and "barbarism," but accept a historical sequence from hunting and gathering to domestication of plants and animals, and most single out writing as heralding the beginning of civilization. Morgan was also correct in his observation that kinship-based societies preceded state organization, that stratification came increasingly more to the fore, that concepts of property were not developed in early times so that inheritance patterns were largely absent, and it is quite likely that descriptive kinship terminology and monogamy are relatively late in their emergence.

The major weakness of Morgan's system rests in the confusion between synchronic and diachronic reconstructions. Extrapolating from living cultures, he felt that past societies could be fully recovered not by archaeological evidence, but by simply accepting the idea that contemporary nonliterate societies *in their totality* were accurate reflections of the past.

Tylor, McLennan, and Maine had been much more careful in the application of the comparative method: they reconstructed sequences of specific institutions or of discrete cultural elements, but not of whole cultures. The most glaring errors in Morgan's work are consequently to be found in his characterizations of contemporary cultures in terms of his historical stages. His correlations did not fit, and can easily be disproven at once even by a cursory glance at the ethnographic evidence. Hawaiians, with a kinship system that was early in Morgan's scheme, developed agriculture, were highly stratified, and possessed a complex form of government. In the Old World, civilizations existed long before the use of iron. The Aztecs worked with native metals and had no knowledge of iron smelting, but nevertheless had a state government and developed a system of writing. Many other examples lie readily at hand.

In spite of these misconceptions, Morgan made substantial contributions. The thousands of kinship studies published since his death eloquently testify to the fact that anthropologists have found much social significance in kinship terminology. His example of field work, of firsthand collection of data, has been energetically followed, even by Boasians who were otherwise critical of him. His evolutionary scheme raised all problems basic to explanations of social change, and conclusive answers for all of these have not yet been found. Implicitly, he recognized cultures as functional wholes, because all institutions were seen as interrelated. It is true that he did not delve deeply into the role of religion, and his remark that all primitive religions are "grotesque and to some extent unintelligible" (Morgan 1963:5) is often quoted. But it is often overlooked that he devoted three chapters of the *League of the Iroquois* to a description of Iroquois religion, and that in *Ancient Society* he dealt with the interrelationships between totemism and kinship. Morgan knew that religion was an important factor in the study of culture, "rich in material for the future student," as he said, but he himself was not prepared to handle a topic dealing with such uncertain elements of knowledge.

Morgan's last book, *Houses and House Life of the Ameri-*

can Aborigines (1881), is another anthropological landmark. He was among the first to realize that products of material culture do not occur in isolation from other social developments, and showed that patterns of architecture interrelate with forms of family organization and social life.

It has already been mentioned that Marx read Morgan's *Ancient Society* and found in it a confirmation of his own materialistic conception of history. When he died he left instructions for Engels to present Morgan's findings to a wider audience, and one year later Engels published *The Origin of the Family, Private Property, and the State, in the Light of the Researches of Lewis Henry Morgan* (1884). It contains a summary of Morgan's arguments and evolutionary theory, and Engels added some examples of Celtic and Germanic tribes from his own knowledge.

Why was Morgan's theory so important to Marx and Engels? Morgan himself was certainly more of a bourgeois than a revolutionary, and he was inclined to consider his own American civilization as an epitome of "safety and happiness." Yet his overall theory could be interpreted as supportive of historical materialism. Morgan's emphasis on the evolution of economic production (fruits and nuts, fishing, agriculture, domestication of animals) and on the tools assisting these modes of subsistence (fire, bow and arrow, pottery, iron) was in line with the Marxian concept that production and the tools necessary for production are the basic factors determining the course of history. Since Morgan had made these criteria diagnostic for his stages, and had made all other aspects of society subordinate to that "base," it was not surprising that Marx was impressed, because he could now present a *total* picture of social evolution in the materialist manner. Since neither he nor Engels possessed much knowledge of primitive or prehistoric cultures, Morgan with his firsthand knowledge of Iroquois was obviously a specialist. Engels called him "the first man who with expert knowledge has attempted to introduce a definite order into the history of primitive man" (Engels 1942:19).

While Engels edited out Morgan's controversial statements, he found many sections that appeared to be full-fledged socialistic. The following passage from *Ancient Society* was quoted by Engels in its entirety; only the italics were added by him:

Since the advent of civilization, the outgrowth of property has been so immense, its forms so diversified, its uses so expanding and its management so intelligent in the interests of its owners, that it has become, on the part of the people, *an unmanageable power. The human mind stands bewildered in the presence of its own creation.* The time will come, nevertheless, when human intelligence will rise to the mastery over property, and define the relations of the state to the property it protects, as well as the obligations and limits of the rights of its owners. The interests of society are paramount to individual interests, and the two must be brought into just and harmonious relations. A mere property career is not the final destiny of mankind, if progress is to be the law of the future as it has been of the past. The time which has passed away since civilization began is but a fragment of the past duration of man's existence; and but a fragment of the ages yet to come. The dissolution of society bids fair to become the termination of a career of which property is the end and aim; because such a career contains the elements of self-destruction. Democracy in government, brotherhood in society, equality in rights and privileges, and universal education foreshadow the next higher plane of society to which experience, intelligence and knowledge are steadily tending. *It will be a revival, in a higher form, of the liberty, equality and fraternity of the ancient gentes.*

(Engels 1942:163)

It is understandable enough that Engels interpreted this passage as supportive of socialism but it could equally well be read as an expression of faith in the progress of democracy. Engels certainly did not quote the very last lines of *Ancient Society*:

. . . we owe our present condition, with its multiplied means of safety and happiness, to the struggles, the sufferings, the heroic exertions and the patient toil of our barbarous, and more remotely, of our savage ancestors. Their labor, their trials and their successes were a part of the plan of the Supreme Intelligence to develop a barbarian out of a savage, and a civilized man out of this barbarian.

(Morgan 1963:563)

Marx and Engels were thus only partially justified in considering Morgan's writings as supportive of their own cause. Although Morgan grasped the importance of economic factors as agents of social change, this alone does not make anyone a historical materialist. As a matter of fact, Morgan was by no means certain in his own mind what constituted the ultimate force behind social change. At different times he cited progress itself, or progress guided by intelligence and knowledge, or plain reason, or natural logic, or brain size, or the plan of the "Supreme Intelligence," sometimes called God. Confused eclecticism rather than historical materialism was the hallmark of his writings.

Engels' study based on Morgan became one of the guidelines for the establishment of new domestic legal codes in the Soviet Union, and the writings of a bourgeois American thus became embedded in Communist ideology. Other quirks of fate decided that the Englishman Tylor had his most enduring influence in the United States, while the writings of the French Émile Durkheim contributed much to the development of social anthropology in England. But the writings of a Scot, James Frazer (1854–1941), became known throughout the civilized world, and his twelve-volume *The Golden Bough* (1890) particularly found wide acclaim. In the reviews of this work his influence upon a host of scholars is often mentioned: Marett, Lang, Haddon, Rivers, Crawley, Junod, Seligman, Van Gennep, Westermarck, Durkheim, Mauss, Freud, Wundt, Anatole France, T. S. Eliot, Ezra Pound . . . the list is endless. More often than not, the extent of this influence is left unspecified, and little more is said than that through Frazer they became aware of anthropology. Marett was not far from the truth when he summed up the impact of the *Golden Bough* as "part of what every schoolboy knows, and what every gentleman must at least have forgotten" (quoted by Kardiner and Preble 1963:81). Frazer was praised for his erudition, his poetic sentiments, and the elegance of his literary style. Witness the opening lines of Book I of the *Golden Bough*:

No one who has seen the calm waters of the Lake of Nemi, lapped in a green hollow of the Alban hills, can ever forget it. Diana herself might still be lingering by that lonely shore, haunting these woodlands wild.

(Frazer 1959:3)

But Frazer was rarely praised for his theoretical insights, which is not surprising, because he himself admitted that data were more interesting to him than theory. He wrote:

The prime want of the study [i.e., of anthropology] is not so much theories as facts.

and again:

. . . it is the fate of theories to be washed away . . . and I am not so presumptuous as to expect or desire for mine an exemption from the common lot. I hold them all very lightly and have used them chiefly as convenient pegs on which to hang my collection of facts.

(Quoted by Kardiner and Preble 1963:80)

Frazer's "convenient pegs" were evolution, the principle of the psychic unity of mankind, and progress, but he never clearly defined these ideas, nor did he develop full theoretical statements about them. His evolution was primarily one of the mental progress of mankind. He described the meaning of the *Golden Bough* as follows:

The cycle of *The Golden Bough* depicts, in its sinuous outline, in its play of alternate light and shadow, the long evolution by which the thoughts and efforts of man have passed through the successive stages of Magic, Religion and Science. It is, in some measure, an epic of humanity which, starting from magic, attains to science in its ripe age . . .

(Quoted by Kardiner and Preble 1963:74)

Frazer explained that early man knew nothing of science, and thus possessed a completely wrong idea of natural causes. He lived primarily by two erroneous principles on which all his magic was based, namely the "law of similarity" and "the law of contact." The first law presumed that like produces like, and magicians were thus convinced that they could control nature by imitating it. Thus, if rain was needed, water was poured out, and to harm an enemy, a doll was fashioned in his image and needles run through its head or heart. The second law posited that connections remain in force even after separation. Thus one could get hold of someone's hair, or nail clippings, or clothing he had worn, and burn or otherwise mutilate such items in the conviction that the same would happen to their former owner.

But when the human mind progressed, people began to realize that they were fairly helpless, that their laws did not always work, and that they could not control nature by their own efforts. The conviction then arose that higher, nonhuman powers ruled the universe, and with this insight religion was born. Magicians became religious specialists, and their supposed ability to contact and persuade supernatural spirits to act on their behalf gave them prestige and authority over people. Gradually, they became divine kings, whose departed souls were revered as gods. The highest development of the human mind was science, which was closely related to magic in as far as man once more began to manipulate nature by his own skills, but now he was equipped with correct laws.

Frazer thus depicted early men and contemporary primitives as rather irrational beings, although he would not deny that they had the same capabilities as modern men. While it is true that science in a modern sense is of late appearance in the history of mankind, it does not follow that nonliterate peoples are wholly ignorant of natural causation. As Malinowski showed later on, they may employ magic to increase their crops, but they also carry out all other rational tasks necessary for production. Moreover, Frazer's stages cannot be found in ethnogaphic reality, and both magic and religion are certainly coexistent with science.

Frazer's evolutionary framework offered him ample opportunity for the display of his data, which he collected from many sources: classic literature, existing ethnographies, folklore, and so forth. He also carried on an extensive correspondence with field workers, missionaries, and other foreign travelers. For their guidance he wrote a pamphlet called "Questions on the Manners, Customs, Religions, Superstitions, etc., of Uncivilized or Semi-Civilized Peoples." In this way he collected an immense quantity of data, using them to illustrate and demonstrate his stages of magic and religion. Many of these were exotica of popular interest, dealing with ghosts, exorcism, scapegoats, human sacrifice, tree worship, taboos, ritual flaying, saturnalia, sex, fertility rites, and the like. While he tore these data out of their cultural contexts he transformed a seemingly meaningless collection of human follies into a meaningful and coherent whole, presenting a fascinating epic of the development of mankind, but one that was completely unverified. Malinowski called the *Golden Bough* "perhaps the greatest scientific Odyssey in modern humanism." After deleting the word "scientific," most anthropologists would agree.

The twelve-volume *Golden Bough* was only part of Frazer's enormous literary output. He also wrote *Totemism and Exogamy* (4 volumes, 1910), *The Belief in Immortality and the Worship of the Dead* (3 volumes, 1913–24), *Folklore in the Old Testament* (3 volumes, 1918), *Aftermath* (a supplement to the *Golden Bough,* 1939), and several more.

In present-day anthropology, Frazer is not forgotten, but he is unpraised and unread. Malinowski was perhaps his last serious defender, but he also was in disagreement with most of Frazer's methods. It appears that contemporary anthropologists are critical of Frazer not only for his methodology, but perhaps even more because his views of nonliterate peoples were so devastating. His belief in "psychic unity" only meant that, given enough time, savages may progress to science and civilization—but they obviously had not yet done so.

CONCLUSIONS

The protagonists of this chapter, Tylor, Morgan, and Frazer, are the men whose personal influence did most to establish anthropology as a separate discipline. Of the three, Tylor is perhaps the most important because of his insight that culture was learned rather than inborn, and socially determined rather than racially. He also championed his science vigorously, and achieved its academic recognition in Great Britain. Morgan pointed the way to the importance of field work and the first-hand collection of data, and was among the first to indicate the importance of kinship and its interrelationships with other cultural institutions. Frazer popularized anthropology so that everyone who read his books became aware that the study of man could be exciting, and that "queer customs" were meaningful and worthy of serious thought.

Even more important was their vision of what a discipline concerned with man should encompass. Anthropology developed into what it is today because these men offered a conceptual framework in which the sum total of human behavior could find its place, and every habit or capability of man, sometimes seemingly trivial, could become relevant for the understanding of humanity. Their orientation was pan-human: culture was everywhere, in the past as in the present, among "savages" as in "civilization."

The theories they presented were strongly attacked in later years, and for a while were suspect. But evolutionism is now no longer unfashionable, and however much modern theories differ from earlier ones, the relevance of their overall approaches is generally recognized.

CHAPTER 9

DIFFUSION
AND MIGRATION

Nineteenth-century evolutionists were well aware that a full understanding of cultures demanded explanations of both their similarities and their differences. Although not all their interpretations were alike, in general it was held that cultural differences existed because of the unequal pace of the march of progress, but degrees of outside influence and adaptation to environment were not neglected. In their views, cultural similarities came about because mental uniformity caused people to react roughly in the same way to like circumstances, aided however by the development of progress of the mind. Cultures in the same stage of development were thus not necessarily historically related, because a greater or lesser part of the cultural inventory was invented independently. When similar traits appeared in areas that were far apart and without known historical contact, it was accepted that they had evolved separately. Similar parallel inventions were the strongest proof for the cherished doctrine of psychic unity.

It was clearly recognized that diffusion was an undeniable fact, and none of the evolutionists even maintained that culture traits were more often invented than imitated. Diffusion did not necessarily interfere with evolution, but it spoiled the neatness of the schemes. But in the thoughts of many evolutionists diffusion seemed to diminish the strength of the arguments in favor of psychic unity. This need not have been so, because if people's minds were indeed dissimilar, culture traits would be mutually unintelligible, and diffusion could not take place at all. But apparently many evolutionists felt that psychic unity was best manifested in human creativity evidenced by independent invention.

Several schools of thought arose that claimed to be anti-evolutionistic, but in fact they often were more critical of psychic unity. They espoused the idea that man was basically uninventive, and that important inventions were made only once. These then spread through the rest of the world by diffusion or by migration. The difference between these two ideas has not always been appreciated, but in fact they represent two different processes of culture change. Diffusion is the taking over of traits by imitation, while migration implies that culture carriers broke away from their original settlements and moved to other parts of the world, taking their cultural inventory with them, but adapting it to new environmental conditions.

The so-called extreme diffusionists used both explanations. They held that civilization arose in one place and spread out over the rest of the world by diffusion, migration, or both. The German *Kulturkreis* school emphasized migration, while the American "culture area" idea was largely based upon diffusion. All three schools of thought were historically oriented and attempted to reconstruct contacts between peoples, paths of diffusion or migration, and the spread of culture items.

The idea that certain aspects of culture originated at one point and in one place existed well before the twentieth century. Max Müller (1823–1900), the German-born philologist who spent most of his life at Oxford, traced all European myths and folklore back to Sanskrit sources. First using linguistic evidence, he became more conjectural later on, and was led to believe that ancient sun worship was the unifying factor of all myth and folktales. Even our habit of saying "good morning" betrayed old pagan beliefs (Dorson 1958:21). Other mythologists soon emerged with rivals for the sun: for Kuhn, storm clouds were at the root of every myth, for

Schwartz it was the wind, for Preller the sky. Hugo Winckler became perhaps the best known of the German nature mythologists, and his pan-Babylonian theory enjoyed a considerable vogue. Examining myths and folktales from all over the world, Winckler became impressed by the fact that heavenly bodies often played a central role in them, even among peoples that had not the slightest notion about astrology or astronomy. He reasoned that astral myths would not have been invented by peoples who had no interest in the heavenly bodies, and their myths must thus have been borrowed. Since it was in Babylonia that scientific knowledge of the heavens was most developed, this must have been the place where these myths arose and whence they spread all over the rest of the world. Other Babylonian culture traits often trailed along, notably the calendar. The Aztecs for one possessed a system of calendrical time reckoning, and comparing the two systems Winckler concluded that the Aztec was an imperfect imitation of the Babylonian one.

While it is true that Babylonian astronomy was amazingly precise and astral myths numerous, it does not follow that myths arise only in scientific contexts. But neither Müller nor Winckler maintained that everything cultural arose from one single nation. This far-fetched idea was championed by Grafton Elliot Smith (1871–1937), by his disciple William James Perry (1887–1949), supported later also by William H. R. Rivers (1864–1922).

Elliot Smith was an anatomist whose scientific accomplishments were well appreciated by his colleagues. At one point in his career he traveled to Egypt and became a great admirer of its ancient civilization. Upon his return to Cambridge, he was struck by similarities between the Egyptian complex of large stone monuments in association with sun worship and that of English megaliths such as Stonehenge. He was certain in his mind that the rude and primitive Druids could not have invented these complex temple structures by themselves, and concluded that the English monuments were crude imitations of Egyptian pyramids and mastabas. He published these findings in 1911, but further investigations revealed to him that megaliths were present not only in Europe, but pyramidal constructions existed all over the world. The Mayan pyramids were of course most striking, but also Japanese pagodas, Cambodian and Balinese temples, and American Indian burial mounds displayed the same basic form, and must thus all be related to Egyptian prototypes. Soon enough, he concluded that all civilization had originated in Egypt and had spread to the far corners of the globe from about 4000 B.C. onward.

Smith knew of course that man was older than that, and also that many nonliterate societies were without pyramids or any other traces of direct Egyptian influence. Harking back to seventeenth-century explanations, Smith called all people outside the influence of civilization "natural men," and described their cultures as a collection of negative traits: no clothing, no ornaments, no law, no art, no agriculture, no cattle, no marriage, no burials. Elliot Smith was rather unique in his attempts to deprive natural men even of magic, which was one trait usually gladly conceded to them even by those who held the lowest opinion of savage life. Yet Smith's concept of "natural man" was romantic rather than hostile. The Punan of Borneo, for instance, were described as peaceful, happy, and well behaved. They were kind to their wives, loved their children, and were faithful monogamists—thus apparently having acquired marriage rules after all.

It was almost miraculous that civilization had come into being at all, but it happened in Egypt in the following way: In the fertile soils of the banks of the Nile, seeds sprouted spontaneously. Following the example of nature, ancient Egyptians began to plant more seeds, and soon learned to predict and control the river's inundations, thus arriving at a full-fledged system of hydraulic agriculture. Stimulated by their success, they invented in rapid succession such necessary items as pottery, weaving, the wheel, the plough, and writing. Then they began to build cities and established the institutions of law, government, and religion, worshiping the sun as their major deity. Their kings became deified because they were personifications of the sun. After death their bodies were mummified and elaborate graves were built for them. Egyptians also invented navigation, and traveled far and wide in search of precious stones and metal, bringing the benefits of their civilization to many areas. The recipients were, however, weak imitators, and nowhere in the ancient world did civilization reach the same heights as in Egypt.

Smith's pan-Egyptian theory (also known as the heliolithic theory) was thus degenerative in two ways: the golden age of happiness and peace of "natural man" was destroyed, and the accomplishments of Egypt deteriorated in the path of their migration. Smith gave no other explanation of culture change, and felt that only the Egyptians had been inventive. He wrote:

We know in the case of every modern invention, that it was made in one definite place and became diffused over a wider and wider area until everyone in any part of the world who is making use of this particular invention is indebted directly or indirectly to one man in one particular place who was originally responsible for initiating the process.

(G. E. Smith 1927:9–10)

Multiple origins, independent invention, multiple diffusions, psychic unity, progress, evolution, and survivals were all abolished in one mighty stroke. W. J. Perry, who was working in the Malayan area, became converted to this view, and popularized it in his book *The Children of the Sun* (1923), which was widely read and often reprinted. It contains such statements as "transmission of culture is always accompanied by degradation," and "no art or craft is really enduring."

W. H. R. Rivers became equally persuaded by this extreme diffusionism toward the end of his life. Like Smith, he was a medical doctor by profession, and he was a member of the famous Torres Strait Expedition (1898), which was the first interdisciplinary anthropological expedition meant to cover all sides of primitive life by trained investigators. Rivers and his students C. S. Meyers and William McDougall were to examine the psychological abilities of the natives, more specifically their sensory capacities. Rivers concluded that there were no racial differences in pure sense acuity. A more important result of this trip was his subsequent article "A Genealogical Method of Collecting Social and Vital Statistics" (1900), which since has become a standard work in this field. Like Morgan, he recorded genealogies and kinship terms, observing specific behavior patterns associated with them, including duties, privileges, status and roles, thus placing such studies in meaningful contexts. His subsequent book *The Todas* (1906) remains a classic monograph, and although these people were strongly influenced by Hinduism, Rivers made no excessive diffusionist claims.

In 1911, however, in an address before the British Association at Portsmouth, Rivers suddenly announced that he had been led independently to the same general position as diffusionists and migrationists. In the following year he published a degeneration-oriented article, "The Disappearance of Useful Arts" (1912), and degeneration together with the uninventiveness of the human mind became the major tools of explanation in his subsequent *History of Melanesian Society* (1914). Noting, for instance, that on some of the Melanesian islands people had no canoes, he reasoned that they once must have known these items so indispensable for any small island population, because without them they could never even have reached their present habitat. Perhaps the canoe craft guilds had died out, but in any case this was a clear example that culture traits frequently disappeared. There were other phenomena, however, that could not be explained so easily. In Australia, for instance, Rivers noted the presence of five different burial rituals in an otherwise homogeneous population within a fairly small geographical region. The simple and uninventive aborigines could not have developed so many variations just by themselves, and Rivers thus conjectured that small successive migrations had occurred. The physical similarities between the people were explained by the conjecture that only males arrived in the canoes, and, since they married local women, their offspring soon lost the racial characteristics of their forefathers. Forced to learn the language of their wives so that their original language disappeared without a trace, the men became thus almost completely assimilated with their host culture, and had no objections to abandoning all their original habits except one, namely burial rites. They had such strong emotional attachment to those practices that they refused to give them up, and the puzzling variations were thus explained away. It remained of course unexplained how the rites had arisen in the first place, and why the original Australian groups so readily gave up *their* own burial rites, to which they must have been equally emotionally attached.

Smith, Perry, and Rivers were unanimous in their convictions that inventiveness was rare and that similarities between cultures could be explained by imitation only. It is, of course, the case that every group borrows more than it invents, but this does not mean that inventions are made only once. The shortcoming of the extreme diffusionists was that they used the hypothetical uninventiveness of man as an explanatory principle of everything they wanted to prove, without investigating other evidence, and without taking into account the entirely different functions and cultural meanings of their diagnostic culture traits. In the instance of Elliot Smith's pyramids, any structure only vaguely resembling them was interpreted as a vestige of the Egyptian prototype, even though the pyramids in Egypt were tombs, those in Yucatán platforms of temples, and those in Indonesia stupas. Another example is Smith's consideration of an African tribe's practice of preserving the femurs of its rulers as a clear example of degeneration, because it represented a weak imitation of Egyptian mummification. The diffusionists thus looked at outward form only, and any vague similarity was to them an undeniable proof of historical contact and imitation.

The somewhat related culture-historical movement that became known as the *Kulturkreis* or "cultural circle" school was much more scholarly. Their adherents examined all culture traits in great detail and with German thoroughness. This movement, too, developed in reaction to evolutionism and questioned the psychic unity and the inventive capacities of man, but its major explanatory device was migration rather than diffusion.

Its inspiration came to a large extent from Friedrich Ratzel (1844–1904), a geographer who made clear-cut distinctions between territorial and social geography. It was the latter branch of his science that held his interest, and he called it "anthropogeography." He saw this mainly as the study of people's relationships to neighboring countries, particularly in terms of trait distributions. Conceding that environment played an important adaptive role, he was nevertheless convinced that people were more influenced by one another than by factors of climate and terrain.

His views on psychic unity were somewhat mixed. On the one hand he professed to "believe" in it, but one can find several statements in his writings that point in the opposite direction: Athabaskan Indians were "poorly endowed," the Negro was "childish and imitative," and the Chinese "highly imaginative." In any case, Ratzel did not use psychic unity as an explanatory principle, and he tended to deny multiple independent inventions. Like the diffusionists, he felt that man is much more given to imitation than to creativity. He specifically attacked Bastian, who in his own inimitable style had maintained that similar inventions came about because people conceived of the *Geist* of a material object, but developed their own form of it. Ratzel stoutly declared that arrows and axes had no souls, and that it was useless to search for them. The one important consideration was to discover from where cultural traits came, and where they went; and there were no spatial limits to the pathways they might take. Single cultural items usually diffused, whole cultural complexes were transplanted by migration. Yet, in every case adaptation to the environment would cause the various culture traits to take on somewhat different outward shapes. How then could their relationships be recognized? Ratzel warned that not every similarity could be taken as proof of historical connection, because objects of material culture, in order to have any utility at all, must possess certain features: a canoe paddle needs a blade, and an arrowhead or a spear must have a point. If, however, there were other similar qualities, unrelated to use, these must evidence historical relationships. Thus if paddles have similar incised ornamentations, or spears have feathers attached to their shafts, this cannot be accidental, and must imply borrowing or migration, even though the respective cultures may be widely separated in time and space. Ratzel called this principle the *Formengedanke* or the "criterion of form." Applying this principle to the history of the African bow and arrow, he noted that the cross-section of the bow shaft, the fastening of the bow strings, and the feathering of the arrows were quite like those in Indonesia, and he assumed borrowing.

Ratzel was not an out-and-out degenerationist. He felt that culture traits may become either simplified or elaborated in their diffusion or migration, depending upon local conditions and the relative sophistication of local technology. He was probably influenced by the biological concept of adaptive radiation, which taught that a common ancestry and relationships between varieties of species can be discovered, and they need not be identical because in species as well as in elements of culture there will be local adjustments.

Ratzel's pupil Leo Frobenius (1873–1938) took these ideas several steps further. He observed that historical connections usually implied much more than transmission of single culture traits, because often enough whole culture complexes were involved. He thus concluded that migration was a more important factor of explanation than diffusion in the explanation of cultural similarities. Finding that not only the forms of bow and arrow were similar in West Africa and Indonesia, but that the areas also resembled each other in their respective house forms, shields, masks, and drums, he concluded that migration had taken place. He thus added another criterion to Ratzel's *Formengedanke,* namely what he first called "geographical statistics," which meant that one should count the number of similarities. Furthermore, he introduced another factor, namely the biological or developmental criterion. By this he meant that internal changes have to be taken into account, because when people migrate into a different environment, their cultures would have to be adjusted. Some traits would change, some that were useless in the new environment would disappear. In this way not only similarities, but significant differences related to ecological adaptation could become indicators of historical connections.

Unlike Ratzel, Frobenius did not confine his research to material culture, and he was particularly interested in mythology. Detecting similarities also between traditional stories in Africa and those in Indonesia, he noted that in the latter area myths were all related and formed an epic, while in Africa the stories appeared singly. Indonesia must thus have been the homeland. It remained unexplained why myths should originate as epics and become splintered in their transmission, except for the preconception that higher cultures were always the originators and lower ones the imitators.

Ratzel's criterion of form and Frobenius' geographical statistics were vigorously combined in the strategy of the *Kulturkreis* school, whose main figures were Fritz Graebner (1877–1934) and Father Wilhelm Schmidt (1868–1954). Graebner spelled out the methodological principles of this movement in his *Methode der Ethnologie* (1911), and he called the two basic criteria those of "quality" and of "quantity." He reasoned that early man invented the basics of culture, such as language and toolmaking, but soon formed a number of small bands that became isolated. Each of those developed their own distinctive cultures, and they were the *Urkulturen* or "primeval cultures" whose members, in time, spread out in all directions, eventually populating all continents. It was the task and aim of culture historians to reconstruct the various *Kreise,* and Graebner wrote that the tracing of such relationships was "the first and most basic problem of ethnology" (Graebner 1911:107).

Realizing that careful description must precede reconstruction, Graebner and all others pursuing this task collected a truly impressive amount of data and described all items in painstaking detail. It is this part of the research that has remained valid and useful until the present day, but the reconstruction of possible *Kreise* and the methods employed have now largely been discarded.

Graebner and his followers were not satisfied with tracking connections, but were also interested in the reconstruction of chronology. Starting his researches in Oceania, Graebner reconstructed six successive cultural developments. The earliest, most primitive *Kreis* was Tasmanian, followed by Australian boomerang culture, totemic hunters, two-class horticulturists, Melanesian bow culture, and Polynesian patrilineal culture. Each of these, alone or in combination with others, had counterparts in Africa and elsewhere. On the way, blending with other cultures had taken place; some traits had become lost, others added or elaborated, still others borrowed. To accommodate these and other complications, a very elaborate vocabulary was constructed: there were primitive, secondary, and tertiary *Kreise,* each of those consisted of sub-circles, and those that did not fit anywhere were either marginal, peripheral, or overlapping *Kreise*. In other words, the system did not work, and in fact all it proved was that cultural spread and development did *not* take place in the ways posited by the *Kulturkreis* scholars.

Wilhelm Schmidt applied the same methods to Africa. Somewhat in competition with Graebner, he claimed to have found an even earlier *Kreis* than the Tasmanian, namely the African Pygmy, who had migrated all over the world. Even their physical type was preserved in several Asian areas. Schmidt held that they were the original inhabitants of Africa, and that all other groups had entered later. Schmidt used a somewhat different nomenclature for the various circles, thus further confusing the issue. Moreover he used criteria of family organization, which are even more difficult to reconstruct than material culture. He also attempted to correlate culture circles with linguistic ones. Making valuable contributions to historical linguistics by establishing certain language families, he himself admitted that one-to-one relationships between cultural and linguistic types could not be found.

Schmidt and Graebner held a lively interest in chronology and developments. Yet they strongly criticized the nineteenth-century evolutionists, not because they were opposed to the concept of evolution itself, but because they considered the methods that had been used entirely wrong. Rightly priding themselves on their elaborate field data, Graebner and Schmidt reproached evolutionists for their lack of precision and for their failure to establish genetic relationships between cultures and stages. They charged that Tylor and Spencer had looked upon culture as if it were one single entity that everywhere displayed the same tendencies toward progress and increasing complexity. *Kulturkreis* research had given conclusive proof that neither of these were constant, and could thus not be used as explanatory devices. Items of material culture sometimes became elaborated, but often enough they were simplified, and degeneration was thus as much a fact of history as was progress. Cultural institutions such as family organization certainly did not increase in complexity: European kinship systems were much simpler than those of Australian aborigines. In the opinion of the *Kulturkreis* writers, evolutionists were at fault also because they used their own culture as normative for all others, and because of their use of survivals as a tool for reconstruction. It implied that some cultures possessed senseless elements, while in reality everything in a culture makes sense within its own context. Traits would become modified once they had lost their former meaning or utility, or else they would completely vanish. Finally, evolutionists were also blamed for establishing their sequences first and then more or less arbitrarily fitting actual cultures into their stages.

Many of these criticisms were telling ones, although *Kulturkreis* writers themselves sometimes fell into the same errors. They, too, attempted to fit cultures into their established sequences, and sometimes used progress as an explanatory device. Schmidt, for instance, wrote that Pygmy burials were simpler than those of any other group, and considered this evidence of their chronological priority. The *Kulturkreis* researchers also overlooked that their aims were different from those of the evolutionists. The *Kulturkreis* writers were concerned with the reconstructions of whole cultures and their historical connections, while Tylor, McLennan, Maine, and Bachofen attempted to reconstruct the development of discrete cultural institutions, be they kinship, marriage rules, law, or religion. They could thus be more eclectic in their use of data, and could select their evidence from ethnography as needed.

Both schools, however, leaned heavily upon the comparative method. Graebner, although admitting that archaeology might be useful, stressed that the starting point of all reconstruction was the examination of presently existing cultures, while Schmidt was convinced that present-day Pygmies represented primeval conditions of mankind. By and large, the culture historians were less interested in absolute origins than the evolutionists, but Father Schmidt, understandably, was very interested in establishing the origin of religion. In his essays on this topic, he reviewed many older theories and took specific issue with Tylor's idea that animism, the belief in spirits, was the earliest form of religion. Backing his own contention with impressive ethnographic evidence, Schmidt showed that the most simple peoples often worshiped a high god as an All-Father, and although there was no clear-cut evidence of monotheism among them, he was convinced that this was the original form of religion. The later addition of other gods and spirits was for him a clear indication of the degenerative tendency of man's thinking on these matters. Schmidt worked out this theory further in his monumental *Der Ursprung der Gottesidee* (*The Origin of the Idea of God*; 12 volumes, 1926–55). Hostile commentators have accused Schmidt of "mysticism" because of his religious commitments, but any unexplained mover of history is "mystical" in this sense, be it progress, degeneration, natural law, or God. Schmidt was historical in the treatment of his data, and honestly attempted to establish the age of the idea of high gods.

Of course, his conclusions about the origin of religion remained as speculative as those of Tylor, Spencer, Lang, and Frazer.

The *Kulturkreis* school is now practically defunct, even in Europe. Some of its principles continue to be used by art historians who attempt to establish relationships between art styles or motifs, but they do not deal with whole cultures. Other than this, the theory has worked mainly to prove itself wrong, because, in spite of the monumental efforts, no culture circles could be established. The shortcoming of the theory rested both in its premises and in its methods. As to the former, it was pure speculation to depict cultural differences as having emanated from four or five early bands each with its own separate migrations. Even the scholarly-sounding criteria of quality and quantity did not always yield realistic results, because too many other influences interfere. It is true enough that a great many similarities in culture items evidence historical contact of some kind: if we found a Gothic cathedral or a Coca-Cola bottle in a remote area of the world, the obvious conclusion would be that they were not independently invented. On the other hand, the mere fact that two or more cultures possess feathered arrows, matrilineality, or myths about an all-father does not necessarily prove historical relationship. Culture change may be convergent, which means that dissimilar forms can become similar in time; but it also can be divergent, which means that similar forms may become dissimilar. Diffusion of course plays havoc with the idea of pure culture circles. Furthermore, the approach was barren insofar as it did not attempt to reach understanding about the dynamics of culture change. It was basically a descriptive or ideographic method that at best gave insight about the spread of culture items, but overlooked analysis of reasons behind their acceptance, rejection, and modifications.

Graebner was a museum curator, and thus concerned with classification of material culture for purposes of meaningful exhibitions. The American culture area theory also received its first impetus from museum methodology. At one time, most museums displayed their items in arrangements dictated by nineteenth-century evolutionism. All arrowheads, for instance, were placed in series of increasing complexity, no matter where they had been found. Coinciding with the Boasian critique of evolution, both the American Museum of Natural History in New York and the Field Museum in Chicago decided simultaneously to use geographical categories instead, so that museum visitors would gain better insights into Indian cultures as wholes. In this manner it was found that cultural items of Indian tribes that lived close to one another were more similar than those of groups who lived farther apart. The geographical regions that displayed such internal similarities were called "culture areas," and their isomorphism was explained by diffusion.

The first full-fledged theoretical treatment and application of this idea was made by Clark Wissler (1870–1947). Dissatisfied with earlier writers who had treated American Indian populations as if they formed one uniform and undifferentiated whole, he felt that the first step to indicate the varieties of their modes of life was to classify their social groupings according to their dominant traits and geographical locations. His original map listed ten culture areas for North America, four for South America, and a separate one for the Caribbean. Seeking for a common denominator for each group, he took subsistence as the most basic factor, not only because it influenced other parts of culture, but also because it was necessarily related to environmental conditions. Reducing his original areas to eight "food areas," his scheme was as follows:

Subsistence	*Area*
Caribou	Eskimo
Bison	Great Plains
Salmon	North Pacific Coast
Wild seeds	California
Eastern maize	Southeast and Eastern Woodland
Intensive agriculture	Southwest, Mexico, Peru
Manioc	Amazon region, Caribbean
Guanaco	Guanaco

(Wissler 1917:370–74)

In order to demonstrate their internal coherences and their differences from each other, Wissler began to list many of their cultural elements. Interested also in the prehistory of the Indians, he made maps based upon archaeology and other maps using ethnographic data. Finding a remarkable degree of coincidence between the past and the present, he concluded that Indian cultures were quite stable, and consequently culture areas were quite stable also. Trying to match his findings with linguistic and racial classification, he found the correlations much weaker. Unable to explain these puzzling facts, he was satisfied that the cultures themselves were relatively homogeneous. Plains Indians, for instance, typically depended upon the buffalo for food, clothing, and tents. They did not fish, had no agriculture, possessed the movable tepee tent, used dogs and the travois for land transportation, had no pottery and no basketry, had highly developed leatherwork, as well as circular shields, geometrical art, men's societies, sweat lodges, and scalp dances. They differed in their ways from North Pacific Coast tribes, who depended on seafood, made much use of berries, cooked in baskets, built rectangular plank houses, had totem poles, dugout canoes, and woven helmets but no shields. Since it was unlikely that such typical trait complexes were invented independently, and since they appeared in groups living in close proximity, diffusion was the most logical explanation, and a separate settling of each area was implied.

Wissler found it necessary to posit a "culture center" for each of his culture areas. This center was the place of early settlement from which the various traits had diffused. Unfortunately it was unproven that all traits emanated from a single center, or even that such a center ever had existed. The center was also the place where all traits typically appeared, and they diminished in number with the increase of distance from the center. Different elements became more numerous, and eventually led to another culture center in a different culture area. Firm boundaries could thus not be established. His scheme resembled that of British diffusionists on a miniature scale: it appeared as if only the inhabitants of culture centers were innovators, and all others imitators. But Wissler did not posit degeneration, because he was clearly aware that traits must be adapted to specific conditions if they are to remain functional.

Kroeber observed that in spite of their differences, culture areas often resembled each other in many ways. He proposed therefore that statistical correlations should be used in order to find the coincidences of "typical" traits, so that culture areas would become more sharply delineated. Traits were minimal definable culture elements, but the question of what constituted "minimal" was not so easily answered. A canoe is a trait, but all its parts, its decorations, the materials used for it, and methods of construction could also be looked upon as traits, as well as such factors as who makes canoes, which rituals are associated with their production and so forth. Impressed, however, by Wissler's dictum that "a culture is not to be comprehended until the list of its traits approaches completeness" (Wissler 1923:51), and eager to make the correct statistical correlations, field workers began to construct ever more elaborate trait lists. In the first California trait list, published in 1935, Klimek included 430 items. Two years later, Gifford and Kroeber made a list for the Pomo and two neighboring tribes, counting 1,094 traits. Working with four tribal groups in Round Valley, Essene recorded 2,174 elements. In other parts of California, Stewart noted 4,662 elements for the Ute and Paiute, Voegelin had a list of 5,263 for tribes of northeast California, while Ray, working in the region north and northeast of the California tribes, increased the number to 7,633. One can sympathize with the complaints of Vernon Ray that the recording of all these items was the most time-consuming and difficult part of his field work, and that it was trying for himself as well as for his informants. But however long the lists were, they could never "approach completeness." It was a barren exercise, because no insight was gained into the dynamics of culture change. No analysis was made of why some culture items were accepted and others rejected, nor of what their functions might be. The dogmatic trait-list approach was soon abandoned, but efforts to classify culture areas continued for at least another decade after the last trait list had appeared. Kroeber revised Wissler's original division and eventually mapped seven "grand areas," twenty-one "areas" and sixty-three "sub-areas" for North and Central America (1939). Stout recognized eleven areas in South America in 1938, which were narrowed down to three by Bennett and Bird in 1949, but increased again to twenty-four by Murdock in 1951. In other parts of the world, Elizabeth Bacon listed six areas and four blend-areas for Asia in 1946, but revised them in 1953. Herskovits mapped nine culture areas in Africa, but he too changed his classification several times. The mere fact that there was no consensus about what constituted a culture area and the constant reworking and realigning of existing classifications were indicative of the problems inherent in the concept. The approach appeared static and without historical depth, migrations sometimes caused entirely different cultures to appear side by side, and the interrelationships between traits and their functions within societies remained unexplained. Graebner criticized culture-area classifications because they were too narrow in scope and neglected to take worldwide similarities into account. He accused American scholars of hydrophobia, because they seemed unwilling to allow culture traits to cross oceans. Graebner overlooked, however, that American culture-area scholars were not concerned with worldwide migrations nor with the reconstruction of total culture history. Their aims were more modest: they wanted to understand the relationships between American Indian cultures, and they used the culture-area concept as a technique for differentiating and describing the range of these cultures. While it sometimes appeared as if the construction of culture areas had become an end in itself, the majority of classifiers did not lose sight of the wider implications.

No significant new culture-area classifications have been made in the last few decades. The approach has not led investigators into a cul-de-sac, however, as was the case for *Kulturkreis* and pan-Egyptian theorists. Its premises were certainly more pedestrian than those of its European counterparts, but they were also more realistic. While there are many exceptions, it is nevertheless true that items of material culture and customs of peoples who live close together tend to resemble one another, and it is reasonable to assume that within a limited geographical area these similarities are most likely due to diffusion. Culture-area scholars did not deny that independent inventions took place, and they were also well aware that migration could be a salient factor for the explanation of culture change. They were also much less dogmatic about their principles than their European colleagues. From the early beginnings onward, they were aware of the shortcomings of their theories and sought to correct them. Wissler realized that his mappings were static and could not explain or even indicate the changes that had occurred through time. Kroeber attempted to remedy this, and suggested that several successive maps should be made and superimposed on each other so that distribution changes would be revealed. He also substituted the concept of cultural "climax" for Wissler's culture "center," reasoning that the latter was by definition static since it supposedly was the single point from which all other traits diffused. Kroeber's climax was to be empirically determined for every separate mapping: it was the place where at a given time the cultural elements appeared in the greatest number and were most sharply expressed. This point of cultural intensity might well change through time.

Most culture-area anthropologists also attempted to understand the interrelationships between culture and environment in the conviction that habitat cannot be neglected in the study of cultural variation. It was fully understood that a variety of cultural adjustments to similar environments could occur, but it was thought that once successful adjustments had been made they tended to persist. Although habitat is only one factor out of many that influences culture, it is one that cannot be neglected. It interacts most strongly with subsistence patterns, particularly in cultures where trade is not widely developed.

The fact that cultural-area boundaries had to remain vague may have been disappointing to those who had expected otherwise, but it was no great obstacle, because culture areas were considered to be methods of classification preliminary to analytic studies. It was also soon realized that Wissler's hypothesis that traits tend to diffuse in all directions from their centers of origin was incorrect. Instead, it was found that diffusion often went in one direction and not in another, that traits diffused at various rates, and often selectively. It thus became essential to examine the reasons for such variations, and in this manner important mechanisms of culture change were highlighted. It came to be understood that diffusion was not a mechanical taking over of some culture traits, but that introduction of new elements often stimulated other internal changes.

Even the much maligned trait-list approach led to increased understanding of cultural phenomena, precisely because it demonstrated that culture traits often appeared in association. These associations in a given culture became studied in terms of "trait complexes" or "culture patterns." Rather than applying historical analysis to "all" traits that might appear in a given culture, several American writers dealt with specific phenomena. Leslie Spier (1893–1961), for one, traced the origin and development of the Ghost Dance religion of Northwest Indians. With extensive documentation he showed how this seemingly new development was in many ways related to the older Prophet Dance religion, and how newer elements were introduced to cope with contingencies that did not exist before, namely the invasion of Western civilization (Spier 1935). Ruth Benedict's study of the religious complex centering around the idea of a "guardian spirit" is also of this nature. No two manifestations of the guardian spirit were identical, but the grouping of traits remained recognizable while adapted to specific cultural constellations. For the Kwakiutl Indians a guardian spirit was a hereditary lineage mark, while the Thompson River Indians sought individual guardian spirits to guide them in their chosen occupations (Benedict 1923). Hallowell wrote in a similar vein about bear ceremonialism (1926), while others dealt with art styles, music, totemism, myths, mortuary rites, and so on. Most sought to explain the inner meanings of these various trait complexes and attempted to trace their relationships to other cultural institutions.

CONCLUSIONS

The schools of thought discussed in this chapter were all critical of nineteenth-century evolutionism, but shared with it an abiding interest in the history and development of culture. British diffusionists and *Kulturkreis* adherents leaned in the direction of degenerationism, but the American culture-area school did not consider this an issue. They stressed that every culture makes its own adaptations, and the question which one progressed more thus becomes futile.

The question about man's psychic unity also attained different dimensions in America. Evolutionists had used it to explain cultural similarities that were not due to diffusion, but in somewhat circular fashion they also held that such similarities proved man's mental unity. American anthropologists, vigorously led by Boas, embraced psychic unity as an ideology. It was not generally used as an explanatory principle, but as a tool to combat racism.

In America, anthropology never lost historical perspective completely out of sight. In England, however, ahistorical functionalism for a while overshadowed all other considerations, as will be discussed next.

CHAPTER 10

FUNCTIONALISM

In the early part of the twentieth century, functionalism became widely accepted as a new and important anthropological method. It was new only insofar as it encompassed a systematic theory, but the notion of function itself was as old as recorded history. Herodotus, Plato, Aristotle, Augustine, Montesquieu, Hobbes, Locke, and most other social philosophers had recognized the interrelationships between cultural institutions and used these in their explanations of society. Montesquieu's dictum that "laws are necessary relationships resulting from the nature of things" can still be considered the basic tenet of functionalism, yet he and his followers were no modern functionalists. They asserted and often demonstrated the "necessary relations" between social institutions, but they did not always seek for the reasons behind them and did not construct a theory about functions. Even Saint-Simon and Comte, while using function as a major methodological tool, were more intent on creating their new science in the image of positivism, and left function itself largely unexplained.

In the writings of Émile Durkheim (1858–1917) the concept of function took on greater methodological significance, and he is widely regarded as a functionalist by sociologists and anthropologists alike. Yet, if a distinction is made between functionalism as a consistent theory and the use of function as a method of explaining certain social phenomena, Durkheim is not a functionalist in the first sense. While he used the notion of function quite extensively, his discussions about the meaning of function are relatively rare.

One of Durkheim's concerns was to establish sociology as an autonomous discipline. Although Comte had baptized the new science and enunciated some of its principles, sociology was not recognized in France until 1887, at which time Durkheim was appointed to a lectureship in social science at the University of Bordeaux. To many of his contemporaries, sociology appeared to be a dangerous innovation, and when Durkheim was called to the University of Paris in 1902, he occupied a chair of ethics and of philosophy of education, because sociology was so far nonexistent in the French capital.

In Durkheim's view, sociology had to be both autonomous and scientific if it was to have any future. Autonomous meant that its data and explanations must be independent from biology, psychology, or from any other science. Social data were to be explained by their own principles, but sociology must be on the same scientific footing as the natural sciences. Positivism dictated that science must deal with concrete and observable things. Durkheim found such "things" in the social realm in what he called "social facts." These facts were marked off from all other phenomena by their "exteriority" and their "constraint." Exteriority meant that they were given to an individual: social beliefs, duties, and practices were waiting for him ready-made at birth. Social facts were also constraining, because they were endowed with coercive powers and imposed themselves upon people regardless of their personal wills or desires.

These formulations create the impression that Durkheim was a superorganicist, conceiving of society as a reified entity residing in a separate realm and bending people to its will. In fact, this was just the opposite of what he had in mind. In his view society was completely inseparable from people not merely because, obviously, society cannot exist without its carriers, but more important because society makes man social.

This view differed sharply from Enlightenment rationalism, which had depicted man as the sole master of his fate, capable of freely selecting better ways of life, to liquidate the past, and to shed the constraints of religion. Durkheim felt strongly that social facts could not be so manipulated, but that there was a continuous interaction between man and society, and a necessary interrelationship between the two. Man was not the sole manager of society, but neither was he a robot, and in fact, it was "individualism" that had caused society to change. Individualism itself, however, was not of a completely personal nature, but was itself somehow a social fact that had progressed and evolved through its interaction with other social institutions.

Durkheim described these developments in his *The Division of Labor in Society* (1893) and demonstrated how individualism both moved the course of social development and was stimulated by the resulting changes. Early societies were small and homogeneous. People had similar tasks, and thus also possessed similar values and emotions. This totality of social similitudes led to what Durkheim called "a collective or common conscience" (Durkheim 1964:79), or a set of social rules held in common and experienced in common. In such a situation, individualism could not find expression, and was weakly developed. The integration of this type of society was one of "mechanical solidarity," based upon the common values, in the absence of a division of labor. Those who attempted to express their individualism and broke social rules were severely punished by "repressive" laws, not so much for the purpose of correction, but because antisocial behavior threatened the solidarity without which these primitive societies could not persist.

In the course of time societies increased in size and complexity, so that social tasks could no longer be the same for everyone. In other words, a division of labor came into being, and the differentiation of social tasks also caused diversification of values and emotions. It was then that individualism could begin to assert itself. Certain personalities broke away from tradition and mechanical solidarity, and became the first political leaders:

Chiefs are, in fact, the first personalities to emerge from the social mass. Their exceptional situation, putting them beyond the level of others, gives them a distinct physiognomy and accordingly confers individuality upon them. In dominating society, they are no longer forced to follow all of its movements. . . . A source of initiative is thus opened which had not existed before then. There is, hereafter, someone who can produce new things and even, in certain measure, deny collective usages. Equilibrium has been broken.

(Durkheim 1964:195)

Mechanical integration could no longer be operative when this trend further developed. A new form of integration had to come into being, because people were no longer of one mind and pursued different goals. These goals themselves were socially organized in and through division of labor. Division of labor reduced competition and assigned different tasks to different people, who thus became increasingly mutually dependent. The new form of integration was called by Durkheim "organic solidarity," which meant that division of labor itself had integrative powers. The term "organic" was borrowed from biology, but Durkheim noted that there was an important difference between the biological and the social realms. In the organism, each cell had a defined role and was unable to change it, while men, even in rigid social systems, were not so predetermined and possessed always a certain degree of liberty. As division of labor increased, liberty increased also.

The change from homogeneous to heterogeneous was thus explained as an interaction between social and individual factors. Individualism, in Durkheim's view, was not a personal pursuit of happiness or a decision to banish religion, but an almost necessary development in the growth of society. The ultimate cause of change was the natural increase in population that brought about an increased "moral density." This was not merely a matter of larger numbers, but also related to degree of communication. If communication increases, people will also have to cooperate more, and if populations also increase in numbers, the communicating and cooperating segments will differentiate themselves from other such segments. Perhaps not overly satisfied with this explanation, Durkheim also appealed to Darwinian theory to explain how differentiation may arise. Since organisms everywhere struggled with one another, such competition would evolve in human societies also. Durkheim thus did not take social change for granted, but searched for explanations of how the transition from mechanical to organic types of society could have taken place. While the change had been a progressive one in as far as social personalities could better express themselves, individuals were not necessarily happier in modern societies than in traditional ones. Durkheim felt that "anomie" —absence of norms—had entered, threatening society with disintegration. Individualism was desirable in itself, but contained inherent dangers because it might divorce people from society. In *Suicide* (1897), Durkheim continued the analysis of pathological aspects of modern society, but the topic was also selected because it demonstrated the coercion of social facts even in these seemingly most personal decisions. Moreover, the occurrence of suicide illustrated in the most striking manner the interrelationships between the individual and the collectivity.

Using statistical tabulations, Durkheim showed how there were no consistent correlations between rates of suicide and organic or psychic dispositions, race, poverty, insanity, personal unhappiness, and similar personal factors, and he also ruled out heredity. There may be psychological or biological predispositions, but since frequencies of suicide remained fairly constant in given societies or regions, they must be due mainly to social determinants.

He distinguished three types of suicide: altruistic, egoistic, and anomic. Each one was related to existing degrees of mechanical or organic solidarity in specific societies. Altruistic suicide was most clearly related to mechanical solidarity. One of his examples was the practice of suttee in India, where a Hindu widow throws herself on the funeral pyre of her husband's body and is cremated with him. She thus follows the commands of her society without asserting her individualism. Egoistic suicide was committed most often in transient types of society, where mechanical solidarity had diminished and organic solidarity was not yet in full force. People who developed strong individualism and were thus not integrated with the social group committed suicide most often in such circumstances. Anomic suicide, finally, was the type that predominated in societies with organic solidarity, and it increased in times of social stress and unrest. This type of suicide was related to the presence of strong individualism which often gave rise to social expectations that could not be realized. The increase in anomic suicide rates revealed the pathological aspects of modern society which in turn were related to lack of integration of the individual with his society. Durkheim attempted to demonstrate that neither family nor religion nor state or government could provide a context of integration in modern societies, and felt that only "corporations" or professional organizations could reintegrate society. This was the Durkheimian version of socialism, and it was also his moral philosophy, namely that social facts must be constraining by their authority, and that man should live willingly, and even happily, by these commands.

Like Comte before him, Durkheim turned to the analysis of religion toward the end of his life. Coming from a family with a long lineage of rabbis, he had broken away from its tradition and become agnostic. But throughout his life he remained convinced that religion was a social fact acting as a moral force. Unlike Comte, Durkheim did not repudiate any of his previous theories when he began to write about religion, but he considered his last book, *The Elementary Forms of the Religious Life* (1912), a summing up of his whole sociology. He wanted to demonstrate that religion was a social fact *par excellence,* and said that Comte was wrong when he believed that one individual could create a new religion. He also attacked Tylor, Spencer, Frazer, and all others who had explained religion in individualistic and cognitive terms as a "belief" in supernatural powers. Moreover, he took exception to any description of religion as a primitive error, based upon false logic or on erroneous interpretations of the world. To the contrary:

The most barbarous and the most fantastic rites and the strangest myths translate some human need, some aspect of life, either individual or social. The reasons with which the faithful justify them may be, and generally are, erroneous; but the true reasons do not cease to exist, and it is the duty of science to discover them. In reality, then, there are no religions which are false. All are true in their own fashion; all answer, though in different ways, to the given conditions of human existence.

(Durkheim 1961:15)

Religion was not an illusion, not an idle fantasy, but an identifiable social fact with important social meanings and functions. The study of religion then is a study of the social reality that it expresses.

Durkheim started the analysis of religion with his well-known distinction between the sacred and the profane. These were two separate realms of cognition: the sacred is a set of rituals and objects set apart from the profane by special prohibitions, dispensations, and prescriptions that do not pertain to everyday life. Religion is then "a unified system of beliefs and practices relative to sacred things . . . which unite into one single moral community . . . all those who adhere to them" (*ibid.*:62) The question was how the sacred could have arisen. To answer this, Durkheim turned to "the most primitive and simple religion which it was possible to find" (*ibid.*: 115), namely the totemism of Australian aborigines. Their society was "perfectly homogeneous," their civilization "most rudimentary," and their social organization was "the most simple which is actually known." They lived in small nomadic groups, but several such groups considered themselves related by bonds of kinship. This larger social unit, the "clan," gathered together at specific times when food was plentiful. Clans had their own names, taken most often from a species of plants or animals, their "totem." Each totem had its visual representation in an emblem, serving as proof of identity with the clan. This collective label was often engraved on objects of stone or wood, tattooed or drawn on the body, or carved on shields and ornaments.

From these ethnographic data (based mainly on the writings of Spencer and Gillen), Durkheim reconstructed what might have been the origin of religion. The small nomadic groups were normally very busy with hunting, fishing, or the gathering of wild seeds, and their life was uniform and dull. When the yearly meetings took place, however, everything was different. People met their kinsmen and heard the latest news, there was plenty of food, wives were exchanged, young men underwent initiation rites, and everyone wore his or her most beautiful decorations. The conditions during the time when the clan was united were thus very far removed from those when the smaller bands wandered around in isolation from each other. The clan gatherings were festive and exciting, and the primitive aborigines almost lost control over themselves and their emotions:

One can readily conceive how, when arrived at this state of exaltation, a man does not recognize himself any longer. Feeling himself dominated and carried away by some sort of external power which makes him think and act differently than in normal times, he naturally has the impression of being himself no longer. It seems to him that he has become a new being: the decorations he puts on and the masks that cover his face figure materially in this interior transformation, and to a still greater extent, they aid in determining its nature. And as at the same time all of his companions feel themselves transformed in the same way and express their sentiment by their cries, their gestures and their general attitude, everything is just as though he really were transported into a special world, entirely different from the one where he ordinarily lives, and into an environment filled with exceptionally intense forces that take hold of him and metamorphose him. How could such experiences as these, especially when they are repeated every day for weeks, fail to leave in him the conviction that there really exist two heterogeneous and mutually incomparable worlds? One is that where his daily life drags wearily along; but he cannot penetrate into the other without at once entering into relations with extraordinary powers that excite him to the point of frenzy. The first is the profane world, the second, that of sacred things.

(Ibid.: 249–50)

The "world of sacred things" thus came into existence through the unification of the clan. The clan itself was symbolized and made visible through the totemic emblems that were all around during these festive meetings, and it became the sacred entity. Religious power—religion itself—was thus nothing other than the collective power of the clan, and the totem representing it became the god of society. It was toward this impersonal power that worship was directed. Since totems (or societies) endure and are more permanent than any one individual, totems (or societies) are external to man and superior to him. Religion is thus a social reality that develops moral forces in man, and because these morals are those of society itself, they must be obeyed.

Durkheim described and analyzed totemism for entirely different reasons than nineteenth-century evolutionists did. The latter tried to establish the absolute origin of religion as a historical fact, in attempts to discover *how* it happened. Durkheim, however, wanted to know *why* it happened, and took a simple society as his point of reference in order to discover the essential social characteristics of religion in general. These characteristics remained the same throughout history. Totemism was not different from the most advanced religions, only the appearances differed. Gods may be personal or impersonal, rituals may be simple or complex, but everywhere religion distinguishes between profane and sacred realms, everywhere it is essentially social, and everywhere it symbolizes moral and social interests. The function of religion is thus that it reaffirms society, and it also reaffirms man as a social being.

It is clear that for Durkheim the concept of function is inseparable from his basic concept of society, namely that it is *sui generis,* representing a reality of its own. Function was thus not the serving of needs of individuals, but of the needs of society. It is this concept that separates Durkheim most sharply from later British functionalists. The latter often transferred Durkheim's social functions to an individual level, and discussed them in terms of biological, psychological, or personal human needs. His French followers understood him better. Henri Hubert (1872–1927) and Marcel Mauss (1872–1950) absorbed their teacher's notion of function as a social phenomenon, and they also turned to the analysis of nonliterate societies as a starting point for the understanding of universal social conditions. Mauss applied Durkheim's theory of religion to Eskimo society (1904), and also wrote a famous essay, "The Gift" (1925), in which he showed that in simple societies economic exchange often takes the form of ritual gift giving. Together with Hubert he wrote on sacrifice (1898), and the two scholars also collaborated on a study of magic (1902–03).

This period of French sociology exhibited a general interest in primitivism. Lucien Lévy-Bruhl (1857–1939) first wrote books on the social philosophy of Jacobi and of Comte, but he became intrigued by primitive modes of thought later in his life, perhaps influenced by Durkheim and Mauss, who were among his many friends. After reading some ethnographic works, Lévy-Bruhl noted strong similarities between the thought patterns of all primitives, and at the same time he found that their ways of thinking were very different from Western ones. Opposing the psychic unity theory which held that the functions of the mind were identical everywhere, Lévy-Bruhl became persuaded that primitive peoples possessed a mentality different not only in degree but also in quality from that of civilized man. Primitive thought was to him collective thought, and it was characterized not merely by a lack of abstraction, but by a logic different from ours. It obeyed a "mystical" principle, which meant that it assumed the belief in invisible forces, and considered them absolutely real. Primitive peoples followed the "law of participation," because in their view things could be at the same time themselves and something else, and this idea is excluded from Western logic. As a result, primitive peoples experienced the world in a manner different from modern man, and Lévy-Bruhl called this mentality "prelogical."

It is not surprising that Lévy-Bruhl has been strongly criticized by anthropologists, because his theories shake at the very foundations of anthropological field work and analysis. If the mind of nonliterate man was of a different nature, civilized anthropologists could never fully grasp its workings. All ethnographies would be erroneous, for field workers have assumed that their data can be meaningfully analyzed in universal terms. But his critics often misunderstood his aims. Lévy-Bruhl felt that cultures can be legitimately studied by analyzing how patterned modes of thinking give rise to patterned social behavior. In this respect he has much in common with the culture-and-personality school of modern anthropology, and he may be called one of the pioneers of this important movement. He certainly misrepresented primitive peoples, but in fact he was attempting to investigate systematically the unproven assumptions of Tylor, Frazer, Morgan, and many others who built imposing schemes of origin and development based upon the idea that primitive man was nonscientific and illogical. Lévy-Bruhl stressed that primitives were capable of reason but possessed different categories of logic.

In a way, Lévy-Bruhl became his own best critic. In his posthumously published *Carnets* (1949) he wrote:

. . . let us expressly rectify what I believed correct in 1910: there is not a primitive mentality distinguishable from the other by two characteristics which are peculiar to it (mystical and prelogical). There is a mystical mentality which is more marked and more easily observable among "primitive peoples" than in our societies, but it is present in every human mind.

Primitive mentality did thus not imply the acceptance of logical contradictions, but nonliterate man accepted ideas that later were proven wrong. In other words, it was not a matter of logic, but of knowledge.

Although Lévy-Bruhl borrowed some ideas from Comte and Durkheim, he did not consider himself a sociologist. Durkheim himself and his French followers remained committed to their science even if they made extensive use of ethnographic data. In England, however, Alfred Reginald Radcliffe-Brown (1881–1955) felt that the social study of nonliterate peoples constituted a separate branch of science, namely "social anthropology." This science was by no means to be confused with the already existing Tylorian anthropology, because, according to Radcliffe-Brown, this was not a true science at all, and in fact it was not even anthropology, but "ethnology."

Radcliffe-Brown began his career as a student of W. H. R. Rivers in psychology, but became his first pupil in social anthropology in the year 1904. Rivers was always strongly interested in history, and in 1906 Radcliffe-Brown was sent out to the Andaman Islands, charged with the task of reconstructing the culture history of their nonliterate inhabitants. In the absence of written records, this was well-nigh impossible, and the young field worker was averse to making hypothetical or conjectural reconstructions. He dutifully recorded Andamanese myths, ceremonies, and customs, but the publication of his findings was delayed for almost fifteen years. Meanwhile, he became acquainted with the writings and theories of Durkheim and Mauss, and concluded that it was more important to study meanings and functions. When *The Andaman Islanders* appeared in print in 1922, it reflected the new insights. Andaman myths and customs were not only recorded but also interpreted, which meant "the discovery not of origins, but of meanings." Defending his position, Radcliffe-Brown wrote that past attempts to reconstruct history not only had been conjectural but were of very doubtful scientific and practical value. Ethnologists had not been historians but pseudo-historians. History was the reconstruction of the past based upon written records, but since nonliterate peoples by definition did not possess such documents, ethnological studies had been anomalous. In contrast, social anthropology was to be based upon strictly scientific principles, and in Radcliffe-Brown's thoughts the two major criteria of science were verifiability and the establishment of universal laws. Biology was in this sense an exemplary science, and Radcliffe-Brown applied its models to the explanation of the workings of society in a very strong way:

> Every custom and belief of a primitive society plays some determinate part in the social life of the community, just as every organ of a living body plays some part in the general life of the organism. The mass of institutions, customs and beliefs forms a single whole or system that determines the life of the society, and the life of the society is not less real, or less subject to natural laws, than the life of an organism.
>
> (Radcliffe-Brown 1964:229–30)

There were other differences as well between social anthropology and ethnology, because ethnology was ideographic, and could at best tell that certain things had happened, which served no practical purposes. Social anthropology, however, was nomothetic or explanatory. As such it could be of immense service, because it would discover universal laws of human behavior. This practicality was not conceived in terms of Durkheimian moral philosophy, but rather within a framework of British colonial policy. Social anthropology might assist in the administration and education of "backward peoples," or it could help the public servant engaged in dealing with the practical problems of the adjustment of the native civilization to the new conditions that resulted from occupation of the country, or assist the missionary to get rid of witchcraft (Radcliffe-Brown 1958:39–41). His faith in applied anthropology was the logical outcome of his admiration of the results of the natural sciences, which had also contributed to the welfare of mankind.

Radcliffe-Brown's arguments for a separation between ethnology and social anthropology resembled Durkheim's differentiation between causal and functional studies. But while Durkheim felt that both were legitimate and useful undertakings, Radcliffe-Brown saw no need for a concern with causes. Social anthropology was to him the sociology of nonliterate peoples, and in these simple societies the general laws of social existence would be much easier to detect than in complex ones. A sociological law was defined by him as "a necessary condition of continued existence" (Radcliffe-Brown 1952:43), but it cannot be said that he discovered any startling new laws. One of his "laws" was that there exists "a certain degree of functional consistency amongst the constituent parts of the social system" (*ibid.*:43). It may well be argued that this statement merely recognizes the regularities of culture, and that it is rather far-fetched to call this a "law." Yet, it is at this point that Radcliffe-Brown made a most profound observation, one that was overlooked or neglected by many of his followers, namely that functional consistency is not the same as logical consistency, and that the two often are in conflict. Social systems never obtain a perfect functional consistency, and it is for this reason that they constantly undergo change. Radcliffe-Brown himself did not often deal with change, because he felt that the first order of business was to describe and order the social phenomena themselves, and to discover their cross-cultural regularities. Later functionalists often emphasized social solidarity and functional integration so much that their analyses were static and precluded the explanation of change.

Radcliffe-Brown also accused ethnologists of psychological reductionism, because they sometimes attempted to explain customs and beliefs in terms of mental processes of the individual. He did not object to psychology in its own right, but felt that social phenomena cannot be explained in psychological terms. Furthermore, individual behavior as studied by psychologists was not scientific in that psychologists neglected to note that seemingly individual notions and actions were conditioned by society. But Radcliffe-Brown did not subordinate the individual to society in the same manner as Durkheim. He recognized that members of a society often consciously initiated social change when they became aware of the inconsistencies of their social system. Particularly in his earlier writings, he often presented what may be called sociopsychological explanations. The Andamanese weeping rite, for instance, demanded that people who had been separated for some time embrace each other and weep together upon meeting again. This obligatory social action served to "relieve emotional tensions." Similarly, dancing at peace-making ceremonies functioned to "appease collective anger," and thus the newly established peaceful relations became realized and internalized.

More frequently, however, Radcliffe-Brown explained the functions of social customs in terms of adaptive mechanisms, enabling human beings to live in an ordered world:

By the function of an institution I mean the part it plays in the total system of social integration of which it is a part. By using that phrase, social integration, I am assuming that the function of culture as a whole is to unite individual human beings into more or less stable structures . . . as to make possible an ordered social life.

(Radcliffe-Brown 1958:62)

In the 1930's Radcliffe-Brown began to develop his concept of social structure, which eventually took on the greatest significance in his theories. Structure in general is the ordered arrangement of the parts as it appears, for instance, in music, in language, or in a building. Similarly, social structure is the ordered arrangement of social elements or processes which together form the unity of a social system. The constituent units of the social parts are human beings who occupy social positions or statuses, and as such the study of social structure can take on various dimensions. It may refer to the interrelationships and functions of persistent social groups such as nations, but also to interpersonal social relationships, as are found in kinship relations. Also the differentiation of individuals and of classes by means of their social roles is an aspect of structure, but they become structural only in as far as they are recurrent.

In order to illustrate the relationship between structure and function, Radcliffe-Brown turned once again to biology. The structure of an organism consists of the ordered arrangements of its parts, and the function of the parts is to interrelate the structure of an organism consists of the ordered arrangements social function is the interconnection between social structure and social life. Physiological phenomena are not simply the result of the nature of the cells, but the cells are organized in specific ways, so that the various organs function to make continued existence possible. Likewise, social structure is not to be studied by considering the nature of individual members of the group, but by examining the arrangements of the functions that make society persistent.

The importance of this differentiation between structure and function is that it can be applied to the study both of continuity in forms of social life and of processes of change. Moreover, it allows for more scientific comparative studies than could be made by Durkheim, whose concept of function implied content as well as meaning. Radcliffe-Brown, however, was well aware that similar things may have different meanings in different cultures, and also that different things may have similar functions. Comparisons, in order to have any value at all, should search for comparable structures, which meant that they must have comparable social functions also, although their *individual* meanings and functions may well be incomparable.

Another important outcome of Radcliffe-Brown's position was that field work was to be carried out by observers fully trained in the theory of social anthropology as well as in methods of scientific observation. Radcliffe-Brown demanded that his students should begin by making intensive studies of single cultures, observing the data, formulating hypotheses, and testing those by further direct observation. Once a sufficient number of cultures had thus been examined, comparisons could be made, and, hopefully, laws would emerge.

Throughout his academic career, Radcliffe-Brown stressed the importance of comparative method, and he gave it new dimensions. In older anthropology, comparative method was the reconstruction of the past by extrapolating from contemporary primitive societies, and things that were similar were generally accepted as indicating historical connections. In social anthropology, however, the purpose of comparison was to explore institutions of present-day societies in terms of their structural-functional similarities and differences. Comparative studies could thus be carried out synchronically and diachronically. In a synchronic study a culture is analyzed at a given moment of its history, so that its regularities and conditions of existence may be defined. A great many diverse types of cultures must then be compared in order to find the universal beneath the multitudinous differences. Diachronic studies seek to discover the ways in which cultures change, and the general laws governing these processes of change. Radcliffe-Brown himself did not make many diachronic studies, and neither did he compare whole cultures. Instead he attempted to establish cross-cultural correlations between specific segments of society such as totemism, political systems, kinship systems, and so forth. Many of his followers also tended toward specialization in specific social institutions, and became averse to the Tylorian notion of culture as a whole, arguing that it was too vast and too vague an entity to be handled by a single field worker.

Radcliffe-Brown's understanding of function was in many ways similar to that of his predecessors. Most every social philosopher had realized that social phenomena are interrelated, and together constitute the social whole. But no one had deemed it necessary to explain what function was. The concept was used eclectically, and it was often considered to be as axiomatic as progress or natural law. Function was a principle of explanation that itself was not explained. To Radcliffe-Brown, function was more than a recognition of reality. It was, to him, a very specific manner of analysis, one that could not be confused with any other method, and above all it was scientific. Function itself thus needed justification, and it is only when principles of explanation themselves are explained that one can identify a method. This is why Radcliffe-

Brown is a "functionalist" and not just a user of function. In fact, since the concept of structure became wedded to that of function, Radcliffe-Brown and his followers are often called "structural-functionalists" mainly to distinguish them from Malinowskian "functionalists."

Radcliffe-Brown considered his specific kind of social analysis superior to all previous methods of explanation. It could relate how and why societies were organized in their specific manner, it could explain cultural similarities and differences, and it could generate "laws" about social behavior. Radcliffe-Brown knew well that his science was still far removed from achieving these goals, because he felt that older field data were not useful and there were not yet enough "scientific" descriptions of cultures made by field workers trained in the methods of social anthropology. "The subject is still in its formative stages," he wrote in 1931, and twenty years later, in 1951: "We do not yet have a systematic general typology of kinship systems, for the construction of such is a laborious undertaking." Some twenty years after his death, his hopes for the discovery of generally valid predictive laws have not been realized. Many variant interpretations of structure and function have since been advanced, and an enormous amount of field work has been carried out that has greatly contributed toward our understanding of structures and functions but has not uncovered any unambiguous laws.

Radcliffe-Brown did not define social anthropology as functionalism, and at one point even claimed to be an antifunctionalist. But this statement had less to do with his concepts of function than with his relationship to Bronislaw Malinowski (1884–1942), who claimed that he was the "father" of functionalism. Radcliffe-Brown strongly disagreed with Malinowski's notions of function, and called functionalism "a myth invented by Malinowski," adding:

As for myself, I reject it entirely, regarding it as useless and worse. As a consistent opponent of Malinowski's functionalism I may be called an antifunctionalist.

(Radcliffe-Brown 1949:320–21)

Many later commentators became as critical as Radcliffe-Brown about Malinowski's brand of functionalism. But even the most severe critics have praised him for the excellence of his field work, which set standards that are still adhered to. Malinowski stayed in the Trobriand Islands for longer than anyone before him had remained in the field, lived among native peoples, and initiated the method of participant observation. He conducted his research in the native language, and from his writings informants emerged as living personalities rather than anonymous data-providers. Paying attention to all kinds of details of everyday life, he described the routine of a man's working day, the care he took of his body, his personal ambitions, passing friendships, as well as the tone of conversations, the laughing and weeping, thus conveying to his readers a sense of the actuality of Trobriand life. He also indicated that the first few weeks of field work were most difficult, but that eventually he began

to take part . . . in the village life, to look forward to the important or festive events, to take personal interest in the group and the developments of small village occurrences; to wake up every morning to a day, presenting itself to me more or less as it does to the native. . . . With this, and with the capacity of enjoying their company and sharing some of their games and amusements, I began to feel that I was indeed in touch with the natives, and this is certainly the preliminary condition of being able to carry on fieldwork.

(Malinowski 1961:7–8)

In 1967, long after his death, Malinowski's widow decided to publish his personal diaries, kept in 1914–15 and 1917–18, which are the years spent mostly on the Trobriand Islands. Written in Polish, Malinowski's native language, and never intended for publication, they gave a unique insight into Malinowski's own personality, and revealed the problems of field work and of adjustment to long periods of isolation in alien surroundings.

Some sample statements:

The old man began to lie about burials. I became enraged. (1967:35)

The stench, smoke, noise of people, dogs and pigs . . . greatly
irritated me.   (*Ibid.*:54)

Sick. Fever. And a violent toothache.   (*Ibid.*:61)

With great effort . . . I wormed out of him material relating to
kinship.   (*Ibid.*:66)

I often long for culture . . . Beethoven's melodies.   (*Ibid.*:150)

I was fed up with the niggers and with my work.   (*Ibid.*:154)

Everyone who prepares to go into the field for the first time
should read the diaries to achieve awareness that far from being
romantic, field work is often frustrating and strenuous, both
physically and psychologically. Malinowski was perhaps more
obsessed about his health than many other people are, and
he was also perhaps overly preoccupied with his relations
to his mother and his future wife, but culture shock and
isolation will tend to magnify a field worker's personal worries.
Malinowski undoubtedly used his diary as an emotional outlet, and it is a unique record of personal honesty.

Malinowski's early writings do not manifest a great deal
of interest in function. In his first Trobriand monograph, *The
Argonauts of the Western Pacific* (1922), he wrote that the
final goal of field work is "to grasp the native's point of view,
of his relation to life, to realize *his* vision of *his* world," adding
that "perhaps through realizing human nature in a shape
very distant and foreign to us, we shall have some light shed
on our own" (Malinowski 1961:25). This can hardly be
called a typical functionalist view, and it is not surprising that
English reviews of the *Argonauts* treated it simply as another
ethnography. Malinowski achieved fame after writing a piece
for the prestigious periodical *Nature* entitled "Psycho-analysis
and Anthropology" (1923). In it he explained that Trobriand
society is matrilineal, and that in their family life the mother's
brother takes on many authoritative tasks and responsibilities
which are assigned to the father in Western society. Having
read Freud's theories about the universality of the Oedipus
complex while he was in the field, Malinowski found that

much of the repressed hatred of the father was among the Trobriands directed against the maternal uncle. The Oedipus theory thus stood in need of reexamination, even more because Trobriand sex life was rather permissive and sexual frustrations were almost absent. This article became the subject of a long series of published controversies of which the English public is so fond. Malinowski quickly took advantage of the attention he received, and wrote a number of books with "sexy" titles, among these *Sex and Repression in Savage Society* (1927) and *The Sexual Life of Savages* (1929). Undoubtedly to the disappointment of some readers, he dealt more with social organization and family life than with sex.

Gradually, however, Malinowski developed his theory of function, in part because he, too, became imbued with the need to make his explanations more scientific. An erudite and well-read scholar, Malinowski was aware of the writings of the French sociologists, but he chose to ally his understanding of function to field-work research. In his thoughts about this matter function was a specific way of understanding institutions and customs of primitive life. In his famous essay "Magic, Science and Religion" (1925) he saw functions largely as fulfilling psychological needs. Magic was "the standardization of optimism," serving to provide man with the necessary confidence to "carry out his important tasks, to maintain his poise and his mental integrity in fits of anger, in the throes of hate, of unrequited love, of despair and anxiety" (1954:90). Also religion opened up escapes from emotional stress. Apart from these functions for the individual, religion also makes social contributions, because it "assists in the maintenance of moral law and order" (*ibid.*:54), and works toward "the identification of the whole tribe as a social unit" (*ibid.*:55). Eventually, Malinowski related psychological and social functions to biological ones. Optimism and confidence enabled Trobrianders to become better food providers, and magic thus also contributed to physical survival. This notion of function as serving biological needs became the core of Malinowski's functional theory. In his posthumous methodological book *A Scientific Theory of*

Culture (1944) he reiterated his conviction that the functional method of investigation is best suited to give an accurate picture of the realities of culture. He warned that the aim of field work was not to discover function, but that function was a heuristic device, a method toward understanding "what actually happens and what can be observed." Yet he realized that even heuristic devices stood in need of explanation, and he began to spell out the basic biological needs of man and their specific cultural responses as follows:

Basic needs	*Cultural responses*
Metabolism	Commissariat
Reproduction	Kinship
Bodily comforts	Shelter
Safety	Protection
Movement	Activities
Growth	Training
Health	Hygiene

(Malinowski 1960:91)

In other words, culture was adaptive, and without the satisfaction of basic biological needs neither man nor culture itself could survive. These responses were universal, showing what the main business of culture is and always has been. A great many cultural activities were directly related to these primary biological wants. Unlike animals, man did not resort directly to nature, but responses to basic needs were made in cultural ways. Hunger must be satisfied, but man prepares his food, making use of fire and cooking utensils; he does not consume his food alone but shares it with others; and he develops ritual attitudes to this communal consumption. Hence his fire, his implements, and his rituals relate culturally to the satisfaction of primary biological wants. There were many other cultural activities that could not be so interpreted. Man has no biological need to build airplanes or submarines or steam engines, yet he has done so. Malinowski called these "derived needs," and held that they were ultimately, not directly, related to the wants of the organism, because they extended man's safety and his comforts, or increased his speed and power of production. Even art, religion, ethics, or research, although several steps removed, could in Malinowski's view be traced back to primary biological necessities.

Although Malinowski did not speculate *how* culture arose, he had no doubts as to *why* it came into being: it was a means to human survival. Man's anatomical endowment, compared to other animals, was somewhat limited: he was naked, unarmed and unprotected, lacking fangs, claws, or similar natural weapons. Instead, he invented tools and implements, relied on cooperation with his comrades, and learned to communicate by means of symbolic language. Once culture had thus come into existence it provided a secondary environment which in turn extended man's needs. These "derived needs" became just as necessary for survival, because they catered to primary biological requirements, albeit often indirectly.

Malinowski has often been criticized for this aspect of his theory, not only because he reasoned in a somewhat circular fashion that culture was "indispensable," but also because when all things contribute toward survival, their functions are always positive, and dysfunction remains unexplained. Nevertheless, it was from this approach that Malinowski derived the important concept of institutions. In his definition, institutions were cultural units of human organization, centered around specific primary or derived needs. Each institution was thus an aspect of culture or a set of behavior patterns organized around an integrating principle. The need for reproduction, for instance, could be seen as such a principle, and it resulted in specific institutions, including the family, courtship, marriage, the extended family, and the clan; while territoriality, another integrating principle, produced bands, villages, towns, districts, or tribes. Other such principles listed included occupation, status, political power; each with their own corresponding sets of institutions. The actual scheme that Malinowski constructed was fairly elaborate, consisting of an outline in columns that could be read vertically and horizontally. The vertical reading would give an overview of the major social institutions of a specific group, while horizontal readings would reveal how these institutions were connected to particular cultural aspects. Thus the family, as one institution based upon the need for reproduction, could be related to its material aspects, to its kinship usages, its religious orientation, its political affiliations, and so on. In other words, Malinowski devised a general framework very suitable for the systematic collection and organization of field data, lending itself also to cross-cultural comparisons.

Intelligent field work and interpretation of its data remained Malinowski's main purpose. The aim of field work was not to discover function or institutions—to the contrary, the theory of function was an aid in field work, a method toward understanding "what actually occurs and what can be observed." It was Malinowski's answer to the trait-list approach: culture was more than a collection of facts or a set of exotic customs. Rather, it was a functioning and thus a functional whole, to be understood in its relationship to man's biology and his environment.

It is this view that sets Malinowski apart from Radcliffe-Brown and the structural functionalists. He was not concerned so much with the discovery of laws, but first and foremost with the understanding of the observable realities of culture. He felt that this understanding must take into account the variables of physical environment and man's biology, since both interacted with one another and with culture. He wrote:

Professor Radcliffe-Brown is, as far as I can see, still developing and deepening the views of the French sociological school. He thus has to neglect the individual and disregard biology. Functionalism differs from other sociological theories more definitely, perhaps, in its conception and definition of the individual than in any other respect. The functionalist includes in his analysis not merely the emotional as well as the intellectual side of mental processes, but also insists that man in his full biological reality has to be drawn into our analysis of culture. The bodily needs and environmental influences, and the cultural relation to them, have thus to be studied side by side.   (Malinowski 1939:939)

Malinowski did not attempt to account for origins of institutions or other cultural items, not only because he felt that they could not be discovered, but also because they were unnecessary for his type of explanation. He was not interested in causality, but in utility; his concern was not with the past, but with the here-and-now. In his earlier years he had followed the then fashionable trend of debunking historical explanations, but later on he admitted that history presented a different approach: history attempted to explain how cultures had become what they were now, while Malinowski wanted to understand why they existed in their present form. It was not so much a question of the truth of history, but of its relevance for the understanding of present-day societies. Malinowski did not consider the two approaches incompatible or mutually exclusive. They were, rather, "complementary and inevitably correlated." Malinowski was thus not antihistorical as is so often maintained, but he was influenced by positivism and frowned upon speculations. It was true enough that evolutionists had been conjectural, and that their reconstructions about origins were not verifiable by scientific method.

It could be asked, however, if the posited functional integration of the cultural whole is itself a verifiable hypothesis. This question is of some importance, because it is directly related to another one: if cultures are such well-functioning integrated wholes, why then do they change? Malinowski was fully aware of this problem and attempted to answer it in a variety of ways. In the first place, he attributed change to diffusion, more particularly "the impact of a higher, active culture upon a simpler, more passive one" (1961:15). But this statement merely begged the question, because it provided no answer as to *why* people should accept elements of the "higher" culture. Malinowski added that some small communities which so far had little contact with Western civilization were in a temporary state of adjustment, and could thus be considered as integral wholes. Moreover, even if missionaries, traders, or Western administrators were present, the society had also adjusted itself to them, and yet had remained a balanced whole. In other words, Malinowski did not explain how change came about, but proposed that once a simple non-Western society was invaded by Western civilization, the interaction between the two, and especially the responses of the natives, could be studied and analyzed. He thus remained present-oriented: the changes of the past were of little concern, but the actuality of ongoing culture contacts and their results were valuable and important topics of research.

Many followers of Malinowski and Radcliffe-Brown neglected and often explicitly rejected historical explanations of any kind, either because they were uninterested in change or unable to explain it. It was a rather happy discovery that previously maligned "savage customs" such as witchcraft, cannibalism, or infanticide had their *raisons d'être* in the cultures where they appeared. If no specific functions could be discovered, it was always possible to state that the existence of a ritual or of warfare contributed to the maintenance of the whole, or else they had psychological functions. Undoubtedly this was all true and logical, and it is important enough to understand the workings of societies other than our own. But the explanations were often facile and circular. Societies were viewed as if they were well-oiled machines, their various parts working well and contemporaneously. Cultural customs and institutions were generally depicted as reducing conflicts and tensions, but why conflicts arose in the first place remained unexplained.

In the course of time many field workers became dissatisfied with this lack of dynamism. The cultures they studied often displayed conflict, and were by no means in perfect balance. In other words, they rediscovered Radcliffe-Brown's distinction between functional and logical consistency, and searched for ways to take both into account so that they could deal with change without abandoning the useful notions of structure and function.

In his *Political Systems of Highland Burma* (1954), E. R. Leach proposed a creative solution by considering conflict itself as a form of structure. The social system in the Highland Burma area was such that it presented individuals with inconsistencies in the schemes of values by which they ordered their lives, and they were thus faced with alternative modes of actions. Leach believed that such decisions were usually made in terms of gaining power to acquire access to office, or of earning social esteem that would lead to increased power (Leach 1954:10). He presented a wealth of evidence that this was indeed one of the primary mechanisms of change among the Kachin and Shan populations of Burma. They consciously attempted to manipulate their myths and marriage choices in manners that would increase their status. Although the cross-cultural validity of Leach's specific explanation has not been proven, his method is very important. He explained change not by preconceived causal factors, but from the realities of Kachin and Shan life. In his hands functionalism became dynamic and diachronic.

Another British social anthropologist who disliked synchronic functionalism was Raymond Firth. He equally proposed that variations of actual behavior should be observed and recorded in order to discover the processes of change. Like Leach, he noted that individuals are often faced with a choice between alternative modes of behavior, but in Firth's view the decisions are not necessarily made in terms of optimization of power but according to personal evaluations of efficiency toward any given goal. These goals themselves are not random, but formulated by the groups and subgroups to which individuals belong. These subgroups are both internally structured and interrelated with one another, so as to structure society as a whole. Individuals belong to several subgroups, determined by criteria of kinship, marriage, occupation, economics, status, class, religion, and so forth. Since memberships in these groups are overlapping, conflicts of choice of action will often arise, because what is efficient within the framework of the one may well be detrimental for membership in another. Firth hoped that intensive studies of these choices and conflicts would lead to the explanation of change not only in single societies, but also on a cross-cultural level, so that "laws" of change may eventually be discovered (Firth 1956:237–58).

The renewed interest in change and diachronic explanations moved several British anthropologists to return to considerations of history. Most explicit and most extreme among those is E. E. Evans-Pritchard, who, although declaring himself to be a functionalist and a follower in the footsteps of Radcliffe-Brown and Malinowski, nevertheless considered the search for "laws" a hopeless and even a rather inane undertaking:

Up to the present nothing even remotely resembling what are called laws in the natural sciences has been adduced—only rather naive deterministic, teleological, and pragmatic assertions. The generalizations which have so far been attempted have, moreover, been so vague and general as to be, even if true, of little use, and they have rather easily tended to become mere tautologies and platitudes on the level of common sense deduction.

(Evans-Pritchard 1964:57)

He diagnosed this failure as resulting from the insistence that social anthropology was a science on a par with all other sciences. This he called "doctrinaire positivism at its worst" (*ibid.*:57). Legal systems were not comparable to planetary or biological ones because social systems were not natural but moral or symbolic systems, and thus by their very nature incomparable. If there were any laws or regularities at all, they were to be sought in history, which would reveal that there are sequences of development in time. "History alone provides a satisfactory experimental situation in which the hypotheses of functional anthropology can be tested" (*ibid.*: 60). Evans-Pritchard thus redefined social anthropology as follows:

. . . social anthropology studies societies as moral, or symbolic, systems and not as natural systems, it is less interested in process than in design and therefore seeks patterns and not laws, demonstrates consistency and not necessary relations between social activities, and interprets rather than explains.   (*Ibid.*:62)

In fact, social anthropology "is best regarded as an art and not as a science" (*ibid.*:85).

Evans-Pritchard fully expected that most of his colleagues would be in disagreement with his statements. Indeed, many rose to the defense of the scientific status of their discipline. Meyer Fortes, for one, stated that "the functionalist point of view has always been concise and consistent" (1953:28), and had as its goal to search for general laws that could be discovered without the aid of history. Significant social analysis could thus be made regardless of the past. Fortes was convinced that social laws must exist because social life is not random. At the same time he was forced to admit that the combination of factors present on any particular occasion can never be predicted. Social laws thus refer to ideally isolated features of social life, and can be stated only in terms of probabilities. In fact, they would not have much reference to social reality at all.

In America, functionalism was accepted earlier by sociologists than by anthropologists. The latter had first to overcome the influence of Boas, who had opposed both evolutionism and functionalism, although he did not lack a functionalist perspective. This will be discussed in the next chapter. The two most influential leaders of American sociological functionalism are Talcott Parsons and Robert K. Merton. Both were critical of certain presuppositions of classical functionalism, and sought to refine its methods. The way was led by Parsons, who in his earlier writings used the concept of function uncritically, but began to scrutinize it later on (1951). Like his British counterparts, he became bothered by the problem of how to relate the static concept of structure to the dynamic aspects of social change, and he, too, formulated his conclusions in terms of conflicting values. Every society has certain necessary preconditions, because without such "functional imperatives" societies are unable to operate. But these imperatives are different for different social institutions. Kinship systems have different requirements than economic or political systems, and situations will arise where individuals will have to decide their course of action in terms of one or the other. In Parsons' system, such decisions are not guided by a desire for power or by any other personal advantage, but by the moral standards of society. The conflicts are, therefore, not between institutions, but between them and social morality. Human action is thus both functional and symbolic, and the tension between the two will lead to continuous change in both, always "straining" toward greater balance.

Robert Merton particularly opposed Malinowski's "postulates" of indispensability, of universality, and of functional integration (Merton 1957:30–37). Citing Malinowski's statement that "magic fulfills an indispensable function within culture. It satisfies a definite need which cannot be satisfied by any other factors of primitive civilization," Merton objects: "This twin concept of the indispensable function and the irreplaceable belief-and-action pattern flatly excludes the concept of functional alternatives" (*ibid.*:34).

Merton meant that social needs can be answered in many different ways, a point that Malinowski and other functionalists would not deny. But Malinowski did not consider magic irreplaceable in an overall sense. Rather, he insisted that in certain *primitive civilizations* functional alternatives for magic were absent and unavailable, and that therefore in those societies magic fulfilled an indispensable function. It was Malinowski's theory that magic was used primarily in precarious situations. The Trobrianders carried out a great deal of open-sea magic because their canoes were relatively fragile and unequipped with modern safety appliances. It was for this reason that magic was indispensable to them, but it could be replaced by scientific inventions, to which the Trobrianders thus far had not been introduced.

The difficulty may perhaps be related to the fact that Merton is a sociologist used to dealing with complex societies where functional alternatives are abundantly present in most every situation, while Malinowski's conceptual framework was that of relatively simple cultures where functional alternatives are much scarcer. Merton's own convincing analysis of functional alternatives and their consequences for change deals largely with the political machinery in American political structure, a situation hardly comparable to Trobriand fishing practices.

Merton further attempted to clarify the concept of function by introducing a distinction between latent and manifest functions. Manifest functions are those consciously recognized by members of a culture, latent ones are "neither intended nor recognized" by participants in the system (Merton 1957: 63). He used this distinction to account for the persistence of certain practices despite the fact that their manifest functions are not always successful. Hopi rain dances, for instance, are overtly carried out in order to produce rain. But rain does not always follow the ritual. Nevertheless, the ceremony has not disappeared, because, although unrecognized by the performers, it has the latent function of promoting group solidarity. There appears to be some logical inconsistency in Merton's explanation. If the rain ceremonies do not produce rain and the Hopi are unaware of its solidarity-promoting properties, the continuation of these practices appears to be a rather irrational affair. As Kaplan and Manners (1972:59) pointed out, there must be other manifest functions to account for their persistence. First of all, rain often follows afterward, and the Hopi may continue the ceremonies because they believe that it works. Moreover, they may well enjoy the getting together and the colorful ritual itself. The fact that the performances may indeed promote group solidarity is an accidental consequence which cannot account for the origin or persistence of the rain dance.

On the whole, American anthropologists have been more critical in their acceptance of "pure" functionalism than some of their British colleagues. Lowie already argued in favor of a "tempered" functionalism (Lowie 1937:230-49), while Kluckhohn, although first making a "functional" study of Navaho witchcraft (1967), became dissatisfied with functional theory because it dealt with structure but not with process (1962:261). He wrote that historical and functional approaches were not mutually exclusive alternatives, but necessary supplements of one another (*ibid*.:260). He made no specific recommendations how their integration could be achieved.

Clifford Geertz provided a stimulating answer to this question. Like many others, he deplored the inability of functionalism to explain change. Most functionalists emphasized the positive, integrative, and psychologically supportive aspects of culture elements, few dealt with the disruptive and dysfunctional aspects. Geertz felt that the major reason for the functionalists' inability to deal with social change was their failure to distinguish between cultural and social aspects of human life (1957:33). Although interrelated, they can be treated as independent variables. Culture is an ordered system of meanings, values, styles, and symbols which guide human action, while the social is the specific form of interaction itself. Individuals define their world and make their judgments in the framework of culture, but the specific form of their actions and interactions takes place within the framework of the actually existing network of social human relationships. The two are no mere mirror images of each other, but may well be conflicting.

Geertz illustrates this by referring to an observed funeral ceremony in a small town in eastern Java. Here culture prescribed that the funeral ritual should be conducted by a certain leader. But the latter refused to do so because of the fact that the family of the deceased belonged to a different religious-political party than the one he himself had come to embrace. The actual situation as Geertz described it was much more complex than that, but the facts remain the same: there was an incongruity between the cultural framework of meaning and the patterning of social interaction, in this specific case due to the persistence of a cultural tradition which clashed with the reality of social interrelationships in an urban environment. Change will thus undoubtedly take place in this instance.

CONCLUSIONS

It is the strength of functionalism that its generalizations are firmly rooted in direct observation of processes of interaction among people. The researches of function-oriented field workers have provided a great deal of penetrating ethnographic descriptions, and the analyses of integration and of interrelations between institutions have given many penetrating insights into the ways in which societies operate and maintain themselves. Malinowski intended functionalism to be heuristic, and it certainly has proven to be a good method of studying societies in the field. Its explanations require empirical facts, and the conjectural and hypothetical reconstructions of the past have thus been superseded.

The major criticisms launched at functional theory were its ahistorical orientation and its alleged inability to explain change. It appears, however, that this failure was not so much a fault inherent in the theory itself as one due to the idiosyncrasies of functionalist writers. Radcliffe-Brown admitted that much when he said that he had a "temperamental preference" for looking forward rather than looking back over the past (Radcliffe-Brown 1958:42). But nearly all important early functionalists included the possibility of dealing with change in their theoretical formulations. One of Durkheim's "rules" of sociological method was that "the determining cause of a social fact should be sought among the social facts preceding it" (Durkheim 1958:110). Radcliffe-Brown wrote that "functional inconsistency exists whenever two aspects of the social system produce a conflict which can only be resolved by some change in the system itself" (Radcliffe-Brown 1958:43), while Malinowski later in his life wrote a whole book under the title *The Dynamics of Culture Change* (1945). It was the fact that synchronic functional analysis was a seductive novelty that made several subsequent field workers prone to the neglect of history and change.

Firth, Leach, Kluckhohn, Parsons, Merton, Geertz, and many others who have not been mentioned, each rediscovered in his own way the potential of functionalism to deal with change. In their hands functionalism became once more the dynamic and nomothetic theory envisaged by its formulators.

CHAPTER II

AMERICAN
ANTHROPOLOGY

American anthropology came into existence almost simultaneously with the birth of the nation. Early American colonizers were no speculative philosophers, but practical men who had to cope with the contingencies of everyday life. They were brought into close and intimate contact with the Indians, and their initial experiences persuaded many of them to the common-sense view that the original inhabitants of the New World were ordinary human beings whose cooperation was important.

Ever since discovery, American Indians had been subjects of lively discussions and debates. William H. Prescott expressed the general excitement about the new discovery quite well when he wrote:

When the Europeans first touched the shores of America it was as if they had alighted on another planet . . . everything there was so different from what they had before seen. They were introduced to new varieties of plants and to unknown races of animals; while man, the lord of all, was equally strange in complexion, language, and institutions. It was what they emphatically styled it, a New World. Taught by their faith to derive all created beings from one source, they felt a natural perplexity as to the manner in which these distant and insulated regions could have obtained their inhabitants. The same curiosity was felt by their countrymen at home, and European scholars bewildered their brains with speculations on the best way of solving this interesting question.

(Quoted by Hallowell 1960:3)

The puzzle of Indian origins was not the only one to "bewilder" the minds of scholars. They were equally intrigued by speculations on the Indian character and the degree of their mental development. Even their status as human beings was not accepted without debate. An official statement by the Church was needed to settle this question: Pope Paul III declared in his bull *Sublimus Deus* (1537) "that the Indians are truly man and are not only capable of understanding the Catholic faith but . . . desire exceedingly to receive it." Yet the belief that Indians were inferior to Europeans remained prevalent. Even missionaries who were intimately acquainted with them often were discouraged, perhaps because the last part of Pope Paul's statement proved to be somewhat removed from reality. Nevertheless, many missionary workers defended the humanity and rational capabilities of their charges, while politicians at home who felt that Indians should be enslaved and dispossessed of their land tended to depict them as being more similar to animals than to Western men.

For Thomas Jefferson it was a "self-evident truth" that all men are created equal. Although he sometimes had mental reservations about the equal status of Negroes, he harbored no such doubts about the Indians. He insisted upon the inclusion of the Lockean phrase in the Declaration of Independence (1776) and remained a defender of Indians throughout his life. He wrote to John Adams: "In the early part of my life I was very familiar with the Indians, and acquired impressions, attachment, and commiseration for them which have never been obliterated" (quoted by Kimball 1947:286). Even more forceful was the following statement:

I am safe in assuming that the proofs of genius given by the Indians of North America place them on a level with whites in the same uncultivated state. The North of Europe furnishes subjects enough for comparison with them, and for a proof of their equality, I have seen some thousands myself, and conversed much with them, and have found in them a masculine, sound understanding. . . . I believe the Indian to be in body and mind equal to the white man.

(Foley 1900:422)

Jefferson became still more defensive of the status of the Indian after learning of the theories of Georges de Buffon (1707–88). This great French naturalist had maintained that natural habitat and climate, particularly the degree of humidity, powerfully influenced the condition of animals and men. The environment of the New World was such that it had stunted its inhabitants' growth. About the Indian he wrote that:

the organs of generation are feeble and small, he has no hair, no beard and no ardor for the female . . . his sensations are less acute, and yet he is more cowardly and more timid. He has no vivacity, no activity of mind . . . the most precious spark of nature is absent . . . his heart is frozen, his society cold, his empire barren. . . . Nature, in denying him the powers of love has treated him worse than any one of the animals.

(Quoted in French by Kimball 1947:287–88)

Jefferson, indignant, exclaimed: "An afflicting picture indeed, which for the honor of human nature I am glad to believe has no original." His personal experience had proven that the Indian was

neither defective in ardor, nor more impotent with his female, than the white reduced to the same diet and exercise; that he is brave . . . that he meets death with more deliberation, and endures tortures with firmness . . . that he is affectionate to his children . . . that his friendships are strong and faithful to the uttermost extremity; that his sensibility is keen . . . that his vivacity and activity of mind is equal of ours in the same situation.

(Quoted by Kimball 1947:288)

From this time onward, Jefferson made every possible effort to encourage and support ethnographic, linguistic, and archaeological research. During his years as President (1801–

09) he organized the Lewis and Clark expedition (1803–06), charging the explorers not only to find a route to the Pacific coast, but also to observe and record ethnographic data. When a wealth of information was indeed brought back, he appealed to the Philosophical Society to foster and support systematic studies of Indian life.

The president of that organization, Samuel Stanhope Smith (1750–1819), was a man who himself had strong anthropological interests. A staunch monogenist, he had defended his position in what was probably the earliest anthropological article in the United States: *Essay on the Causes of the Variety of Complexion and Figure in the Human Species* (1787). He visualized a future anthropology when he wrote in 1784:

As the character, and manners, and state of society among the savages, would make a very important part of the history of human nature, it appears to me to be an object that merits the attention of literary societies, not less than the discovery of new islands and seas. Hitherto the Indians have been observed, chiefly within the compass of the United States, and by traders or soldiers, who had objects very different from philosophy in their view. The character of the observers has necessarily confined their observation, in a great measure, to that part of the Indian tribes that has been corrupted by our interests, or intimidated by our injuries. . . . But I conceive it would not be unworthy of societies established for extending human knowledge, to employ good philosophers, who should be hardy enough for the undertaking, to travel among their remotest nations, which have never had any intercourse with Europeans; to reside among them on a familiar footing; to dress and live as they do; and to observe them when they should be under no bias or constraint. We should then see whether there be any essential difference between them and the tribes with which we are already acquainted. We should discover, in the comparison of their languages, their different degrees of improvement; their affinities with one another; and, at the same time, the objects with which each has chiefly conversed, that have occasioned a variety in their terms and phrases. But above all, we should discover the nature and extent of their religious ideas, which have been ascertained with less accuracy than others, by travelers who have not known to set a proper value upon them. (Quoted by Hallowell 1960:34–35)

American anthropology thus received its distinctive coloring from developing in the presence of the Indians. The study of their cultures, languages, and history remained the focus of this discipline until the early twentieth century. The motivations for this early interest represented a mixture of genuine scholarly curiosity, the practical necessity to deal with the Indians, a sincere desire to elevate the Indians to a higher level of civilization, and a degree of self-interest. Practical-minded Benjamin Franklin (1706–90), cosigner of the Declaration of Independence, wrote that

securing the friendship of the Indians is of the greatest consequence to these Colonies; and that the surest means of doing it, are, to regulate the Indian trade, so as to convince them, by experience, that they may have the best and cheapest goods, and the fairest dealings from the English; and to unite the several governments, so as to form a strength that the Indians may depend on for protection . . . (Quoted by Labaree 1961:117)

Earlier than in Europe, American scholars emphasized the necessity for firsthand observations, facilitated of course by the promixity of the Indians. Many early ethnographers also were keenly aware that aboriginal cultures and languages were rapidly changing or disappearing, and that the valuable data should be retrieved before it was too late.

Earlier also was the objectivity with which the native Americans were viewed, but, regretfully, this humanistic attitude was not long sustained, and the "unalienable rights" of Indian men were soon forgotten.

The objectivity with which most early American ethnologists and linguists carried out their research did not result in anthropological theories superior to their European counterparts, but were more often derived from them. The idea that Indians were descendants from the Lost Tribes of Israel enjoyed a considerable vogue. It must also have crossed Jefferson's mind, because in the instructions which he prepared for the Lewis and Clark expedition he suggested that the explorers should search for the affinities between Indian religious ceremonies and those of the ancient Jews. Like many an Enlightenment philosopher, Jefferson also ascribed to a progressive stage-theory of cultural development, but he gave no further explanations. With some pride he noted that all "stages" were represented in his own country, and he felt that a rather orderly spatial succession of these stages could be observed between the Rocky Mountains and the eastern seaboard. The earliest stage lived "under no law but that of nature, subsisting and covering themselves with the flesh and skin of wild beasts." Next came the pastoralists, then the semi-barbarians, while in the eastern seaport towns Indians lived in the "as yet most improved state." This situation represented to him the general course of human progress "from the infancy of creation to the present day." The strength of early American anthropology rested not in its contribution to theory, but in its vigorous data retrieval, comparative treatments, and classifications.

The fact that scholarly interests often prevailed over practical ones becomes manifest in the early emphasis upon linguistic studies. Jefferson himself collected some forty different vocabularies, devising a word list of "such objects as, being present everywhere, would probably have a name in every language," thus anticipating the basic vocabulary lists of twentieth-century glottochronologists. The tragic story of the loss of his trunk containing his most valuable linguistic documents may serve as a warning to all field workers to make copies of their field notes and to dispatch them by different routes. Boatsmen stole Jefferson's trunk, which he sent from Washington to Monticello in 1809, and they scattered the papers in the mud along the banks of the James River. Although some were retrieved (and are now on display in the Smithsonian Institution), most of the results of thirty years' labor were irretrievably lost. Jefferson's purpose in collecting Indian vocabularies was based upon his conviction that language was best suited to establish relationships between Indian groups and could also reveal connections between them and Asiatic nations, so that their origins might be found in this manner. Other American linguists included John Pickering (1776–1846), who devised a phonetic alphabet for the recording of Indian sound systems; and Peter Stephen Duponceau (1760–1844), who is best known for inventing the term "polysynthetic" to characterize the agglutinative qualities of many aboriginal tongues. The first to classify North American languages was Albert Gallatin (1761–1849), secretary of state under Jefferson, and cofounder of the American Ethnological Society in 1842. He also served as the first president of this organization, which was the first professional group of anthropologists in the United States. He recognized the existence of thirty-two distinct language families in this country.

Jefferson's many-sided interests also included archaeology. In 1784 he excavated a "barrow" (or what we now call a burial mound) in Virginia. In the account of this undertaking he reported his techniques in detail, anticipating some of the modern archaeological methods, and making some valid inferences (Heizer 1959:218–21). Later archaeology remained focused on burial mounds for quite a while, fostered by a romantic interest in the past. Many speculations were made about the identity of the ancient Mound Builders (Shetrone 1930).

Ethnology, linguistics, and archaeology were thus well represented in early American anthropology, and Samuel Smith's treatise on human variation was certainly related to physical anthropology. Yet the latter branch lagged somewhat behind the others, and when systematic collections of human remains were made and the results analyzed, a note of racism appeared almost at once.

On the brighter side, Indians also inspired many artists, novelists, dramatists, and poets. The first American novelist to gain world reputation was James Fenimore Cooper (1789–1851), whose five-volume Leatherstocking Tales were particularly popular, even if he had no firsthand knowledge about Indian life. Between 1820 and 1840, at least thirty plays with Indian themes appeared on the stage. George Catlin

(1796–1872) achieved distinction as a painter of Indians in their still undisturbed state in the "Wild West." In 1837 he opened an Indian Gallery in New York, exhibiting not only many hundreds of his paintings, but also items of material culture that he had collected. Before the invention of photography, exploring expeditions were often accompanied by one or more artists who sketched landscapes, house types, rituals, and portraits of Indians.

Henry Rowe Schoolcraft (1793–1864) was an early recorder of Indian mythology. An Indian agent, he discovered, rather to his amazement, that the Ojibwa and other Indian tribes possessed a traditional oral literature, and he wrote in his journal that this spoke more for the intellect of the race than any other trait he had heard of. Although he censored some of the stories, omitting what he considered indecent, his two-volume collection *Algic Researches* (1839) remains valuable for folklorists. It became the inspiration for Longfellow's long poem *Hiawatha* (1855), whose character molded the popular image of Indians at home and abroad.

Schoolcraft was not merely a collector. He was convinced that myths and folktales rendered significant insights into Indian thought patterns and reasoning, and that the origin of their institutions could possibly be discovered from these traditional stories. Furthermore, he compared Indian myths with ancient Christian and Oriental literature, and discovered several "correspondences." Menstruation taboos, for instance, were mentioned in the Bible as well as in Algonkian myths, as were other sex taboos and purification rites. Cremation was both an Oriental and an Indian custom, and this as well as other similarities confirmed his theory that the Indians originated in Asia, although he did not rule out the possibility of their ultimate Jewish origin.

When he resigned from his post as Indian agent in 1841, he turned more vigorously to writing and to furthering the science of ethnology. His publications included *Historical and Statistical Information Respecting the History, Condition, and Prospects of the Indian Tribes of the United States* (1851–

57), a monumental work in six folio volumes of about six hundred pages each. He was elected to the American Philosophical Society, assisted Gallatin in organizing the American Ethnological Society (1842), traveled to Europe and read a paper at the meetings of the British Association for the Advancement of Science, and excavated several mounds in Virginia and Ohio. He drew up a "Plan for the Investigation of American Ethnology," which he presented to the regents of the newly organized Smithsonian Institution at its first meeting in 1846. From its contents it is clear that Schoolcraft envisaged anthropology as a separate science. Unlike European scholars of his time, Schoolcraft did not agonize about the scientific status of the discipline, although he insisted that ethnology should consist of "ascertained facts," and should include evidence of linguistics, archaeology, and history.

Lewis Henry Morgan equally began his anthropological career with a romantic interest in Indian life. Like Schoolcraft, he first aimed at investigating the relationships between Indian and Asiatic cultures, and became an evolutionist only in his later life. His contributions have already been discussed, but it may be added at this point that he profoundly influenced a number of other scholars, among them Adolf Francis Bandelier (1840–1914), who began to correspond with Morgan in 1870. Under his guidance, Bandelier studied the social organization of the Aztecs and published three monographs: "On the Art of War of the Ancient Mexicans" (1877), "On the Distribution and Tenure of Lands among the Ancient Mexicans" (1878), and "On the Social Organization of the Ancient Mexicans" (1879). In these studies Bandelier took a stand against the popular notion that Aztec political structure was best understood in terms of European or Egyptian models. William Prescott (1796–1859), for one, depicted the Aztec rulers as Sun Kings comparable to Louis XIV of France, while Lewis Wallace (1827–1905), best known for his book *Ben-Hur,* wrote a now forgotten novel, *The Fair God* (1873), in which Aztec kings were likened to Egyptian Pharaohs. Bandelier insisted that such comparisons were false and unscientific, and

a barrier to true understanding of Indian cultures. Nevertheless, he himself wrote a novel of prehistoric Pueblo Indians,
his famous *The Delight Makers* (1890). In the preface to the
first edition he explained that its purpose was to make the
"truth about the Pueblo Indians" more accessible and acceptable to the general public. He stressed that the romantic
plot was of his own making, but that the description of Pueblo
manners, customs, creeds, and rites was based upon factual
observations (1971:xxi). Bandelier also was an ardent archaeologist, and his researches in this field remain important for all
scholars interested in Southwest Indian prehistory and culture.

Another admirer of Morgan was John Wesley Powell
(1834–1902), founder of the Bureau of American Ethnology
(1879) and its first director. He collected many Indian songs
and myths, particularly among Shoshoneans, whose language
he had learned; recorded their marriage and burial customs;
and described items of material culture. But his major contributions were in linguistics. He made a comprehensive
classification of Indian languages north of Mexico, and
grouped them into fifty-six separate linguistic families (1891).
Although modifications were suggested later on by such
scholars as Boas, Sapir, Kroeber, and many others, Powell's
classification still retains its validity. Harry Hoijer wrote that
"in no case has a stock established by Powell been discredited
by later work" (1946:10). His classification is often referred
to in linguistic works, while that of Gallatin has been well-
nigh forgotten.

It appears that a friend of Powell's, Joseph Henry (1797–
1878), was the first American to use the word "anthropology"
in a professional sense. He was the first secretary of the Smithsonian Institution, and in his previously submitted plan for
organization proposed the inclusion of "anthropology" in
terms of systematic research of Indian cultures. In his Annual
Report of 1877 he wrote:

. . . anthropology, or what may be considered the natural history
of man, is at present the most popular branch of science. It absorbs

a large share of public attention and many original investigators are assiduously devoted to it. Its object is to reconstruct, as it were, the past history of man, to determine his specific peculiarities and general tendencies. . . . American anthropology early occupied the attention of the Smithsonian Institution . . . and to collect all the facts which could be gathered in regard to the archeology of North America, and also of its ethnology, or, in other words, an account of its present Indian inhabitants, was considered a prominent object in the plan of operations of the establishment.

(Quoted by Hallowell 1906:31)

Henry himself was not an anthropologist, but a physicist imbued with the ideals of science rather than with those of the humanities. In a conversation with Thomas Huxley, Henry admitted that Kant's *Critiques* or Mill's *Logic* would not have been acceptable for publication in the Smithsonian *Contributions to Knowledge* (Hellman 1966:127), because they were far too speculative. It was clear, then, that anthropology was considered a science. Witness also its recognition by the American Association for the Advancement of Science since 1851, where its own independent "Section H" was established in 1882. The New York Academy of Sciences also recognized anthropology as a scientific discipline, and continues to sponsor monthly anthropological meetings at its own premises.

When Franz Boas (1858–1942) received his first academic appointment at Clark University in 1888, anthropology was already firmly established in its four-field approach. The first volume of the *American Anthropologist* (1888) contained articles dealing with linguistics, archaeology, physical anthropology, and ethnology. Anthropology was empirical and emphasized field work; many good monographs had already been published. Nevertheless, Boas became the most influential figure of twentieth-century anthropology. During his reign at Columbia University from 1896 till his death in 1942, he trained a great many famous anthropologists, among them Alfred Kroeber, Alexander Goldenweiser, Frank Speck, Robert Lowie, Paul Radin, Edward Sapir, Leslie Spier, Melville

Herskovits, M. F. Ashley Montagu, Margaret Mead, Ruth Underhill, Ruth Bunzel, and Ruth Benedict. His literary output consists of some seven hundred articles, several books, and extensive myth collections. He founded the American Folklore Society (1888), revitalized the American Ethnological Society (1900), and advised W. J. McGee, then chief of the Bureau of Ethnology, on the creation of a national professional organization, the American Anthropological Association. Boas was at odds with McGee over the question of membership, recommending that only professionals should be invited to join, while McGee wanted to give the organization a much wider scope. The association was incorporated in 1902 without Boas' participation, and although McGee maintained that this had been an inadvertent omission, it is possible that this was not the case (Stocking 1960:7). McGee became the organization's first president; Boas was elected to this position in 1907.

Boas was born in Germany, studied at the universities of Heidelberg, Bonn, and Kiel, first majoring in physics and mathematics, later shifting to geography. He wrote his forty-two-page doctoral dissertation on the color of sea water (1881), joined an arctic expedition to Baffinland as a geographer in 1883–84, and first visited the Indians of the Northwest Coast in 1886, returning two years later at the request of Tylor. In 1893 he organized the anthropological collections for the Chicago World's Fair, and his appointment to Columbia came in 1896.

Many of his later associates and students tried to pinpoint the circumstances and reasons for his "conversion" to anthropology. Some held that during his first expedition he discovered that the Eskimos had a different set of color categories which influenced their perception of the color of sea water, and from that began to recognize the importance of culture. Herskovits (1953:9–10) considers this story to be legendary, but adds that Boas himself never discouraged this interpretation. In any case it is true that he was brought in close association with the native people during his trip, particularly during the winter months when the harbors were frozen. Boas himself wrote of that period:

Now I began in earnest to make my ethnographical studies. . . . Every night I spent with the natives who told me about the configuration of the land. . . . They related the old stories handed over to them by their ancestors, sang the old songs after the old monotonous tunes, and I saw them playing the old games, which with they shorten the long, dark winter nights.

(Boas 1884:253)

He became attracted to the study of people rather than their environment because, as he wrote in 1936, he had become disillusioned about the significance of geographic determinants (1940:306). In his earliest monographs on Baffinland (1884 and 1885) he explained Eskimo life largely in geographical terms, and this attitude of geographical determinism was still recognizable in *The Central Eskimo* (1888), although to a lesser degree. Harris (1968:267) suggests that at the time when he was writing this book he was hoping to obtain a position as a geographer at the University of Berlin, and thus did not want to undercut this discipline. After settling in America he never again stressed the geographical milieu as a factor influencing culture.

His broad education had made Boas fully aware of the traditional German distinction between *Geisteswissenschaften* and *Naturwissenschaften,* roughly corresponding to the "humanities" and the "sciences" in English-speaking countries. It is true, however, as Stocking (1968:41) points out, that in nineteenth-century Germany there was a considerable overlap between geography and ethnology, particularly through the creation of anthropogeography. Boas' shift from physics to geography was thus more incisive than the later one from geography to anthropology.

At the beginning of his anthropological career in America Boas described the aims of ethnology as follows:

The task of ethnology is the study of the total range of phenomena of social life. Language, customs, migrations, bodily characteristics are subjects of our studies. Thus its first and most immediate object is the study of the history of mankind; not that of civilized nations alone, but that of the whole of mankind, from its earliest traces found in the deposits of the ice age, up to modern times. We must follow the gradual development of the manifestations of culture.   (Boas 1940:627–28)

This formulation was not in contradiction to the aims of evolutionists, and, like them, Boas felt at that time that the search for laws of cultural evolution was a legitimate undertaking:

A comparison of the social life of different peoples proves that the foundations of their cultural development are remarkably uniform. It follows from this that there are laws to which this development is subject. Their discovery is the second, perhaps the more important aim of our science.   (*Ibid*.: 633–34)

His acceptance of the possibility of lawful sequences of events was reiterated in 1896, but he now attacked the comparative method which evolutionists had used for the reconstruction of their worldwide stages. The major error of this method was its assumption that cultural similarities always arose from the same causes. Boas added that evolutionists had never bothered to prove their hypothesis, and had simply concluded that cultural similarities, no matter where they were found, indicated the existence of one grand system according to which human culture had evolved everywhere. From this point onward, they simply forced all data into the straitjacket of their unproven convictions (*ibid.*:276–77).

Boas recommended that the comparative method be replaced by the historical method. The latter was to be based upon the principle that like phenomena were *not* always due to the same causes, and that in every single instance a common cause must be empirically established. Admittedly this was a slow and laborious undertaking, but it would reconstruct the history of cultural development with great accuracy.

Only one common cause for cultural similarities was acceptable to Boas, namely common origin in history. He rejected uniformity of the mind as an explanation because man does not obey the same laws everywhere. Similarity of environment was equally ruled out, because it could be shown that different forms of culture existed in similar environments, and vice versa. Common historical origin itself could never be taken for granted, but should be established first in small and well-defined geographical areas, and continuity of distribution was the major proof for historical connection. When there was a break in this continuity, it should be presumed that similar traits had arisen independently.

There was a great deal of truth in Boas' critique of the methods used by the evolutionists, but he misunderstood their scientific philosophy. Like Boas, they correctly observed that cultural similarities do exist in diverse areas of the world, and they searched for a generalized factor or an independent cause to account for these similarities, regardless of the presence or absence of known historical connections. This is certainly not unscientific, as Boas charged, and although the causal explanations that were advanced (progress, psychic unity, economic determinants, environment) have not proven to be sufficient explanations, the principles of their method cannot be blamed. The same cannot be said about the execution of these principles, which indeed could not always pass the test of scientific objectivity.

Boas' own historical method by its very formulation denied the existence of general laws, because similar phenomena were precisely *not* due to similar causes, except in very limited geographical areas. He arrived thus at a position known as historical particularism, proposing a research design that at best could explain isolated parts of human history, but never its totality. Boas himself became increasingly pessimistic about the value of the historical method. In 1920 he phrased the problem in those terms: "It is, of course, true that we can never hope to obtain incontrovertible data relating to the chronological sequence of events, but certain general broad outlines can be ascertained with a high degree of probability, even of certainty" (*ibid.*:284). But at that time he had also discovered the role of the individual in culture change, and once this was taken into account, the search for laws became almost ephemeral. In the same article he wrote: "The activities of the individual are determined to a great extent by his social environment, but in turn his own activities influence the society in which he lives, and may bring about modifications in its form" (*ibid.*:285).

By 1932, Boas had given up all hope for the discovery of any laws, general or particular: "The phenomena of our science are so individualized, so exposed to outer accident, that no set of laws could explain them . . . it seems to me doubtful whether valid cultural laws can be found" (*ibid.*: 257). Yet, he never grew tired of showing that the general sequences proposed by evolutionists were all wrong. Where most evolutionists had postulated the priority of matrilineality over other patterns of kinship, Boas proved that in Kwakiutl society patrilineality had changed into matrilineality (*ibid.*: 356–60). When art historians quarreled about whether realism in art had preceded geometric abstract designs or vice versa, Boas proved both wrong, showing that the development may take place either way (Boas 1908, 1927).

When Boas became disillusioned about history and historical reconstruction, his interest in the role of the individual increased. Although calling Freud's psychoanalytical approach "one-sided," and taking particular issue with his theory of symbolism (Boas 1940:288–89), Boas was cognizant of the influence of culture on personality, and he knew also that individuals react to their cultures in different ways. These insights were more systematically examined by later anthropologists, leading to the development of the "culture and personality" branch of anthropology.

Lowie (1937:142–44) saw in Boas' theories a strong functionalist component, but he ascribed this position to his teacher on slim evidence: Boas realized that "cultures were not mere aggregates of separate elements but integrated wholes." This insight is not necessarily related to functionalism, and Boas in fact criticized it because of its presumed antihistorical bias. But there is another important element in Lowie's statement that he himself overlooks, namely that Boas used the plural form "cultures." Boas shifted attention from the general idea of "culture" to the more specific fact that every society possesses its own culture, thus implying that each culture is an integrated way of life, valid and meaningful in its own right. This was the positive side of historical particularism, and it followed logically from the rejection of earlier evolutionism's division of mankind on an unequal basis, savages and barbarians being "lower" than civilized man. Strongly repudiating this idea, Boas expressed the point of view that has since become axiomatic in anthropology: "There is no fundamental difference in the ways of thinking of primitive and civilized man. A close connection between race and personality has never been established" (Boas 1963:17). It is not surprising that Boas' books were included in the book burning ordered by the Nazis in Germany in 1933.

Boas' recognition of the pluralities of cultures closely interrelates with his emphasis upon field work. Leslie White vindictively attempted to impugn Boas' competence as a field worker, implying that he had inflated the amount of time actually spent in the field (White 1963:9–11), and chiding him for missing important aspects of Kwakiutl social organization (*ibid.*:67). Nevertheless, Boas accomplished more in collecting vast amounts of data than almost anyone else. He did not originate the practice of field work, but attempted to achieve higher standards by insisting that theory must be based upon objective empirical data. He advocated that field work should be part of every anthropological training program, and recommended that students spend at least a full year with the people under study, living with them as closely as possible, and learning to communicate with them in their own language.

Boas' ethnographic researches were mainly directed toward kinship organization, art, and myth. The latter was closely related to his interest in language, because he felt that the best linguistic data could be obtained by the recording of a peo-

ple's oral literature. Keenly aware also that much of this traditional material would soon be forgotten because Indian cultures were rapidly changing or disappearing, he collected
myths, legends, folktales, prayers, folk medicine, and similar
folkloristic materials from many Indian groups (Chinook
1894, Bella Coola 1898, Tsimshian 1902, Kwakiutl 1905, and
so on). Many of these publications appeared with interlinear
translations, so that they are also of great value to linguistic
analysis. Boas also conceived of the then novel idea of training
native peoples to record their own culture.

Boas' theoretical contributions to mythology and folklore
are relatively small. He opposed the view that the essential
unity of the human mind had produced similarities in folktales throughout the world, and he equally objected to the
theory that myth had arisen from a universal tendency to
anthropomorphize nature. He saw clearly that borrowing of
myths and folktales was never an automatic process, but that
the themes of stories were commonly adapted to the culture
of the borrowers. Myths were thus in part culturally determined, and in part they arose from human imagination. Boas
hoped to be able to discriminate between these two elements,
but he never did.

Several of anthropology's most familiar concepts and
methods are the heritage of Boas. Yet there is no "Boasian
school," nor are there any theories closely associated with his
name. But his influence is generally recognized by those who
studied under him. He was able to communicate to them the
urgency and importance of anthropological research "not by
preachment," as Margaret Mead put it, "but by tempo, tone,
and gesture, and this urgency remained with us" (Mead 1959:
43). His interests were so wide that no single individual could
possibly pursue them all. Some followed up on his distribution
and diffusion studies, others concentrated on historical reconstructions or studied individual cultures in detail, still
others began to examine the influence of personality on culture, thus injecting psychological factors into anthropology.

The latter was viewed with some alarm by Alfred Louis

Kroeber (1876–1960), the first to receive a doctoral degree in anthropology under Boas. Unlike his mentor, Kroeber did not have a scientific background but came to anthropology via the humanities. His twenty-eight-page doctoral dissertation, "Decorative Symbols of the Arapaho" (1901), evidenced both his humanistic interests and Boas' influence. He showed how in the art of these Plains Indians realistic symbolism and decorative abstractions appeared together, and concluded that the origin of either style thus could not be established, and thus also that a uniform development of art styles could not have occurred. Eight years later, Boas made a similar point in his study of Alaskan needlecases.

After graduation Kroeber moved to California, where he built a department of anthropology, much as Boas did at Columbia. Beginning his career with a Boasian emphasis on data collection, he encouraged the trait-list approach, in the conviction that facts must precede theory. Concentrating first on California, he and his students amassed a wealth of detailed information, and the subsequent *Handbook of the Indians of California* (1925), a thousand-page volume, contained almost everything that was then known about these groups. The same detailed description of most other North American Indians was present in his later work *Cultural and Natural Areas of Native North America* (1939). In both books he mapped culture areas, and he gave the concept greater historical depth by introducing the theories of cultural climax and cultural intensity. Nevertheless, the culture area trait-list approach involved a mechanistic view of culture that was not compatible with Kroeber's humanistic inclinations. He felt that culture could not be wholly understood by even the most complete summation of the observable elements, because every culture contained other elements that could not be caught by trait lists. Kroeber called these the "sensitive indicators" of culture, and they included art, music, religion, ethos, philosophy, and similar aspects of intellectual life that do not easily lend themselves to statistical treatment. Kroeber even became convinced that these sensitive elements were more characteristic of cultures than the concrete elements, and more diagnostic of cultural intensity.

Undoubtedly, Kroeber was right that these intangibles cannot be excluded, but their evaluation is of necessity subjective. There can be no scientific agreement about the relative worth of an art style or the value of a worldview. Kroeber did all he could to show that the two approaches were not in opposition, but he could not unify them. His view of culture remained thus somewhat dichotomized, consisting of "value culture" and "reality culture."

After it became clear that territorial plotting of culture elements raised more problems than it could solve, Kroeber turned away from the study of minutiae, and pursued his interests in the more macroscopic view of culture history, which resulted in the publication of his monumental *Configurations of Culture Growth* (1944). In it, he dealt not with Indian cultures, but with the civilizations of Egypt, Mesopotamia, Greece, Rome, China, and several European nations. He had long been intrigued by the fact that these civilizations had known periods of high achievement in art, music, drama, literature, science, philosophy, but later on declined again. This phenomenon had been noted by others, and Kroeber's contemporary, the German philosopher Oswald Spengler (1880–1936), had advanced the explanation that civilizations can be equated with organisms that are born, pass through childhood, maturity and old age, finally to die (Spengler 1918). Kroeber felt strongly that this theory was not only false, but reductionistic to the utmost. Culture and culture change could not be explained by reference to biology or psychology. In Kroeber's view, culture constituted a separate realm of phenomena, namely the superorganic, and as such it could be explained only in terms of its own laws.

The concept of the superorganic itself was not new. It had been named by Spencer, defined by Tylor, applied by Sumner, and it was implicit in the writings of Comte and Durkheim. On its simplest level, it was nothing more than a recognition of culture as a learned tradition and a realization that it cannot be explained totally by reference to biology or chemistry. But in the hands of convinced superorganicists the concept took on the more dogmatic meaning that *nothing* in culture can be explained by reference to other disciplines. Neither biology, nor psychology, nor environment, nor even man himself could serve as an explanatory factor for culture and cultural developments: culture set its own laws. In this view, culture thus became endowed with a dynamic inner force that determined its own existence and regulated its own changes. Human volition or human genius had no decisive influence upon culture, and superorganicists never tired of attacking the "great man" theory, which held precisely the opposite view.

Kroeber was already fully committed to the superorganic view when he began to write his *Configurations,* and it was meant to be a final defense of his position. As early as 1915 he expressed his conviction that "the personal or individual has no historical value, save as an illustration" (1915:283–88). Two years later, in his article "The Superorganic" (1917), he produced a long list of Western inventions that had been made simultaneously by scholars working independently of each other: the telescope, invented by three people in 1608; oxygen, discovered twice in 1774; the steamboat, developed by four different people; Neptune, discovered twice in the same year; as well as the invention of photography, the telephone, the phonograph, and the discovery of the North and South Poles almost simultaneously (1948:342; 1952:44–45). This "principle of simultaneity of invention" as Kroeber called it was to him the best proof that invention or discovery was not due to "some mysterious inherent faculty of individual minds," but to "the presence of majestic forces or sequences pervading civilization" (Kroeber 1952:45).

Edward Sapir reacted at once to this view (1917), and argued for the significance of the individual in culture and cultural processes. Pointing out that Kroeber had used only technological inventions that often depend upon previous ones (Neptune could not be discovered before the invention of the telescope), he challenged Kroeber to occupy himself instead with man's religious, aesthetic, or philosophical activities, which could never be abstracted from human beings.

Kroeber answered with a publication about women's fashions (1919), reporting that certain measurements such as décolleté or skirt lengths went up and down in regular curves over periods of time. In 1940, together with Jane Richardson, he covered three hundred years of such changes, confirming the regularity of the pattern. Fashion designers, convinced of their own aesthetic creativity, were in fact hapless victims of the laws of culture.

In *Configurations* Kroeber examined all other cultural phenomena that Sapir had set at defiance. But although Kroeber remained convinced that the florescent periods of culture indicated that culture itself determines the expression of genius, he was unable to discover any cultural laws that might lie behind such periodization. At the beginning of the book (on which he worked for seven years), he optimistically wrote that behind the movements of culture "there seem to lie certain forms of happenings which are more or less recurrent or generic, perhaps necessary and universal" (Kroeber 1963: 3). At the end, under "Review and Conclusions," he stated:

> I wish to say at the outset that I see no evidence of any true law in the phenomena dealt with; nothing cyclical, regularly repetitive, or necessary. There is nothing to show either that every culture must develop patterns within which a florescence of quality is possible, or that, having once so flowered, it must wither without chance for survival.   (*Ibid.*: 761)

He also admitted later on that he had underrated the significance of human beings in the cultural process, and that psychological factors could sometimes contribute toward the understanding of culture.

Superorganic explanations have not found general acceptance among anthropologists, and Kroeber himself was strongly attacked by his contemporaries. Both Boas (1928:235) and Ruth Benedict (1934:231) felt that it was "mysticism" to consider culture as existing outside of man. Bidney (1944:42), equally disapprovingly, accused Kroeber of idealism because he reified culture, while Morris Opler (1963:902) bemoaned the fact that superorganicism stripped anthropology of its warmth and purpose, its concern with humanity.

The idea that man should be nothing but an implement of culture or an illustration of history was repugnant to most, but dislike is no disproof. One of the more naïve attempts to demolish the superorganic was the argument that culture is not "real": culture does not enamel its fingernails, but people do. Kroeber answered that this was a point which he cheerfully conceded to his critics, but that it could not diminish his interest in cultural phenomena (1952:114). Of course he had never denied human reality: "cultural values, along with cultural forms and cultural content, surely exist only through men and reside in men" (*ibid.*:129).

Involved in this kind of critique and in Kroeber's own position was the old philosophical question about the nature of reality. Nominalists maintained that culture was not tangible, could not be observed in action ("only people paint their nails"), and as such it was a mere logical construct that could neither cause nor explain anything. This position was expressed *in extremis* by Radcliffe-Brown who wrote: "To say of culture patterns that they act upon an individual . . . is as absurd as to hold a quadratic equation capable of committing a murder" (Radcliffe-Brown 1957:30).

Kroeber himself began to waver on his formerly held stance about the reality of culture, and eventually retreated into the compromise of the "as if" philosophy. Culture could be studied *as if* it were real (1952:113), *as if* cultural data constituted a self-contained system (*ibid.*:126), *as if* individual personalities did not have a hand in cultural events (*ibid.*:133). It appears that Kroeber felt that the explanatory powers of conceptual entities are more important than questions about their ontological status. Indeed, White's monographs on the Pueblo Indians (1942, 1962) do not reveal his superorganic conviction, nor does Morris Opler's study of the Apache (1941) show his antisuperorganic orientation.

Another question related to superorganicism was the problem of reductionism. Kroeber was rather horrified by the attempts of some of his contemporaries to explain culture largely in psychological terms, and warned that such practice may explain culture away, as biological reductionism had attempted in the past. But, as Kaplan (1965:958–76) pointed out, reductionism is not necessarily a reprehensible scientific practice. Physicists agree that laws of thermodynamics are reducible to laws of mechanics, but this does not make the phenomena of the former false, nor are they "explained away." About cultural phenomena Kaplan wrote that some are not explainable by reference to psychology or biology—concepts like the clan, or cross-cousin marriage, or spelling rules—while other cultural institutions may be better understood by adding psychological or biological explanations.

The staunchest of modern superorganicists is Leslie White. He has sometimes been accused of failing to admit the influence of psychology, biology, or environment upon culture, but White has never held that phenomena of one level are not explainable in terms of other ones, only that such explanations are not culturological. Culturology to White is the science of culture and of culture alone, and cultural anthropologists, if they want to maintain their discipline as a separate one, must study culture in its own terms (White 1949:397–415). To White, culture is a separate realm because man possesses the unique capability to symbolize, and "all human behavior consists of, or is dependent upon, the use of symbols" (*ibid.*:22).

It is impossible for a dog, horse, bird, or even an ape, to have any understanding of the meaning of the sign of the cross to a Christian. . . . No chimpanzee or laboratory rat can appreciate the difference between Holy water and distilled water, or grasp the meaning of Tuesday, 3, or sin.

(*Ibid.*: 23–24)

White makes a sharp, qualitative break between cultural behavior and all other behavior, in this manner justifying his view that culture constitutes a superorganic realm.

Yet the idea that anthropologists should not concern themselves with any other explanations than culturological ones seems to narrow down the discipline unnecessarily. Anthropology does not seem to stand in any danger of "total reduction" when psychological, biological, and environmental explanations are added to cultural and historical ones. Anthropologists are no longer insisting upon the exclusiveness of their discipline; since they aim at a total understanding of mankind, no significant factor adding to such understanding can be arbitrarily ruled out.

Kroeber's writings indicate both the influence of Boas and a deliberate departure from some of his most cherished ideas. It may be said that this was typical for all who followed after Boas, no matter if they were directly or indirectly influenced by him. His interests went in many different directions, but his theories were rarely definitive, so that it became possible to follow up on some of his suggestions and to make methodological innovations at the same time. As a result, anthropological theories proliferated, and only some of these will be mentioned.

Ruth Fulton Benedict (1887–1948) was a student of Boas at the time when he had turned to historical particularism. She accepted his view that cultures are discrete entities and integrated wholes, but her friendship with Margaret Mead made her aware of the close relationships between individual mentality and cultural ethos. These two concepts together inspired her to examine the relationships between cultures and the psychology of their members. The results were published in her most famous book, *Patterns of Culture* (1934).

A "pattern" was to her the specific way in which a culture was integrated: consistent within itself and with the overall temperament of its participants. This she demonstrated for three different cultures: the Pueblo Zuni, the Kwakiutl of the Northwest Coast, and the Melanesian Dobu. Characterizing their ethos in Nietzschean terms, the Zuni were Apollonian, averse to violent emotions, peaceful and nonaggressive; while the Kwakiutl and the Dobu were Dionysian, loving excess and valuing the illuminations of frenzy. The bragging Kwakiutl were also typified as "megalomaniac" while the magic-ridden Dobu culture was "paranoid." The Zuni were exempted from such psychopathological invective: Benedict clearly preferred them over the other two.

Subsequent field workers showed that her characterizations were overdrawn. The Zuni were sometimes violent and drunk, the Kwakiutl sometimes humble. But most agreed that the tendencies she described were strikingly present. She pointed the way to a possible method of explaining cultural similarities and differences, and she felt that cross-cultural comparisons could be made on the basis of this new way of looking at cultures. It is not without reason that *Patterns of Culture* became what is probably the all-time anthropological bestseller. It is the more regrettable that she depicted two cultures in terms of psychopathology. Not only does it seem illogical to think of whole cultures as sick or disturbed personalities, but her imagery is also detrimental to the concept of the equality of man and the worthiness of primitive cultures in their own right.

Leslie Spier (1893–1961) followed Boas' suggestions about the study of diffusion. He compared two religious cult-complexes, the so-called Prophet Dance and the Ghost Dance which appeared among Northwest Indian groups (Spier 1935). He plotted the geographical distribution of these cults, and showed how the Ghost Dance had developed upon the older foundations of the Prophet Dance, and how its meanings and functions had changed in the process. His treatment of diffusion was both more creative and more enduring than the culture-area approach that had also used diffusion as its major explanation.

Paul Radin (1883–1959) applied Boas' technique of using literate Indians to record aspects of their own culture. Radin induced Crashing Thunder, a Winnebago Indian, to write his autobiography. This became the first published account of an

Indian culture viewed from within (1927). It showed that many differences existed between cultural rules and their acceptance and interpretation by individuals. Earlier, it had been taken more or less for granted that nonliterate cultures were homogeneous wholes. Crashing Thunder showed that this was not so. In the Winnebago culture it was important that young men seek a vision, often by means of prolonged fasting, which gave them a certain mystical power. Crashing Thunder told how he only pretended to have a vision. This, and other cultural deviances, led Radin to the recognition of variations of cultural behavior and thus also to an interest in personality and psychology. His example of presenting autobiographies was followed, among others, by Walter Dyk's *Son of Old Man Hat* (1938), a Navaho; Leo Simmons' *Sun Chief* (1942), a Hopi; and more recently by Nancy Lurie's *Mountain Wolf Woman* (1966) (she was a sister of Crashing Thunder); and Charles Brant's *Jim Whitewolf: The Life of a Kiowa Apache Indian* (1969).

Robert H. Lowie (1883–1957) absorbed the antievolutionist mood of some of Boas' writings, and his *Primitive Society* (1920) was in a sense a sustained critique of Morgan's *Ancient Society*. It would be an error, however, to typify Lowie as an antievolutionist. He used some of the basic premises of the evolutionary method, revised and refined some of Morgan's sequences, rejected the notion that group marriage was the earliest form of marriage, and so forth; but he was more opposed to the neglect of diffusion and the lack of scientific rigor on the part of early evolutionists than to the concept of evolution itself. Lowie departed from Boas' dictum that similar phenomena are generally not due to similar causes, and showed that many cultural traits were functionally interrelated, so that like phenomena could well be the product of like antecedents. It was thus possible that separate cultures could have evolved in a somewhat parallel manner (Lowie 1966:88), and it was Lowie rather than Steward who coined the term "multilineal evolution" to indicate that there may have been several developmental sequences in the evolution of social life (Murphy 1972:75). Lowie felt, however, that such parallelisms had taken place on a very limited scale because diffusion interfered with the order of the sequences.

Unlike Kroeber and White, Lowie did not worry about the independent status of anthropology as a discipline. He knew that true knowledge could not be compartmentalized, and that the aim of anthropology was not the safeguarding of its own methodological purity, but the understanding of man and his culture. Insights of other disciplines should thus be accepted and freely used if they contributed to such understanding. The seemingly remote and extraneous field of metallurgy had assisted anthropology in the study of ancient tools; geology and chemistry had provided important dating techniques for archaeological finds; botany had helped to distinguish between wild and domesticated plants, thus shedding light on the origins of agriculture; and geography, astrology, philosophy, psychology, and history had also made important contributions.

Lowie's willingness to accept evidence from a wide variety of sources broke the earlier isolated position of the discipline. In the early decades of its professional existence, anthropologists rarely acknowledged the sister sciences, in spite of the multifarious interests that often overlapped. The first break came when anthropology joined with psychology and psychiatry to study the relationships between personality and culture. It moved closer to sociology when it entered into the study of modern and complex communities, and soon afterward it recognized and utilized the insights provided by economists, political scientists, and jurists.

However many different directions anthropological research interests took, the notion of culture as learned behavior remained central in all undertakings. After Tylor had defined culture in 1871, almost half a century elapsed before anthropologists in America began to formulate their own definitions. Once the idea that culture was a learned phenomenon had been set forth, it was so obvious that no further elaborations appeared necessary. Even Boas did not venture a definition of his own until he was seventy-two years old. It seems that Clark Wissler was the first American to do so when he wrote that culture was "all social activities in the broadest sense" (Wissler 1920:3), which retained the Tylorian spirit, but was certainly no improvement. From this time onward, however, definitions rapidly proliferated, because it became recognized that culture had many other properties and meanings over and above the fact that it was learned. In 1952, Kroeber and Kluckhohn listed 164 different definitions as well as over a hundred statements about culture. These numbers are much larger at present, and indicate both the protean nature of culture and the scholarly concerns about it. Kroeber himself wrote extensively on the nature of culture (Kroeber 1948:253–310, and 1952). He showed that culture is open and receptive, so that it can undergo change by diffusion and invention; that its parts are interconnected and merge into each other without definite breaks so as to form a coherent whole; that it is cumulative and additive because past knowledge does not get lost; that it is also composite, diversified, symbolic, coherent, and integrated; it possesses meanings, values, and functions; and it molds the personality of individuals.

Clyde Kluckhohn's (1905–60) *Mirror for Man* (1949) went a long way to popularize anthropology and to bring the notion of culture to the attention of the general public. In simple and nontechnical language he showed that anthropology is more than a collection of queer customs, potsherds, and skulls: it can provide a scientific basis for dealing with contemporary problems. Portraying the great variety of existing cultural behavior patterns, he pleaded not only for recognition and tolerance of nonliterate cultures, but also for an understanding even of the cruelties of Germans and Japanese during the Second World War. Admitting that this was difficult, Kluckhohn declared that the great lesson of culture is that the goals toward which men strive and fight are not biologically "given." If Germans and Japanese behaved as they did because of their biological heredity, the outlook for restoring them as peaceful nations would be hopeless. The concept of culture thus carried a note of hope: proper understanding of its meaning could assist in the struggle to diminish bigotry, anti-Semitism, and racism (Kluckhohn 1949:40). If political leaders of the world today could be convinced of this very simple fact, and realize that war is also learned behavior and thus not innate and natural, international tensions could become eased and our chances for survival greatly improved.

While political leaders seem impervious to such understanding, the concept of culture has exercised an enormous influence on American thought, and the clarification and popularization of this idea is one of the most seminal contributions of anthropology. Lawyers, doctors, dentists, nurses, social workers, and all others dealing with people have come to understand that it is necessary to know something about the cultural background of their clients if their interrelationships with them are to be successful. Social scientists and philosophers have become aware of the cultural dimensions of their own researches, and many realize that their findings may be culture-bound and thus not necessarily universal. Many others are cognizant of the fact that their own ways of observing and behaving are not normative for the rest of the world.

Neither Boas nor his followers were opposed to functionalism, and its methods were used quite frequently and casually. American anthropologists have left it largely to their colleagues in sociology to define or redefine "function" and to make theoretical elaborations. Most anthropological textbooks and published collections of "readings" contain no sections dealing with functionalism per se (Kroeber 1953; Tax 1964; Hammond 1964; Fried 1968 and 1973; Jennings and Hoebel 1972; Hughes 1972; Barnouw 1971; Hockett 1973; Weaver 1973; and many others). Those that do deal with it reprint articles by British social anthropologists or sociologists (Thomas 1956; Manners and Kaplan 1968) or discuss *their* theoretical contributions (Lowie 1937; Harris 1968). The indices of the *American Anthropologist* for the years 1949–69 list functionalism only four times, which does not mean that functional analyses are absent in their pages, but indicates a lack of theoretical concern. Radcliffe-Brown taught at the University of Chicago from 1931 till 1937, and his version of functionalism became generally more accepted in this country than that of Malinowski. But American anthropologists had been fully aware of the importance of function long before the theories of Radcliffe-Brown and Malinowski became widely known here. Morgan had already enunciated one of its principles when he wrote "every institution of mankind which attained permanence will be found linked with a perpetual want" (Morgan 1963:98), and his whole evolutionary scheme was predicated on an understanding of functional interrelationships between such social institutions as family structure and kinship, or between family interaction and house types. Boas repeatedly demonstrated how several aspects of culture influence one another, and his criticism of British functionalism was directed at its lack of historical insights and its futile search for laws. Kroeber explained the integration of Mohave culture by tracing the interrelationships between its myths, songs, and dreams, while Cora DuBois showed that the prestige of wealth could serve as an independent variable that went a long way to explain tribal ideology and other cultural elements in Northwest Indian cultures.

Their view that functional analysis is an approach that can meaningfully be combined with others has remained present in most subsequent anthropological writings. George Peter Murdock's influential *Social Structure* (1949) was most explicit on this point. In this book, historical, functional, psychological, and statistical methods are brought together to form a harmonious synthesis of cross-cultural comparisons. The statistical element entered because of Murdock's participation in the Yale University Institute in Human Relations, which he later on directed. The Human Relations Area Files (HR-AF) consist of a classification system of ethnographic data in all culture areas of the world. Vast bodies of material, taken from both published and unpublished sources, are coded and cross-filed, so that researchers have easy access to data that otherwise would take them a lifetime to accumulate. At the time when Murdock wrote *Social Structure* he used data from some 250 different societies about which the coded material was already available.

Murdock's approach may be illustrated by his analysis of incest taboos. Prohibitions of sexual intercourse within the nuclear family are universal, but in every known society these taboos are extended beyond the father-daughter, mother-son, and brother-sister relationships. These extensions are not the same everywhere. Sometimes they include maternal cousins only, or paternal ones only, or sometimes other relatives, not always biologically related. Many scholars attempted to account for this seemingly strange phenomenon. Some held that the horror of incest was instinctive, but in that case the taboos would not need to be stated, and the extensions remained unexplained. Others felt that people living in close proximity for long periods of time lost all sexual interest in one another —which is simply untrue. Murdock grasped the complexity of the problem and showed that it could not be explained by anthropology alone. He credited Sigmund Freud with the explanation of the universality of incest taboos, because he had shown that the nuclear family was constituted in such a way that it generated the Oedipus complex, so that rather than having instinctive aversions, a boy desired his mother sexually. Social training strongly repressed this desire, which accounted for the emotional quality of the prohibition of incest and the often very severe punishments for breaking the rules. Sociology (which Murdock equated with functionalism) had shown that without incest taboos, sexual competition within the family would weaken this important institution, thus endangering the whole society. It remained to be explained why the prohibitions extended beyond the nuclear family. Using data from HRAF, Murdock demonstrated that extension in the direction of maternal relatives is most common in matrilineal societies, in the paternal direction in patrilineal societies, and in both directions in cases of double descent. These and many other such findings of cross-cultural regularities are in turn functionally interrelated with other cultural rules such as exogamy, preferential marriage, family organization, and residence rules.

There is perhaps no other aspect of social structure that has fascinated anthropologists quite as much as the analysis of kinship. Murdock's *Social Structure*, although giving new dimensions to this subject, is but one in a very long list of publications emphasizing kinship. Some of these studies are quite abstract, written in a kind of kinship algebra that can be deciphered only by other specialists in this field. In fact, American anthropologists long remained rather aloof from any directly practical applications of their science. They tended toward the persuasion that it was their primary task to study nonliterate cultures, preferably those that had not been strongly contaminated by Western contacts. When some anthropologists turned their attention to acculturation studies, the American Anthropological Association was not altogether certain that this was a legitimate field of concern for their discipline. The question was officially raised and discussed at the annual meeting of the organization in 1936, after Leslie Spier, then editor of the *American Anthropologist*, officially asked the participants if he should accept articles dealing with acculturation studies for publication, or if they were better referred to sociological journals. A motion was made and seconded to the effect that the topic indeed did lie within the scope of anthropology, but the motion was tabled and never taken up again in subsequent meetings (Beals 1953:623). Although acculturation studies proliferated from this time onward, they were accepted as appropriate to the discipline only after some soul searching.

Acculturation deals with the effects of firsthand and continuous contact between two or more cultures. It is thus somewhat different from diffusion, which is a process of voluntary and usually selective borrowing. "Firsthand and continuous contact" is more typical of colonial and conquest situations, or of a large influx of immigrants. In theory cultures thus in contact exercise mutual influence, but in reality many ac-

culturation studies dealt with the impact of Western civilization upon native cultures. This encroachment caused adminis-
trative, political, and ideological concerns, and it was clear
that acculturation studies could have great practical value.
Their value was recognized by the U.S. Bureau of Indian
Affairs, and John Collier, who was at that time the commis-
sioner of the Bureau, requested two ethnologists to serve as
consultants to his agency. As good anthropologists, they
insisted that the traditions, beliefs, and culture patterns of
Indians should be recognized and taken into consideration.
Government officials failed, however, to see the importance
of the Indian ways of life, and believed that both Indians and
America as a whole would be best served if the Indians could
be persuaded (or forced) to total assimilation with the white
man's way of life. This was, and still is, the American "melt-
ing pot" ideology, namely the ethnocentric conviction that the
American way of life is best for everyone. Anthropological
experience in native societies has made it manifest that every
culture, however simple its technology, possesses its own
dignity, values, and meanings. No valid way has as yet been
discovered to prove that one system is intrinsically better than
any other. Anthropologists have also observed that attempts
to impose drastic culture change have led in many instances
to severe cultural crises, accompanied by social unrest, hostility, demoralization, or sheer hopelessness. Their insistence
upon these views has not been well received by government
administrators, who sometimes even accuse anthropologists of
wanting to preserve native cultures for their own study purposes. Nevertheless, various government agencies continue
to use anthropologists as consultants, but their advice is not
often heeded. Most cultural anthropologists have remained
wary of lending their services in any direct manner to organizations actively involved in human engineering, and continue
their acculturation studies on a theoretical level. The results
of these studies are of course available to all government
officials and policy makers. *Acculturation in Seven American
Tribes* (Linton 1940) defined various types of contact and

explained the reasons for their different consequences. *Acculturation in the Americas* (Tax 1952), *Human Problems in Technological Change* (Spicer 1952), *Perspectives in American Indian Culture Change* (Spicer 1961), *Cultural Patterns and Technical Change* (Mead 1955), and many others describe and analyze conditions of contact, and add significantly to the understanding of culture change and of acculturation. Hallowell (1957) is one of the few to present the other side of the coin. He wrote on the many contributions made by American Indians to the culture of America. He mentioned not only corn, tobacco, moccasins, and the log cabin, but also showed how American culture has been influenced by Indian music, art, folklore, language, and even by modes of thought.

It became increasingly understood that the analysis of acculturation and culture change required knowledge of both cultures in contact, and many anthropologists turned to the study of complex societies. A variety of reasons impelled them to do so, including the emergence of new nations, the rapid rate of change accompanying these developments, and perhaps also the decrease of simpler societies—very few are left untouched by Western influence. Moreover, anthropologists became convinced that the insights gained from their close acquaintance with non-literate cultures could profitably be extended to include more complex situations. They realized, however, that their methods of analysis had to be modified. In simpler societies it had been possible for the field worker to become familiar with the full round of culture, while in large and heterogeneous societies the social whole cannot be so observed even by a team of anthropologists. The question arose if and how the traditional holistic approach could be maintained in the study of complex cultures. A stimulating answer was provided by the theory of the community study method.

An early formulation of this method appeared in the first volume of the famous *Yankee City* series (Warner and others 1941–59). The authors explained that a territorially defined unit such as a community was a laboratory for the study of the social whole because it was in many respects a microcosm of the larger society. This view was already implicit in Conrad Arensberg's *The Irish Countryman* (1937), and he became in later years the most vigorous defender of the method (Arensberg 1954, 1955, 1961). He explained that community study is not the study of a community, but a method of research in complex societies. It is thus not to be confused with efforts to study a village as if it formed a total social system in and of itself, although such studies do exist and have their own place in the literature. Community study method, however, treats a village or any other geographical subunit as an integral part of the wider social system. As such, a well-chosen community will reflect the larger culture to a significant degree. Community studies thus examine not only the internal structure of a community, but also its participation in the network of communications, interactions, and all other relationships with the surrounding villages and towns. According to Arensberg, a carefully selected and sampled community stands in a one-to-one correspondence to the culture as a whole, and is the microcosm of the macrocosmic whole (Arensberg 1955:1143). More often than not, groups of communities will have a similar historical descent, similar value systems, and comparable social structures. This in turn implies that every culture has its own characteristic community type. Arensberg suggested that there are several distinctive types of community in the United States, each representative of a recognized American subculture. These include New England towns, county seats of the Deep South, crossroad hamlets of the Appalachians, and Main Street towns and mill towns of the great American middle country (*ibid.*:1143–62).

This approach has come under attack from anthropologists and other social scientists doing research in complex areas (Steward 1950, Manners 1957, Dumont and Pocock 1957). Although in full agreement with the principle that communities are functionally interrelated to each other and to the total culture, they found that in most instances the idea of the microcosm did not reflect reality. Some recommended that the networks of such institutions as marriage, trade, politics, and religion should be carefully examined, suggesting that the interrelationships between these networks would provide a better way of analyzing whole cultures (Mariott 1959:66–74). Others conceptualized these relationships in terms of social roles (Pitkin 1959:14–19), or in terms of circulation of people and the exchange of goods, services, information, values, and symbols (Casagrande 1959:1–10). Robert Redfield (1955) suggested a great many ways in which the relationship between community and the larger culture could be conceptualized: by looking at a community as an ecological system, a social structure, a typical biography, a kind of person, an outlook on life, and so forth.

The study of complex cultures also brought renewal of the old question of social typology. Confucius, Plato, Aristotle, Cicero, Augustine, Thomas Aquinas, and many others had recognized the existence of two different social types. In more recent times, Tönnies had made the distinction between *Gemeinschaft* and *Gesellschaft* (Tönnies 1887), Durkheim between societies with mechanical and organic solidarity, Spencer between homogeneous and heterogeneous ones, the American sociologist Charles Cooley between primary and nonprimary groups, and so on. Anthropologists used a variety of terms to distinguish the peoples whom they preferred to study from all others, and used terms such as "primitive," "nonliterate," or "simple" to refer to them. But their experience with modern cultures taught them that the common areas of so-called primitive cultures and modern ones were greater than their areas of difference. Moreover, they had met with so many different types of society that they realized that simple dichotomies could not be made. As a partial answer to this problem, Redfield (1953) formulated the idea of a folk-urban continuum, a polar-ideal type of construction which implied that no known society precisely corresponds to the description of the extreme ends, but all fall near one or the other of the two poles or in between. He then continued to sum up the typical characteristics of "folk" and "urban," and used their dominant outlooks on life as his main criteria, calling these the "moral" and the "technical" order respectively. The moral order, typical of folk society, signified "all the binding together of men through implicit convictions as to what is right, through explicit ideals, or through similarities of conscience" (*ibid.*:20), which meant in turn that members of folk societies pursued their own ideals of "the good life." The technical order of urban life was composed of the opposite attributes. The bonds that held urban societies together did not rest upon convictions of "the good life," and were not characterized by a foundation in human sentiments. They resulted instead from mutual usefulness, deliberate coercion, or from necessity and expediency (*ibid.*:21).

Subsequently, Redfield himself as well as such scholars as Eric Wolf, Sidney Mintz, George M. Foster, and Manning Nash added an intermediate type of society, namely that of peasantry. Wolf (1966) clearly explained why. The Redfieldian construct had remained rather vague about the vast intermediate ranges of social forms between the ideal polar ends, and there was at least one other typical cultural form that had absorbed some of the characteristics of both "folk" and "urban." In a sense also an ideal construct, peasantry was nevertheless an existing and observable form of social life. Peasants raise crops like most post-Neolithic groups, but they do use their surpluses not for the discharge of ritual and kinship obligations, but for trading with cities. Peasants are also to be distinguished from farmers, who are businessmen in an industrial setting, cultivating their crops for profit only. Peasant societies are relatively self-contained and possess their own indigenous culture structures and values, but they stand in a subordinate relationship to the city, which often controls their land and labor and determines the prices of their agricultural products. They are thus structurally related to the more complex cities. Not only do they trade with them, but they also consider the city as the primary source of innovations because of the prestige of city life. The recognition of peasantry as a social type has led to many important studies contributing also to increased knowledge about economics, ecology, and culture change.

There are not many peasant societies left in America. During World War II, when anthropologists could not freely travel to do field work among peasant or folk societies, they responded creatively by devising a new method that became known as the study of culture "at a distance" (Mead and Métraux 1953). This approach was initiated by Ruth Benedict, who was asked by the U.S. Office of War Information to undertake research on occupied or enemy nations. She selected Japan as her first target, and wrote *The Chrysanthemum and the Sword* (1946), depicting the culture of that nation in a holistic manner, although she had never been there in person. Instead of direct field observation she used Japanese immigrants in the U.S. as her informants, and interviewed many government officials and other persons who had firsthand knowledge of Japan. She also examined historical documents, Japanese literature, and other art forms. The direction of this kind of study was followed by the Columbia University Research in Contemporary Cultures, inaugurated by a grant from the Office of Naval Research, and directed by Margaret Mead after Benedict's death. The first book-length publication arising from this project was Zborowski and Herzog's *Life Is with People* (1952). This is an anthropological study of a culture that no longer exists, the *shtetl,* or the small-town Jewish community of eastern Europe. The authors relied upon their own memories, but they also interviewed many eastern European Jews who now lived in the United States. To many of them, the *shtetl* was not remote, because its values still survived in their memories and in their household practices. Supplementing their findings also with fifty life histories, Jewish literature, drama, humor, and historical documents, the authors not only produced a delightful and very readable book, but demonstrated a new technique of reconstructing vanishing or vanished cultures.

CONCLUSIONS

In dealing with the history of anthropology in America from its early beginnings till the end of World War II, European influences have not been emphasized. This strategy was adopted because one purpose of this chapter was to indicate that American anthropology has its own roots and foundations. Although it adopted many concepts and borrowed many ideas that had their origin in European thought, anthropology in the United States was never a mere imitation, and it possesses many distinct features not generally shared with its counterparts in other countries.

First and foremost among these is that American anthropology has both developed and maintained the four-field approach, which was already in existence long before Boas came to the United States. It arose almost spontaneously through the enthusiastic curiosity about everything pertaining to man and his behavior, together with the insight of leaders like Jefferson that it was necessary to understand the culture and history of the Indians if they were ever to be made into full participants of the developing new nation. The latter ideal has not been fulfilled, partly because of greed, partly because it was not understood that the Indian was proud of his cultural tradition and did not want to be assimilated, and partly also because theories of racism (which will be discussed in the next chapter) sometimes superseded cultural ones.

In any case, this four-field approach became more consciously formulated: since anthropology was a science aiming at the total understanding of mankind, all aspects of human existence that could further such understanding had to be taken into account. At the minimal level, these included man's biological nature, his unique ability to use symbolic language, his history and prehistory, and his cultural behavior patterns.

A second characteristic of American anthropology is that it has never lost sight of the historical perspective. Although many American scholars became interested in functionalism and its emphasis upon synchronic analysis, they continued to relate their findings to such historical concerns as diffusion, reconstruction, culture change, evolution, and the results of civilizations in contact. Most cultural anthropologists keep themselves informed about the findings of archaeologists in the areas of their own interest and specialization, and consider it standard procedure to examine available documents in archives and government offices during the course of their field work.

Related to this is the holistic approach in the description and analysis of individual cultures. American ethnographers and ethnologists strive to deal with the whole range of cultural phenomena, not only with the traditional subjects of economy, the family, kinship, and politics. They regularly include observations about religion, art, folklore, child training, gestures, language, house types, and "any other capabilities and habits of man."

After the initial focus on American Indian cultures, American anthropologists have not imposed any geographical limitations upon their interest in mankind. This attitude stands in fairly sharp contrast to that of anthropologists of former European colonial powers, who carried out most of their researches in societies located in areas of colonial dependency.

It is also noteworthy that American anthropologists have sired more theories and concepts than their colleagues in other parts of the world. Several of their approaches have led into dead alleys, and the profusion of theories has often befuddled the general public and the beginning student alike. Yet this state of affairs indicates that anthropology in this country is not a static discipline, and many of the new approaches have contributed to understanding. Not all of these have been discussed so far. Some will have to remain unmentioned, but some of the more recent developments will be dealt with in the final chapter of this book.

Finally, it has been typical for anthropologists in America to take full account of theories and findings of other disciplines in related fields. Among those, the biological theories of race and the psychological theories of the mind have been of the greatest moment. They warrant separate discussion, and will be the subjects of the next two chapters.

ANTHROPOLOGY AND THE CONCEPT OF RACE

Race is a category of biological classification, related to other taxonomic categories such as phylum, class, order, genus, and species. Technically, the term race denotes the statistically significant genetic variations within a species. Although biologists are not in full agreement about the correct definitions of their classificatory terminology, no one can object to their attempts to understand nature. However, the concept of race as applied to the human species has given rise to the most acrimonious debates, has sired innumerable theories relative to the nature of man and of culture, and has been used as a rationalization for human deprivations of the worst possible kind.

The major fallacy of racist theories rests in the assumption that physical and mental characteristics are correlated, and that both are passed on from generation to generation by hereditary factors. Add to this the equally unscientific notion that the white race is superior to all others, and all ingredients for racism are at hand. Racism may be defined as the ranking of human groups according to their presumed superiority or inferiority, based upon the idea that the features that cause these differences are hereditary. In other words, the ranking criteria are conceived as natural: present "in the blood," or in the genes, or God-given, but in any case unalterable.

Not all ranking of human groups is racist in these terms. Ethnocentrism, geographical determinism, or concepts of degeneration generally allow for improvement. The Greeks were ethnocentric in their conviction that their culture was superior to all others. They called all non-Greeks "barbarians" —people who did not speak the Greek language and whose speech sounded like "bar-bar-bar." But barbarians who learned Greek, accepted the Greek gods, and assimilated to Greek culture patterns were admitted as citizens, no matter if they were physically different. Some achieved such fame that they were honored by a state funeral after death. Augustine made a distinction between "pagans" and "Christians," and cultural value judgments were by no means absent from his religious typology. But he fervently hoped for the conversion of the pagans, which would elevate them to a higher spiritual and cultural level. Geographical determinists traced human differences to influences of climate, temperature, terrain, diet, or disease; but this generally implied that changes in these seeming causal conditions would alter the inferior physical and cultural status of those living in unfavorable parts of the world. Degeneration theories were often predicated on the Christian doctrine of monogenesis. In this view, all human beings were descended from one original couple, and in this sense all were "created equal." Some groups, however, became inferior either through sin, or else through environmental factors. Mission work or improvement of the environment could remedy the situation.

These theories all imply unwarranted and prejudiced value judgments, but they also signify a humanitarian philosophy, calling for programs of welfare and improvement. True racist theories posit that group differences are unalterable, and they were often used as justifications for slavery or other forms of oppression of those who were considered to be inferior by their very nature. The theory of polygenesis attributes human differences to special creations or separate origins, and thus lends itself well to racist interpretations. Biological racism (sometimes called scientific racism) arose with the classification of man in the animal kingdom and the recognition of human variety. It was Linnaeus, the great classifier of nature, who moved the question of relative cultural superiority into the realm of systematic biology. In the first edition of his *Systema naturae* (1735) he introduced his famous system of nomenclature, and recognizing that men belonged to one species, he designated them as *Homo sapiens*. In the subsequent edition of 1738, he added a notation about the "varieties" of man, indicating a fourfold subdivision of the species. He also gave his impressions of the mentality of the four major varieties, as follows:

Homo sapiens americanus: tenacious, contented, free
Homo sapiens europaeus: light, lively, inventive
Homo sapiens asiaticus: stern, haughty, stingy
Homo sapiens afer: cunning, slow, negligent

There are no indications that Linnaeus was a racist bent on the denigration of other human groups. Of course he was convinced that Europeans were superior, because that was the unquestioned dogma of his age. His concept of "variety" arose directly from his botanic studies, and he believed that the observed differences in plants were not hereditary, but caused by climate, sun, or the winds. Moreover, upon the return of the plant to its original habitat it would revert, so he thought, to its original type (Glass 1968:146). While Linnaeus did not apply these ideas to the human species, it is reasonable to conclude that he assigned no hereditary factors to human variability.

According to Ashley Montagu (1964:3), it was the French naturalist Buffon who first used "race" in the sense of Linnaeus' "varieties." Buffon wrote: "In Lapland, and on the northern coast of Tartary, we find a race of man of uncouth figure, and small stature" (1749), and he continued to describe five other groups in a rather impressionistic manner, including their mentality as well. Unlike Linnaeus, Buffon held no great interest in taxonomy, and in a nominalistic vein he explained that species, families, or races had no reality in nature, but were merely invented for the sake of convenience. Nevertheless, Buffon agreed that all human beings belong to a single species, and he explained their physical and mental differences as being caused by environmental factors. It has already been shown how he evoked the wrath of Jefferson by his warped judgment of American Indians, whose physical and intellectual growth had been hampered by the high humidity of the American continent.

The first systematic classifier of human races according to skin color was Johann Friedrich Blumenbach (1752–1840). His five races were Caucasian or white, Mongolian or yellow, Ethiopian or black, American or red, and Malayan or brown (Blumenbach 1775). He stressed that these categories were purely arbitrary, because he knew well that it was impossible to draw a clear-cut line between skin colors since multiple gradations occurred between the extremes. He wrote:

No variety of mankind exists, whether of color, countenance, or stature, etc., so singular as not to be connected with others of the same kind by such an imperceptible transition, that it is very clear that all are related, and only differ from each other in degree.
(Blumenbach 1865:98–99)

Blumenbach and many of his contemporaries (Herder, Goethe, the Humboldt brothers, Cuvier) foresaw the dangers of racial classifications, and expressed their strong beliefs in the essential unity of the human species. Herder, for one, wrote:

I could wish the distinctions between the human species, that have been made from a laudable zeal for discriminating science, not be carried beyond due bounds. Some for instance have thought fit, to employ the term *races* for four or five divisions, originally made in consequence of country or complexion: but I see no reason for this appellation. Race refers to a difference in origin, which in this case does not exist, or in each of those countries, and under each of these complexions, comprises the most different races. . . . In short, there are neither four or five races, nor exclusive varieties, on this Earth. Complexions run into each other: forms follow the genetic character: and upon the whole, all are at last but shades of the same great picture, extending through all ages, and over all parts of

the Earth. They belong not, therefore, so properly to systematic
natural history, as to the physico-geographical history of man.

(Herder 1803:298)

But it was already too late. In the early period of scientific
racism, it was taken more or less for granted that physical
differences went hand in hand with mental ones. It was difficult, however, to know the precise nature of these relationships. It was generally believed that thought emanated from
the soul, a rather elusive entity that was not subject to scientific
observation. The soul transmitted its ideas to the head, but
mental characteristics were not determined by the brain mass.
A contemporary of Blumenbach's, Franz Joseph Gall (1758–
1828), put an end to this mystic conception by his science of
phrenology. Mustering up both anatomic and psychological
evidence, he showed that not the soul but the brain was the
seat of thought, and that there was thus a definite physical
basis for mental activity. Consequently, thought and mentality became amenable to scientific analysis. This aspect of
Gall's work was a genuine breakthrough, and contributed
much to developments in the fields of psychology and medicine. He went on to speculate, however, that different parts
of the brain each had their own mental function, and that the
relative size of these parts determined the degree of development of their respective faculties. Observations and measurements of "bumps" on skulls and heads could thus provide
rather accurate estimates of personality and character. Phrenology enjoyed a period of considerable vogue: it was a new and
seemingly scientific way of fortune telling. Painters such as
Jacques Louis David (1748–1825) attempted to indicate the
character of their human subjects by subtle enlargements of
those parts of the head responsible for their personalities.
Phrenology also motivated scientists to collect and study
skulls in order to make racial classifications and to determine
the "national character" of these groups.

Phrenological measuring techniques, however, were very
imprecise, and more accurate procedures were soon invented.

Andres Retzius (1796–1860) devised a simple formula to express the cephalic index, which is the ratio of the length to the width of the head. Long and narrow heads are dolichocephalic, broad ones brachycephalic. He also measured the relative protrusion of the mandibles, which he expressed as orthognathic (straight jawed) and prognathic (protruding jaws). In 1836, F. Tiedemann described a method to calculate cranial capacity. The procedure was simply to fill a skull with millet seeds, and subsequently to measure them, so that absolute brain size could be determined.

The shape and size of the skull were considered the best indicators of mental superiority of one race over another. The phrenological dictum "the bigger the better" was generally accepted as the basis for these conclusions. Increasing numbers of measurements became added to already existing ones, not only of skulls, but of every bone of the skeleton. Anthropometry (measurement of bones) and somatometry (measurement of the living body) became skills which every physical anthropologist learned to master, and they are still taught in several American colleges. Probably no one else went to the extremes of Dr. A. von Török, who reported to the scientific world that he had taken more than five thousand measurements on a single skull (quoted by Barzun 1965:117).

The interest in skulls resulted in the establishment of some excellent collections, both in Europe and in America. Many catalogues of skulls appeared: Sandifort's *Tabulae craniorum diversarum gentium* (1830), the *Atlas der Cranioskopie* (1864) by Carus, *Crania Britannica* (1856) by Davis and Thurman, and several others. One thing became abundantly clear from the measurements: head shapes and other cranial features displayed great variations and these tended to correlate with geographical racial divisions. This discovery contributed to an ever increasing concern about the unity of the species, and in the first half of the nineteenth century the problem was most often debated in terms of monogenesis versus polygenesis. The latter position involved the rejection of the account of Creation in the book of Genesis, a step not lightly taken at that time. Henry Home, Lord Kames (1696–1782), a Scottish judge, solved this dilemma to a degree by making a compromise between polygenism and orthodoxy. He wrote that available evidence made it most reasonable to conclude that all races were separately created, but the evidence of the Bible could not be denied. However, the book of Genesis also told how God had dispersed people all over the earth as a punishment for their attempts to construct the Tower of Babel. At that time He had given them different languages, but in His mercy God had also bestowed "an immediate change of constitution" upon the different linguistic groups, thus adapting them both physically and mentally for survival in their new environments (Kames 1774). Kames' book was immensely popular, and went through many editions before the turn of the century.

For a time, the polygenists' position appeared indeed "most reasonable," because they had ready-made explanations for observable human differences which monogenists had to justify by other means. A mixture of environmentalism and theology was the best defense they could muster, and it often seemed far from convincing.

The Reverend Samuel Stanhope Smith (1750–1819), professor of moral philosophy at Princeton and later its president, was a monogenist, and a strong believer in the unity of man. The theological part of his defense of this position was that God would not have created separate species that could interbreed. Animal species could not do so, and to make man diverge from this law of nature would imply slovenly workmanship. The theory of polygenesis was thus a slur on the wisdom and the economic sense of the Creator. Smith's pious views left the observable differences between human groups unexplained, and like most monogenists of his time he fell back on environmentalism. Dark skin color was caused by sunlight. Even the blackest Negro was white at birth, and did not turn dark until exposed to the outside, he explained. The good pastor gave no reason why Caucasian infants did not turn into blacks as soon as they went outdoors. Undaunted,

Smith said that everyone knows that sunshine causes freckles, and the dark skin of the Negro was nothing but a "universal freckle" (Stanton 1960:4).

The case of Henry Moss, a Negro whose skin was turning white, must have been a "godsend" to Smith. After examining him, he declared that Moss was in good health, and noted that "wherever there were rents in the thin clothes which covered him there were generally seen the largest spots of black," a sure indication that the sun was responsible for color (*ibid.*:6). Smith's reasoning is hard to follow. If the sun reached the skin through torn clothes thus turning the spots dark, Moss's feet should have been white, his face and hands black. The idea that sunlight is directly responsible for racial differences in skin color is the most naïve of all environmental explanations.

Meanwhile, Moss himself profited from his rare condition. Setting himself up at the Black Horse Tavern in Philadelphia, he charged the substantial admission price of $1.25 per person, and soon he was able to buy his freedom from the proceeds. Among the many scientists who came to view the miracle was Dr. Benjamin Rush, a close friend of Jefferson's. At a subsequent meeting of the American Philosophical Society Rush explained to the learned audience that the black color of Negroes is derived from a mild form of leprosy, which produced an excess of pigment. Moss was undergoing a spontaneous cure (*ibid.*:7).

Smith was closer to the truth when he observed that "it is impossible to draw the line precisely between the various races of men, or even to enumerate them with certainty" (1810:240n). Later in his life, Smith modified his environmentalism to a significant degree, because he had learned to appreciate the power of cultural factors. He wrote:

... the state of society, which may augment or correct the influence of climate ... is itself a separate and independent cause of many conspicuous distinctions among mankind. These causes may be infinitely varied in degree; and their effects may likewise be diversified by various combinations. And, in the continual migrations of mankind, these effects may be still further modified, by changes which have antecedently taken place in a prior climate, and a prior state of society.

(*Ibid.*:244)

He further explained, not unlike Tylor, that "the state of society" included "diet, clothing, lodging, manners, government, arts, religion, agricultural improvements, commercial pursuits, habits of thinking, and ideas of all kinds . . ." (*ibid.*: 176), but he did not realize that these were learned patterns. Yet he anticipated what became the strongest refutation of racism by his insight into the influence of social phenomena, or what later anthropologists called "culture."

Smith's monogenism and his defense of the unity of man found as many sympathizers as detractors. Most influential among the latter was a Philadelphian physician, Samuel G. Morton (1799–1851). Morton had become interested in skulls through his contacts with George Combe (1788–1858), a disciple of Gall. Although Morton cannot be ranked with the phrenologists, he was convinced that "there was a singular harmony between the mental character of the Indian, and his cranial developments" (Hallowell 1960:63). Collecting skulls from all over the world, Morton took some thirteen measurements on 276 specimens, and calculated the cranial capacity of each. When his *Crania Americana* appeared in 1839, it was a model of documented evidence, containing charts and tables, descriptions of his measuring techniques, as well as seventy-one beautiful lithographs depicting Indian types, made by John Collins. From the evidence at hand, Morton concluded that all American Indians belonged to one race, separate from all other races, and not including Eskimos.

Morton was averse to controversy, but was forced to take a stand on the pivotal question of monogenesis versus polygenesis. He followed Kames in giving a nod of recognition to the biblical account of Creation, but he felt that it was after the deluge that God had adapted the races rather than at the Tower of Babel. Later on, Morton found a seemingly more scientific explanation of polygenism. Still operating within the restriction of biblical chronology, which assigned the creation of man to about 4000 B.C., Morton noted that ancient Egyptian art, dating back perhaps to 3000 B.C., already clearly depicted the separate races. It seemed a "physical impossibility" that races could have developed in the thous-and-odd years before that.

Based upon inferences from his physical measurements, Morton also described the moral character of all races. It was unquestioned that Caucasians had achieved the highest mental and moral development, and measurements of their skulls were the standards of high achievement. The degree of deviation from these norms thus indicated the relative want of intellect. The mental faculties of American Indians were, he thought, of "a decidedly inferior cast when compared with those of the Caucasian or Mongolian races" (Morton 1839:81). The Indians were restless, revengeful, fond of war, and since contact with Europeans had had no ennobling effects on them, it could be concluded that they "turn with convulsion from the restraints of civilized life" (*ibid*.:63).

In his *Crania Americana,* Morton included an essay by George Combe called "Phrenological Remarks," and in spite of their differences in method there was a remarkable congruence between their estimation of the races. The Indian came off much worse than the Negro. Morton had called the latter "joyous, flexible and indolent." Combe added that the Negro brain showed less destructiveness and greater benevolence and power of reflection than the brain of the native Americans. Their relatively benign judgment of Negroes may bear some relationship to the fact that both men were strongly opposed to slavery.

To those in favor of slavery, however, polygenism seemed to provide a better "scientific defense" than monogenism. An admirer of Morton's, Josiah Clark Nott (1804–73), was a physician in Mobile, Alabama. A confirmed polygenist, he favored slavery on the ground that Negroes were by nature an inferior race that had "risen but little above the beasts of the field." Their own well-being depended upon the protection offered to them on the plantations, and emancipation would endanger blacks and whites alike, to the point of extermination of both. Nott's first article on this matter contained a warning in its very title: "The Mulatto a Hybrid—Probable Extermination of the Two Races if the Whites and Blacks are allowed to intermarry" (1843:252–56). Together with another friend of Morton's, George R. Gliddon, Nott published *Types of Mankind* (1854), which had gone through ten editions by 1871. It would serve no purpose to repeat all absurd unscientific theories and base denunciations of the Negro that can be found in this book. It is important to note, however, that Nott and Gliddon were in any case honest enough to break completely with biblical traditions. They did not indulge in Kamesian hedging, and made no attempts to reconcile their views with selected parts of Genesis. To the contrary, they held that it was the duty of every Christian to inquire "honestly" into the subject of the unity of man, using the tools of science rather than relying upon the unproven tenets of the Scriptures.

Another learned proslavery southerner, Thomas Cobb, had no need of skull measurements to defend his position. Nature itself gave the example that the enslavement of blacks was normal and regular: "The red ant will issue in regular battle array, to conquer and subjugate the black negro ant . . . these negro slaves perform all the labor of the communities into which they are brought" (Cobb 1858:8–9).

In Europe, the development of racism kept pace with that in America, and the debates also centered around the unity of the human species.

The leading and most influential monogenist in England was James Cowles Prichard (1786–1848). His interest in anthropology developed when, as a young man, he heard debates between monogenists and polygenists. What struck him most was the fact that the opponents both called upon the Scriptures in their defense and Prichard decided to investigate the matter for himself. Although his own position of monogenism was orthodox, he denounced all a priori arguments from biblical sources. Truth was to be found by scientific method only, and the Bible was not involved with scientific research.

He wrote extensively on the question of the unity of man. In his *Researches into the Physical History of Man* (5 volumes, 1836–47), many data about the races of mankind were systematized. Examining in great detail the value of the criteria of color, hair, stature, head shape, and so on, he concluded that environment could not serve as an explanation for the observed differences. He correctly noted that physical features such as skin color remain constant through many generations in different latitudes and climates, so that the degree of sunshine could not be a causal factor. Thus giving up the common standby of monogenists, Prichard had to account for human differences in another way. He developed a theory that shows startling similarities to Darwin's later theory of sexual selection—so much so that it seems difficult to ascribe the two to independent invention, although the historian E. B. Poulton (1896) holds that this is the case.

Be this as it may, Prichard began his explanations by noting that domesticated plants and animals show greater variations within the boundaries of their species than wild ones. Man was a self-domesticated animal, and the process of his domestication found its strongest expression in civilization. It was at this time that many varieties in physical appearance arose. Furthermore, man had been endowed from the beginning with an innate sense of aesthetics that had made him prefer light over dark. Mating and marriage choices tended thus to favor lighter types, eventually producing a distinctive white group which kept itself separate from its darker brothers, so as not to endanger its achieved beauty. Prichard's own sense of aesthetics, innate or not, coupled with his belief in progress, made him conclude that black skin was not a degeneration from white skin, but white skin was progressively derived from black: "The process of Nature in the human species is the transition of the characteristics of the Negro into those of Europeans." The earliest progenitors of the human race, Adam and Eve, thus were blacks. Since the process of

becoming lighter was also coupled with the onset of civilization, Prichard, like all others who adhered to the ideology of
progress, concluded that earlier and darker races were inferior
to lighter and civilized ones. Nevertheless, he was strongly
opposed to slavery and a stout defender of human rights.
Despite the many shortcomings and inconsistencies that are
present in Prichard's theories he was a remarkable figure, not
the least because of his early application of evolution and selection to human development. Had he added the struggle for
existence to his theories, he would have been a Darwinian before Darwin.

The polygenist camp was well developed in England.
Charles White of Manchester argued in 1799 that there were
four distinct and separate races: Europeans, Asians, American
Indians, and Africans, listed in descending order of intelligence. Compared to other races, Negroes had the smallest
brains and the largest genitals, a clear indication of the direction of their interests. White was nevertheless opposed to
slavery. James Hunt (1833–69), a polygenist who strongly
championed the cause of the South, is much better known
than White. His anthropological fame rests primarily on the
fact that he broke away from the existing British Ethnological
Society (founded in 1843) and established the Anthropological
Society of London in 1863. The Ethnological Society was
heavily under the influence of Prichard, and the break was
really based on the diverging views of the Negro question
(Penniman 1965:91). But Hunt couched his arguments in
different terms: he felt that the work of the Ethnological
Society was too narrow in scope. In the opening address to the
renegade Anthropological Society (Hunt was its first president) he declared that anthropology was the whole science of
man, and must include biology, anatomy, chemistry, natural
philosophy, and physiology. Ethnology treated only the history or science of nations or races, while anthropology must
deal with the whole matter of the origin and development of
humanity, with the aid of the geologist, archaeologist, anatomist, physiologist, and philologist (1863, quoted in Penni-

man 1965:91). After the death of Hunt at the early age of thirty-six, the two rival societies were amalgamated as the Anthropological Institute of Great Britain and Ireland in 1871, and this organization, still flourishing, was permitted to add the title "Royal" in 1907. It was henceforward to be devoted to seeking the truth for its own sake.

Earlier than elsewhere, perhaps, racism in France tended to move into the direction of national and class differences. Pierre Paul Broca (1824–88) turned his attention to physical anthropology when 125 skeletons, excavated from an ancient cemetery in Paris, were placed at his disposal. Assigning them to twelfth-century aristocracy, he compared the skulls with 259 others dug up from nineteenth-century paupers' graves, and concluded that the upper-class skulls were superior to the lower-class ones. He was a meticulous scientist, and devised many accurate measuring techniques, invented several instruments to that end, defined the points to be used in taking measurements, and presented methods for collecting and preserving brittle bones. He also realized the limitations of conclusions based upon the measurement of only one or a few skulls, and introduced statistical techniques to calculate skull averages that would indicate the mean characteristics of racial groups rather than absolute ones. He taught that no fewer than twenty skulls of the same population were necessary to establish a race. Broca was also aware that environment, climate, and cultural factors may influence head shapes, and gave hints how to recognize artificial deformations. He also founded the *Société d'Anthropologie de Paris* in 1859, because he could no longer stand the bland preracialist orientations of the existing *Société des Observateurs de l'Homme.*

Although Broca thus made many positive contributions, he remained a victim of the phrenological fallacy that head shape is a good indicator of mentality. Toward the end of his life, Broca began to realize that skull measurements were futile, and turned his attention to the study of the brain itself. But he remained a convinced polygenist throughout his life.

While Broca was devoted to laboratory work and empirical

research, Count Joseph Arthur de Gobineau (1816–82) was
a man of letters, interested in the arts, and a very prolific
writer. He is singled out by many as the Iago of racism, but
his notoriety is partly due to a biased translation of his best-
known work *Essai sur l'inégalité des races humaines* (4 vols.,
1853–55). The English translation of 1915 is entitled *On the
Inequality of Human Races,* but the French word *inégalité*
may also mean "nonuniformity." The title of the earlier English edition is actually closer to the import of the book: *The
Moral and Intellectual Diversity of the Races* (1856).

In this work, de Gobineau divided mankind into three
great races: white, yellow, and black. In his time, racists and
nonracists alike considered the white race superior to all others,
and de Gobineau was no exception: members of the white
race were energetic and born leaders. But compared to some
other writers on this topic, his judgments of the other races
were very mild indeed. The blacks were artistic and sensual, the
yellows stable and fertile. Each race thus had its positive aspects, and all could have lived side by side without great problems. But the white race had been spoiled by interbreeding
with other races. The primitive Aryans, early progenitors of
the superior white race, had allowed themselves to be contaminated by Negro and Asiatic blood, and the results of this
unfortunate mixture were clearly visible in the social and
political decadence of Europe. The influence of the Semites—
whom he classified as Negroid—had been particularly strong
in southern Europe, not excepting France. Although denounc-
ing the Semites and Asiatics, de Gobineau was most vehement
in his descriptions of the thoroughly semitized and melanized
populations of the Latin countries, thus expressing his own
disgust for the mediocrity and decadence in France.

Of course he was a racist, but a pessimistic one. He seems
to have felt that he himself was a relatively pure Nordic-
Aryan, but he did not advocate preserving or perpetuating
racial purity. He knew well that the process of "mixing" had
taken place everywhere: there were very few pure Aryans left.
De Gobineau did not use his theories to support oppression of

others, but presented a racial theory of history, explaining historical changes not only by the contact of cultures, but also by the contact of races, thus biologizing the process.

While his views deserve no praise, his position has often been misunderstood. Although his *Essai* became the bible of later racists, his interpreters and followers often used his writings selectively. Nott, for instance, abridged the four-volume *Essai* for its American publication and selected mainly those pages that supported his own unmitigated racism. Writing a long appendix, Nott explained that de Gobineau's monogenism could not be taken seriously because the author was a Catholic who, moreover, had no accurate knowledge of biology.

Richard Wagner (1813–83), after becoming acquainted with de Gobineau and his work, interpreted it as a glorification of "the German race," and wrote essays of his own with blatant anti-Semitic overtones. His son-in-law, the "renegade Englishman" Houston Stewart Chamberlain (1855–1927), wrote his own version of racial history in *The Foundations of the Nineteenth Century* (1899). He became so popular with German aristocracy and rulers that he was known as "the Kaiser's anthropologist." But that was in 1899. Meanwhile, the political and scientific climate had undergone significant changes in Europe as well as in the rest of the world.

Pre-Darwinian discussions of race exhibit a mixture of sincere scientific interests in the nature of man and abject prejudices. The dividing line between the two is not always easy to draw. Polygenist theories lent themselves well to the support of slavery, but many polygenists were strongly in favor of emancipation. It is of course true that scientists generally react to the ethos of their times. In this sense, racism is a product of human beings responding to conditions that they themselves created. These conditions involved not only the slavery issue or how to deal with American Indians, but included the social configuration in its totality. Among its various components, the influence of economics presents itself with great strength. The laissez-faire doctrine, best known through the writings of the Scottish economist Adam Smith (1723–90), came to be one of the main principles of classical economics. In his famous *An Inquiry into the Nature and Causes of the Wealth of Nations* (1776), Smith maintained that competition motivated by private interest was the key to economic success both on the personal and the national level. The ideals of the Protestant ethic were compatible with this economic philosophy, and together they made individual competition and economic success both desirable and respectable.

When Darwin's *Origin of Species,* subtitled *The Preservation of Favored Races in the Struggle for Life,* appeared, his theories seemed to provide further justifications for competition and individualism. The struggle for life in the biological realm appeared to be a natural law applicable also to social life. The economic success of some and the poverty of others, the spread of Western technology over all parts of the earth, the continued oppression of the American Indians, imperialism, class struggles, and civil wars all seemed to be part and parcel of the same law, even if Darwin himself at first made no such extensions. In fact, he expressed surprise that his views might be relevant to social questions (Himmelfarb 1968:413). In the *Origin* he was timid about even including man in the biological process of evolution. All he said about man was that all animals were probably descended from one primordial form, and that "light will be thrown on the origin of man." But Wallace, Spencer, Huxley, Lyell, and several others, less pusillanimous, at once began to construe the social implications of biological evolution. Darwin himself followed suit only in 1871 with the publication of *The Descent of Man.* By that time he realized that there was not much new to contribute to the subject, and declared that he wrote the book mainly to vindicate himself from accusations that he was concealing his opinions (Himmelfarb 1968:354).

Darwin vindicated himself by stating outright that man was descended from a "hairy, tailed quadruped, probably arboreal in its habits," and was ultimately related to a hermaphrodite aquatic animal, not unlike the larvae of the existing marine Ascidians (sea squirts) (Darwin 1871:911).

This book centered around two major topics: the evolution of human mentality and the origin of human races. As to the former, Darwin was cautious in his dealings with inherited mental patterns, expressing his belief that deeply ingrained habits might transmit tendencies, but never the habits themselves. But his overall position was quite clear: conscience, morality, religion, reasoning powers, and similar mental phenomena were subject to the evolutionary process, and good qualities aid in survival. It is true that Darwin often qualified the importance of natural selection on the psychological plane. Perhaps his acquaintance with what he repeatedly called "the interesting works of Mr. Tylor" had made him dimly aware that culture could not be overlooked. Hedgingly he admitted that such factors as imitation, or deliberate cultivation of mental and moral excellence, might interfere with natural laws.

Darwin's discussions of race are notable for his retreat from natural selection:

For my own part, I conclude that of all the causes which have led to the differences in external appearance between the races of man, and to a certain extent between man and the lower animals, sexual selection has been the most efficient.

(Ibid.:908)

His four-hundred-page argument may be summed up as follows: Each primitive group possessed its own standards of beauty. Some held that black skin and flat noses were most attractive, others favored yellow or white skin and long noses. Those individuals who came closest to the local aesthetic ideals were favored as mates, and in time the unappreciated traits disappeared.

The important thing to note here is that Darwin accounted for mental and physical differences in entirely different ways, thus breaking the insidious correlation between intellectual and physical features that had been generally accepted since

Linnaeus. So different were the respective developments, according to Darwin, that they were subject to separate evolutionary processes, the one by natural, the other by sexual selection.

While this was an important breakthrough, it did not impede further growth of racism, because Darwin as well as many of his contemporaries and followers remained convinced of the intellectual superiority of the Caucasians, no matter whether or not it was related to physical appearance. It was, Darwin wrote, "the grade of their civilization" that seemed to be the most important element in the success of the competing nations (*ibid.*:543), and although thus weakening the older biological arguments for the explanation of "the unequal progress of the races," he placed the burden upon history. The Tasmanians, for one, had become extinct, and this proved without a doubt that they had been less fit for survival and thus inferior. Darwin also never doubted that the race most favored to survive was the European. History had shown that this race possessed superior mental faculties and the most advanced civilization. In a letter to W. Graham, he wrote:

I could show fight on natural selection having done more for the progress of civilization than you seem inclined to admit. Remember what risk the nations of Europe ran, not so many centuries ago, of being overwhelmed by the Turks, and how ridiculous such an idea now is! The more civilized so-called Caucasian races have beaten the Turkish hollow in the struggle for existence. Looking to the world at no very distant date, what an endless number of the lower races will have been eliminated by the higher civilized races throughout the world.

(1881, quoted by Himmelfarb 1968:416)

On the whole it may be said that the polemic in the *Origin* was far superior to that of the *Descent*. In the latter, Darwin's arguments are confused and confusing, and often contradict one another. Clearly, he was a great biologist, but not a social philosopher. In fact, it was Herbert Spencer rather than Darwin who bestowed scientific respectability upon the application of biological evolution to social life.

Spencer had used the catch phrases "struggle for existence" and "survival of the fittest" earlier than Darwin. Long before the publication of the *Origin,* Spencer had speculated that pressure of subsistence exercised beneficial effects upon humanity because this struggle for existence placed a premium upon skill and intelligence. Individuals possessing the greatest degree of these adaptive features were the fittest and survived. The laws of evolution thus operated alike in the biological and social realms.

Spencer not only takes temporal precedence over Darwin in matters of social evolution, but his writings possessed certain qualities that made his theories more persuasive. First, Spencer's system possessed a strong internal consistency once his basic premise that the universe and all it contains moves from simplicity to complexity was accepted. Everything now seemed to fall in place, and philosophy could indeed become "synthetic." Moreover, Spencer presented his theories in a language free from jargon, so that they could be understood more easily.

The evolutionary theories of Darwin and Spencer together reflected the sociopolitical conditions of their times, and were interpreted within the framework of dominant concerns. Their combined writings were so rich in content and ideas that they could supply support for the ideas of scholars of most different persuasions, much as the Bible had done earlier. Natural selection and survival of the fittest were not the causes of post-Darwinian racial theories, but they became instruments in the hands of those bent on proving that might makes right. Although there were no sharp breaks, racism after Darwin and Spencer was marked by a movement in the direction of national and class distinctions. Slavery had been abolished everywhere, but Caucasians were competing among themselves and attempted to find justification in the laws of nature for fierce competition, rapid expansion, and imperialism. While the importance of physical criteria as indicators of relative intelligence became somewhat curtailed, races cannot be recognized without external markers, and especially the cephalic index captured the imagination of those who searched for distinctions among Europeans. Reliance on history as proof for racial superiority or inferiority also became more pronounced after Darwin, and a relatively new element entered in the form of eugenics, or efforts to maintain or promote racial purity. But counterarguments also became more persuasive. Physical anthropologists, frustrated in their efforts to pinpoint races, lost confidence in the concept, while the growing insight into the nature of culture convinced many that the correlation between mental and physical evolution stood in need of reexamination.

These various developments occurred not only side by side, but often hand in hand, and the resulting theories reflected this by their hybridity and self-contradiction. In France, Joseph Deniker (1852–1918) objected to the term "race" for several reasons. His researches and measurements had shown that any racial group exhibited numerous variations, and he began to feel that race was a hypothetical concept, and classification an unattainable ideal. He further noted that groups of people commonly called "races" were in fact held together by cultural rather than physical criteria. He wrote:

Do these real and palpable groupings represent unions of individuals which, in spite of some slight dissimilarities, are capable of forming what zoologists call "species," "subspecies," "varieties," in the case of wild animals, or "races" in the case of domestic animals? One need not be a professional anthropologist to reply negatively to this question. They are *ethnic groups* formed by virtue of community of language, religion, social institutions, etc., which have the power of uniting human beings of one or several species, races, or varieties, and are by no means zoological species . . .

(Deniker 1900:2–3)

Nevertheless, these remarks were made in the preface of his book called *The Races of Man* (1900), and he identified ten races in Europe alone. His American counterpart, William Zebina Ripley (1867–1941), also had his doubts about the factual reality of race, since individual members rarely, if ever, embodied all diagnostic criteria in their person. Race was an abstraction existing mainly in the mind of the observer. But this abstraction figured also in the title of Ripley's book *The Races of Europe* (1899), although its subtitle was *A Sociological Study*. As much as he could, he included social and environmental factors to account for physical differences, but he regularly confused biological inheritance and socially learned behavior. Yet he was among the first, along with Boas, to argue that race, culture, and language bore no intrinsic hereditary relations to each other. He found three races in Europe: Teutons, Alpines, and Mediterraneans.

He also decided to test what had become known as "Ammon's law." Otto Ammon (1842–1916), a German journalist, had compared head measurements of contemporary urban and rural populations, and found more longheads in cities, more roundheads among peasants. This seemed to him a convincing proof that dolichocephalics were more intelligent. Jumping to conclusions, he wrote:

The longheads [dolichocephalics] of German descent represent the bearers of higher spiritual life, the occupants of dominant positions, to which they are destined by nature, the innate defenders of the fatherland and the social order. Their whole character predetermines them to aristocracy. . . . From purely scientific interests, to which the longheads are driven by their desire for knowledge and to which they devote all the impetus of their character, the roundheads keep more aloof. Their inclination to the democratic theory of equality is due to the fact that they themselves do not exceed mediocrity and feel nothing but an aversion, if not hatred, against grandness which they cannot understand.

(Quoted by Weidenreich 1946:101–02)

Ripley similarly compared city and country dwellers' heads in the United States, and he too found more dolichocephalics in urban centers. Unable to shake off the notion that this must relate to intelligence, he was forced to the same conclusions as Ammon, although without the blatant nationalistic overtones. Ripley stated that longheads may be more inclined to migrate to cities, but he also felt that the greater challenges of urban life may influence the cephalic index of the children of roundheads. The latter idea was an improvement over earlier ones, because it implied that headshape may be affected by environment, and was thus not strictly a hereditary factor.

German writers of the period tended to be much less careful in their estimations of class superiority. The German dentist C. Röse calculated cephalic indices of business leaders and successful intellectuals, comparing them with those of office workers and manual laborers. He boldly concluded: "the higher the position and the greater the salary, the longer are the heads." Others, perhaps round-headed themselves, came to opposite conclusions and demonstrated to their own satisfaction that brachycephalics were the more intelligent ones.

Whatever the conclusions, it became generally accepted that "the races of Europe" were a rather mixed lot. De Gobineau had blamed the social and political upheavals in Europe on the intermingling of the races, and since the process could no longer be reversed, he feared for the future of the Continent. His countryman Georges Vacher de Lapouge shared this pessimistic outlook. The three major races of Europe were, in his view, quite unequal in temperament. The blond dolichocephalic Protestant Nordics were brave and creative, one step below were the brachycephalic Catholic Alpines, dull, conservative, and obedient. Lowest on the scale were the Mediterraneans. Their head shape was mesocephalic, somewhat in between round and long, and they were restless and treacherous. Discussing the struggle for existence between the three races in terms of politics, economy, religion, and morality, Lapouge concluded that the Nordics were in danger of being overwhelmed by the Alpines in sheer numerical terms. The Alpines produced so many offspring and interbred so frequently with others that the Nordics might be bred out of existence. Although Lapouge regretted this, he too believed that the tide could not be turned.

Francis Galton (1822–1911), a cousin and admirer of Darwin's, was more optimistic. He laid the foundations of a movement known as eugenics that promised to save or possibly even improve the better-endowed races. Taking his cues from natural selection, Galton felt that the theories of his famous relative stood in need of practical application. If nature worked toward survival of the fittest, it stood to reason that man could emulate the process by selective breeding, even if Darwin and Spencer had held that nature is better left alone.

Galton first wanted to make certain that desirable mental and moral qualities were indeed hereditary. In his first book, *Hereditary Genius* (1869), he explained that he had examined some three hundred families of eminent men. He defined "eminence" as achievement of a prominent social position or artistic success. Finding that close relatives of such famous men achieved eminence more often than distant ones, he concluded that genius was due to "nature" or heredity rather than to "nurture" or environment. It followed that members of families naturally endowed with eminent qualities should practice "judicious mating," and he proposed that registers of superior families should be established for these purposes.

Galton's writings were received with much acclaim both in Europe and in the United States, and around the turn of the century many eugenic societies were founded and eugenic records offices established. Although the inclusion in these records had a great amount of snob appeal, the advice to seek one's marriage partner from these listings was not generally heeded. It was then that an alternative method became popularized: the unfit should in any case be prevented from multiplying. Identifying the fit with the upper classes, and criminality, physical illness, and mental deficiency with the lower ones, eugenists perpetuated the idea that the poor were biologically destined to their miserable conditions. Although some eugenic societies were philanthropically inclined, many advocated the institution of sterilization laws, expecting that this would eliminate crime, insanity, feeblemindedness, abnormal sexuality, and all other social evils in less than a century.

The eugenics movement drew fire from several angles, earliest from those who had begun to understand the influence of social conditions upon performance, later also from biologists and physical anthropologists. Lester Ward (1841–1913), for one, examined Galton's statistics and demonstrated that in all his cases of "hereditary genius" people had money, education, were literate, and had access to books, without which genius could not succeed (1906). Ward also disagreed with Spencer, showing repeatedly that physical and mental evolution did not proceed along the same lines. Modern geneticists demonstrated that the eugenic ideals are unattainable, even from the point of view of physical fitness alone. Dunn and Dobzhansky (1952:87) noted that many mental and physical disabilities are due to recessive genes which remain undetected in parents. Ashley Montagu (1960:275) added that sterilization of defective individuals would do very little to delete unfavorable genes from the total population, while Birdsell (1942:476) concluded that a scrupulous application of eugenic principles would involve sterilization of all human beings. Moreover, it is clear that physical or mental unfitness did not prevent Dostoyevsky, Van Gogh, Toulouse-Lautrec, Kierkegaard, Helen Keller, and many others from unfolding their genius in intellectual and artistic realms.

While eugenic societies still exist, they have lost much of their popular appeal. The most prominent modern eugenist is Hermann J. Muller, who won the Nobel Prize for his discovery of the influence of radiation on mutation. He did not promote sterilization, but advocated selective breeding like the earlier eugenists. It had become known that sperm can be frozen for long periods of time without losing its generative powers, and Muller recommended that sperm of highly endowed males should be preserved in this manner. It can then be utilized in artificial insemination, implanting it in "desirable females" who would certainly not refuse to bear a child of a man like Leonardo, Descartes, Pasteur, Lincoln, or Einstein.

The difficulties involved in all eugenic schemes, including Muller's, are not only ethical, but pertain also to the inconclusive status of the relationship between genetic factors and mental capabilities. Although genes and ability are related in some ways, genes set potentialities only, and do not determine final results. The stimulus of the environment will work on the genetic potential, and environment is anything that acts upon the individual, including opportunity for education, economic conditions, home environment, and culture in general.

The term Social Darwinism is sometimes applied to all theories that equate social and biological evolution, but it is more specifically identified with the theories of those social scientists who paid little or no attention to physical characteristics, but applied the principles of natural selection and survival of the fittest directly to the social realm. In the latter sense, William Graham Sumner (1840–1910) was the most influential Social Darwinist in America. His teachings at Yale University turned this institution into a citadel—some say a hotbed—of this movement. Opposed to eugenics, Sumner took the more orthodox Spencerian stand that evolution would inevitably run its course, and any interference by governments or well-meaning philanthropists would be of no avail, and might even be dangerous. The Spencerian principle that evolution advanced from the simple to the complex was quite welcome in the ethnically diverse United States, and the thought that heterogeneity spelled progress, and that backward races would disappear because of their unfitness, gave comfort to many Anglo-Saxons, who felt that they themselves were eminently "fit."

In a sense, Sumner read the evolutionary principles of Darwin and Spencer back to front. He argued that survival of the fittest could have no meaning unless there was social inequality. The existing unequal distribution of wealth set the laws of nature in motion, and economic competition was nature's major tool in the social realm. Sumner concluded that money was the surest indication of social fitness:

The millionaires are a product of natural selection, acting on the whole body of men to pick out those who can meet the require-

ment of certain work to be done. . . . It is because they are thus
selected that wealth—both their own and that entrusted to them—
aggregates under their hands. . . . They may fairly be regarded as
the naturally selected agents of society . . .

(Sumner 1914:90)

Consequently, Sumner condemned all welfare acts, poor
laws, and, as he put it, "any other device whose aim it is to save
individuals from any of the difficulties or hardships of the
struggle for existence." He added that the Jeffersonian idea
that all men were equal was simply a falsehood.

Cultural anthropologists who turned their attention to
evolution on a universal scale were much less involved than
Social Darwinists with contemporary problems. They were
more interested in remote primitive cultures, but they did not
escape the influence of the dominant ideologies of their times.
There were no doubts in their minds about the superiority of
Western civilization over the cultures of savages and barbarians, but they also generally subscribed to the doctrine of
psychic unity, and began to realize that culture is learned
rather than biologically determined behavior. Tylor pioneered
the latter insight, and made the conclusion that inevitably
follows, namely that considerations of race should be eliminated from the study of culture (Tylor 1958 I:7). But after
a while, Tylor retreated from this position, and came to believe
that culture was inborn and somehow related to physical
characteristics after all. Referring to findings of "eminent
anatomists," he wrote that the European brain is both larger
and more complex in its convolutions than the brain of a
Negro or a Hottentot. Admitting that these observations had
not yet been perfected, they showed, nevertheless, "a connection between a more full and intricate system of brain cells
and fibers, and a higher intellectual power" (Tylor 1916:60).
Tylor also spoke of "inbred temperament" and "inbred
capacity of mind," and held that children of "lower races"
learn as well as children of "the ruling race" until the age
of about twelve years, but then they fall off and are left far
behind. He added that "this fits well with what anatomy

teaches of the lesser development of the brain in the Australian and African than in the European" (*ibid.*:75).

With such views of biologically determined inferiority, Tylor could not become a challenger of racism. Among anthropologists, it was Boas who led the first conscious and consistent attacks, dealing with both the physical and the cultural aspects of racist theories. Biological racism had set great stock by skull and head measurements because of the implied correlations with intelligence, but also because it was believed that head shape was strictly hereditary and impervious to environmental influences. Boas measured heads of foreign-born Hungarians, Poles, Italians, Slovaks, and Scotsmen, and compared these with measurements of their American-born children. He found that significant differences in cephalic index existed between the immigrants and their offspring, and these tended to be greater the longer they had lived in the United States (Boas 1963). Boas' results have been confirmed by others, among those C. E. Guthe (1918), N. D. M. Hirsch (1927), and Harry L. Shapiro (1939). The latter made a very detailed study of a group of Japanese immigrants to Hawaii, and compared their measurements with those of their relatives who had remained behind in Japan and with those of their Hawaiian-born offspring. He, too, found significant differences in cephalic index, nasal dimensions, sitting height, and other physical measurements. Allowing for chance variations, his sample was large enough to prove without doubt that head shape is not entirely dependent upon heredity but may respond to environmental factors and diet even within one generation.

Boas further showed that the size of the brain is no indicator of mental excellence. Some eminent people had large brains, other fell way below the average, and also in mentally defective people brain size varied from large to small. Moreover, Boas pointed out that all racial groups showed so much internal variation in physical characteristics that no major discontinuity between races could be found, and clear-cut classifications did thus not exist.

On the cultural level, Boas cogently argued that every

group of people, no matter what their physical appearance, developed cultures enabling them to survive, and that there were no ways of measuring which cultures were better than others. Primitive peoples had made many inventions and often produced excellent art, their social institutions were often quite complex, and above all, they were fully capable of learning Western civilization or any other cultural form if given the opportunity. In other words, Boas fully accepted the early Tylorian insight that culture was acquired, and thus bore no correlation to physical appearance or language.

Subsequent anthropologists have fully confirmed and endorsed Boas' antiracism, and have demonstrated time and again that all social groups and individuals are fully capable of learning every possible culture trait or habit in the world. Since their evidence was indeed overwhelming, the idea that head shape may indicate intelligence has become extinct. It could also no longer be argued that some races had no capacity for civilization; particularly in America the many immigrants proved otherwise. But since American Negroes generally have lower incomes and poorer housing than whites, racists began to search for different genetic justifications to account for this disparity. The answer was found in "intelligence testing." Intelligence, according to early psychologists, was an innate factor that could be measured by asking questions of an intellectual nature. Particularly the early Stanford-Binet tests measured I.Q. by questions involving word meanings, mathematics, and abstract symbolic material, and thus equated intelligence with knowledge. U.S. Army intelligence testing during World War I showed that black recruits scored much lower than white ones, and racists gleefully concluded that the mental inferiority of the Negro was now fully demonstrated. Other intelligence tests showed that American Indians and Mexicans also had low I.Q.s, while in Europe the tests also provided the expected results: Nordics scored higher than Alpines and Mediterraneans.

Biological explanations were not wanting. Robert Bean, who had made an early study in which he claimed that

Negroes have smaller frontal lobes of the brain than whites (Bean 1906), was frequently cited with approval. F. W. Vint (1934), also working on brain morphology, concluded that "the pyramidal cells of the supragranular cortex" are smaller in the brains of Kenya natives than in European brains. Although Vint himself made no correlations of this fact with relative intelligence, racist writers seized upon it as highly significant.

Otto Klineberg, a psychologist with anthropological training, scrutinized the various results of I.Q. testing and demonstrated that an individual's performance in the tests was strongly influenced by many extraneous factors besides knowledge, including level of education, motivation, social environment, rapport with the investigator, and familiarity with the language. He gave many examples of how different cultural training and experience determined the answers to the test questions. American Indian children were asked to select two words that identified a crowd most closely from the following five: "closeness," "dust," "excitement," "danger," "number." Many chose the words "dust" and "excitement" and although their experience with crowds would make these choices correct, they did not score. Southern Negro children were asked to complete this sentence: "———should prevail in churches and libraries." The "right" answer was "silence" but since the children did not have much experience with libraries, and in their churches silence was neither expected nor desired, they gave "wrong" answers (Klineberg 1935:158). Even non-linguistic tests presented the same culture-bound problems. The so-called draw-a-man test of Goodenough is based upon the concept of a fully clothed man; but when this test was administered to Australian aborigines, they invariably drew the man naked and lost points given for the correct drawing of clothes. Examples could be multiplied, but it is clear that evaluation of "intelligence" was largely based upon the cultural standards of the investigators.

Klineberg also reexamined the results of the army tests, and breaking the figures down to geographical locations, he found that Negroes in northern states scored higher than those living in the South, that New York Negroes did better in the tests than Alabama whites, and that northern whites outscored southern whites. These and many similar findings gave evidence that the white man possessed no biologically determined intellectual superiority, but that opportunity for education was among the most important factors in the determination of I.Q.

For a while, it seemed that scientific racism had been put to silence. After the downfall of Nazism, racists were reduced to cursing Boas, Klineberg, Dobzhansky, and all others who had exposed the fallacies of the old racist arguments. The United Nations proclaimed the "Universal Declaration of Human Rights" based upon the findings of scientists, and the UNESCO "Statements on Race" (1950, 1951, 1964, and 1967) adopted an equally clear position on human equality. Several psychologists admitted that their testing procedures had been ethnocentric (Klineberg 1966:186–91). But racists did not remain silent for long. In 1960, a newly established journal, *The Mankind Quarterly,* published several articles (Garrett 1960:15–22; Purves 1960:51–54; etc.) that claimed that what Garrett called "the scandalous crime rate of the Negro" (1960:20) was due to genetic factors alone. In 1969, the *Harvard Educational Review* published an article by Arthur R. Jensen (1969:1–123), a psychologist teaching at the Institute of Human Learning at Berkeley, California. Jensen argued that, for any individual, intelligence is determined for eighty per cent by genetic factors, and that "social class and racial variations in intelligence cannot be accounted for by differences in the environment" (*ibid.*:123). Compensatory education programs such as SEEK or Head Start were thus quite useless.

Anthropologists reacted swiftly and strongly to this renewed outbreak of racism. The American Anthropological Association devoted one of its publications to a critique of "jensenism" (Brace *et al.* 1971), while *Current Anthropology,* a world journal of the sciences of man, published an article by Comas (1961:303–40), where he attacked the racist orientation of *The Mankind Quarterly*. Support for the position of anthropologists came from zoologists, geneticists, and psychologists. Each showed from his own discipline that the racists' arguments were erroneous, that their statistics were biased, their tests culture-bound, and that the important distinction between individual and group performances had been overlooked. Anthropologists stressed once again that sociocultural factors cannot be neglected in evaluations of any test results. Low performance tends to correlate with low socioeconomic conditions in all groups, and not just among blacks. In the case of American Negroes, their background of slavery and the physical and psychological insults that have barred them from the white man's civilization for many centuries are additional handicaps. Social rewards generally motivate behavior; but since the rewards of scholastic performance have been unequally distributed in favor of the whites, this motivation is certainly less developed on part of the Negro.

In the course of the history of racial discussions, speculations, and researches, a great many of the older principles have been overcome by the self-correcting process of science. The idea that human brain size is related to intelligence has been proven wrong; no consistent correlation between cranial capacity and intellectual performance has been found to exist. Some Neanderthal men reached a cranial capacity of more than 1800 cc, while the brain of Anatole France was only 1100 cc in volume. Researches in brain morphology also have not established clear-cut criteria of correlation with intelligence, and cephalic index figures give good insights into the degree of human variation, but tell us nothing about intelligence.

Racial taxonomy is still in a state of confusion. The racial divisions of Linnaeus and Blumenbach are no longer considered to be very useful, because they were based upon geography. Linnaeus' *Homo sapiens americanus* is clearly outnumbered on its home grounds by *Homo sapiens europaeus* and *Homo sapiens afer,* and every other continent harbors many different physical types. Moreover, their divisions were based upon one arbitrarily selected criterion, namely skin color. In view of the hundreds of existing physical variations, one physical feature is clearly insufficent to establish a race, but how many are necessary remains an open question. Disagreement on this matter has led some taxonomists to recognize only two races, others have listed four, five, six, thirty, or even two hundred.

Population geneticists have proposed to restrict the term "race" to Mendelian breeding populations, by which they mean a relatively isolated group within which most mating takes place. A "race" is then a restrictive community set apart from others by the frequency of some genes in their common gene pool. This model has been of vital importance for the understanding of the formation of human physical similarities and differences, but has complicated rather than clarified any possible racial taxonomy. Some groups are more isolated than others, but interbreeding has taken place most everywhere. The genes of all the inhabitants of a village, town, country, continent, or of the whole world can thus be considered as belonging to smaller or larger gene pools.

All groping attempts at classification have made one thing abundantly clear: pure races do not exist, and evidence from studies of fossil human remains shows that mixing took place at a very early time in human history. The uncertain status of the biological concept of race has moved some scholars to propose abandonment of the term altogether. Ashley Montagu, for one, holds that "race" has no existence in nature, and that all classifications have been arbitrary and artificial, because the variations in human physique are continuous and gradual. He proposes to use "major groups" for overall geographical populations and "ethnic groups" for the varieties of men entering into the composition of these major groups (1952:5). The major objection to this view has been that one does not change anything by changing names and that words cannot easily be banned from a language.

On the older question of monogenism versus polygenism,

at present there is virtual agreement that man had a single origin. Carleton Coon, who is sometimes called a polygenist, holds that at the beginning man was a single species, *Homo erectus*. In his view, all present-day living men also belong to a single species, *Homo sapiens,* and all descended from the earlier *Homo erectus*. Most physical anthropologists have no serious quarrel with this view, although there is no absolute agreement on nomenclature. But Coon goes on to argue that there are five races in living man: Australoid, Mongoloid, Caucasoid, Congoid (Negroes and Pygmies), and Capoid (Bushmen and Hottentots), and that each passed from the *erectus* to the *sapiens* state independently and at different times. The Caucasoid race (or subspecies) crossed the border line first during the second interglacial period, about 250,000 years ago, whereas the Congoids arrived at this advanced state some 200,000 years later. In Coon's own words:

> It is a fair inference that fossil men now extinct were less gifted than their descendants who have larger brains, that the subspecies which crossed the evolutionary threshold into the category of *Homo sapiens* the earliest have evolved the most, and that the obvious correlation between the length of time a subspecies has been in the *sapiens* state and the levels of civilization attained by some of its populations may be related phenomena.
>
> (Coon 1962a:ix–x)

Although Coon also mixes physical criteria with cultural ones, there is nothing further in his book indicating a belief in the superiority or inferiority of living races. In fact, he observed that until the present century all five races of man included populations with very simple hunting and gathering cultures, which would serve to show that there is no one-to-one correlation between race and the degree of cultural development. Expectedly, however, the idea that Negroes reached the *sapiens* state 200,000 years later than whites was received with great enthusiasm by racists and segregationists. They found in it a new scientific explanation for Negro slums, African "backwardness," Haiti's poverty, and anything else they could find to denounce the blacks and to bolster their arguments in favor of segregation.

No such conclusions follow from Coon's book by necessity. Dobzhansky (1963:172) pointed out that if Coon's thesis were correct (which he does not believe), it would follow that the Negro had evolved his culture five times as rapidly as the Caucasoid, and would thus seem mentally superior rather than inferior.

Theory is the life blood of science, and no one should eschew investigations for fear that his findings may be misused. Coon, as a scientist, is fully entitled to his scientific convictions about the separate origins of the races. But the issues involved are of great social relevance, touching the lives of many human beings. Scientists have social responsibilities as well as scientific ones, and it is regrettable that Coon has remained silent about the damaging use that racists have made of his theories. He maintains the ivory tower position, and wrote that "it is not our business to worry about what politicians will do with our data" (1962b:26).

CONCLUSIONS

In historical perspective, a significant body of anthropological research developed around the question of race. It is certainly true that several physical and cultural anthropologists of the past have helped to bestow scientific dignity upon human prejudice and discrimination, sometimes unwittingly, sometimes with a vengeance. At the same time there were numerous others who carried out their cultural researches without involvement in racial issues. Several of those have been mentioned in earlier chapters, and include Schoolcraft, Maine, Bastian, McLennan, Fustel de Coulanges, Codrington, Powell, Bandelier, Cushing, Durkheim, *Kulturkreis* theorists, the early Tylor, Morgan, and a host of others. They were probably all convinced of the superiority of their own culture, but most were equally persuaded that primitive peoples were not predetermined by heredity to remain in their lower stage of cultural development. In fact, the evidence that culture is a learned phenomenon is so overwhelming that this alone should suffice to prove that there are no racial differences in terms of achievement. None of the existing differences in the broad spectrum of cultural variations in time and space can be correlated with physical appearance. Cultures of Mongoloid peoples, for instance, cover a complete range of cultural complexity from the simplest hunters and gatherers to the most advanced industrialists.

However simple cultures may be in their technological developments, they all possess their own learned skills. Many nonliterate peoples in Africa or the Caribbean speak five or six different languages; few American intellectuals possess such linguistic versatility. Australian aborigines know how to make boomerangs and use them successfully in the hunt; not many white people have acquired that skill. Anthropology students often find it very hard to understand the complexities of American Indian kinship systems, and very few people can make an efficient stone tool. Ignorance on these matters is certainly not gene determined, but merely a lack of cultural training. All these skills can be acquired by anyone who sets his mind to it, and skills of Western society can equally be learned by non-Western man. Members of recently "primitive" cultures have fully demonstrated their ability to do so. Mohawk Indians specialize in construction work on bridges and skyscrapers, an Australian aboriginal girl has become a tennis champion—examples could be multiplied.

The evidence of acculturation and of cultural learning is thus most persuasive in disproving the racist myth that physical types and mental characteristics can be equated. Scholars who have examined a wide range of cultures and have firsthand experience with so-called primitives generally disavow racism and construct relevant explanations of cultural similarities and differences in cultural behavior without having to contemplate skin color or cephalic index. Indeed, if physical

criteria were causal factors of cultural variety, the social
sciences could not even exist. Anthropologists have vindicated
themselves by exposing the fallacies of their old errors, and
they have gained in the process because they have achieved
greater awareness about the status and responsibilities of their
discipline.

CHAPTER 13

PSYCHOLOGICAL

ANTHROPOLOGY

The primary aim of psychological anthropology is to examine the interrelationships between culture and personality. Rather than seeking to analyze culture as it is manifested in material items or social institutions as do other anthropological studies, psychological anthropology studies culture as it is embodied in the character of its members.

Long before psychological anthropology became systematized, it was generally recognized that human groups could be characterized by overall personality traits. Often enough, this resulted in the formation of unanalyzed stereotypes, depicting whole nations as brave, proud, cruel, sentimental, aggressive, or meek.

Several pre-Freudian scholars were well aware that national personalities were formed largely through cultural training. John Locke wrote in 1693 that little or almost insensible impressions on our tender infancies have very important and lasting consequences. Alexander Pope rhymed:

> *'Tis education forms the common mind;*
> *Just as the twig is bent, the tree's inclined.*

David Hume in an essay with the modern-sounding title "Of National Characters" made the same point when he said that men acquire similar manners through their relations with one another.

The German philosopher Immanuel Kant in his book *Anthropology* (1789) dealt with the character of peoples and related them to historical factors as well as to consciously directed cultivation, or what we now call enculturation. His description of German national character remains of interest today, and it was based upon observation of many behavioral data: The German is home-loving; solid but not brilliant; industrious, thrifty, cleanly, without much flash of genius; intelligent, capable, but lacking in wit or taste; overmethodical, pedantic, without impulse toward equality, but addicted to a painstaking hierarchical grading of society that sets title and rank above natural talent; docile under government, accepting despotism rather than resisting the established order of authority (Quoted by Kroeber 1948:586).

The Swiss historian Jacob Burckhardt (1818–97) was even more modern in his approach to cultural personality. He compared the overall character of medieval peoples in Italy with that of the Renaissance. In the Middle Ages, men tended to identify themselves closely with collective social entities such as their ethnic or national groups, corporations, and extended families. The Renaissance was marked by the rise of individualism. Italians became less dependent upon their social affiliations, and were thus enabled to view their governments with greater objectivity (Burckhardt 1943:145–47). Burckhardt demonstrated these personality changes by analyzing various cultural manifestations, including art and literature, folk festivals, forms of dress, etiquette, humor, and similar factors which later on received much attention in psychological anthropology.

Although anthropological culture and personality studies have their roots in earlier thought and scholarship, they began to proliferate when the writings of Sigmund Freud (1856–

1939) became known. In the United States, psychological anthropology was launched in a spirit of criticism; Freud's long essay "Totem and Taboo" (1913) particularly set off angry reactions. Its subtitle "Resemblances between the Psychic Life of Savages and Neurotics" alone was enough to send anthropologists up in arms.

His thesis about the origin of totemism, incest taboo, exogamy, and the Oedipus complex is well known. He posited the existence of a primal horde, the leader of which was the oldest male, who assumed exclusive sexual rights over all females in the group. Frustrated, the sons murdered and ate their father; but overcome by guilt afterward, they decided to obey his commands and abstain from sexual intercourse with their mothers and sisters. Selecting a totem animal as a symbolic father substitute, they declared that it must be protected during the year and consumed only on ritual occasions. These ritual totem meals thus reenacted their original deed and reinforced their self-imposed incest prohibitions. Freud went as far as to say that all culture originated from this sacrificial meal.

"Totem and Taboo" became widely known in the United States at the end of World War I, at a time when Boas had already sharply criticized other theories that had attempted to establish a single origin for totemic practices. Although Boas was not uninterested in psychology, he reacted to Freud's essay by stating that his method was one-sided and could do nothing to advance understanding of cultural development (Boas 1940:288–89). Kroeber (1952:301–05) wrote that Freud's conjectures evidenced a "bewilderingly fertile imagination," and made some twelve detailed criticisms. At the same time he realized the importance of the psychological dimensions of culture, and said that they could now no longer be ignored without stultification.

Freud's concept of evolution was perhaps most unacceptable of all. It represented a mixture of biological determinism and strict unilinealism and he was much more dogmatic than any of the early anthropological evolutionists. According to Freud, mankind had developed along the same lines as infants growing into adults. Contemporary "savages" represented an arrested stage of the childhood of man, while Western man had attained mental maturity. As adulthood could not be reached without passing through infancy and childhood, so cultures must go through predetermined biological stages of mental and social development. Not only did "savages" resemble children, but their fears, compulsions, lack of motivation, and attraction to what is forbidden were traits that Freud had frequently encountered in his neurotic patients. It followed, then, that "savage" habits could be profitably studied by psychoanalytic methods.

Another Freudian principle that engendered a great deal of discussion was that of the supposed universality of the Oedipus complex. This involved the idea that a son hates his father for his strict authority, is jealous of his sexual prerogatives over the mother, and yet loves and admires him for his strength and protection. Intrigued, Malinowski decided to test this out in the matrilineal Trobriand society, where interpersonal relationships were structured quite differently than in the Western families of Freud's acquaintance. Among Trobrianders, the father was not an authoritarian figure, but rather a benevolent friend, while the mother's brother, from whom the son would inherit, took on the role of disciplinarian. Moreover, Trobrianders were, according to Malinowski, ignorant of the procreative role of the father, while a young boy had long and intimate contacts with his mother, often sleeping with her and being nursed until he no longer desired it. Consequently, the Oedipus complex was directed toward different relatives. The ambivalent love/hate sentiments were directed toward maternal uncles, while incestuous wishes concentrated on sisters rather than on mothers. Malinowski considered this to be "a notable confirmation of the main tenet of Freudian psychology," modified only because of the changed family situation (1955:77).

Ernest Jones (1879–1958), a follower of Freud, resisted

Malinowski's findings, and wrote that it was his ignorance of psychoanalysis that had led him to the wrong conclusions. Dogmatically, Jones insisted that the Oedipus complex existed in its pure form in every man's psyche even if the primary authority resided in an uncle. The uncle merely symbolized the father, and the sisters symbolized the mother (Jones 1925: 109–30).

Somewhat peeved, Malinowski answered that in the strict Freudian definition of the term, the Oedipus complex was certainly not universal, attacked "Totem and Taboo" and other psychoanalytic writings, and turned against psychoanalytic interpretations (1955:123–57). Abram Kardiner (1939:481) agreed with Malinowski, and Dorothy Eggan (1953:286) showed that the Oedipus complex was also absent in Hopi personality. Orthodox Freudians, viewing the ambivalence toward the father as an innate factor, continued to believe in the absolute universality of this psychic phenomenon. Géza Róheim, for one, maintained that anthropologists who denied this were suppressing the recognition of the Oedipal complex in their own lives.

Subsequent anthropological field work was carried out in order to demonstrate that the relationship between culture and personality was of an entirely different nature. It was culture itself that molded personality to a significant degree, and there were few absolute universals. Margaret Mead's (1928) pioneer study on Samoa dealt with the question of whether the rebellion that marked adolescent personality in Western cultures was a product of the biological changes occurring at puberty or a result of cultural circumstances. She found that the whole cultural mood on Samoa was much less emotional than that in America. Facts of birth, death, and sex were not hidden from Samoan children, premarital sex was considered natural and did not demand strong emotional involvements, and adolescents were not confronted with the necessity of selecting from a variety of often conflicting standards of ethics and values. Adolescence was thus not marked by storm and stress on Samoa, but was simply a part of the gradual development of life. The major point of the study was, in Mead's own words (1939:x), "the documentation over and over of the fact that human nature is not rigid and unyielding." Her next major study (1930) also emphasized this point.

Apart from Mead, Edward Sapir was among the first to realize that anthropological studies of personality represented a whole new approach to the understanding of culture. Well aware of the errors of Freud's evolutionary ideas, Sapir nonetheless praised his insights into the psychic mechanisms of personality formations and concluded that the application of psychoanalytic methods would add a new dimension to ethnological field work and analysis. All too often ethnologists of the past had presented culture as a more or less mechanized sum of patterns of behavior, and thus depicted Zuni, Eskimo, or Nuer as if they were mere robots, thoughtlessly carrying out the rules of their cultures. In fact, in every society people differ from each other in their interpretations and assessments of social reality, and the significance of individual personality cannot be left out of attempts to achieve a truly objective understanding of the cultural whole (Mandelbaum 1951:590–97). It was Sapir, together with John Dollard, who directed the first seminars on culture and personality at Yale University in the early 1930's, influencing many other students.

Sapir himself applied his insights into the importance of psychology to linguistics, and examined the ways in which people's thoughts and perceptions were patterned by language. Benjamin Whorf (1897–1941) developed Sapir's line of thought on this matter, and the so-called Sapir-Whorf hypothesis holds that language and culture are inextricably interrelated, and that the often unconscious patterns of grammar strongly influence the ways in which speakers of a particular language experience their world (Whorf 1956). This idea engendered a great deal of research in psycholinguistics, but the hypothesis has also been criticized for its resulting cultural relativism. Moreover, as Hoijer (1954:102–04) pointed out, peoples with similar cultures sometimes speak totally un-

related languages, while closely related languages are sometimes spoken by peoples whose cultures are entirely different.

Sapir's theoretical insights and the results of Mead's early
field work as well as various other demonstrations of the influence of culture upon the formation of personality did not
escape the attention of trained psychoanalysts. Many ventured
into the field of analysis of non-Western cultures, sometimes
remaining orthodox Freudians, convinced of the universality
of symbolism and accepting the relationship between neurotics
and primitive peoples as a given fact. Others modified their
views, and became strongly involved with anthropological
interests in enculturation, or the relationships between childhood training and adult personality. Following Freud's dictum
that early years, when a child is enculturated without being
conscious of it, were the most crucial for personality development, anthropologists and psychoanalysts alike embarked on
intensive studies of child training, stressing such matters as
breast feeding, weaning, swaddling, toilet training, sibling
rivalry, modes of punishment, degrees of indulgence, and
similar character-conditioning variables. It became over-
whelmingly clear that personality traits were neither uniform
nor fixed by instinct, but the analysis of the precise relationships between child training and adult personality were often
overdrawn, making it appear as if a few selected practices of
child treatment fixed their characters forever, and permeated
all adult cultural behavior.

Thus, Erik Erikson (1939:101–56; 1949:206–38) studied
the Sioux Indians, who treated their children with great indulgence. A child was fed whenever it cried, and nursing was
prolonged, often coinciding with teething. When a boy bit his
mother's breast he was thumped on the head, which often led
to a temper tantrum. These outbursts were not viewed with
any alarm by the Sioux—to the contrary, it was believed that
they made a child strong. Sioux youngsters were also often
placed on a cradleboard, which encased their limbs. Induced
rage could thus not be abreacted by muscular movements.
Erikson concluded that the backlog of unreleased rage which

was thus built up related to the readiness for anger in adult Sioux character and to the cruelty and aggressiveness of their warriors. In turn, these personality traits were related to the self-torture that was a regular part of their rituals and initiation rites. During the Sun Dance ceremony, men drove wooden skewers through their skin, connecting these by ropes to the Sun Pole, and then pulled until their flesh was ripped. In Erikson's words, this self-torture represented "a sacred and collective turning against the self of the 'original sin' of biting temper which had compromised the paradise of babyhood" (quoted by Honigmann 1954:50). Although Erikson himself later on called his study "impressionistic and speculative" (Erikson 1949:207) and admitted that the individual is not merely the sum total of his childhood experiences, he conveyed the impression that the cradleboard was an immediate causal factor of single aspects of adult personality, so that it seemed as if the human psyche consisted of separate and disconnected elements, each traceable to specific childhood events.

While this is not a very satisfactory view of personality, Erikson was much more cautious than Geoffrey Gorer, who connected childhood practices among Russian peasants not only with natural character, but also with some momentous events of Russian history (Gorer and Rickman 1962). Russian peasants swaddle their infants during the first year after birth, wrapping them tightly in long strips of cloth, thus immobilizing them almost completely. This swaddling is so frustrating to the child that it reacts with destructive rage which is not directed toward any individual person, but remains undetermined and generalized. Eventually, this pent-up rage gives rise to destructive wishes, but the child also fears that if he gives in to these he himself will be destroyed. Restraint is thus essential for his own safety. The unfocused guilt which Gorer considered typical of adult Russians was related to the early unfocused rage. Release was sought in religious rituals, but also in indulgence in alcohol and sex. Furthermore, the

Bolshevik revolution and the Stalin purge trials in which many Russians readily admitted their guilt could also be understood as related to the rage-and-guilt complex.

Gorer's "swaddling hypothesis" achieved great notoriety and was strongly attacked by anthropologists, psychologists, and historians alike. These critics were undoubtedly correct when they observed that historical and cultural factors more cogently explained developments in Russian history. They overlooked, however, that Gorer certainly did not deny this, but merely wanted to show that personality factors might bring additional insights. He wrote that swaddling is but one of a number of antecedents to the development of Russian character, and denied that he had any direct causality in mind. The vehemence of his critics can be partly explained by the fact that Gorer presented something entirely novel. Historical events were customarily analyzed in terms of such accepted variables as politics, economy, class struggle, or industrialization. The idea that a few strips of cotton cloth could be brought into the picture at all seemed either preposterous or very humorous. While Gorer reached his conclusions too hastily, in principle there is nothing wrong with attempts to seek additional explanations for complex events in terms of personality.

Erikson's and Gorer's studies presented examples of attempts to discover the relationship between childhood experiences and adult character. Others took it more or less for granted that cultural behavior was largely derived from innate tendencies, and sought to explain specific cultural phenomena by psychoanalytic methods. This approach was particularly favored by psychoanalysts. Géza Róheim (1891–1953), for one, was a practicing analyst and an orthodox Freudian who fully accepted the universality of the Oedipus complex as well as the relationship between savage and neurotic thinking. Like Freud, he emphasized the importance of human sexuality. Explaining the origin of such important cultural inventions as agriculture, animal domestication, economy, medicine, and religion, he rejected all functional theories in the conviction that all human institutions evolved on the genital level (Róheim 1943).

Agriculture, for instance, was first nothing else but an expression of Oedipal frustrations. The earth, always considered female in mythology, symbolizes the mother, and various forms of cultivation were displaced attempts to have intercourse with her. Yams were at one time growing wild in the Trobriand Islands. Their shape is clearly phallic, but the result of inserting these tubers into the ground could not have been foreseen by the preagricultural Trobriand people. In their myths about the origin of yam cultivation a child is the inventor of the art. Based upon these data Róheim reconstructs the origin of yam agriculture as follows: Frustrated Trobriand boys began to play with wild yams, made holes in the earth, and placed the yams inside. Eventually these yams took root and multiplied. While this accounted for one aspect of the Oedipus complex, namely the incestuous desire to possess the mother, explanations for the expression of father-hatred had still to be found. Before yam gardens can be planted, the ground had to be cleared with an ax, and tree cutting was "clearly" symbolic of father castration. Soon enough, agriculture was regularly carried out by means of such phallic agricultural implements as the digging stick and the hoe (Róheim 1943:53–60). In Egypt, the plough was invented, and the ox, a *castrated* animal, was pulling it. It was quite evident to Róheim that "the type of agriculture which forms the basis of our own cilivization, with the plough and the ox, was evolved on the genital level, on the basis of the Oedipus attitude, and the castration complex" (*ibid.*:62). All other professions of mankind were more or less distorted or projected equivalents of the infantile situation:

A soldier is re-enacting his body-destruction phantasies or his Oedipus complex, a lawyer makes a profession of the endopsychical struggle between Super-Ego, Id and Ego, a scientist is a voyeur prying into the secrets of Mother Nature, a painter continues to play with his feces—a writer of fiction never renounces his day-dreams, and so forth.

(*Ibid.*:72)

Cultures and personalities were thus not unique, and the Boasians had simply been misled. Theories about borrowing, diffusion, migration, function, evolution, and all other traditional anthropological approaches could not lead to any basic understanding of cultural practices. This could come only from psychoanalytic methods.

In fact, Róheim felt that all research carried out by anthropologists was not merely useless, but potentially dangerous. Granting that anthropologists are well-meaning people, Róheim felt that their concept of culture was not so very far removed from stereotyped racism:

If Ashley Montagu has called *racism* "Man's most dangerous myth," anthropological nationalism is nearly as great a danger. . . . Instead of race we now have culture, but most anthropologists fail to see *mankind* and fail to see the *individual*.

(Róheim 1950:394)

Understandably, anthropologists did not receive the whole-sale denunciation of their discipline with great kindness, and acrimonious debates followed. But Róheim's trump card was always the same: the more anthropologists protested, the stronger was the proof that they had repressed their own Oedipal complexes. In fact, Róheim did not hold his own colleagues either in very high esteem. In his judgment, Bruno Bettelheim was the only other psychoanalyst capable of making correct interpretations of culture.

In his book *Symbolic Wounds* (1962), Bettelheim searched for the explanation of such sexual preoccupations as circumcision, subincision, and similar genital mutilations. Upholding Freud's correlation between neurotic and primitive thought, Bettelheim used the behavior of four schizophrenic adolescents as the basic explication of his thesis that circumcision is rooted in male envy of female fecundity. His patients, two boys and two girls, formed a "secret society" at the time when the girls began to menstruate, planning to hold monthly meetings at which occasions the boys would cut their fingers and mix their blood with that of the menses. They were convinced that this ritual would assure sexual pleasure and success in the adult world.

As the disturbed boys were envious of the maturity of the girls, so circumcision, a frequent feature of initiation rites among nonliterate peoples, symbolized the same jealousy. The bleeding occurring at circumcision was somehow symbolic of the males' attempts to convince themselves that they were as mature and fertile as women. In the course of mental development, men came to understand that they were in fact equally fertile, and recognized their biological contribution to procreation. At this time the phallus became admired and often venerated, and circumcision continued because it emphasized masculinity by making the glans permanently more visible.

Bettelheim's study was not written to refute anthropological interpretations; it was, rather, a reexamination of Freud's theory that circumcision was an attempt to create castration anxiety. But since this book dealt with an area of definite anthropological interest, it was widely read by anthropologists. By and large, however, interpretations of this kind did not inspire much confidence and were criticized for their intuitive methods, their circular reasoning, as well as for the assumption that the behavior of schizophrenics could help to explain cultural institutions of contemporary nonliterate people. Moreover, Boasians who stressed the uniqueness of cultures and cultural personalities distrusted the emphasis on what was common in man. Nevertheless, there were many others who had become dissatisfied with cultural relativism, and they recognized that psychoanalysis presented a view that was consistent with what used to be called the "psychic unity" of mankind. While it remained an open question whether or not this unity resided in the Oedipus complex, it could not be denied that certain constants of the mind must be evoked in order to make valid cross-cultural comparisons. Most psychoanalysts, for their part, accepted the anthropological insight that culture was a salient factor in personality formation. Greater cooperation between the two disciplines could thus develop, and a number of interdisciplinary seminars were organized. One of those was led by Abram Kardiner, a practicing analyst; participants included Ralph Linton, Ruth Benedict, Ruth Bunzel, Cora DuBois, and James West.

Kardiner was a neo-Freudian, a term applied to those who accepted some of Freud's theories but rejected or modified others. Kardiner believed that the early years of life were most crucial in the formation of personality, but he dropped the emphasis on the Oedipus complex and the sexual determinants of culture. Well aware that a degree of individual variation in character exists in every society, he developed the concept of "basic personality structure" to indicate their common grounds (Kardiner 1945:107–22).

He argued that techniques of child rearing, duration of breastfeeding, methods of weaning, sexual training, and similar conditioning factors are roughly similar in a given group. Adults thus have had certain important common experiences that give rise to a common basic personality type. These institutionalized common determinants were in Kardiner's terminology the "primary institutions," but the special personality structure thus formed projected itself in the "secondary institutions," which included art, myth, folklore, religion, ethics, and worldview in general.

Kardiner thus went far beyond simple childhood determinisms, presenting instead a dynamic model that could also serve to explain culture change: if primary institutions changed, the resultant changes in basic personality structure would also alter secondary institutions. Thus if the economy of a certain group demanded that mothers spend much time away from home, older siblings or others would be charged with caring for the infants. In these circumstances many tensions may develop, and a child might feel ambiguous toward the mother, which in turn could well become reflected in myths or religious beliefs. Should there be a shift in economic patterns allowing mothers to become more fully nurturant, the basic personality would change, and with it also the secondary institutions.

The logic of Kardiner's scheme was certainly an important improvement over some previous efforts that labeled religious practices or myths "irrational" or resulting from a kind of infantile neurosis, as Freud would have it.

Nevertheless, those anthropologists who were not given to psychological interpretations could point out that Kardiner's theory plausibly explained the existence of certain cultural institutions, but could account for them only in psychological terms. Thus if neglecting mothers gave rise to a concept of a threatening female deity, all that could be said was that this was possibly a "projection" of hostile feelings, or an "outlet" for them, "reflecting" insecurity, and so on. Cultural functions were thus neglected, and it appeared as if primary institutions had no other functions than to form the personality, while secondary institutions served mainly to cope with the frustrations of that personality. Moreover, Kardiner's system could not account for the existing differences among primary institutions, and provided no answer as to why some societies were patrilineal, others matrilineal, or why some practiced cross-cousin marriage, and others not.

It followed, however, from Kardiner's view, that the contents of secondary institutions could be examined for possible clues about basic personality and primary institutions, even in those instances where myth and folklore were the only available documents left of an extinct group.

Kardiner himself made no such interpretations. He often analyzed the field data of anthropologists who had gathered full information about a specific group (Kardiner 1945), but he did not attempt to interpret myth or folklore outside of their cultural context.

But there were others who ventured out on this dangerous path, taking their cues mainly from Freud, who had held that all irrational stories and fantasies expressed unconscious wishes which were predominantly of a sexual nature. In this vein Erich Fromm "translated" the European fairy tale of

Little Red Riding Hood in sexual terms. Little Red-Cap is a maiden who has become sexually mature (red = menstruation), but she has had no sexual experience (she carries an unbroken bottle of wine to grandmother = virginity). She meets a wolf (man) in the forest (trees = phalli). The wolf eventually eats her (aggressive intercourse), and, later on, he is punished by Red-Cap, who puts stones (sterility) in his belly. He dies. The story symbolizes "the triumph of man-hating women, ending with their victory" (Fromm 1951:240-41).

A more sophisticated attempt to reconstruct cultural personality was developed by the Columbia University Research in Contemporary Cultures project, inaugurated by Ruth Benedict shortly after the outbreak of World War II. Its participants included Margaret Mead, Rhoda Métraux, Gregory Bateson, Jane Belo, Geoffrey Gorer, and others (Mead and Métraux 1953). Their approach became known as "the study of culture at a distance," and it answered a very pressing need. The war sharply curtailed travel and field research, and yet there was a strong demand to arrive at a better understanding of both enemies and allies. Culture-at-a-distance studies concentrated on film analysis, and the participants scanned newspapers, letters, propaganda material, humor, and similar documents, supplementing their findings by interviews with immigrants, asking them to write life histories, and to take psychological tests. A new model was thus provided for the analysis of cultural regularities in the character of societies inaccessible to direct observation.

In further developments of psychological anthropology, Kardiner's concept of basic personality received a great deal of attention. Cora DuBois, a member of his seminar, carried out field work in a village on the Indonesian island of Alor, and recorded not only the more traditional ethnographic facts, but also collected eight lengthy biographies, dreams, and children's drawings and administered a number of projective tests (DuBois 1944). Upon her return she submitted the life histories to Kardiner for his analysis, the test results were given to Dr. Emil Oberholzer, while she asked the assistance

of Trude Schmidl-Waehner for the interpretation of the
Alorese drawings. Each of these specialists worked "blind,"
i.e., without knowledge of the ethnographic data, and without consulting one another. The results showed a great deal
of correspondence: all noted the shallowness of Alorese emotional life, insecurity, apathy, and suspiciousness. These conclusions were made by pooling all individual responses to
the various tests and averaging them so that the resulting
"psychogram" described the most prevalent personality features of the group. DuBois called this the "modal" personality, because it was directly derived from testing, while
Kardiner's "basic" personality was inferred from cultural data.

The agreement among the specialists who had blindly
interpreted the Alorese material inspired confidence in projective testing, and a large amount of test material was brought
back by subsequent field workers. It was felt that testing was
a scientific method that reduced the impressionistic qualities
of earlier studies, and that the modal personality was a true
reflection of the personality features of the majority of people
in a culture. Among the various tests available, the Rorschach
was particularly favored. Named after its inventor, it consists
of presenting the subject with ten nonpictorial "inkblot"
cards, and inviting him to describe what he sees in them. The
test is not difficult to administer, not culture-bound, and does
not measure intelligence but thoughts, feelings, and views. The
answers were counted and scored, and interpreted in terms of
degree of originality, imagination, repression, conformity,
aggression, emotional control, and similar underlying characteristics of the personality. Other tests often used included
Murray's Thematic Apperception test, Bender's Gestalt test,
immanent judgment tests, supplemented by data derived from
doll play, free drawing, autobiographies, and dreams.

Once the modal personality was established it became relatively easy to relate its features to dominant social patterns.
Frequency of warfare, belief in sorcery, or harsh initiation
rites could be plausibly explained by such modal personality
features as aggression, insecurity, or guilt feelings. Although

the results were very neat, they were not very satisfactory. They were not predictive in any sense, and at best they stressed the great diversity of modal personalities between cultural groups, thus representing a version of Boasian historical particularism on a psychological level. Most anthropologists became dissatisfied with this dead-end approach, and began to reappraise their theories and methods.

It was found, first of all, that adult personality cannot be fully predicted in terms of early childhood experiences. Margaret Mead, among others, directed attention to the importance of the *totality* of expectations and pressures communicated to individuals sharing the same culture. Explanations of personality must then take into account the cultural conditions under which attitudes and feelings are learned and experienced during the individual's lifetime, and should include adult interpersonal relationships and adult interactions. This insight was strengthened by the neobehaviorist theory, developed under the leadership of Clark Hull. Older behaviorists had stressed action alone, but Hull and his followers noted that an individual actor constantly registers what is happening to him and that this alters his subsequent acts. In anthropological terms, this meant that the study of personality development must consider the whole range of social interactions.

Hull had developed his theories of learning and behavior on the basis of learning experiments with rats. John W. M. Whiting applied these theories to a set of concrete ethnographic data of the Kwoma, a mountain tribe in New Guinea (Whiting 1941). His application of Hull's learning theory to cultural analysis was perhaps too literal, and not many other studies have been made along these lines. But Whiting's monograph contributed to the insight that stricter scientific approaches were possible in the study of personality and culture.

These findings led to a closer scrutiny of basic and modal personality. So far, the notion that a core of homogeneous personality characteristics existed in each culture had been taken rather for granted, but when the statistical averages were checked against actual individual performances the discrepancies were embarrassingly large. Anthony Wallace (1952) analyzed Rorschach records of Tuscarora Indians and found that only thirty-seven per cent of the sample fell within the limits of the previously computed modal personality. He recommended that score averages should be accompanied by measures of variability, thus calling for more appropriate and more rigorous statistical procedures. Bert Kaplan (1954) even asked whether a modal personality exists at all, and questioned the appropriateness of the tests. He showed that their interpretations were often ethnocentric, discussed the difficulty of interpreting the responses made by people in societies drastically different from that of the interpreter, and drew attention to the sampling problem.

Furthermore, psychological anthropologists began to take note of organic influences on personality formation. Psychiatrists themselves had neglected this for some time, treating their patients almost exclusively by psychoanalysis, as if mental illness and health were psychological factors only. In the 1930's, however, they began to supplement analysis by such physical treatments as insulin and electroshock, and later by tranquilizing or energizing drug treatments. Research in this area also uncovered the possible relationships between mental states and metabolism, endocrine functions, and blood composition, so that it became evident that organic parameters played a role in the expression of personality.

Not many anthropologists have consistently applied the "organic approach" to their field research. One notable exception is found in the work of Wallace (1961:255-95), who also demonstrated that the study of psychopathology in other cultures cannot be based upon generalizations, because mental illness and health are often defined along entirely different lines than in Western cultures. But even those culture and personality scholars who had no specific interest in psychopathology could no longer assume with complacency that basic or modal personality was relatively easy to establish.

A further complicating factor was environment, to which the human organism was inextricably related, not only in terms of climate, but also in respect to diet and nutrition, the use of alcohol and narcotics, and similar cultural-environmental features that affect personality and behavior.

In the face of these innumerable odds, John Whiting and his collaborators were able to take most of these newer insights into account and to arrive at a new synthesis without relinquishing all previous work that had been done. In this approach, child training was still considered an important determinant, but it encompassed much more than the more or less conscious feeding or weaning patterns. Sleeping arrangements, for instance, might be quite significant, and these may in turn be related to specific forms of family organization. In polygynous societies, a husband will generally sleep with his various wives in turn, and under such arrangements postpartum sexual taboos may be quite long. A mother will then sleep with her newborn child for longer periods of time than in monogamous situations. Whiting did not take these facts for granted, but examined the Human Relations Area Files and perused monographs for statistical correlations which indeed were found to exist: polygynous societies practiced longer postpartum taboos than monogamous ones. Further statistical research indicated that such societies showed a positive correlation to the presence of male initiation rites. To account for this seemingly startling fact, two hypotheses were advanced. Either the sleeping arrangements increased the Oedipal rivalry between father and son, so that the puberty rites served to prevent revolt against paternal authority, or the sleeping patterns led to an excessive dependence upon and identification with the mother so that initiation rites were needed to break or counteract these socially disruptive dependencies. The first interpretation was least likely to be true, because in polygynous societies with postpartum sexual taboos a father has more than one wife by definition. The presence of the infant will not lead to sexual deprivation, and rivalry will not develop. The second hypothesis seemed thus to be the more plausible one (Whiting, Kluckhohn, and Anthony 1958).

In an even more ambitious study, Whiting (1964) took organic and environmental factors into account as well. Humid tropical areas where agricultural products are the staple food were low in protein intake and were positively correlated with the occurrence of kwashiorkor, a disease caused by protein deficiency. Prolonged postpartum taboos imply prolonged nursing, and statistics proved further that the duration of the sex taboo increases as the protein in the available natural resources decreases. Lactation provides the child with protein, particularly important for its health in its early years. The sex taboo prevents the mother from becoming pregnant while she is nursing, and polygyny is compatible with this situation. Finally, polygyny is positively correlated with patrilocal residence, and patrilocality is in turn correlated with patrilineality. Such societies are thus strongly male-centered, and boys who have spent long periods of time sleeping with their mother will need intensification of their adult male roles, which is provided by their initiation rites (Whiting, 1964).

While Whiting's complex demonstrations have sometimes been likened to a Rube Goldberg machine (Barnouw 1963: 356), his studies represent a major advance in methodology. The data from the Human Relations Area Files that he uses may not always be perfect, and the statistical approach has its own shortcomings and limitations. Nevertheless, Whiting transcended earlier deterministic interpretations by his emphasis on interaction rather than on causality. His theory is by its very nature cross-cultural, and thus more meaningful than descriptions of how societies differ and what they have in common. Moreover, Whiting found a way to account for the conditions that gave rise to what Kardiner had called "primary institutions" which Kardiner himself had been unable to explain (Kardiner 1939:471).

CONCLUSIONS

The interaction between psychology and anthropology gave new dimensions to the study of man and his culture. Many explanations are incomplete, but the basic insight that human personality is interrelated with cultural factors cannot be left out if culture is to be fully comprehended, even if the question as to which is the major determinant remains so far unanswered. While many cultural anthropologists still remain aloof from psychological interpretations, a great deal of research is carried out that keeps personality problems in mind, even by those who do not identify themselves with psychological anthropology. Several studies stress the influence of the total cultural setting upon personality and behavior. Oscar Lewis in his Mexican (1959, 1963, 1967) and Puerto Rican (1965) studies demonstrated how poor economic conditions will give rise to similar behavior and expectations. He found this so pervasive cross-culturally that he coined the phrase "culture of poverty" to indicate the regularities of personality among peoples living under deprived social conditions. Studies of class and caste in the South, like the one made by Dollard (1937), emphasize the influence of social distance. Bernard James (1961) interpreted the personality of Ojibwa Indians in terms of their life on a reservation, Elkins (1961) traced the consequences of slavery for personality, while Spiro (1958) dealt with life in the kibbutz along the same lines. A substantial amount of literature deals with the personalities of peasants as compared with those of city dwellers (Redfield 1953, 1956; Foster 1965).

Applications to modern problems in complex societies have also not been wanting. Cross-cultural studies on the function of alcohol (Horton 1953), the relationship between national character and modern political systems (Inkeles 1961), the effects of Western education upon American Indian children

(Thompson 1951), psychological adjustments of soldiers, im-migrants, and prisoners are but some of the areas that have been scrutinized by psychological anthropologists.

Psychiatrists and psychologists have acknowledged the tremendous influence of culture and personality studies upon their disciplines (Campbell 1961). Confrontation with an-thropological literature has substantially altered the implicit ethnocentrism contained in the earlier assumption that West-ern behavior is the norm by which all other forms of behavior can be measured. The documentation of the importance of cultural determinants in personality formation is probably the major achievement of psychological anthropology, and has given wider perspectives not only to psychology and psy-chiatry, but to anthropology as a whole. By focusing on per-sonality, anthropologists came to realize that social systems do not operate on their own power, and that superorganic or structural explanations are incomplete. It has been observed (Spiro 1969) that psychological anthropologists have often shown greater concern with the definition and analysis of per-sonality than with sociocultural systems, and have focused mainly on those institutions that seemed to be the major deter-minants of personality. Spiro suggests that the study of social structure would be broadened if the situation were reversed, and the emphasis placed upon the explanation of social sys-tems in terms of personality dynamics.

Psychological anthropology is still largely considered as a subdiscipline of cultural anthropology, but if there were stronger attempts to examine the ways in which cultural per-sonality systems enable cultural institutions to serve their social functions, psychological anthropology could become a partner in a joint venture rather than remaining a "branch" of anthropology.

CHAPTER 14

THE NEW
ANTHROPOLOGY

In the decades after World War II, specialists in the several subfields of anthropology critically evaluated their methods with the result that conscious efforts were made to create new approaches. W. Taylor (1948) laid the foundations for a "new archaeology," S. Washburn (1951) called for a "new physical anthropology," linguists and cultural anthropologists equally sought new directions. To a significant degree, these efforts led to a closer cooperation, tending to reaffirm and strengthen the four-field approach which for a while stood under the threat of dissolution. New archaeologists view their findings as representative of cultural systems, and attempt to grasp the meanings of archaeological remains not as ends in themselves, but as a means to understanding the human beings who made them, and the societies in which they lived. The new trend in physical anthropology is to project human evolution against the background of culture and ecology, while field studies of living primates search for the interrelationships between animal and human social behavior. Many present-day linguists concern themselves with cultural and psychological elements of language, while cultural anthropologists often take linguistic methodology as a model for their own studies.

Anthropological efforts to revise and refine older concepts have gone in many different directions, but the overall concern is the attempt to discover units of explanation that can be used cross-culturally in an objective and unbiased manner. Dissatisfied with historical particularism, anthropologists now feel that meaningful cross-cultural comparisons can not rest upon often undefined categories that were used earlier, categories such as trait, pattern, theme, custom, or folkways.

The interest in cross-cultural analysis turned the interest of scholars toward the attempt to discover universals in culture, in the realization that human behavior is flexible but not ultimately so, and that cultures vary but also possess common grounds of existence. These developments were not unrelated to the increasing concern for bringing the study of primitive societies into greater relationship with complex ones. For a long while, anthropologists had described primitive cultures as if they were timeless and unchanging isolates, but such a romantic outlook could no longer be maintained. The tremendous changes going on in the world after World War II touched primitives, peasants, townsmen, and industrialized city dwellers alike, and studies of acculturation, of how primitives become members of modern society, how migrants adjust to new surroundings, how peasants become industrialized farmers, have come to replace the timeless descriptions of "the" Nuer or "the" Eskimo to a significant degree.

The community study method was perhaps the first conscious attempt to extend the insights gained from the study of homogeneous societies to more complex ones. The method signaled a breaking away from particularized concerns with tribal groups, and demonstrated that cultures were functionally dependent parts of larger wholes. In itself, however, the method contained no directions as to how the various larger wholes could be brought into relationship with each other in a meaningful way. Searching for a wider framework, one in which the findings of archaeology, linguistics, and physical anthropology also could be encompassed, anthropologists rediscovered evolution.

Although Boas and his followers were not quite so anti-evolutionist as they are sometimes made out to be, they made few efforts to discover possible regularities of development and change. Nevertheless, the evolutionary concerns that had marked the beginning of anthropology as an independent discipline were never completely lost from sight. V. Gordon Childe (1892–1957) and Leslie White kept this tradition alive in England and America respectively. Childe (1951) described evolution in terms of three major events: the invention of food production, urbanization, and industrialization. Analyzing the transitions that took place under the impact of these "revolutions," Childe presented an overall view of the evolutionary process and delineated its common factors.

Leslie White went a step further. Although he was a student of Boas, he was a greater admirer of Tylor and Morgan. Like them, White believed in the progressive course of evolution, but he tried to explain what caused progress itself and how it worked. Searching for a universal principle of explanation, he found it in "energy." He reasoned that culture is basically a survival mechanism, and that energy is required to provide man with the necessities for his continued existence. In the earliest stage of human development, man used his own body as the major source of energy, but soon he began to capture other natural resources of energy, and utilized fire, water, and wind for his own purposes. Tools became increasingly efficient, animals were domesticated, engines constructed, and so forth, so that the amount of energy harnessed per capita and the efficiency of technology increased as culture evolved. Each type of technology, moreover, conditioned a specific type of social organization: pastoralism, agriculture, metallurgy, industry, and militarism each found a corresponding expression in a social system (White 1949:363–93).

It is the latter proposal that is somewhat dubious, and the one-to-one correlation between technology and social organization has not been supported by ethnographic evidence. Agricultural societies, for instance, are widely divergent in their forms of social organization, and, furthermore, technological types are widely overlapping: pastoralism, agriculture, metallurgy, and industry often occur side by side. But White's greater relevance is that he continued the work begun by Tylor and Morgan. Rather than repudiating the concept of universal evolution, he improved it by using observable material factors as parameters of change rather than referring to abstract notions of progress.

By its very nature, White's overall view of evolution did not account for particular events. He dealt with advance, not with divergence, and with general process, not with adaptation. He took the position that evolution does occur on a planetary scale, and that this is a worthy object of study. He regarded the amount of energy available to a human group at a given period in cultural development a convenient macrocosmic framework for the discussion of a long-term evolutionary history.

It is obvious enough that overall views of evolution obscure particular events. But the interest in macroscopic culture history had waned in the postwar period, and White's work roused little enthusiasm and a great deal of criticism because of its inability to account for short-time developments. Julian Steward (1902–72), for one, wrote that both nineteenth-century "unilinear" evolution and White's "general" evolution dealt with culture rather than with cultures, and that the concern with overall cultural developments could at best provide limited insights (Steward 1953:313–26). Instead, Steward pleaded for "multilinear" evolutionism, which approach would establish sequences of parallel developments that could be investigated in empirical reality. It was Steward's thesis that societies with a similar technology existing in similar environments would parallel one another also in their forms of social and political organization. Thus it appeared to him that hunter-gatherers tended to form patrilineal bands, and that widely scattered Indian societies that had accepted the horse after its introduction into America were comparable in their sociopolitical organizations. His argument was strengthened by the researches of Karl Wittfogel (1957), who showed that societies located near inundating rivers which carried out hydraulic (irrigation) agriculture originated state organizations, thus demonstrating the interaction between environment, technology, and political organization.

Steward's multilineal approach differs from earlier ones but does not necessarily discredit them. White stressed the general, Steward the particular, and the debates between evolutionists with different predilections were nothing more than semantic squabbles. White (1959:106–25) maintained that Steward confused history with evolution, because history, according to White, is concerned with particulars while evolution seeks to generalize; Steward felt that White's generalizations were barren. But, as Sahlins and Service (1960) pointed out, White and Steward simply dealt with evolution in different ways. White observed the overall directional advance of culture in absolute terms, Steward dealt with related historical sequences. Mead (1964:23) added that a third approach is possible, namely the study of actual processes of change as they occur in one generation or between adjacent generations.

Subsequent neoevolutionists have not brought these approaches into harmony. White's followers tend to stress material factors and technology as determinants of social organization, but theirs is often a functional rather than an evolutionary approach. Multievolutionists have generally acknowledged the interrelationships between environment and technology, so that the latter became viewed as a variable rather than as an ultimate cause of evolution. Others searched for different parameters of change. Naroll (1956) saw occupational specialization and urbanization as the basic indicators of cultural advance. Carneiro (1962, 1967) offered a list of 205 qualitatively different cultural features that may measure degrees of cultural development, suggesting that such "scale analysis" would also reveal the functional interrelationships between traits. Barnett (1953) examined the innovative processes themselves, while Service (1971) published an ethnographic compendium in which he presented descriptions in various cultures in ascending orders of political complexity: bands, tribes, chiefdoms, primitive states, and modern folk societies. Mead's suggested short-time studies are not generally termed evolutionary, but are more often considered as instances of culture change.

The various new approaches to the study of evolution called attention to the question of how to combine the particular with the general, or how the study of individual cultures could yield meaningful information about culture writ large. The issue became sharpened by the writings of Marvin Harris, who drew attention to Radcliffe-Brown's earlier distinction between nomothetic and ideographic approaches to the study of culture. The literal meaning of nomothetic is "law-giving," and nomothetic research thus attempts to discover general social laws. Ideography, on the other hand, means description in particular terms, and is thus not necessarily analytic. Strongly favoring the former over the latter, Harris did not advocate the abandonment of detailed descriptions, but indicated that data must be collected in such a way that they become cross-culturally comparable and thus can lead to valid cross-cultural comparisons. Earlier attempts to do so had been thwarted by impressionism and vague categorizations, while in reality there had been no consensus about what constituted a "trait," an "institution," or a "role."

In *The Nature of Cultural Things* (1964) Harris took the movements of the body as an incontrovertible unit of observation. Body motions constitute nonverbal behavior, which is indeed an important aspect of all cultural descriptions, although it is generally explained by seeking verbal information about its meanings or by taking note of the words that regularly accompany it. But Harris wanted to take an unambiguous and depersonalized view of culture, and since language is often ambiguous he left out linguistic verification or explanation given by informants.

Where Kluckhohn (1949:300) maintained that the first responsibility of an anthropologist is to record events as seen by the people themselves, Harris denied this explicitly (Harris

1964:93). He felt that the actor-oriented approach led to great confusion, not only because language is ambiguous, but also because the actors themselves do not generally know the social purposes or meanings of their behavior. In Harris' observer-oriented approach, it is the first responsibility of the anthropologist to set down events as seen by the observer.

Since the older terminology ("trait," "custom," and so forth) was considered redundant, Harris constructed a new vocabulary to express classes of behavior. The smallest items are *actones,* just visible behavior, and recurrent actones are *actonemes.* Two of his twenty-two examples of actonemes are (1964:47–49):

ACTONEME	BODY PART	BODY MOTION	ENVIRONMENTAL EFFECT
pick up	hand	hand elevated while fingers grasp	object is raised
drink	mouth	mouth opens	liquid disappears inside mouth

From these basic units more complex classes of behavior are constructed: actonemes following each other in sequence are actone chains, and in order of complexity follow episodes, nodes, nodal chains, scenes, serials, nomoclones, permaclones, paragroups, nomoclonic types, permaclonic types, permaclonic systems, and permaclonic supersystems. If all of those are operationally described we have "culture" (1964:168).

Harris admits that in practice such detailed analysis of cultural behavior is well-nigh impossible, and cites budgetary limitations and lack of manpower as the main reasons for the dubious future of actonic research. The significance of his position is, however, a theoretical one. He demonstrates that a consistent scientific approach to cultural taxonomy is indeed possible, but at a cost that is more than financial, namely that of the subjective meaning of culture.

Already in *The Nature of Cultural Things,* but more explicitly in his later book *The Rise of Anthropological Theory*

(1968), Harris deals with the contrast between "etic" and "emic" approaches. These terms were coined by the linguist Kenneth Pike (1954), utilizing the last part of the words "phonetic" and "phonemic." In linguistics, phonetics is the description of all speech sounds as they are produced by the human speech organs, while phonemics is the sorting out of these sounds in order to arrive at their distinctive differences. Phonetic systems can be universally applied because the human organs of speech are similar everywhere, but phonemic systems differ from language to language because sound combinations and distinctive differences are unique for every linguistic group. In terms of cultural behavior, etics would provide a set of criteria capable of classifying all data into a single system, while emics would attempt to discover the meaningful structure of specific cultures. To Pike, etics is the handmaiden of emics. Etics is classificatory and nonstructural, emics reflects the internal structural relationships found in specific cultural systems (Pike 1954:8–9).

It may already be surmised that Harris' position is quite the opposite, and that he favors etics over emics. Phonetic and etic analysis can proceed purely by observation, and meaning does not enter the picture. This is very similar to Harris' actonic approach, while phonemics and emics are particularistic. Pike explicitly stated that emic units relate to the actors' purposes and meanings: "It is absolutely essential, if one is to study behavior *as it actually functions,* that the analyst can detect the presence and to some degree the nature and meaning of purpose" (Pike 1954:80).

But of course, as soon as meanings and purposes enter the picture, individual actors become involved and scientific purity fades away. Emic studies, according to Harris, deal with inner psychological states, and assume that an actor knows his own inner state better than the observer does, and that it is essential for the observer to know the actor's inner state. But this is an impossibility, because the actor's meaning will not generally coincide with social meanings, and the essential structural features of a culture are generally unknown to informants.

Moreover, human thought is sometimes rational and logical, sometimes irrational and illogical, and it occurs on conscious, unconscious, and preconscious levels. Inner psychological states are thus poor and unreliable guides, and emic research will lead to unscientific results which are ideographic, mentalistic, idealistic, and particularistic. Etics, however, is nomothetic, materialistic, general, and scientific.

The whole status of anthropological research is thus put in doubt. Etic research is too cumbersome and too expensive; emic research is useless. Harris himself retreated from this uncompromising position by stating that both emic and etic phenomena form part of the adaptive process of cultural systems, but warns that emic and etic aspects of behavior must never be confused, because each will lead to an entirely different type of analysis (Harris 1971:149).

While Harris stressed the difficulties of "entering inside the heads of informants," many modern investigators are attempting to do precisely that (Frake 1964:133), thus stressing the emic approach. These "ethnoscientists" as they are sometimes called (Sturtevant 1964:99–131), also take their cues from language, and are not examining "inner psychological states" à la Freud, but focus on cognition as it is expressed in linguistic categories. In kinship analysis, for instance, they searched to identify cognitively contrasting components of specific kinship systems, and the most successful method is known as componential analysis (Goodenough 1956). This method avoids the use of ethnocentric kinship terms such as "uncle" or "cousin," because those relatives whom we call "uncle" may be classed quite differently elsewhere. All kinship terms are classified in terms of distinctions such as sex, generation, lineality, collaterality, affinity, and other culturally appropriate criteria, resulting in a diagram that shows the formal cognitive rules of a kinship system as it is utilized by members of the group. In this manner then, the researcher discovers what goes on inside someone's head, whether or not this process is conscious. Componential analysis goes further than that, because it does not merely point the way to recognize relatives, but systematically describes the structural relationships between relatives in the total kinship system.

Ethnoscience thus accounts for cultural items and cultural relationships in terms of the information used by members of a culture in their linguistic categories. This information itself is related to culturally significant behavior, which demands delineation of the conditions under which such behavior occurs. Among the best-known examples of such research in domains other than kinship is Harold Conklin's (1955) study of color categories among the Hanunóo in the Philippines. He found significant differences in the ways in which the Hanunóo classified colors as compared to Western categorizations. The latter depend on hue, brightness, and saturation, but the Hanunóo use moisture, surface texture, and lightness as the critical attributes for naming colors. Their classification, moreover, is associated with other cultural phenomena, particularly in plant life and its desirability in terms of consumption. In a similar vein Frake (1961), working among the Subanun of Mindanao in the southern Philippines, showed how these people diagnosed disease according to a specific set of cultural criteria expressed in terms of mutually exclusive linguistic categories, and indicated how their system of diagnosis related also to treatment and therapy. Many other studies demonstrated that different cultures structure their fields of cognition in entirely different manners. Art, food tastes, plant and animal classification, supernatural entities, mental illness, deviancy, crime, and many other cultural categorizations are conceptualized in different cultures by different criteria. Several anthropological subfields have developed based upon this insight, each stressing a separate and specific cultural aspect, and all using the prefix "ethno-" to indicate their alliance with ethnoscience: ethnomusicology, ethnobotany, ethnozoology, ethnomedicine, ethnopsychology, ethnoecology, ethnofolklore, and so forth.

The great advantage over previous ethnographic research is that the procedures of discovery can be precisely described, so that subsequent field workers can replicate and verify the analysis, build upon it, and note changes if and when they occur. Although complete ethnoscientific ethnographies are scarce, it should be possible to correlate all cultural cognitions with one another and thus to achieve a meaningful cultural analysis.

The new ethnologists have been relatively silent, however, about the possibilities of cross-cultural comparisons. If each culture is described in its own terms, how can cultures be compared? One possible answer is that if the descriptive techniques are universal, the resulting systems should be comparable. Another answer is that the principles of cognition or of thought may be comparable, and it is in this field that Claude Lévi-Strauss has made his contributions.

To Lévi-Strauss, the most fundamental problem is the understanding of the modes of human thought. His particular approach has become known as structuralism, but his concept of structure differs from that of Radcliffe-Brown on several points. Lévi-Strauss would agree with Radcliffe-Brown that "structure is an ordered arrangement of parts or components" (Radcliffe-Brown 1952:9), but Radcliffe-Brown took interpersonal social relationships as his point of departure. He examined social structure in order to discover social functions, and these functions always possessed an aura of utility, at a minimum serving to maintain the coherence of the social whole. Lévi-Strauss is not concerned with such functions, and considers them self-understood: "Function is to produce the consequences which it does produce" (1969a:141). He is interested in structure not from the aspect of interpersonal relationships, but he wants, first and foremost, to discover the structure of human thought processes.

Although occasionally borrowing from Freud's insights into the human psyche, Lévi-Strauss' structuralism is not reducible to psychology. Neither does he maintain that structures of thought determine culture, but holds instead that they operate within a cultural context. Cultural forms express the characteristics of mind, but not as a simple mirror reflection, so that detailed ethnographic studies are necessary in order to show how they operate.

Much like American ethnoscientists, and unlike Hegel or Freud, Lévi-Strauss does not start his researches with a priori categories or ideas. Each human group has its own contingent history and its own physical and social environment which interact with structured modes of thought. In his published work, he pays attention to minute ethnographic details, in the conviction that each culture represents a new situation which can be understood only after painstaking scrutiny. When a cultural system different from one's own is first encountered, it appears to be incoherent, but structural analysis shows that it possesses its own internal logic. Lévi-Strauss holds that this coherence transcends all utility and function, and it follows that the principles of this logic can be accounted for only in terms of the inherent and unconscious structure of the human mind itself.

Lévi-Strauss borrows his most important methodological tool from linguistics, with particular reference to phonemics. The so-called Prague School of linguistics, led by N. Troubetzkoy and Roman Jacobson, demonstrated that the structure of language cannot be found by a mere inventory of its sounds, but that it is the relationship between sounds that provides significance. These relationships are not normally conscious in the minds of speakers, but they form the basis for discovering cross-culturally valid invariant rules (Lévi-Strauss 1963:33).

Turning first to the study of kinship organization and marriage rules, Lévi-Strauss likewise examined the structural relationships of their constituent elements rather than considering them in isolation. Traditionally, kinship systems had been studied in the manner of prestructural linguistics: the sets were broken down into their smallest units and the nature of these elements was then discussed in terms of interpersonal relationships, or related to other social meanings and functions. Lévi-Strauss, however, attempts to unravel the unconscious logic behind kinship classifications and marriage rules by considering the relationships between their constituent units. These relationships consist of oppositions and correlations, permutations and transformations, and the correspondences are thus not explained in terms of mechanical causality, but in terms of logic. Since this logic is universal, both intra- and inter-cultural comparisons become possible.

Starting with his first important book, *The Elementary Structures of Kinship* (1969a; originally published in 1949), Lévi-Strauss took the incest taboo as his point of departure. This is not an a priori category, because it has been empirically established that incest taboos appear in every known society, although specific rules differ from culture to culture. Although incest taboos do possess social functions, these cannot account for their origins, because it is impossible to believe that early men who instituted these rules could have known their possible social advantages. Instead, incest taboos ultimately depend upon the property of the human mind to think in opposites, and the most fundamental dichotomy, one that must be recognized in order for man to become human and to develop culture, is that between "self" and "others." Only when this distinction is made does true symbolic communication become possible, and communication is reciprocal exchange that takes place on three fundamental levels: exchange of messages, goods, and women (Lévi-Strauss 1953: 536).

Incest taboos have to do with exchange of women. Among animals, mating is random and promiscuous, while incest taboo by its very nature dictates an ordered exchange of women, thus also instituting marriage rules. This reciprocity sets in motion a cycle of reciprocal exchange on other levels. Incest taboos thus mark the difference between man and animals, which is also the difference between nature and culture, and this most basic dichotomy is present in many cultural systems: in totemism, in myth and art, in ritual, and even in such unexpected areas as the ways in which people name their pet animals (Lévi-Strauss 1966b:191–216).

While it thus appears to be a basic property of the human mind to think in dyads, the resulting systems are by no means simple. The dualism itself is often subdivided, its elements may be unequal or asymmetrical, and triadic divisions may intertwine with all others. It is evident that "dualism" is not a mere catchword. The dichotomizing tendency of the human mind is of a structural nature, and while it is not necessarily conscious, it gives a specific shape to the arrangement of social phenomena. Any dualism evokes new arangements and new complications, and hence it does not lead to identical social organizations, but produces ever new forms. The most important activity of the human mind is to organize the raw materials of experience provided by history and environment, but the laws of organization are common to all human beings.

Lévi-Strauss' search for the nature of the unconscious mind led him almost inevitably to the study of myth. Of all activities of the human mind, myth making is least ruled by functional necessities and nearest to the unconscious. Kinship systems, marriage rules, and village organizations are at least partially influenced by the contingencies of social life as it has to be lived, but myth stands apart from such considerations. The myth-making mind is constrained mainly by its own inherent principles and not by social utility: "Mythology has no obvious practical function . . ." (Lévi-Strauss 1969b:10). If, then, the human mind proves to be structured in the function-free realm of myth, it must also be so determined in all other spheres of mental activity (ibid.:10).

Describing his basic method in an article called "The Structural Study of Myth" (1963:206–31), Lévi-Strauss took various versions of the Oedipus myth as his example. The myth is not to be read as a story, but must be broken down into its basic constituent elements or "mythemes," and the relationships between them must be examined. They represent the nature-culture dichotomy, hinging on the incest taboo. In his subsequent 4-volume Mythologiques (1964, 1966a, 1968, 1972), Lévi-Strauss shows the full strength of his method. In The Raw and the Cooked (1969), he explores 187 South

American myths, and in the subsequent volumes a further six hundred Indian myths are examined and analyzed. While they are often very different in content, Lévi-Strauss endeavors to demonstrate that their underlying structures display significant similarities. Together, they are like an orchestral score, where each instrument says something different, but what it says is part of a structured whole.

The differences between the myths are brought into harmony by analyzing them in terms of relatively simple oppositions, among which that between nature and culture figures quite prominently. This implies that it must be shown that unlike mythical elements possess the same structural significance. It is at this level that the greatest difficulties arise. Although Lévi-Strauss stresses again and again that overt meanings are not important, it is nevertheless necessary to deal with semantic meanings in order to show that the myths are structurally equivalent. Mythemes are thus "translated," transposed, and transformed to indicate their common grounds, and although Lévi-Strauss does this with great elegance and eloquence, the transformations often appear arbitrary and farfetched. Thus, since honey is always consumed "raw," it represents nature. But honey is also enticing and seductive, and hence all myths dealing with seduction stand in the same structural position as honey. Ashes, however, are produced by fire. Fire is one of man's earliest inventions, and both ashes and fire signify culture. Tobacco needs fire for its consumption, and wild pig meat is never eaten uncooked. Myths dealing with tobacco or with the origin of the wild pig are thus related to those dealing with fire, ashes, cooking, smoke, and burning. Even myths explaining the origin of feather necklaces are so related, because feathers are often burned in order to produce smoke.

The crux of the structural position does not rest on the question of whether or not all of Lévi-Strauss' transformations are acceptable to others. Rather, it must be asked if the method itself can increase our understanding about man and his culture. Those anthropologists who see their discipline as a positivistic science are generally very critical of structuralism, because the reality that Lévi-Strauss presents is an unconscious one, and thus unverifiable. In his own words: "The unconscious . . . is always empty—or, more accurately, it is as alien to mental images as is the stomach to the foods which pass through it" (1963:203).

His unconscious is thus of a different nature from that depicted by Freud, for whom it was anything but empty. To the contrary, in Freud's view no experience is ever wholly obliterated, and the very method of psychoanalysis is aimed at retrieving what may have been forgotten or repressed. Neither does Lévi-Strauss deal with the latent aspects of social structure or function, those that were neither intended nor recognized. But there is nothing in the theories of Durkheim or Radcliffe-Brown (who dealt with these latent functions) that precludes recognition of structure and function on part of the culture bearers. In language, children and untutored adults are unaware of their use of grammatical rules, but these are readily recognized when they are taught. But how can Lévi-Strauss' "empty" unconscious ever become manifest? It seems doubtful that American Indians would agree that feather necklaces and wild pigs have the same significance, even if structuralism was taught to them.

It appears, then, that the reality into which Lévi-Strauss has led us, a reality that he himself considers to be more real than that of the concrete world, is devoid both of human consciousness and of social living. The absence of the former is axiomatic, and about the latter he says that social structure "has nothing to do with empirical reality" (1953:297).

Lévi-Strauss concedes that his methods are not always easy to follow. Although "guided by reality," his conclusions "blindly derive their substance from myth" (1969b:2). He also realizes that his transformations may seem arbitrary. But that does not matter, because, in the final analysis, "it is immaterial whether . . . the thought processes of the South American Indians take shape through the medium of my thought, or whether mine take place through the medium of theirs" (*ibid.*:13).

While many anthropologists have difficulties in accepting Lévi-Strauss' postulates, it is particularly displeasing to them that structuralism seems to have no relevance to the empirical world. The close acquaintance that many field workers have with living American Indians and with other traditional societies has convinced them that these peoples' thought and behavior patterns are firmly rooted in the world of concrete experience and that they classify and observe the phenomena of the world in categories meaningful to themselves. This observation does not necessarily prove that Lévi-Strauss is wrong, but it rather indicates that thus far his theories and methods have not been persuasive to most positivist-minded anthropologists. Nevertheless, some have also realized that positivism is a scientific method using verifiability as its code, and that it is possible that other codes for understanding exist. Perhaps, then, Lévi-Strauss is embarked on a scientific revolution, although at present it seems to be a faltering one. So far, he does not say much more about the human mind than that it *is* structured, and that its tendency is to think in binary patterns.

Although Lévi-Strauss stresses that the unconscious logic of the mind is of much greater importance than the analysis of the content of myth, and thus seemingly attempts to remove myth (or kinship or totemic beliefs) away from concrete and empirical reality, he himself did not remain satisfied with structure devoid of social meaning. He well realizes that incest taboos, once they are instituted, possess certain social advantages, and that art or myth reflects other things than the unconscious structures of the mind. In pursuing those aspects Lévi-Strauss is much closer to what anthropologists consider the core of their discipline, and here he is most brilliant and creative. Where Boas did not really know quite what to do with the Indian myths that he so painstakingly collected, Lévi-Strauss shows how each myth reflects and interacts with features of the environment, and is meaningful also on a concrete social level. Particularly when he analyzes single myths, and when he places them within their own ecological and sociocultural matrix, he shows that they can have explanatory functions that had not been previously realized and that they are much more systematic than had been supposed. But for these kinds of explanations it is not necessary to invoke the unconscious structure of the mind.

Although with different emphasis, this aspect of Lévi-Strauss' cultural analysis is not unrelated to the work of cognitive ethnoscientists who also elicit the rationality of folk classifications and relate them to other social facts.

Meanwhile, the search for a priori principles of the mind has also been taken up by linguists. In the forefront of this undertaking stands Noam Chomsky, who is also known for his vigorous protests against the Vietnam war. It is as a scholar of linguistics, however, that he is counted by some as the Galileo of his discipline, while others have denounced his theory as one "spawned by a generation of vipers" (Hockett 1968). Essentially, the debate is centered around the relationship between thought and experience in terms of rationalism versus empiricism. The difference between the two positions is that rationalists claim that the mind is the major source of human knowledge and behavior, while empiricists feel that there are no innate properties of the human mind and that all knowledge derives from experience. Chomsky defends the rationalist camp, and declares that contemporary linguistic research supports the theory that the mind possesses certain given properties which, although limited in number, underlie all languages. These basic principles are present in the mind at birth, and the mind is thus not a "tabula rasa" or an "empty cabinet," as Locke and Hume maintained. Chomsky allies himself more closely to the position of Descartes, who argued that the human understanding of the world rests upon "innate ideas" (Chomsky 1966).

Concentrating on the descriptive aspects of linguistics

(phonetics, phonemics, syntax), pre-Chomskian linguists had little to say about the acquisition of language and even less about its semantic structures. Chomsky, however, was struck by man's extraordinary ability to use sentences that have not been taught, and to understand an infinite number of utterances that have not been heard before. By the age of five or six, children are able to construct and understand new sentences, and to reject those word orders and grammatical structures that are linguistically unacceptable. Human linguistic abilities thus go far beyond anything taught or experienced, and Chomsky concludes that there must be independent processes at work, removed from experience.

The next obvious step is to discover the logic of these innate structures, and Chomsky shows that all sentences in the languages that he and his associates have scrutinized can be derived from a relatively small number of "kernel" sentences and a set of rules of operations. The crucial assertion is that every sentence has both a "surface" structure and a "deep" structure. The former consists of the words we say and hear, and corresponds to the parsing of sentences we learn in school. The deep structure expresses the relationships between these "parts of speech," and is thus more abstract. The operational rules are limited in number, but they can generate an infinite number of human utterances, in a way similar to mathematical operations (addition, subtraction, equivalence, and so on), which also give rise to unlimited constructions.

Although not all languages have been thus examined, Chomsky believes that the four thousand or so presently known languages all rest upon the same basic principles, which he calls "formal universals." Chomsky does not clearly commit himself to the view that such innateness is biological or neurochemical. The processes are likely to be of great intricacy, and may well be located in an intermediary zone between "mental" and "physical," or between "psychic" and "neurochemical," or perhaps this vocabulary is outmoded and there may be no ultimate distinction between "body" and "mind."

While this question remains an open one, Chomsky is

convinced that some invariant properties are at the root of all languages and that they are present at birth. This very premise has made him one of the most devastating critics of neobehaviorism, notably that of B. F. Skinner. Rooted in the empiricism of Locke and Hume, who argued that man's understanding of the external world is based upon perceptions only, Skinner claims that language is acquired in a similar manner, namely by experience (Skinner 1957). Extrapolating from his studies of stimulus-and-response behavior in animals, Skinner feels that language acquisition is not very different from the ways in which rats learn to run a maze, namely by punishment and reward. A child learns a language because it is "rewarded" when it makes the correct noises, and because correct speech is effective and incoherent speech is not. Language and speech are thus nothing but a complex set of conditioned responses.

Chomsky considers this view of man shocking. Precisely in linguistic behavior man is unique, and different from all other animals. From childhood on, the human use of language goes beyond everything that is taught, and behaviorism cannot account for this astonishing creativity. Moreover, Chomsky continues, Skinner did not base his theory of language learning on actual observation, but on analogies to laboratory studies of lower organisms who do not display any verbal behavior (Chomsky 1959).

A good deal of Chomsky's further criticism is of an extremely technical nature, but throughout he insists upon his thesis that language is not just a simple habit, but one that depends upon a given structure or condition of the mind. Evidence for the presence of linguistic universals has come from other linguists as well as from psychologists, but the question of language acquisition remains a puzzle.

By and large, cultural anthropologists have been more inclined to accept Chomsky's rational view of man than Skinner's behaviorism, which depicts man as an intelligent and highly trained rat, but they are not overly enthusiastic about what logically follows from Chomsky's theories, namely that if language is based upon certain innate rules, culture must equally be so predetermined, which is Lévi-Strauss' position. Nevertheless, whatever the future holds in store for the attempts to discover the structure of the mind, they have served to compel anthropologists to reexamine the often unexpressed axioms of their own methodology. The principles in which modern anthropology founded itself were strongly influenced by a rejection of the concept of human nature. As viewed by earlier philosophers, human nature was something inborn or instinctual, and hence rather inflexible. Freud and his followers were convinced that the human psyche was a kind of biological entity with universal properties such as the Oedipus complex, while racists with polygenic persuasions posited a plurality of unmodifiable human natures.

It was against the fatal consequences of such views that anthropology took its stand, and the concept of culture as learned rather than as innate behavior provided a powerful alternative explanation. But often enough, culture was viewed as something external to man. Durkheim wrote that the first and foremost principle of the study of society was "to consider social facts as things" (1958:14), adding that the most important characteristic of a social thing is "the impossibility of its modification by the human will" (*ibid*.:28). Boas rejected the racist view of human nature as well as Bastian's "psychic unity," stressing the diversities of cultures rather than their uniformities. Early psychological anthropologists set out to refute Freud, showing that human nature was influenced by cultural training, and thus flexible to a very significant degree. Kroeber and White depicted all human behavior as caused by culture. White in particular saw culture as a greater tyrant than human nature had ever been, calling the idea that man could exercise any control over the social order "an anthropocentric illusion" (White 1949:330–59). Few anthropologists have gone to such extremes, but there was nevertheless a very strong tendency to regard human nature as a function of culture only, and it was also felt that any allusion to a universal "human nature" had no explanatory value. In these views, culture was not so much the fact that man acquires or learns his habits, but rather the results of that learning: culture is everything that man does, makes, and thinks (Herskovits 1948:154), or "the *total* way of life of any society" (Linton 1945:30). Human behavior could thus be objectified, labeled, and described in an orderly fashion that made sense to professionals and laymen alike. If social facts were "things," human behavior consisted of "acts," and it became possible to study their interrelationships, their functions, their histories, and their changes.

There is no doubt that these various undertakings have significantly contributed to the understanding of how culture has evolved, how it operates, and how and why it may change. But "the death-knell of theories about human nature" having been sounded, as Herskovits (1948:618) expressed it, it seemed that the curiosity about the general and universal propensities of the mind had died also. If Lévi-Strauss and Chomsky admittedly have not found any definite answers, they have resurrected an interest in man not merely as a culture "carrier," but as a culture "maker." The strength of traditional explanations is not undermined by the realization that human nature, now defined as "common structures of the mind," may be involved in cultural behavior, but, rather, the possibility of seeing such behavior in wider context has been opened up. In fact, the postulate of a common "human nature" is prerequisite to all anthropological understanding. Without it, the very perception of "humanity" would be in doubt.

In principle, anthropologists never denied this, but they saw the unity of mankind as existing exclusively in man's ability to use symbols and thus to create culture. This defined man uniquely: language and culture were considered to be *sui generis* phenomena which had no parallels in the animal world. Not many cultural anthropologists found it necessary to investigate the origins of these dimensions of culture. This resulted in a curious and paradoxical position in connection with the theory of evolution. Darwin's theory of physical continuity was universally accepted, but cultural anthropologists stressed the mental and behavioral discontinuity between man and the animal world.

The problem was not neglected by other disciplines. Darwin himself had suggested that language, behavior, and intelligence could be viewed in evolutionary perspective, and although he was strongly criticized for his gross anthropomorphism, he stimulated great interest in this area of research. As early as 1883, G. J. Romanes proposed the term "comparative psychology" for studies dealing with the relations between animal and human behavior, while zoologists and physical anthropologists later on coined the term "ethology" (the study of character) to specify their interest in this topic. Predictably, the kinds of studies undertaken vary with the disciplinary background of the investigators. Comparative psychologists are generally behavioristic in orientation, and thus more concerned with conditioning and learning processes. This implies that they work most often with animals in captivity, because experiments must be carried out under controlled conditions. Ethologists, however, are more interested in possible continuities between animal and human social behavior. Since laboratory conditions are always artificial, they study animals as much as possible in their native habitats, observing their interactions, reproductive behavior, patterns of communication, and the relation of these processes to group integration. The controversies that have arisen between the two disciplines resemble nineteenth-century quarrels over the primacy of nature or nurture, ethologists backing the former, psychologists the latter position. Fortunately, most researchers now realize that such dichotomies are artificial, and that animal and human behavior is better understood as resulting from an interaction between a number of variables, including genetic structures, learning patterns, and both physical and social environments.

Early animal studies in the nineteenth century did not yet distinguish between psychological and social behavior.

Darwin's evolutionary theories had brought man and beast closer together, and when their physical relationship was generally accepted the topic of animal intelligence became immensely popular. Several writers depicted animals as highly rational creatures with an innate sense of morals, justice, and social responsibility. W. L. Lindsay, an English physician, wrote several volumes (1879) on the mind of animals and gave many examples in order to show that they were endowed with the same higher mental faculties as man, and that their actions were governed by reason rather than by instinct. P. A. Kropotkin wrote a series of popular essays on this theme, later published in book form (1919). His major thesis was a reversal of the Darwinian "struggle for survival": in his view social evolution had taken place through mutual cooperation rather than by competition and brute force. The importance of these and other writings was that they recognized the social components of animal behavior, but unfortunately most of their examples were purely anecdotal. While they made delightful reading, serious scholars soon began to ridicule them for their fertile imagination and unscientific attitudes.

When Edward Lee Thorndike (1874–1949) began to experiment with animals in his laboratories, his methods and findings took center stage for several decades, and animal sociology became neglected. He conditioned animals by punishment and reward tactics and successfully modified their behavior. Somewhat hastily he concluded that the behavior of all organisms was regulated by the same "law of exercise and effort" (Thorndike 1911:280), and his theory became known as behaviorism. It received much further impetus from the researches and writings of John B. Watson (1878–1958), who also was convinced that there were no fundamental differences between animal and human behavior and learning. He wrote on this matter that "in passing from the unicellular organisms to man, no new principle is needed" (Watson 1914:318). This became an article of faith to many subsequent psychologists. Dollard and Miller based their accounts of human personality on the assumption that "any general phenomena of learning found in rats will also be found in people" (1950:63), and their psychotherapy was predicated by this principle.

One crucial question remained unexplained. If learning processes were similar, why were apes not capable of learning human language? Maybe they had not been given adequate opportunities to do so. Human children do not speak spontaneously either, but are taught the art by their parents. A number of so-called ape-rearing experiments were subsequently carried out, mostly with chimpanzees, who are great imitators. The Kelloggs (1933) took a young chimpanzee, Gua, into their home and raised it along with their infant son, Donald. Keith and Cathy Hayes similarly "adopted" a three-day-old chimp, Viki, and kept her for 6½ years. Some five or six similar experiments occurred, all with the objective of teaching the apes to speak. The Kelloggs reported that Gua adapted herself readily to her surroundings, imitated acts performed by adults, learned certain tasks, but never copied human speech sounds. The Hayeses taught Viki to say "mama," "papa," and "cup" by manipulating her lips, and after considerable effort she also learned to associate these words with their correct objects. But the experimenters concluded that the words were extremely hard for an ape to master, and that they would never occur naturally (Hayes 1951; Hayes and Hayes 1950). All researchers reported that apes communicate by gesture signals: biting or chewing at clothing meant "hungry," protruding lips toward cup "drink," and so forth. The chimps also learned to react to simple commands like "come here," or "close the door," but it was clear that they were utterly incapable of human speech.

In recent years other psychologists conceived of the idea that the inability of chimps to speak did not necessarily imply that they were deficient in learning. Allen and Beatrice Gardner (1969) trained a young chimpanzee, whom they called Washoe, to use American Sign Language (ASL). This is a

gesture language used by the deaf, and does not involve spelling. Movements substitute for an entire word: "open" is
signaled by opening closed hands, "please" by rubbing the
hand across the chest in a circular motion. The results were
phenomenal. In 1968, after sixteen months of training, Washoe
was able to use nineteen signs reliably; in 1971 she had 150
signs in her repertoire. She is able to extend the meanings of
her "words": the sign for "open" was taught to her in relation to a specific door, but soon she was able to request "open"
also in reference to bottles, boxes, refrigerators, and all other
doors. She formulated sentences such as "hurry gimme sweet
please," and she knows her name as well as the names of the
experimenters, making the appropriate signs when asked
"Who is that?" or "Who are you?" She recognizes pictures
of dogs, dolls, hats, as well as the real objects. For the first
time in history a two-way communication between man and
an animal was scientifically established. Another couple, Ann
and David Premack (1972), reported similar findings with a
chimp called Sarah. They did not use sign language, but
variously shaped and colored pieces of plastic, each representing a word.

These fascinating experiments have indicated that up to
the age of about three years the mental development of
chimpanzees is not far behind that of a human child, and
their muscular development is much more rapid. But the
experimenters themselves are well aware of the vast differences between their own systems of communication and that
of chimps. What is missing in the latter is what Chomsky has
called "creativity" and what anthropologists (Sapir 1921,
White 1949) and philosophers (Cassirer 1953, Langer 1951)
call the symbolic aspects of human language. Creativity, as has
been pointed out, refers to the human capacity to construct
and create new utterances, while symbolization is the ability
to abstract from the immediate situation, so that man can
learn not only by means of direct experience, but through language itself. There is no indication that Washoe can learn in
the abstract: she knows only those things and their signs that

have been directly shown to her, but cannot rely on verbal explanation alone.

It is worth stressing that not all of man's language and behavior is abstract and symbolic. Children learn to speak in a way similar to that of the chimps, namely by direct association, and this aspect of language never gets lost. When someone is thirsty he will ask "give me a drink, please" and Washoe can ask this also. But man can speak outside of the immediate stimulus situation, and thus he can know about things not directly encountered. Emily Dickinson expressed this unique human capability most poignantly when she wrote:

> *I never saw a moor*
> *I never saw the sea;*
> *Yet I know how the heather looks,*
> *And what a wave must be.*

These are the qualities of human language that make culture possible. Symbolic learning enables man to store knowledge and to generate new situations and ideas. He can recall the past, plan for the future, learn to go to the moon before actually going, and he can communicate about things seen, unseen, and unseeable. Some anthropomorphic-minded scholars have claimed that the fact that apes learn part of their behavior patterns indicates that they have culture (Nissen 1951:426). Although it is true that culture involves learned behavior, it does not logically follow that all learned behavior is culture. It is the kind of learning that makes the difference. As Morton Fried (1972:8) pointed out, three different kinds of learning processes can be distinguished. The first one is situational, i.e., the acquisition of new behavioral responses through experience. It is exclusive to the organism and cannot be communicated, although it may be passed on through biogenetic means. All simple and complex organisms learn in this manner. The second process is social learning, which is basically imitation. Higher primates and man learn this way, and its possibility for transmission is limited by the presence of the concrete stimulus. Only man can also learn on the symbolic level, and this process does not depend upon experience or imitation, except in its initial stages.

While comparative psychologists experimented with animals, trying to condition or alter their behavior or to teach them human tricks, ethologists studied their naturally occurring behavior. This meant observing animals in their natural habitat, not under artificial laboratory or human family conditions. It was primarily through the inspiration of R. M. Yerkes (1929) that the first field expeditions were initiated, resulting in a number of significant monographs (Nissen 1931, Bingham 1932, Carpenter 1940, etc.). The major difficulty of these undertakings was that the animals usually ran away when human beings approached and could be observed only from a distance with telescopic equipment.

Recently researchers in this field made a major breakthrough by modeling their approach along lines of anthropological field work among human beings. They went out to live in close proximity to the animals over considerable periods of time so that, in the long run, their presence was no longer disturbing. This is a slow process. Jane Goodall, working among chimpanzees in Africa, reported that after eight months she could approach no closer than fifty yards, by fourteen months she was able to get within thirty to fifty feet, and after eighteen months she was "accepted": the chimps took food from her hand and greeted her almost as another chimpanzee (Goodall 1963, 1965). Phyllis Jay did similar work among Indian langurs (1962, 1965), George Schaller among the mountain gorillas (1964), and from these and many other studies came important information about the animals' social behavior and communication systems.

On the whole it was much easier to draw parallels between human and animal social behavior than between communication systems. Several primate groups exhibited a kind of family structure, there were hierarchies of dominance, they trained their young, cooperated in defense, and so forth. But the communication systems differed so significantly that Jane Lancaster concluded:

The more that is known about the communication systems of non-human primates the more obvious it is that these systems have little relationship with human language, but much with the ways human beings express emotion through gesture, facial expression, and tone of voice. There is no evidence that human displays expressing emotion, such as laughing, smiling, or crying, are any more or less complex than are displays of monkeys and apes or that they differ in form or function. It is human language, a highly specialized aspect of the human system of communication, that has no obvious counterpart in the communication systems of man's closest relatives, the Old World monkeys and apes.

(Lancaster 1968:446)

More precisely, the acts of communication in a social group of nonhuman primates take place between members of that group and rarely with strangers, even if they are of the same species. The members of such a group generally spend their entire lives within the same social context. Not only do they communicate with one another by sound, but gestures, posture, and facial expression are essential parts of the complete signal. In fact, as many field and laboratory workers have emphasized, vocalization is more often than not the least important part of primate communication, serving primarily to call attention to the signaler, or to enhance visual signs.

In contrast, human language is essentially a system of sounds. Words and combinations of words alone are capable of conveying the full meaning of a message. Gestures or facial expressions may signify emotions, but they are not otherwise semantically necessary: we understand written messages as well as spoken ones.

Once again, these findings confirm the unique qualities of human language and culture. Animal social behavior is learned and carried out under immediate stimulus conditions, and includes sexual behavior, food getting, mother-offspring relations, interaction based upon dominance, and so on. No animal has developed those elements of culture that are independent of immediate experience such as religion, art, myth, ritual, ethics, presidential elections, economic investments, and space travel.

This knowledge about the uniqueness of human learning has caused anthropologists to be wary of facile correlations between human and animal behavior, particularly when proposals are made to condition people in analogy to animal conditioning. Ultrabehaviorists, such as B. F. Skinner (1971), still maintain that there is no fundamental difference between man and the animals. Humanly concerned about the many social problems of our age, Skinner feels that man can no longer afford his freedom, and a new technology of behavior should condition people to behave in more constructive and socially acceptable ways. He has already invented a teaching machine and an "air crib" (a mechanical baby tender) toward this end. The objections to this scheme are not merely ideological and ethical (whose social standards are acceptable?), but it should be clear by now that the proposal is based upon a misunderstanding of human nature and culture. Skinner has appropriately selected his subjects from pigeons and rats, who can only make direct responses to stimuli. In order for man to be manipulated and conditioned in similar ways, it would indeed be necessary to reduce him to a status similar to those captive animals, and reduce him to the precultural, presymbolic, and precreative level of existence.

Some ethologists have also taken an extreme position vis-à-vis human behavior and have underrated culture. Konrad Lorenz (1966), for one, proposed that intraspecies aggression is instinctive in man, as it appears to be in some but by no means all animal species. More blatant was the playwright Robert Ardrey (1966), who speculated that territoriality was the basic human instinct that could explain many historical events as well as modern warfare, private property, capitalism, and independence movements. Lorenz is much more careful, and recognizes the existence of culture and of symbolic behavior, but holds that this is not incompatible with the presence of instincts. In his view, warfare may well be considered as an expression of innate or genetically determined aggression.

Objections to this view have been made from several angles. Instincts are poorly understood. There is no genetic evidence for innate aggression: many of man's closest relatives in the animal world are rarely aggressive (Hall 1968:23), and some human groups are much less aggressive or warlike than others. Even within these groups there are great individual differences. It is much more likely that warfare is a cultural invention rather than an inevitable consequence of man's so-called animal nature.

This leaves anthropologists with the question of why man does so often engage in warfare. If it is not instinctive, the explanations must be placed within a cultural framework. Traditionally, anthropologists have done just that, and have demonstrated convincingly that in terms of overall group survival, primitive warfare had certain positive functions. It often regulated economic inequalities between groups: when one society possessed more cattle or camels than necessary for survival, warlike raiding redistributed these resources; or warfare functioned to control the size of a group in a specific ecological niche; or it was a powerful agent in the exchange of new ideas and useful inventions; and often it served religious and ceremonial purposes (Bohannan 1967).

While these explanations were often plausible, they are utterly irrelevant to modern warfare, which does not redistribute resources but destroys forests and crops by the use of napalm and chemical defoliants, and is bent on the deliberate destruction of cultural and genetic heritages rather than contributing to the exchange of useful inventions. Neither does modern warfare serve any religious or ritual needs, and the lack of any purpose or motivation has rendered war so meaningless for its "drafted" participants that they seek their escape from it in drugs.

For quite a while, most anthropologists turned their backs to professional involvements with problems relevant to contemporary world events. But the Vietnam war, the threat of large-scale atomic destruction as well as the conflicts in countries and places where anthropologists habitually have carried out their field work, have compelled them to ask serious questions about their own social responsibilities (cf. Fried, Harris, and Murphy 1968; Berreman, Gjessing, and Gough 1968). Although members of our discipline do not profess any single political line with respect to war and other world problems, as human beings they share a concern about the future of the world and the human species. But there is sharp disagreement about *professional* involvement with these questions. Some maintain that their science, like all other science, is and should be value-free, or hold that anthropology has not yet far enough advanced to take a stand on complex modern problems (Gulick 1968). Others feel that anthropology should become politicalized, concentrate exclusively on the solution of problems in our own society, and thus become relevant to a changing world. They point out that neither science as a whole, nor anthropology itself, has ever been value-free. The passionate pleas of those committed and sometimes revolutionary anthropologists strike a responsive chord in all of us who are disgusted about the cruelties of war, about racism, economic colonialism, the threat of pollution, and the unequal status of women.

But disgust is an inappropriate attitude for anyone who truly wants to understand. Throughout its professional existence, anthropology has trained its students to look without disgust at those cultural phenomena that are personally disgusting, such as the human sacrifice of the Aztecs, the self-torture of the Plains Indians, the gerontocide of the Eskimos, the headhunting practices of the Jivaro, the cannibalism of the Amahuaca, and the witchcraft beliefs of many Africans. Although the understanding they have achieved may be only a partial one, the dispassionate view of field workers has certainly been more relevant than that of any other approach. Anthropologists are now faced with the much more difficult task of analyzing with scientific neutrality phenomena in their own society which often personally disgust them.

While this may seem humanly impossible, it is worth recalling the position of Max Weber. It was he who coined the term *Wertfreiheit,* to indicate that the social sciences should be value-free. But his position has been misinterpreted by subsequent social scientists, who felt that this ideal entitled them to an ivory tower position. Weber's value-free social science meant that statements of social fact should not be contaminated by emotional judgments. But he never meant to imply that social research was irrelevant to social values, much less that social scientists should be morally uncommitted. Weber himself was a deeply committed person, and he also coined the term *Wertbezogenheit,* or value relevance. What he meant is that any analysis of social situations must be viewed without disgust, without emotion, and without philosophical ideals, and that such research is of necessity most relevant to the values of the task at hand. It is with these very difficult problems in mind that anthropologists are now plotting their future tasks.

BIBLIOGRAPHY

INDEX

Adelung, Johann Christoph
1782 *Versuch einer Geschichte der Cultur des menschlichen Geschlechts.* Leipzig: C. G. Hertel.

Ardrey, Robert
1966 *The Territorial Imperative.* New York: Dell Publishing Company.

Arensberg, Conrad
1937 *The Irish Countryman.* New York: The Macmillan Company.
1954 "The Community Study Method." *American Journal of Sociology,* 60:109–24.
1955 "American Communities." *American Anthropologist,* 57:1143–62.
1961 "The Community as Object and Sample." *American Anthropologist,* 63:241–64.

Aron, Raymond
1968 *Main Currents in Sociological Thought.* Volume 1. Garden City, New York: Doubleday Anchor Books.

Azurara, Gomez Eannes de
1896 (written 1453) *The Chronicle of the Discovery and Conquest of Guiana.* C. R. Beazly and Edgar Prestage, translators. London: Hakluyt Society.

Bachofen, Johann Jacob
1861　*Das Mutterrecht.* Basel: Benno Schwabe.

Bacon, Elizabeth E.
1946　"A Preliminary Attempt to Determine the Culture Areas of Asia." *Southwestern Journal of Anthropology,* 2:117–32.
1953　"Problems Related to Delimiting the Culture Areas of Asia." *Society for American Archaeology,* Memoir 9:17–23.

Bacon, Francis
1879–80　(original 1605) "Advancement of Learning." In James Spedding, R. L. Ellis, and D. D. Heath, eds., *Works of Francis Bacon.* Volume 4. London.
1939　(original 1620) "The Great Instauration." In Edwin A. Burtt, ed., *The English Philosophers from Bacon to Mill.* New York: The Modern Library.
1963a　(original 1620) *"Novum Organum."* (The New Organon or True Directions concerning the Interpretation of Nature.) In *The Complete Essays of Francis Bacon,* 178–264. New York: Washington Square Press.
1963b　(original 1624) "New Atlantis." In *The Complete Essays of Francis Bacon,* 267–307. New York: Washington Square Press.

Bandelier, Adolf Francis
1877　"On the Art of War and Mode of Warfare of the Ancient Mexicans." Cambridge, Massachusetts: *Tenth Annual Report of the Peabody Museum of American Archaeology and Ethnology,* Volume 2:95–161.
1878　"On the Distribution and Tenure of Lands, and the Customs with Respect to Inheritance, among the Ancient Mexicans." Cambridge, Massachusetts: *Eleventh Annual Report of the Peabody Museum of American Archaeology and Ethnology,* Volume 2:385–448.
1879　"On the Social Organization and Mode of Government of the Ancient Mexicans." Cambridge, Massachusetts: *Twelfth Annual Report of the Peabody Museum of American Archaeology and Ethnology,* Volume 2:557–699.
1971　(original 1890) *The Delight Makers: A Novel of Prehistoric Pueblo Indians.* New York: Harcourt Brace Jovanovich.

Barnett, Homer G.
1953　*Innovation: The Basis of Cultural Change.* New York: McGraw-Hill Book Company.

Barnouw, Victor
1963　*Culture and Personality.* Homewood, Illinois: The Dorsey Press.

1971 *An Introduction to Anthropology*. Volume 2: *Ethnology*. Homewood, Illinois: The Dorsey Press.

Barzun, Jacques
1965 *Race: A Study in Superstition*. New York: Harper and Row.

Beals, Ralph L.
1953 "Acculturation." In Alfred L. Kroeber, ed., *Anthropology Today*, 621–41. Chicago: The University of Chicago Press.

Bean, Robert B.
1906 "Some Racial Peculiarities of the Negro Brain." *American Journal of Anatomy*, 5:353–415.

Benedict, Ruth
1923 *The Concept of the Guardian Spirit in North America*. Memoirs of the American Anthropological Association, 29.
1934 *Patterns of Culture*. Boston: Houghton Mifflin.
1946 *The Chrysanthemum and the Sword: Patterns of Japanese Behavior*. Boston: Houghton Mifflin.

Bennett, Wendell C., and Junius B. Bird
1949 *Andean Culture History*. New York: The American Museum of Natural History, Handbook Series 15.

Berreman, Gerald D., Gutorm Gjessing, and Kathleen Gough
1968 "Social Responsibilities Symposium." *Current Anthropology*, 9:391–435.

Bettelheim, Bruno
1962 *Symbolic Wounds: Puberty Rites and the Envious Male*. New York: Collier Books.

Bidney, David
1944 "Concept of Culture and Some Cultural Fallacies." *American Anthropologist*, 46:30–44.

Bingham, Harold C.
1932 "Gorillas in a Native Habitat." Washington, D.C.: *Publications of the Carnegie Institute*, 426:1–66.

Birdsell, Joseph B.
1972 *Human Evolution*. Chicago: Rand McNally and Company.

Blumenbach, Johann Friedrich
1865 (original 1775) *The Anthropological Treatises of Johann Friedrich Blumenbach*. Thomas Bendyshe, translator and ed. London: Longman, Green, Longman, Roberts and Green.

Boas, Franz

1881 *Beiträge zur Erkenntnis der Farbe des Wassers.* Minden: Körber und Freytag.

1884 "A Journey in Cumberland Sound and on the West Shore of Davis Strait in 1883 and 1884." *Bulletin of the American Geographical Society,* 3:241–72.

1885 "Baffin-Land. Geographische Ergebnisse einer in den Jahren 1883 und 1884 ausgeführten Forschungsreise." Ergänzungsheft 80 zu *Petermanns Mitteilungen,* 1–100. (Ergänzungsband XVII). Gotha: Justus Perthes.

1894a "Human Faculty as Determined by Race." *Proceedings of the American Association for the Advancement of Science,* 43:- 301–27.

1894b *Chinook Texts.* Washington, D.C.: Bureau of American Ethnology, Bulletin 20.

1898 *The Mythology of the Bella Coola Indians.* Publications of the Jesup North Pacific Expedition, 1:25–127.

1902 *Tsimshian Texts.* Washington, D.C.: Bureau of American Ethnology, Bulletin 27.

1905 *Kwakiutl Texts.* Publications of the Jesup North Pacific Expedition, 3:5–532.

1908 "Decorative Designs of Alaskan Needle-Cases." *Proceedings of the U.S. National Museum,* 34:321–44.

1927 *Primitive Art.* Oslo: H. Aschehoug and Company.

1940 *Race, Language and Culture.* New York: The Macmillan Company.

1962 (original 1928) *Anthropology and Modern Life.* New York: W. W. Norton and Company.

1963 (original 1911) *The Mind of Primitive Man.* New York: The Free Press.

1964 (original 1888) *The Central Eskimo.* Lincoln: University of Nebraska Press.

Bohannan, Paul (ed.)

1967 *Law and Warfare: Studies in the Anthropology of Conflict.* Garden City, New York: The Natural History Press.

Boucher de Perthes, Jacques

1841 *De la création: essai sur l'origine et la progression des êtres.* Five volumes. Paris: Treuttel et Würtz.

1847–64 *Antiquités Celtiques et Anté-diluviennes: Mémoire sur l'industrie primitive et les arts à leur origine.* 3 volumes. Paris: Treuttel et Würtz.

Brace, C. Loring, George R. Gamble, and James T. Bond (eds.)

1971 *Race and Intelligence*. Washington, D.C.: American Anthropological Association, Anthropological Studies 8.

Brant, Charles S.

1969 *Jim Whitewolf: The Life of a Kiowa Apache Indian*. New York: Dover Publications.

Brerewood, Edward

1614 *Enquiries touching the diversity of languages, and religions through the cheife parts of the world*. London: John Bill.

Brinton, Daniel G.

1896 "The Aims of Anthropology." *Proceedings of the 44th Meeting of the American Association for the Advancement of Science*, 1–17.

Bronowski, J., and Bruce Mazlish

1962 *The Western Intellectual Tradition: From Leonardo to Hegel*. New York: Harper Torchbooks.

Brosses, Charles de

1760 *Du Culte des dieux fétiches, ou, Parallèle de l'ancienne religion de l'Egypte avec la religion actuelle de Nigritie*. Paris.

Buffon, Georges Louis Leclerc

1749–1804 *Histoire naturelle, générale et particulière*. Paris: De l'Imprimerie Royale.

Burckhardt, Jacob

1943 (original 1860) *The Civilization of the Renaissance in Italy*. Oxford: Phaidon Press.

Bury, John Bagnell

1955 (original 1932) *The Idea of Progress*. New York: Dover Publications.

Campbell, Donald T.

1961 "The Mutual Methodological Relevance of Anthropology and Psychology." In Francis L. K. Hsu, ed. *Psychological Anthropology: Approaches to Culture and Personality*, 333–52. Homewood, Illinois: The Dorsey Press.

Carneiro, Robert L.

1962 "Scale Analysis as an Instrument for the Study of Cultural Evolution." *Southwestern Journal of Anthropology*, 18:149–69.

Carneiro, Robert L. (*continued*)

1970   "Scale Analysis, Evolutionary Sequences, and the Ratings of Cultures." In Raoul Naroll and Ronald Cohen, eds., *A Handbook of Method in Cultural Anthropology*, 834–71. Garden City, New York: The Natural History Press.

Carneiro, Robert L. (ed.)

1967   *The Evolution of Society: Selections from Herbert Spencer's Principles of Sociology.* Chicago: The University of Chicago Press.

Carpenter, Clarence Ray

1940   "A Field Study in Siam of the Behavior and Social Relations of the Gibbon." *Comparative Psychology Monograph*, 16:1–212.

Carus, Karl Gustav

1864   *Neuer Atlas der Cranioskopie.* Leipzig: Fleischer.

Casagrande, Joseph B.

1959   "Some Observations on the Study of Intermediate Societies." In Verne F. Ray, ed., *Intermediate Societies, Social Mobility, and Communication*, 1–10. Seattle, Washington: American Ethnological Society.

Cassirer, Ernst

1953   *An Essay on Man.* Garden City, New York: Doubleday and Company.

Chamberlain, Houston Stewart

1912   (original 1899) *The Foundations of the Nineteenth Century.* John Lees, translator. New York: J. Lane Company.

Childe, V. Gordon

1951   (original 1936) *Man Makes Himself.* New York: The New American Library.

Chomsky, Noam

1959   "A Review of B. F. Skinner's *Verbal Behavior.*" *Language,* 35: 26–58.

1966   *Cartesian Linguistics.* New York: Harper and Row.

Cobb, Thomas

1858   *An Inquiry into the Law of Negro Slavery in the United States of America.* Philadelphia: Johnson and Company.

Collingwood, Robin George

1956   *The Idea of History.* New York: Oxford University Press.

Comas, Juan
1961 " 'Scientific' Racism Again?" *Current Anthropology*, 2:303–40.

Committee of the Royal Anthropological Institution of Great Britain and Ireland (eds.)
1967 *Notes and Queries on Anthropology*. Sixth edition. London: Routledge & Kegan Paul.

Comte, Auguste
1835–52 *Cours de philosophie positive*. 6 volumes. Paris: Bachelier.

Condorcet, Marie Jean Antoine Nicolas Caritat
1955 (original 1795) *Sketch for a Historical Picture of the Progress of the Human Mind*. June Barraclough, translator. London: Weidenfeld and Nicolson.

Conklin, Harold C.
1955 "Hanunóo Color Categories." *Southwestern Journal of Anthropology*, 11:339–44.

Coon, Carleton S.
1962a *The Origin of Races*. New York: Alfred A. Knopf.
1962b Comment on article by A. Wiercinski, "The Racial Analysis of Human Populations in Relation to Their Ethnogenesis." *Current Anthropology*, 3:26.

Darwin, Charles
1859 *The Origin of Species by Means of Natural Selection, or the Preservation of Favored Races in the Struggle for Life*. (Quotations are taken from the undated Random House edition.) London: John Murray.
1871 *The Descent of Man and Selection in Relation to Sex*. (Quotations are from the undated Random House edition.) New York: D. Appleton.

De Maistre, Joseph C.
1959 (original 1810) *On God and Society, Essay on the Generative Principle of Political Constitutions and Other Human Institutions*. Chicago: Henry Regnery Company.

Deniker, Joseph
1900 *The Races of Man*. London: Walter Scott.

Dobzhansky, Theodosius
1963 Review of *The Origin of Races*, by Carleton S. Coon. *Scientific American*, 208:169–72.

Dollard, John

1937 *Caste and Class in a Southern Town*. New York: Harper and Brothers.

Dollard, John, and Neal E. Miller

1950 *Personality and Psychotherapy: An Analysis in Terms of Learning, Thinking and Culture*. New York: McGraw-Hill Book Company.

Dorson, Richard M.

1958 "The Eclipse of Solar Mythology." In Thomas A. Sebeok, ed., *Myth: A Symposium*, 15–38. Bloomington, Indiana: Indiana University Press.

DuBois, Cora

1944 *The People of Alor: A Social-Psychological Study of an East Indian Island*. Minneapolis: University of Minnesota Press.

Dumont, Louis, and D. Pocock (eds.)

1957 *Contributions to Indian Sociology*. Oxford: Institute of Social Anthropology.

Dunn, Leslie C., and Theodosius Dobzhansky

1952 *Heredity, Race and Society*. New York: The New American Library.

Durkheim, Émile

1951 (original 1897) *Suicide*. John A. Spaulding and George Simpson, translators. Glencoe, Illinois: The Free Press.

1958 (original 1895) *The Rules of Sociological Method*. Sarah A. Solovay and John H. Mueller, translators. Glencoe, Illinois: The Free Press.

1960 (original 1893) *Montesquieu and Rousseau*. Ann Arbor: The University of Michigan Press.

1961 (original 1912) *The Elementary Forms of the Religious Life*. Joseph Ward Swain, translator. New York: Collier Books.

1964 (original 1893) *The Division of Labor in Society*. George Simpson, translator. New York: Collier Books.

Dyk, Walter

1967 (original 1938) *Son of Old Man Hat*. Lincoln: University of Nebraska Press.

Eggan, Dorothy

1953 "The General Problem of Hopi Adjustment." In Clyde Kluckhohn and Henry A. Murray, eds., *Personality in Nature, Society, and Culture*, 276–91. New York: Alfred A. Knopf.

Elkins, Stanley
1961 "Slavery and Personality." In Bert Kaplan, ed., *Studying Personality Cross-Culturally,* 243–67. Evanston, Illinois: Row, Peterson and Company.

Engels, Friedrich
1942 (original 1884) *The Origin of the Family, Private Property and the State: In the Light of the Researches of Lewis H. Morgan.* New York: International Publishers.

Erasmus, Desiderius
1958 (original 1511) *The Praise of Folly.* Ann Arbor: The University of Michigan Press.

Erikson, Erik Homburger
1939 "Observations on Sioux Education." *Journal of Psychology,* 7:101–56.
1949 "Childhood and Tradition in Two American Indian Tribes." In Douglas G. Haring, ed., *Personal Character and Cultural Milieu,* 206–39. Syracuse, New York: Syracuse University Press.

Essene, Frank
1942 "Culture Element Distributions, XXI: Round Valley." *Anthropological Records,* 8:1–96.

Evans-Pritchard, Edward Evan
1964 *Social Anthropology and Other Essays.* Glencoe, Illinois: The Free Press.

Fenton, William N.
1962 Introduction to L. H. Morgan's *League of the Iroquois.* New York: Corinth Books.

Firth, Raymond
1956 "Function." In William L. Thomas, Jr., ed., *Current Anthropology,* 237–58. Chicago: The University of Chicago Press.
1963 *Elements of Social Organization.* Boston: Beacon Press.

Foley, John P. (ed.)
1900 *The Jefferson Cyclopedia.* New York: Funk and Wagnall's Company.

Fortes, Meyer
1953 *Social Anthropology at Cambridge since 1900: An Inaugural Lecture.* Cambridge, England: Cambridge University Press.

Fortes, Meyer (*continued*)

1969 *Kinship and the Social Order: The Legacy of Lewis Henry Morgan.* Chicago: Aldine Publishing Company.

Foster, George M.

1965 "Peasant Society and the Image of Limited Good." *American Anthropologist,* 67:293–315.

Frake, Charles O.

1961 "The Diagnosis of Disease among the Subanun of Mindanao." *American Anthropologist,* 63:113–32.

1964 "Notes on Queries in Ethnography." *American Anthropologist,* 66, number 3, part 2:132–45.

Frazer, James

1910 *Totemism and Exogamy.* 4 volumes. London: Macmillan and Company.

1913–24 *The Belief in Immortality and the Worship of the Dead.* 3 volumes. London: Macmillan and Company.

1918 *Folk-Lore in the Old Testament.* 3 volumes. London: Macmillan and Company.

1959 *The New Golden Bough.* T. H. Gaster, ed. Abridged version of the 12-volume *The Golden Bough,* 1890. New York: Criterion Books.

Freud, Sigmund

1938 (original 1911) "Totem and Taboo: Resemblances between the Psychic Life of Savages and Neurotics." In A. A. Brill, translator and ed., *The Basic Writings of Sigmund Freud,* 807–930. New York: The Modern Library.

Fried, Morton H.

1972 *The Study of Anthropology.* New York: Thomas Y. Crowell Company.

Fried, Morton H. (ed.)

1968 *Readings in Anthropology, Volume 2: Cultural Anthropology.* 2d edition. New York: Thomas Y. Crowell Company.

1973 *Explorations in Anthropology: Readings in Culture, Man, and Nature.* New York: Thomas Y. Crowell Company.

Fried, Morton H., Marvin Harris, and Robert Murphy (eds.)

1968 *War: The Anthropology of Armed Conflict and Aggression.* Garden City, New York: The Natural History Press.

Fromm, Erich

1951 *The Forgotten Language: An Introduction to the Understanding of Dreams, Fairy Tales and Myths.* New York: Grove Press.

Galton, Francis
1952 (original 1869) *Hereditary Genius: An Inquiry into its Laws and Consequences*. New York: Horizon Press.

Gardner, R. Allen, and Beatrice T. Gardner
1969 "Teaching Sign Language to a Chimpanzee." *Science,* 165: 664–72.

Garrett, Henry Edward
1960 "Klineberg's Chapter on Race and Psychology." *Mankind Quarterly,* 1:15–22.

Geertz, Clifford
1957 "Ritual and Social Change: A Javanese Example." *American Anthropologist,* 59:32–54.

Gifford, Edward W., and Alfred L. Kroeber
1937 "Culture Element Distributions, IV: Pomo." *University of California Publications in American Archaeology and Ethnology,* 35:117–254.

Glass, Bentley
1968 "Heredity and Variation in the Eighteenth Century Concept of the Species." In Bentley Glass, Owsei Temkin, and William L. Straus, Jr., eds., *Forerunners of Darwin,* 144–72. Baltimore, Maryland: The Johns Hopkins Press.

Gobineau, Joseph Arthur de
1856 *The Moral and Intellectual Diversity of the Races.* H. Holtz, translator. Philadelphia: J. B. Lippincott.
1915 *The Inequality of Human Races.* Adrian Collins, translator. New York: G. P. Putnam's Sons. (The above are two different English translations of Gobineau's *Essai sur l'inégalité des races,* 4 volumes, 1853–55.)

Goodall, Jane
1963 "My Life Among Wild Chimpanzees." *National Geographic Magazine,* 124:273–308.
1965 "Chimpanzees of the Gombe Stream Reserve." In Irvin DeVore, ed., *Primate Behavior: Field Studies of Monkeys and Apes,* 425–73. New York: Holt, Rinehart and Winston.

Goodenough, Ward H.
1956 "Componential Analysis and the Study of Meaning." *Language,* 32:195–216.

Gorer, Geoffrey, and John Rickman
1962 *The People of Great Russia: A Psychological Study*. New York: W. W. Norton and Company.

Graebner, Fritz
1911 *Methode der Ethnologie*. Heidelberg: Carl Winter's Universitäts Buchhandlung.

Grotius, Hugo
1715 (original 1625) *Of the Rights of War and Peace*. London: D. Brown.

Gulick, John
1968 Comments on "Social Responsibilities Symposium." *Current Anthropology*, 9:414.

Guthe, Carl Eugen
1918 "Notes on the Cephalic Index of Russian Jews in Boston." *American Journal of Physical Anthropology*, 1:213–23.

Hall, K. Ronald L.
1968 "Social Organization of the Old-World Monkeys and Apes." In Phyllis C. Jay, ed., *Primates: Studies in Adaptation and Variability*, 7–31. New York: Holt, Rinehart and Winston.

Hallowell, A. Irving
1926 "Bear Ceremonialism in the Northern Hemisphere." *American Anthropologist*, 28:1–175.
1957 "The Impact of the American Indian on American Culture." *American Anthropologist*, 59:201–17.
1960 "The Beginnings of Anthropology in America." In Frederica de Laguna, ed., *Selected Papers from the American Anthropologist 1888–1920*. Evanston, Illinois: Row, Peterson and Company.

Hammond, Peter B. (ed.)
1964 *Cultural and Social Anthropology: Selected Readings*. New York: The Macmillan Company.

Harris, Marvin
1964 *The Nature of Cultural Things*. New York: Random House.
1968 *The Rise of Anthropological Theory*. New York: Thomas Y. Crowell Company.
1971 *Culture, Man, and Nature*. New York: Thomas Y. Crowell Company.

Hayes, Cathy
1951 *The Ape in Our House*. New York: Harper and Row.

Hayes, Keith J., and Cathy Hayes
1950 "The Intellectual Development of a Home-Raised Chimpanzee." *Proceedings of the American Philosophical Society*, 95:105–09.

Hegel, Georg Wilhelm Friedrich
1956 (original 1837) *The Philosophy of History*. J. Sibree, translator. New York: Dover Publications.

Heizer, Robert F. (ed.)
1959 *The Archaeologist at Work*. New York: Harper and Brothers.

Hellman, Geoffrey T.
1966 "The Enigmatic Bequest." *The New Yorker*, December 3, 1966: 66–150. (Part 1 of a series of three articles on the Smithsonian Institution. The other parts appeared in the December 10 and December 17 issues.)

Herbert of Cherbury, Edward
1705 (original 1663) *The Ancient Religion of the Gentiles*. William Lewis, translator. London: John Nutt.

Herder, Johann Gottfried
1803 (original 1784–91) *Ideas of the Philosophy of the History of Mankind*. T. Churchill, translator. London: Luke Hansard.

Herodotus
1965 *The Histories*. Aubrey de Sélincourt, translator. Baltimore, Maryland: Penguin Books.

Herskovits, Melville J.
1924 "A Preliminary Consideration of the Culture Areas of Africa." *American Anthropologist*, 26:50–63.
1948 *Man and His Works*. New York: Alfred A. Knopf.
1953 *Franz Boas: The Science of Man in the Making*. New York: Charles Scribner's Sons.

Himmelfarb, Gertrude
1968 *Darwin and the Darwinian Revolution*. New York: The Norton Library.

Hirsch, Nathaniel David Mttron
1927 "Cephalic Index of American-born Children of Three Foreign Groups." *American Journal of Physical Anthropology*, 10:79–90.

Hobbes, Thomas
1967 (original 1651) *Leviathan*. Michael Oakeshott, ed. New York: Collier Books.

Hockett, Charles F.
1968　*The State of the Art.* The Hague: Mouton.
1973　*Man's Place in Nature.* New York: McGraw-Hill Book Company.

Hodgen, Margaret T.
1964　*Early Anthropology in the Sixteenth and Seventeenth Centuries.* Philadelphia: University of Pennsylvania Press.

Hoijer, Harry
1954　"The Sapir-Whorf Hypothesis." In Harry Hoijer, ed., *Language in Culture.* American Anthropological Association, Memoir 79: 102–04.

Hoijer, Harry, *et al.*
1946　*Linguistic Structures of Native America.* New York: Viking Fund Publications in Anthropology, 6.

Honigmann, John J.
1954　*Culture and Personality.* New York: Harper and Brothers.

Horton, Donald
1953　"The Functions of Alcohol in Primitive Societies: A Cross-Cultural Study." In Clyde Kluckhohn and Henry A. Murray, eds., *Personality in Nature, Society, and Culture,* 680–90. New York: Alfred A. Knopf.

Hubert, Henri, and Marcel Mauss
1902–03　"Equisse d'une théorie générale de la magie." *L'Année sociologique,* 7:1–146.
1964　(original 1898) *Sacrifice: Its Nature and Function.* W. D. Halls, translator. Chicago: The University of Chicago Press.

Hughes, Charles C. (ed.)
1972　*Make Men of Them: Introductory Readings for Cultural Anthropology.* Chicago: Rand McNally and Company.

Hume, David
1748　*An Enquiry Concerning Human Understanding* and *An Enquiry Concerning the Principles of Morals.* Reprinted in *The Empiricists* (no editor, no date). Garden City, New York: Doubleday and Company.
1875　(original 1742) "Of National Characters." In T. G. Green and T. H. Grose, eds., *Essays, Moral, Political, and Literary.* London: Longmans, Green, and Company.

1964 (original 1757) "The Natural History of Religion." In Richard Wollheim, ed., *Hume on Religion*, 31–98. New York: The World Publishing Company.

Hutton, James
1788 "Theory of the Earth, or an Investigation of the Laws Observable in the Composition, Dissolution and Restoration of Land upon the Globe." *Royal Society of Edinburgh, Transactions,* 1.

Inkeles, Alex
1961 "National Character and Modern Political Systems." In Francis L. K. Hsu, ed., *Psychological Anthropology: Approaches to Culture and Personality*, 172–208. Homewood, Illinois: The Dorsey Press.

James, Bernard J.
1961 "Social-Psychological Dimensions of Ojibwa Acculturation." *American Anthropologist,* 63:721–46.

Jay, Phyllis C.
1962 "Aspects of Maternal Behavior among Langurs." *Annals of the New York Academy of Sciences*, 102:468–76.
1965 "The Common Langur of North India." In B. Irven DeVore, ed., *Primate Behavior: Field Studies of Monkeys and Apes*, 197–249. New York: Holt, Rinehart and Winston.

Jefferson, Thomas
1955 (original 1785) *Notes on the State of Virginia*. Chapel Hill: University of North Carolina Press.

Jennings, Jesse D., and E. Adamson Hoebel (eds.)
1972 *Readings in Anthropology*. 3d edition. New York: McGraw-Hill Book Company.

Jensen, Arthur R.
1969 "How Much Can We Boost IQ and Scholarly Achievement?" *Harvard Educational Review*, 39:1–123.
1971 "Can We and Should We Study Race Differences?" In C. Loring Brace, George R. Gamble, and James T. Bond, eds., *Race and Intelligence*, 10–31. Washington, D.C.: American Anthropological Association, Anthropological Studies, 8.

Jones, Ernest
1925 "Mother-Right and the Sexual Ignorance of Savages." *International Journal of Psycho-Analysis*, 6, part 2:109–30.

Jones, Richard Foster
1965 *Ancients and Moderns.* Berkeley: University of California Press.

Kames, Lord (Henry Home)
1774 *Sketches of the History of Man.* 2 volumes. Edinburgh: W. Creech.

Kant, Immanuel
1789 *Anthropologie in pragmatischer Hinsicht abgefasst.* Königsberg: F. Nicolovius.
1934 (original 1781) *The Critique of Pure Reason.* N. K. Smith, translator. New York: The Macmillan Company.

Kaplan, Bert
1954 *A Study of Rorschach Responses in Four Cultures.* Cambridge, Massachusetts: Papers of the Peabody Museum of American Archaeology and Ethnology, 42.

Kaplan, David
1965 "The Superorganic: Science or Metaphysics?" *American Anthropologist,* 67:958–76.

Kaplan, David, and Robert A. Manners
1972 *Culture Theory.* Englewood Cliffs, New Jersey: Prentice-Hall.

Kardiner, Abram
1945 *The Psychological Frontiers of Society.* New York: Columbia University Press.

Kardiner, Abram (ed.)
1939 *The Individual and His Society.* New York: Columbia University Press.

Kardiner, Abram, and Edward Preble
1963 *They Studied Man.* Toronto, Ontario: The New American Library.

Kellogg, Winthrop Niles, and L. A. Kellogg
1933 *The Ape and the Child: A Study of Environmental Influence upon Early Behavior.* New York: McGraw-Hill Book Company.

Kimball, Marie
1947 *Jefferson: War and Peace, 1776 to 1784.* New York: Coward-McCann.

Klimek, Stanislaw

1935–37   "Culture Element Distributions, I: The Structure of California Indian Culture." *University of California Publications in American Archaeology and Ethnology,* 37:1–70.

Klineberg, Otto

1935   *Race Differences.* New York: Harper and Brothers.

1966   "Race Differences: The Present Position of the Problem." In Thomas W. McKern, ed., *Readings in Physical Anthropology,* 186–91. Englewood Cliffs, New Jersey: Prentice-Hall.

Kluckhohn, Clyde

1949   *Mirror for Man: A Survey of Human Behavior and Social Attitudes.* New York: McGraw-Hill Book Company.

1962   *Culture and Behavior: The Collected Essays of Clyde Kluckhohn.* Richard Kluckhohn, ed. Glencoe, Illinois: The Free Press of Glencoe.

1967   (original 1944)   *Navaho Witchcraft.* Boston: Beacon Press.

Kroeber, Alfred Louis

1901   "Decorative Symbolism of the Arapaho." *American Anthropologist,* 3:308–36.

1915   "The Eighteen Professions." *American Anthropologist,* 17: 283–88.

1917   "The Superorganic." *American Anthropologist,* 19:163–213.

1919   "On the Principle of Order in Civilization as Exemplified by Changes of Fashion." *American Anthropologist,* 21:235–63.

1939   "Cultural and Natural Areas of Native North America." *University of California Publications in American Archaeology and Ethnology,* 38:1–242.

1948   *Anthropology.* Revised edition. New York: Harcourt, Brace and Company.

1952   *The Nature of Culture.* Chicago: The University of Chicago Press.

1963   (original 1944)   *Configurations of Culture Growth.* Berkeley: University of California Press.

Kroeber, Alfred Louis (ed.)

1925   *Handbook of the Indians of California.* Washington, D.C.: Bureau of American Ethnology, Bulletin 78.

1953   *Anthropology Today: An Encyclopedic Inventory.* Chicago: The University of Chicago Press.

Kroeber, Alfred Louis, and Clyde Kluckhohn

1963   *Culture: A Critical Review of Concepts and Definitions.* New York: Random House.

Kroeber, Alfred Louis, and Jane Richardson
1940 "Three Centuries of Women's Dress Fashions: A Quantitative Analysis." *University of California Anthropological Records*, 5:111–54.

Kropotkin, Petr A.
1919 *Mutual Aid: A Factor of Evolution*. London: Heinemann.

Labaree, Leonard W., et al. (eds.)
1961 *The Papers of Benjamin Franklin*. Volume 4. New Haven, Connecticut: Yale University Press.

Lamarck, Jean Baptiste de
1963 (original 1809) *Zoological Philosophy*. Hugh Elliot, translator. New York: Hafner Publishing Company.

La Mettrie, Julien Offray de
1912 (original 1748) *Man a Machine*. G. Bussey, ed. and translator. Chicago: The Open Court Publishing Company.

Lancaster, Jane B.
1968 "Primate Communication Systems and the Emergence of Human Language." In Phyllis C. Jay, ed., *Primates: Studies in Adaptation and Variability*, 439–57. New York: Holt, Rinehart and Winston.

Lang, Andrew
1898 *The Making of Religion*. London: Longmans, Green.

Langer, Susanne K.
1951 *Philosophy in a New Key: A Study in the Symbolism of Reason, Rite, and Art*. New York: The New American Library.

Leach, Edmund R.
1954 *Political Systems of Highland Burma: A Study of Kachin Social Structure*. Cambridge, Massachusetts: Harvard University Press.

Lévi-Strauss, Claude
1953 "Social Structure." In Alfred L. Kroeber, ed., *Anthropology Today*, 524–53. Chicago: The University of Chicago Press.
1963 *Structural Anthropology*. Claire Jacobson and Brooke Grundfest Schoepf, translators. New York: Basic Books.
1964 *Mythologiques: Le Cru et le Cuit*. Paris: Librairie Plon.
1966a *Mythologiques: Du Miel aux Cendres*. Paris: Librairie Plon.
1966b *The Savage Mind*. George Weidenfeld and Nicolson Ltd., translators. Chicago: The University of Chicago Press.

1968 *Mythologiques: L'Origine des Manières de Table.* Paris: Librairie Plon.

1969a (original 1949) *The Elementary Structures of Kinship.* James Harle Bell and John Richard von Sturmer, translators; Rodney Needham, ed. Boston: Beacon Press.

1969b *The Raw and the Cooked: Introduction to a Science of Mythology.* Volume 1. John and Doreen Weightman, translators. New York: Harper and Row.

1972 *Mythologiques: L'Homme Nu.* Paris: Librairie Plon.

1973 *From Honey to Ashes: Introduction to a Science of Mythology.* Volume 2. John and Doreen Weightman, translators. New York: Harper and Row.

Lévy-Bruhl, Lucien
1949 *Les Carnets de Lucien Lévy-Bruhl.* Maurice Leenhardt, ed. Paris: Presses Universitaires de France.

Lewis, Oscar
1959 *Five Families: Mexican Case Studies in the Culture of Poverty.* New York: Basic Books.

1963 *The Children of Sanchez: Autobiography of a Mexican Family.* New York: Random House.

1965 *La Vida: A Puerto Rican Family in the Culture of Poverty—San Juan and New York.* New York: Random House.

1967 *Pedro Martínez: A Mexican Peasant and His Family.* New York: Random House.

Lindsay, William L.
1879 *Mind in the Lower Animals in Health and Disease.* Volume 1. London: Kegan Paul.

Linton, Ralph
1945 *The Cultural Background of Personality.* New York: Appleton-Century-Crofts.

Linton, Ralph (ed.)
1940 *Acculturation in Seven American Indian Tribes.* New York: D. Appleton-Century Company.

Locke, John
1894 (original 1690) *An Essay Concerning Human Understanding.* Oxford, England: Clarendon Press.

Lorenz, Konrad
1966 *On Aggression.* Marjorie Kerr Wilson, translator. New York: Bantam Books.

Lowie, Robert H.
1920   *Primitive Society*. New York: Liveright Publishing Corporation.
1937   *The History of Ethnological Theory*. New York: Rinehart and Company.
1948   *Social Organization*. New York: Rinehart and Company.
1966   (original 1917) *Culture and Ethnology*. New York: Basic Books.

Lucretius (Titus Lucretius Carus)
1957   *Of the Nature of Things*. William Ellery Leonard, translator. New York: E. P. Dutton and Company.

Lurie, Nancy Oestreich
1966   *Mountain Wolf Woman: Sister of Crashing Thunder*. Ann Arbor: The University of Michigan Press.

Machiavelli, Niccolò
1971   (original 1513) *The Prince*. Daniel Donne, translator. New York: Modern Library.

Maine, Henry Sumner
1888   (original 1861) *Ancient Law*. New York: Henry Holt and Company.
1890   *Popular Government*. London: J. Murray.

Malefijt, Annemarie de Waal
1968   "Homo monstrosus." *Scientific American*, 219:112–18.

Malinowski, Bronislaw
1923   "Psycho-analysis and Anthropology." *Nature*, 112:650–51.
1929   *The Sexual Life of Savages*. London: George Routledge.
1939   "The Group and the Individual in Functional Analysis." *American Journal of Sociology*, 44:938–64.
1945   *The Dynamics of Culture Change: An Inquiry into Race Relations in Africa*. New Haven, Connecticut: Yale University Press.
1954   *Magic, Science and Religion, and Other Essays*. Garden City, New York: Doubleday and Company.
1955   (original 1927) *Sex and Repression in Savage Society*. New York: The Noonday Press.
1960   (original 1944) *A Scientific Theory of Culture and Other Essays*. New York: Oxford University Press.
1961   (original 1922) *Argonauts of the Western Pacific*. New York: E. P. Dutton and Company.
1967   *A Diary in the Strict Sense of the Term*. Norbert Guterman, translator. New York: Harcourt, Brace and World.

Malthus, Thomas Robert
1960 (original 1798) *On Population*. New York: Modern Library.

Mandelbaum, David G.
1951 *Selected Writings of Edward Sapir in Language, Culture, and Personality*. Berkeley: University of California Press.

Mandeville, John
1964 (original 1499) *The Travels of Sir John Mandeville*. New York: Dover Publications.

Manners, Robert A.
1957 "Methods of Community Analysis in the Caribbean." In Vera Rubin, ed., *Caribbean Studies: A Symposium*, 80–92. Seattle, Washington: University of Washington Press.

Manners, Robert A., and David Kaplan (eds.)
1968 *Theory in Anthropology: A Sourcebook*. Chicago: Aldine Publishing Company.

Manuel, Frank E.
1959 *The Eighteenth Century Confronts the Gods*. Cambridge, Massachusetts: Harvard University Press.

Marcuse, Herbert
1960 *Reason and Revolution: Hegel and the Rise of Social Theory*. Boston: Beacon Press.

Marett, Robert Ranulph
1936 *Tylor*. London: Chapman.

Marriott, McKim
1959 "Changing Channels of Cultural Transmission in Indian Civilization." In Verne F. Ray, ed., *Intermediate Societies, Social Mobility, and Communication*, 66–74. Seattle, Washington: American Ethnological Society.

Mauss, Marcel
1904 "Essai sur les variations saisonnières des sociétés eskimos: Étude de morphologie sociale." *L'Année Sociologique*, 9:39–132.
1954 (original 1925) *The Gift: Forms and Functions of Exchange in Archaic Societies*. Ian Cunnison, translator. London: Cohen and West.

McLennan, John F.
1865 *Primitive Marriage: An Inquiry into the Origin of the Form of Capture in Marriage Ceremonies*. Edinburgh: Adam and Charles Black.

Mead, Margaret
1928 *Coming of Age in Samoa.* New York: William Morrow and Company.
1930 *Growing Up in New Guinea.* New York: William Morrow and Company.
1939 *From the South Seas.* New York: William Morrow and Company.
1959 "Apprenticeship under Boas." In Walter Goldschmidt, ed., *The Anthropology of Franz Boas,* 29–45. The American Anthropological Association, Memoir 89.
1964 *Continuities in Cultural Evolution.* New Haven, Connecticut: Yale University Press.

Mead, Margaret (ed.)
1955 *Cultural Patterns and Technical Change.* New York: The New American Library.

Mead, Margaret, and Rhoda Métraux (eds.)
1953 *The Study of Culture at a Distance.* Chicago: The University of Chicago Press.

Meier, Albert
1589 *Certaine Briefe and Speciall Instructions for Gentlemen, Merchants, Students, Souldiers, Marriners, etc., Employed in Services Abraode, or anieway occasioned to Converse in the Kingdomes, and Governments of Foreign Princes.* London: Iohn Woolfe.

Meiners, Christoph
1785 *Grundriss der Geschichte der Menschheit.* Lemgo: Meyerschen Buchhandlung.

Merton, Robert K.
1957 *Social Theory and Social Structure.* Glencoe, Illinois: The Free Press.

Montagu, M. F. Ashley
1952 *Man's Most Dangerous Myth: The Fallacy of Race.* New York: Harper and Brothers.
1960 *Human Heredity.* New York: The New American Library.

Montagu, M. F. Ashley (ed.)
1964 *The Concept of Race.* London: Collier-Macmillan.

Montaigne, Michel de
1968 (original 1580) "Of Cannibals." In *The Complete Essays of Montaigne,* 150–59. Donald M. Frame, translator. Stanford, California: Stanford University Press.

Montesquieu, Charles de

1964   (original 1721)   *The Persian Letters.* George R. Healy, translator. Indianapolis: Bobbs-Merrill.

1966   (original 1748)   *The Spirit of the Laws.* Thomas Nugent, translator. New York: Hafner Publishing Company.

More, Thomas

1903   (original 1516)   *Utopia.* London: Chiswick Press.

Morgan, Lewis Henry

1868   "A Conjectural Solution to the Origin of the Classificatory System of Relationship." *Proceedings of the American Academy of Arts and Sciences,* 7:436–77.

1870   *Systems of Consanguinity and Affinity of the Human Family.* Washington, D.C.: Smithsonian Institution.

1962   (original 1851)   *League of the Ho-dé-no-sau-nee, or Iroquois.* New York: Corinth Books.

1963   (original 1877)   *Ancient Society: Researches in the Lines of Human Progress from Savagery through Barbarism to Civilization.* New York: The World Publishing Company.

1965   (original 1881)   *Houses and House-Life of the American Aborigines.* Chicago: The University of Chicago Press.

Morton, Samuel George

1839   *Crania Americana.* Philadelphia: J. Penington.

Muller, Hermann J.

1960   "The Guidance of Human Evolution." In Sol Tax, ed., *The Evolution of Man,* 423–62. Chicago: The University of Chicago Press.

Murdock, George Peter

1949   *Social Structure.* New York: The Macmillan Company.

1951   "South American Culture Areas." *Southwestern Journal of Anthropology,* 7:415–36.

Murphy, Robert F.

1972   *Robert H. Lowie.* New York: Columbia University Press.

Naroll, Raoul

1956   "A Preliminary Index of Social Development." *American Anthropologist,* 58:687–715.

Nissen, Henry W.

1931   "A Field Study of the Chimpanzee." *Comparative Psychology Monograph,* 8:1–122.

Nissen, Henry W. (*continued*)

1951 "Social Behavior of Primates." In C. P. Stone, ed., *Comparative Psychology*, 423–57. Englewood Cliffs, New Jersey: Prentice-Hall.

Nott, Josiah Clark

1843 "The Mulatto a Hybrid—Probable Extermination of the Two Races If the Whites and Blacks Are Allowed to Intermarry." *American Journal of the Medical Sciences*, 6:252–56.

Nott, Josiah Clark, and George R. Gliddon

1854 *Types of Mankind*. Philadelphia: J. B. Lippincott.

Opler, Morris E.

1941 *An Apache Life-Way: The Economic, Social, and Religious Institutions of the Chiricahua Indians*. Chicago: The University of Chicago Press.

1963 "Cultural Anthropology: an addendum to a 'working paper.'" *American Anthropologist*, 65:897–903.

Parsons, Talcott

1951 *The Social System*. Glencoe, Illinois: The Free Press.

Penniman, T. K.

1965 *A Hundred Years of Anthropology*. London: Gerald Duckworth.

Perry, William James

1923 *The Children of the Sun*. London: Methuen and Company.

Pike, Kenneth L.

1954 *Language in Relation to a Unified Theory of the Structure of Human Behavior*, Part 1. Glendale, California: Summer Institute of Linguistics.

Pitkin, Donald S.

1959 "The Intermediate Society: A Study in Articulation." In Verne F. Ray, ed., *Intermediate Societies, Social Mobility, and Communication*, 14–19. Seattle, Washington: American Ethnological Society.

Poulton, Edward Bagnall

1896 *Charles Darwin and the Theory of Natural Selection*. London: Cassell and Company.

Powell, John Wesley

1891 *Indian Linguistic Families of America North of Mexico*. Seventh Annual Report of the Bureau of American Ethnology, 7–142.

Praz, Mario
1928 "Machiavelli and the Elizabethans." London: *Proceedings of the British Academy*, 1928:49–97.

Premack, Ann J., and David Premack
1972 "Teaching Language to an Ape." *Scientific American*, October 1972:92–99.

Prichard, James Cowles
1836–47 *Researches into the Physical History of Mankind*. 5 volumes. London: Sherwood, Gilbert and Piper.

Purves, D.
1960 "The Evolutionary Basis of Race Consciousness." *The Mankind Quarterly*, 1:51–54.

Radcliffe-Brown, Alfred Reginald
1949 "Functionalism: A Protest." *American Anthropologist,* 51: 320–23.
1952 *Structure and Function in Primitive Society*. Glencoe, Illinois: The Free Press.
1957 *A Natural Science of Society*. Glencoe, Illinois: The Free Press.
1958 *Method in Social Anthropology*. M. N. Srinivas, ed. Chicago: The University of Chicago Press.
1964 (original 1922) *The Andaman Islanders*. Glencoe, Illinois: The Free Press.

Radin, Paul
1963 (original 1927) *The Autobiography of a Winnebago Indian*. New York: Dover Publications.

Raleigh, Sir Walter
1614 *The History of the World*. London: William Stansby for Walter Burre.

Ray, Verne F.
1942 "Culture Element Distributions, XXII: Plateau." *Anthropological Records*, 8:99–257.

Redfield, Robert
1953 *The Primitive World and Its Transformations*. Ithaca, New York: Cornell University Press.
1955 *The Little Community: Viewpoints for the Study of a Human Whole*. Chicago: The University of Chicago Press.

Redfield, Robert (*continued*)

1956 *Peasant Society and Culture.* Chicago: The University of Chicago Press.

Resek, Carl

1960 *Lewis Henry Morgan: American Scholar.* Chicago: The University of Chicago Press.

Ripley, William Zebina

1899 *The Races of Europe: A Sociological Study.* New York: D. Appleton.

Rivers, William Halse Rivers

1900 "A Genealogical Method of Collecting Social and Vital Statistics." *Journal of the Royal Anthropological Institute of Great Britain and Ireland,* 30:74–82.

1906 *The Todas.* London: Macmillan and Company.

1912 "The Disappearance of Useful Arts." *Festskrift tillägnad Edvard Westermarck,* 109–30. Helsingfors.

1914 *The History of Melanesian Society.* Cambridge, England: Cambridge University Press.

Róheim, Géza

1943 *The Origin and Function of Culture.* New York: Nervous and Mental Disease Monographs, 69.

1950 *Psychoanalysis and Anthropology.* New York: International University Press.

Romanes, George John

1883 *Animal Intelligence.* New York: D. Appleton.

Rousseau, Jean-Jacques

1967 *The Social Contract* (original 1762) and *Discourse on the Origin of Inequality* (original 1755). Lester G. Crocker, ed. New York: Washington Square Press.

Rubruquis, William de

1808–14 (original 1258?) "The Remarkable Travels of William de Rubruquis." In John Pinkerton, ed., *A General Collection of the best and most interesting Voyages and Travels.* London.

Sahlins, Marshall D., and Elman R. Service (eds.)

1960 *Evolution and Culture.* Ann Arbor: The University of Michigan Press.

Saint-Simon, Claude Henri de

1964 (original 1825) "New Christianity." In Felix Markham, ed.

and translator, *Social Organization: The Science of Man and other writings*, 81–116. New York: Harper Torchbooks.

Sapir, Edward

1917 "Do we need a Superorganic?" *American Anthropologist*, 19: 441–47.

1921 *Language*. New York: Harcourt, Brace and Company.

Schaller, George B.

1964 *The Year of the Gorilla*. Chicago: The University of Chicago Press.

Schmidt, Wilhelm

1926–55 *Der Ursprung der Gottesidee: Eine Historisch-kritische und Positive Studie*. 12 volumes. Münster in Westfalen: Aschendorff-sche Verlags-Buchhandlung.

Schoolcraft, Henry Rowe

1839 *Algic Researches, Comprising Inquiries Respecting the Mental Characteristics of the North American Indians. 1st Series: Indian Tales and Legends*. 2 volumes. New York: Harper.

1851–57 *Historical and Statistical Information Respecting the History, Condition, and Prospects of the Indian Tribes of the United States*. 6 volumes. Philadelphia: J. B. Lippincott.

Schrier, Arnold, *et al*. (eds.)

1963 *Modern European Civilization*. Fairlawn, New Jersey: Scott, Foresman and Company.

Service, Elman R.

1971 *Profiles in Ethnology*. Revised edition. New York: Harper and Row.

Seznec, Jean

1961 *The Survival of the Pagan Gods*. Barbara F. Sessions, translator. New York: Harper Torchbooks.

Shapiro, Harry L.

1939 *Migration and Environment*. London: Oxford University Press.

Shetrone, Henry C.

1930 *The Mound-Builders*. New York: Appleton.

Simmons, Leo

1942 *Sun Chief: The Autobiography of a Hopi Indian*. New Haven, Connecticut: Yale University Press.

Simpson, George Gaylord
1960 *The Meaning of Evolution.* New Haven, Connecticut: Yale University Press.

Skinner, Burrhus Frederic
1957 *Verbal Behavior.* New York: Appleton-Century-Crofts.
1971 *Beyond Freedom and Dignity.* New York: Bantam/Vintage Books.

Slotkin, James Sydney
1965 *Readings in Early Anthropology.* Viking Fund Publications in Anthropology, 40. New York: Wenner-Gren Foundation for Anthropological Research.

Smith, Adam
1776 *An Inquiry into the Nature and Causes of the Wealth of Nations.* London: W. Strahan and T. Cadell.

Smith, Grafton Elliot
1911 *The Ancient Egyptians and Their Influence upon Civilizations in Europe.* London: Harper and Brothers.
1927 "The Diffusion of Culture." In G. E. Smith, Bronislaw Malinowski, Herbert J. Spinden, and Alex. Goldenweiser, eds., *Culture: The Diffusion Controversy*, 9–25. New York: W. W. Norton & Company.

Smith, Samuel Stanhope
1810 (original 1787) *An Essay on the Causes of the Variety of Complexion and Figure in the Human Species.* New Brunswick.

Smith, William
1816 *Strata Identified by Organized Fossils.* London: W. Arding.

Spencer, Herbert
1852 "A Theory of Population Deduced from the General Law of Animal Fertility." *Westminster Review*, 57:468–501.
1857 "Progress: Its Laws and Causes." *Westminster Review*, 67: 445–85.
1862 *Synthetic Philosophy: First Principles.* New York: DeWitt Revolving Fund.
1864–67 *The Principles of Biology.* 2 volumes. New York: D. Appleton.
1870–72 *The Principles of Psychology.* 2 volumes. New York: D. Appleton.
1876–96 *The Principles of Sociology.* 3 volumes. New York: D. Appleton.

1891 (original 1852) "The Development Hypothesis." In *Essays: Scientific, Political, and Speculative*, volume 1:1–7. London: Williams and Norgate.

1892–93 *The Principles of Ethics*. 2 volumes. New York: D. Appleton.

Spengler, Oswald
1966 (original 1918) *The Decline of the West*. Charles Francis Atkinson, translator. New York: Alfred A. Knopf.

Spicer, Edward Holland (ed.)
1952 *Human Problems in Technological Change*. New York: John Wiley and Sons.
1961 *Perspectives in American Indian Culture Change*. Chicago: The University of Chicago Press.

Spier, Leslie
1935 "The Prophet Dance of the Northwest and Its Derivatives: The Source of the Ghost Dance." *American Anthropological Association, General Series in Anthropology*, 1.

Spiro, Melford E.
1958 *Children of the Kibbutz*. Cambridge, Massachusetts: Harvard University Press.
1969 "An Overview and a Suggested Reorientation." In Francis L. K. Hsu, ed., *Psychological Anthropology: Approaches to Culture and Personality*, 459–92. Homewood, Illinois: The Dorsey Press.

Stanton, William
1960 *The Leopard's Spots: Scientific Attitudes Toward Race in America 1815–59*. Chicago: The University of Chicago Press.

Steward, Julian H.
1950 *Area Research: Theory and Practice*. New York: Social Science Research Council, Bulletin 63.
1953 "Evolution and Process." In Alfred L. Kroeber, ed., *Anthropology Today*, 313–26. Chicago: The University of Chicago Press.

Stewart, Omer C.
1942 "Culture Element Distributions, XVIII: Ute-Southern Paiute." *Anthropological Records*, 6:231–360.

Stocking, George W., Jr.
1960 "Franz Boas and the Founding of the American Anthropological Association." *American Anthropologist*, 62:1–17.
1968 *Race, Culture, and Evolution*. New York: The Free Press.

Stout, David B.

1938 "Culture Types and Culture Areas in South America." *Papers of the Michigan Academy of Science, Arts, and Letters*, 23:73–86.

Sturtevant, William C.

1964 "Studies in Ethnoscience." *American Anthropologist*, 66, part 2:99–131.

Sumner, William Graham

1914 *The Challenge of Facts and Other Essays*. New Haven, Connecticut: Yale University Press.

Tagliacozzo, Giorgio (ed.)

1969 *Giambattista Vico: An International Symposium*. Baltimore, Maryland: The Johns Hopkins Press.

Tax, Sol (ed.)

1952 *Acculturation in the Americas*. Chicago: The University of Chicago Press.

1964 *Horizons of Anthropology*. Chicago: Aldine Publishing Company.

Taylor, Walter W.

1948 "A Study of Archaeology." *Memoirs of the American Anthropological Association*, 69.

Thomas, William L., Jr. (ed.)

1956 *Current Anthropology*. Chicago: The University of Chicago Press.

Thompson, Laura

1951 *Personality and Government*. Mexico, D. F., Ediciones del Instituto Indigenista Interamericano.

Thorndike, Edward Lee

1911 *Animal Intelligence*. New York: The Macmillan Company.

Tönnies, Ferdinand

1967 (original 1887) *Community and Society*. Charles P. Loomis, translator. New York: Harper Torchbooks.

Turgot, Anne Robert Jacques

1844 (original 1750) *Plan de Deux Discours sur l'Histoire Universelle*. Paris: Guillaumin.

Tylor, Edward Burnett

1861 *Anahuac: or Mexico and the Mexicans, Ancient and Modern*. London: Longman, Green, Longman, and Roberts.

1879 "On the Game of Patolli in Ancient America and its Probable Asiatic Origin." *Journal of the Royal Anthropological Institute of Great Britain and Ireland*, 8:116–29.

1889 "On a Method of Investigating the Development of Institutions; Applied to the Laws of Marriage and Descent." *Journal of the Royal Anthropological Institute of Great Britain and Ireland*, 18:245–72.

1916 (original 1881) *Anthropology: An Introduction to the Study of Man and Civilization*. New York: D. Appleton.

1958 (original 1871) *Primitive Culture*. Reprinted in 2 volumes: 1. *The Origins of Culture*, 2. *Religion in Primitive Culture*. New York: Harper Torchbooks.

1964 (original 1865) *Researches into the Early History of Mankind and the Development of Civilization*. Paul Bohannan, ed. Chicago: The University of Chicago Press.

Vico, Giambattista

1961 (original 1725) *The New Science of Giambattista Vico*. Translated from the 3d edition of 1744 by Thomas Goddard Bergin and Max Harold Fisch. Garden City, New York: Doubleday and Company.

Vint, F. W.

1934 "The Brain of the Kenya Native." *Journal of Anatomy*, 68, part 2:216–23.

Voegelin, Erminie B. W.

1942 "Culture Element Distributions, XX: Northeast California." *Anthropological Records*, 7:47–251.

Voltaire (François Marie Arouet)

1963 (original 1756) *Essai sur les moeurs et l'esprit des nations* (Essay on the Customs and Spirit of Nations). Paris: Garner.

Waitz, Theodor

1859–72 *Anthropologie der Naturvölker*. 6 volumes. Leipzig: F. Fleischer.

Wallace, Anthony F. C.

1952 *The Modal Personality Structure of the Tuscarora Indians as Revealed by the Rorschach Test*. Washington, D.C.: Bureau of American Ethnology, Bulletin 150.

1961 "Mental Illness, Biology and Culture." In Francis L. K. Hsu, ed., *Psychological Anthropology: Approaches to Culture and Personality*, 255–95. Homewood, Illinois: The Dorsey Press.

Wallace, Lewis
1873 *The Fair God, or, The Last of the 'Tzins.* Boston: J. R. Osgood.

Ward, Lester
1906 *Applied Sociology.* Boston: Ginn and Company.

Warner, William Lloyd, *et al.*
1941–59 *Yankee City.* 5 volumes. New Haven, Connecticut: Yale University Press.

Washburn, Sherwood L.
1951 "The New Physical Anthropology." *Transactions of the New York Academy of Sciences,* 13:298–304.

Watson, John Broadus
1914 *Behavior: An Introduction to Comparative Psychology.* New York: H. Holt and Company.

Wauchope, Robert
1962 *Lost Tribes and Sunken Continents.* Chicago: The University of Chicago Press.

Weaver, Thomas (ed.)
1973 *To See Ourselves.* Glenview, Illinois: Scott, Foresman and Company.

Weidenreich, Franz
1946 *Apes, Giants, and Men.* Chicago: The University of Chicago Press.

White, Charles
1799 *An Account of the Regular Gradation in Man, and in Different Animals and Vegetables; and from the Former to the Latter.* London: C. Dilly.

White, Leslie A.
1942 *The Pueblo of Santa Ana, New Mexico.* American Anthropological Association, Memoir 60.
1949 *The Science of Culture.* New York: Grove Press.
1959 "The Concept of Evolution in Cultural Anthropology." In Betty J. Meggers, ed., *Evolution and Anthropology: A Centennial Appraisal,* 106–25. Washington, D.C.: The Anthropological Society of Washington.
1962 *The Pueblo of Sia, New Mexico.* Washington, D.C.: Bureau of American Ethnology, Bulletin 184.
1963 *The Ethnography and Ethnology of Franz Boas.* Texas Memorial Museum, Bulletin 6, The University of Texas.

Whiting, John W. M.

1941 *Becoming a Kwoma.* New Haven, Connecticut: Yale University Press.

1964 "Effects of Climate on Certain Cultural Practices." In Ward H. Goodenough, ed., *Explorations in Cultural Anthropology,* 511–44. New York: McGraw-Hill Book Company.

Whiting, John W. M., Richard Kluckhohn, and Albert Anthony

1958 "The Function of Male Initiation Ceremonies at Puberty." In Eleanor E. Maccoby, T. M. Newcomb, and E. L. Hartley, eds., *Readings in Social Psychology,* 359–70. New York: Henry Holt and Company.

Whorf, Benjamin Lee

1956 *Language, Thought, and Reality.* John B. Carroll, ed. New York: John Wiley and Sons.

Wissler, Clark

1917 *The American Indian: An Introduction to the Anthropology of the New World.* New York: D. C. McMurtrie.

1920 "Opportunities for Coordination of Anthropological and Psychological Research." *American Anthropologist,* 22:1–12.

1923 *Man and Culture.* New York: Thomas Y. Crowell Company.

Wittfogel, Karl A.

1957 *Oriental Despotism: A Comparative Study of Total Power.* New Haven, Connecticut: Yale University Press.

Wolf, Eric

1966 *Peasants.* Englewood Cliffs, New Jersey: Prentice-Hall.

Yerkes, Robert M., and Ada W. Yerkes

1929 *The Great Apes: A Study of Anthropoid Life.* New Haven, Connecticut: Yale University Press.

Zborowski, Mark, and Elizabeth Herzog

1952 *Life Is with People: The Culture of the Shtetl.* New York: International Universities Press.

A NOTE ON THE TYPE

This book was set on the Linotype in Granjon, a type named in compliment to Robert Granjon, type cutter and printer—in Antwerp, Lyons, Rome, Paris—active from 1523 to 1590. Granjon, the boldest and most original designer of his time, was one of the first to practice the trade of type founder apart from that of printer.

Linotype Granjon was designed by George W. Jones, who based his drawings on a face used by Claude Garamond (1510–1561) in his beautiful French books. Granjon more closely resembles Garamond's own type than do any of the various modern faces that bear his name.

The book was designed by Betty Anderson and was composed, printed, and bound by The Haddon Craftsmen, Inc., Scranton, Pennsylvania.